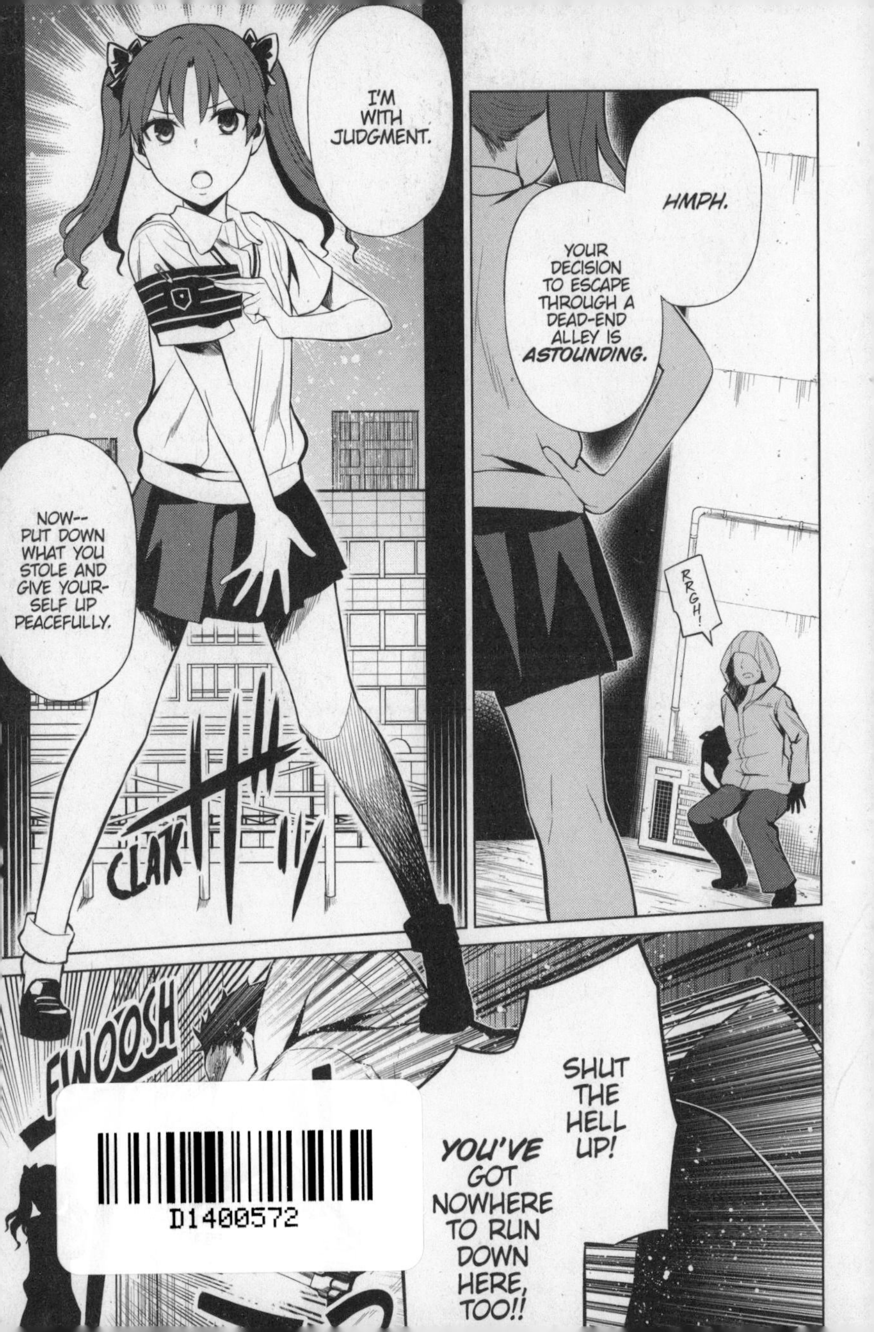
HMPH.
YOUR DECISION TO ESCAPE THROUGH A DEAD-END ALLEY IS ASTOUNDING.
RRGH!
I'M WITH JUDGMENT.
NOW-- PUT DOWN WHAT YOU STOLE AND GIVE YOUR-SELF UP PEACEFULLY.
CLAK
SHUT THE HELL UP!
YOU'VE GOT NOWHERE TO RUN DOWN HERE, TOO!!
FINOOSH

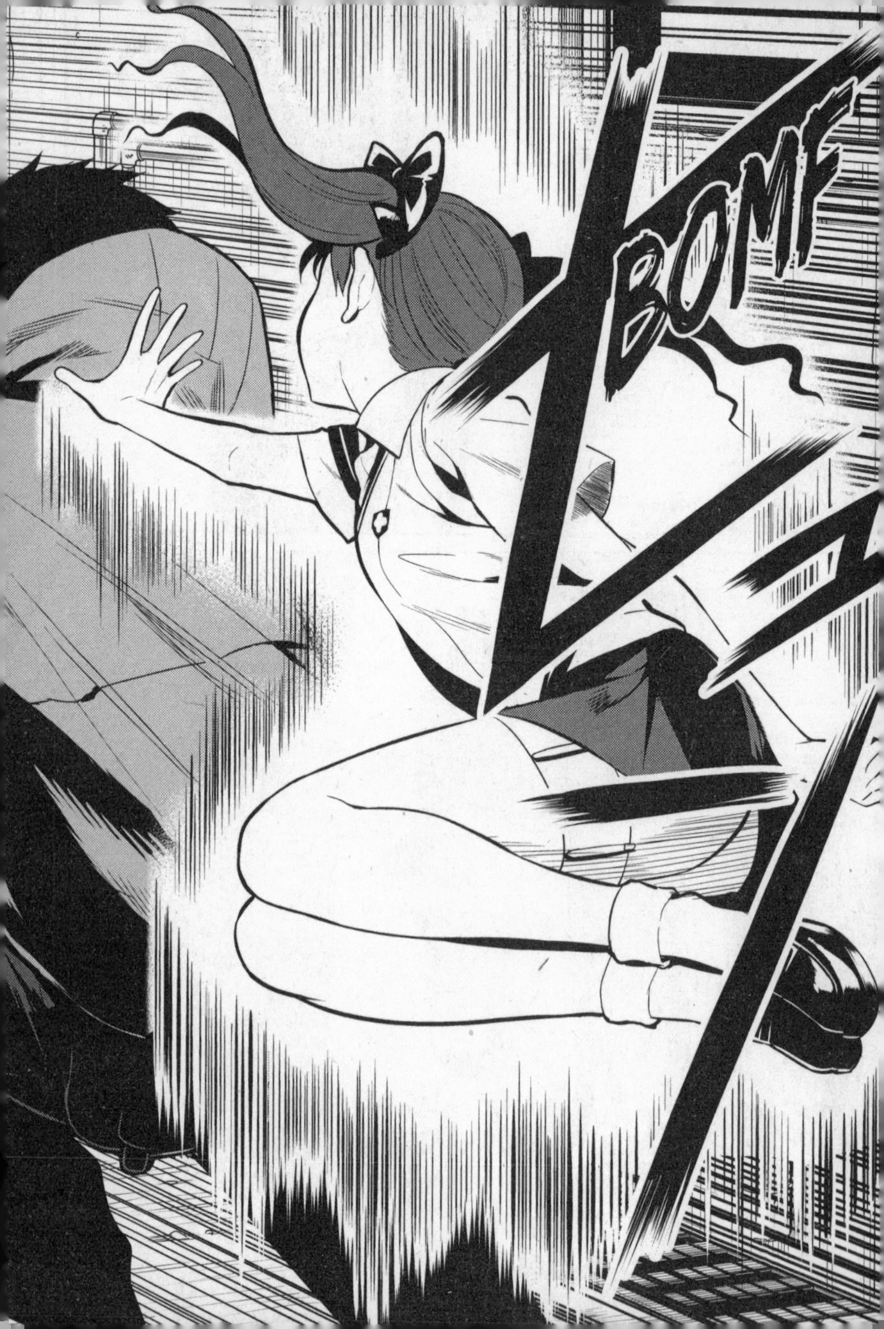
BOMF

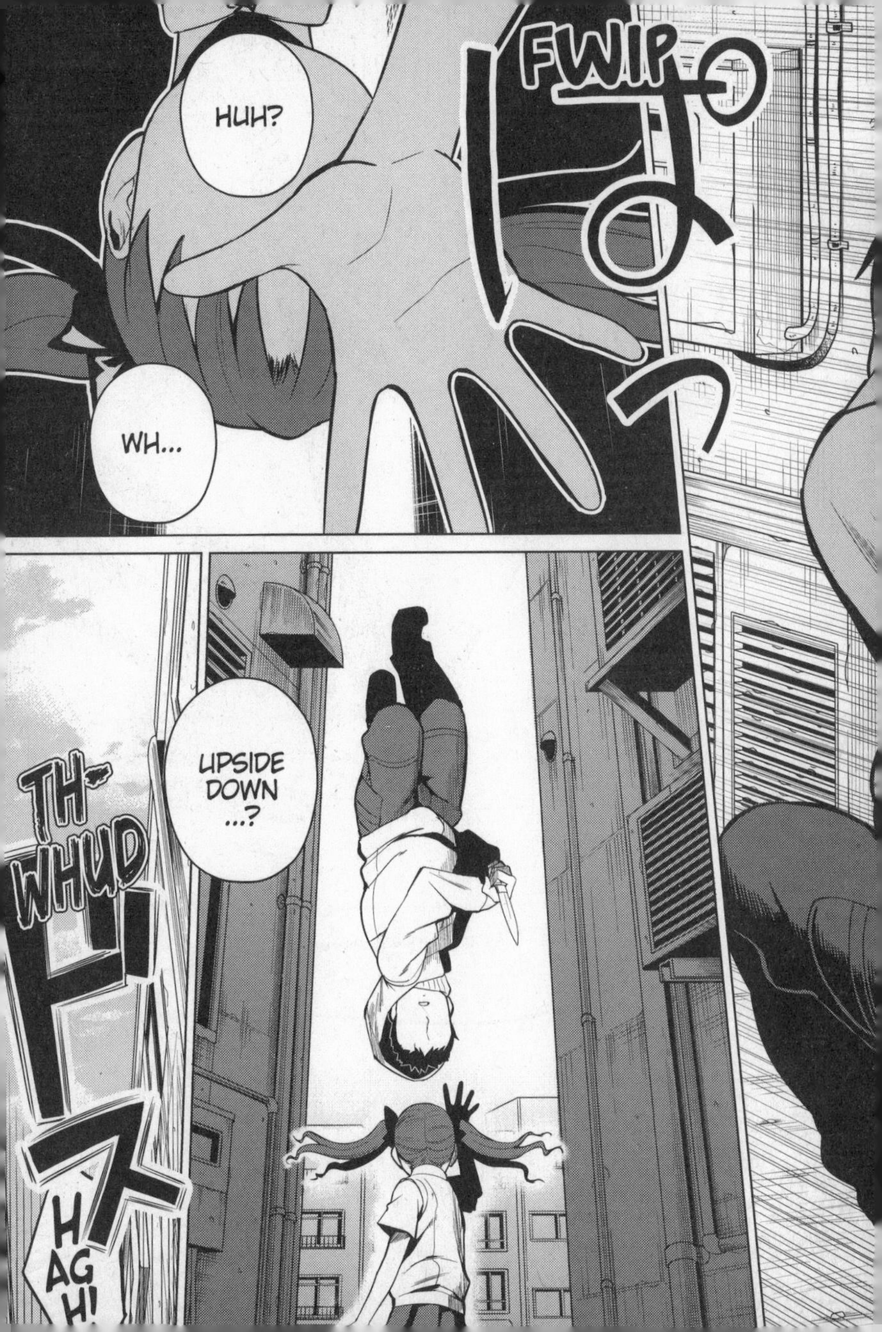
FWIP
HUH?
WH...
UPSIDE DOWN ...?
TH-WHUD
HAGH!

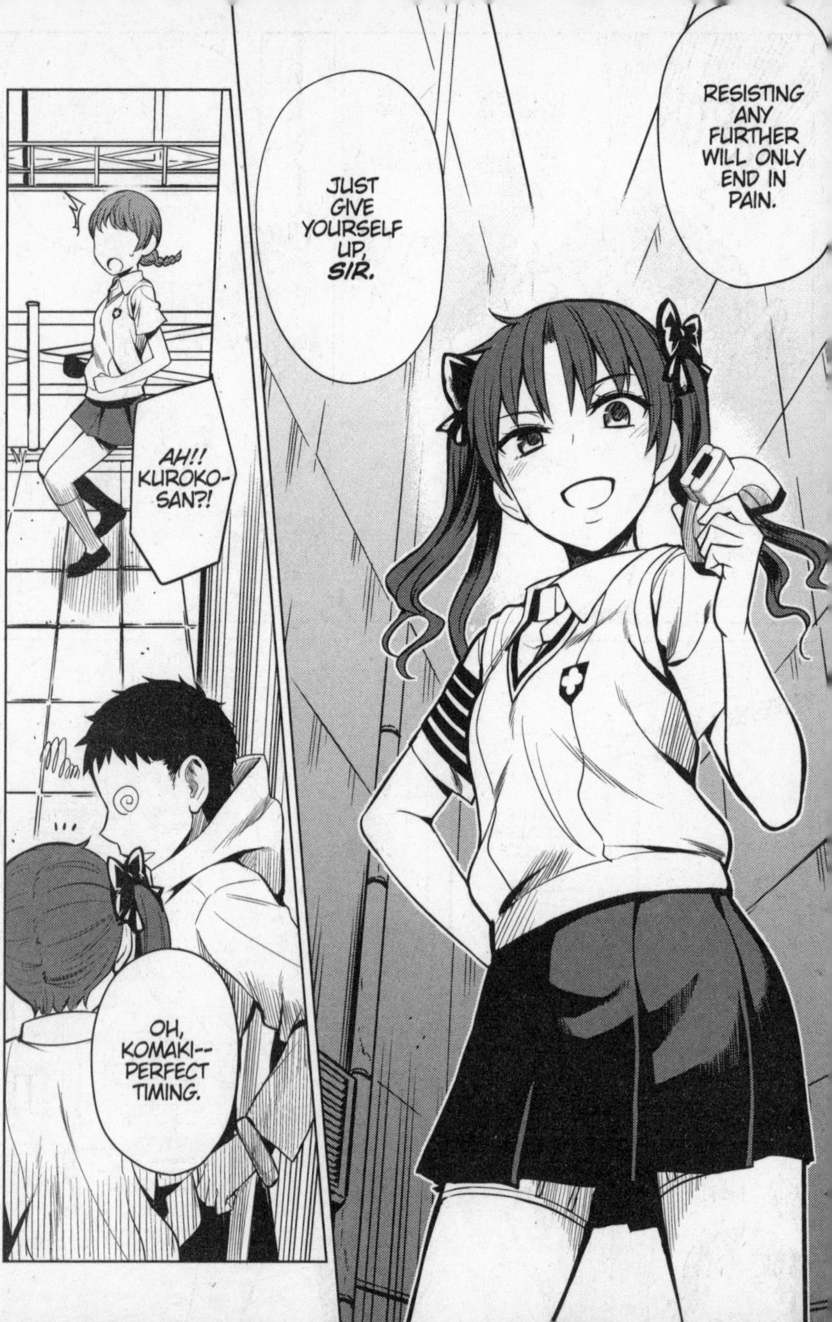
RESISTING ANY FURTHER WILL ONLY END IN PAIN.
JUST GIVE YOURSELF UP, *SIR.*
AH!! KUROKO-SAN?!
OH, KOMAKI--PERFECT TIMING.

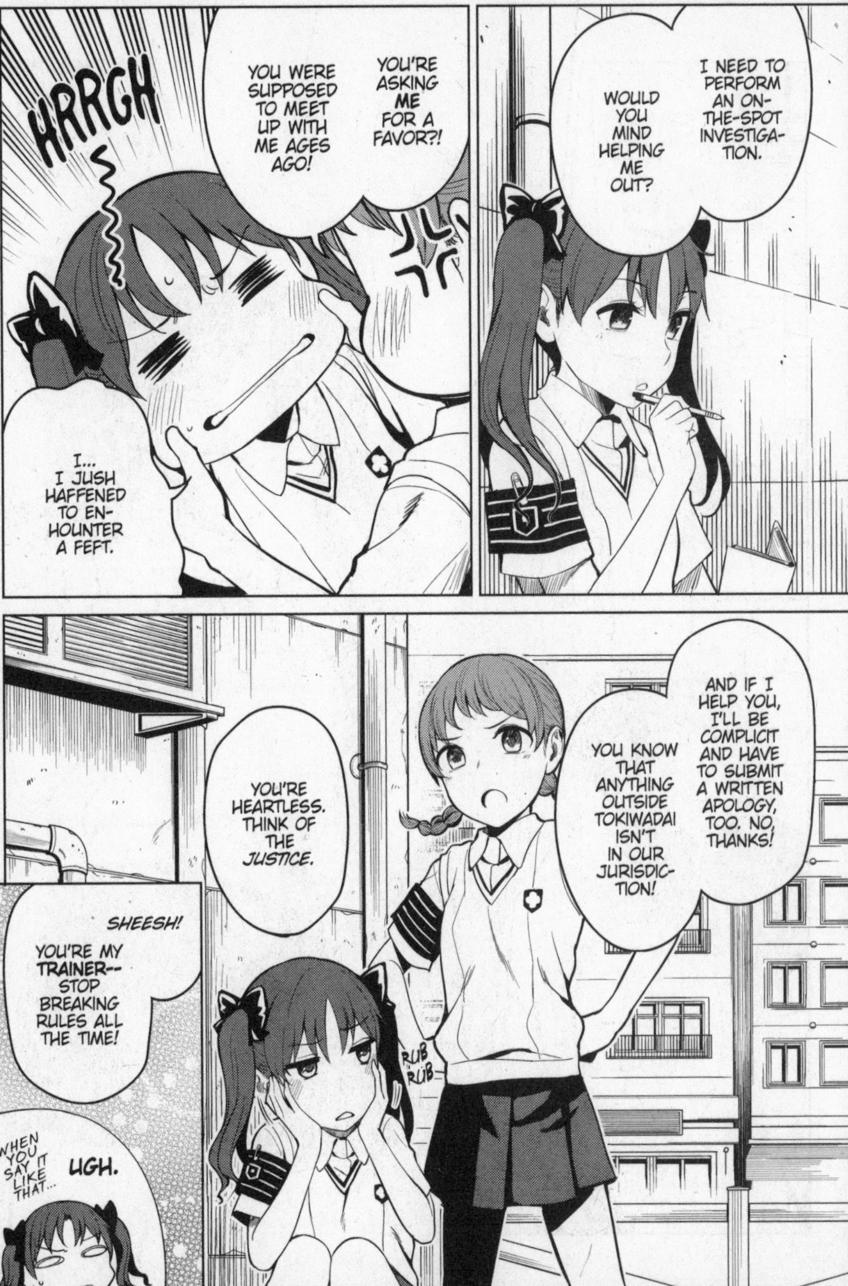
I NEED TO PERFORM AN ON-THE-SPOT INVESTIGATION.
WOULD YOU MIND HELPING ME OUT?
YOU'RE ASKING ME FOR A FAVOR?!
YOU WERE SUPPOSED TO MEET UP WITH ME AGES AGO!
HRRGH
I... I JUSH HAFFENED TO EN-HOUNTER A FEFT.
YOU KNOW THAT ANYTHING OUTSIDE TOKIWADAI ISN'T IN OUR JURISDICTION!
AND IF I HELP YOU, I'LL BE COMPLICIT AND HAVE TO SUBMIT A WRITTEN APOLOGY, TOO. NO, THANKS!
YOU'RE HEARTLESS. THINK OF THE JUSTICE.
SHEESH! YOU'RE MY TRAINER-- STOP BREAKING RULES ALL THE TIME!
RUB RUB
UGH.
WHEN YOU SAY IT LIKE THAT...

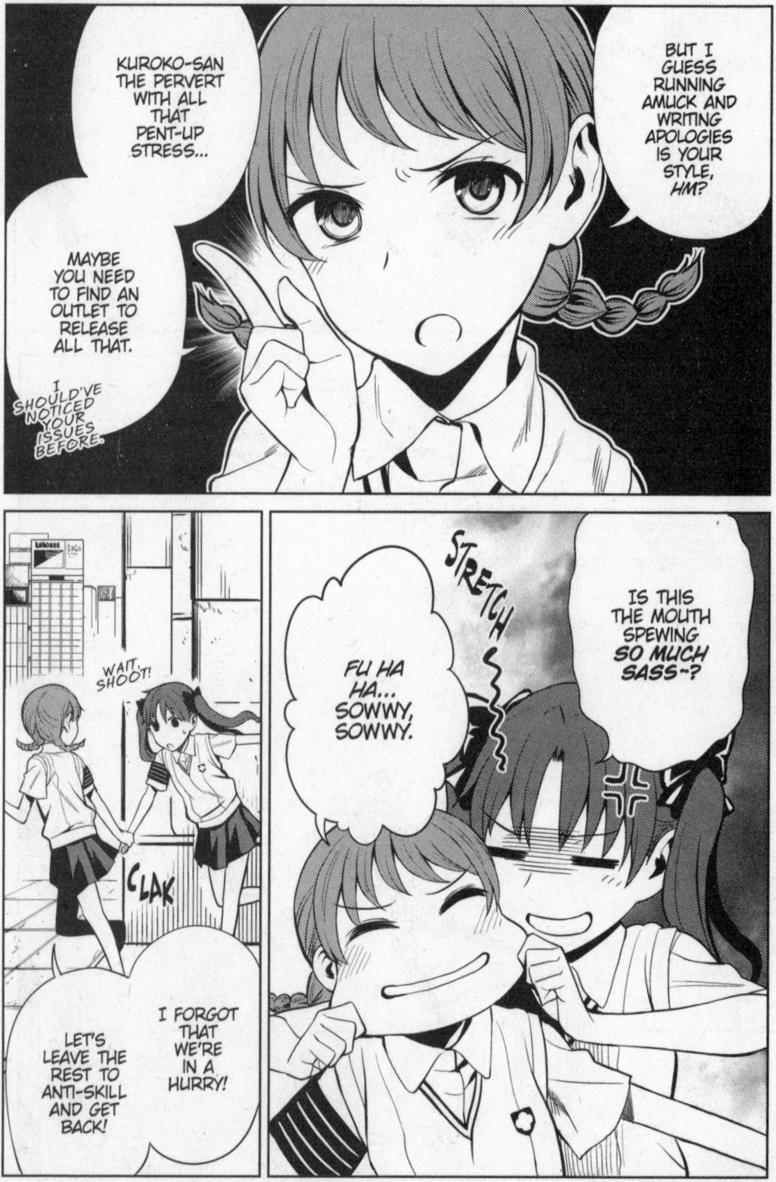
BUT I GUESS RUNNING AMUCK AND WRITING APOLOGIES IS YOUR STYLE, HM?
KUROKO-SAN THE PERVERT WITH ALL THAT PENT-UP STRESS...
MAYBE YOU NEED TO FIND AN OUTLET TO RELEASE ALL THAT.
I SHOULD'VE NOTICED YOUR ISSUES BEFORE.
IS THIS THE MOUTH SPEWING SO MUCH SASS~?
STRETCH
FU HA HA... SOWWY, SOWWY.
WAIT, SHOOT!
CLAK
I FORGOT THAT WE'RE IN A HURRY!
LET'S LEAVE THE REST TO ANTI-SKILL AND GET BACK!

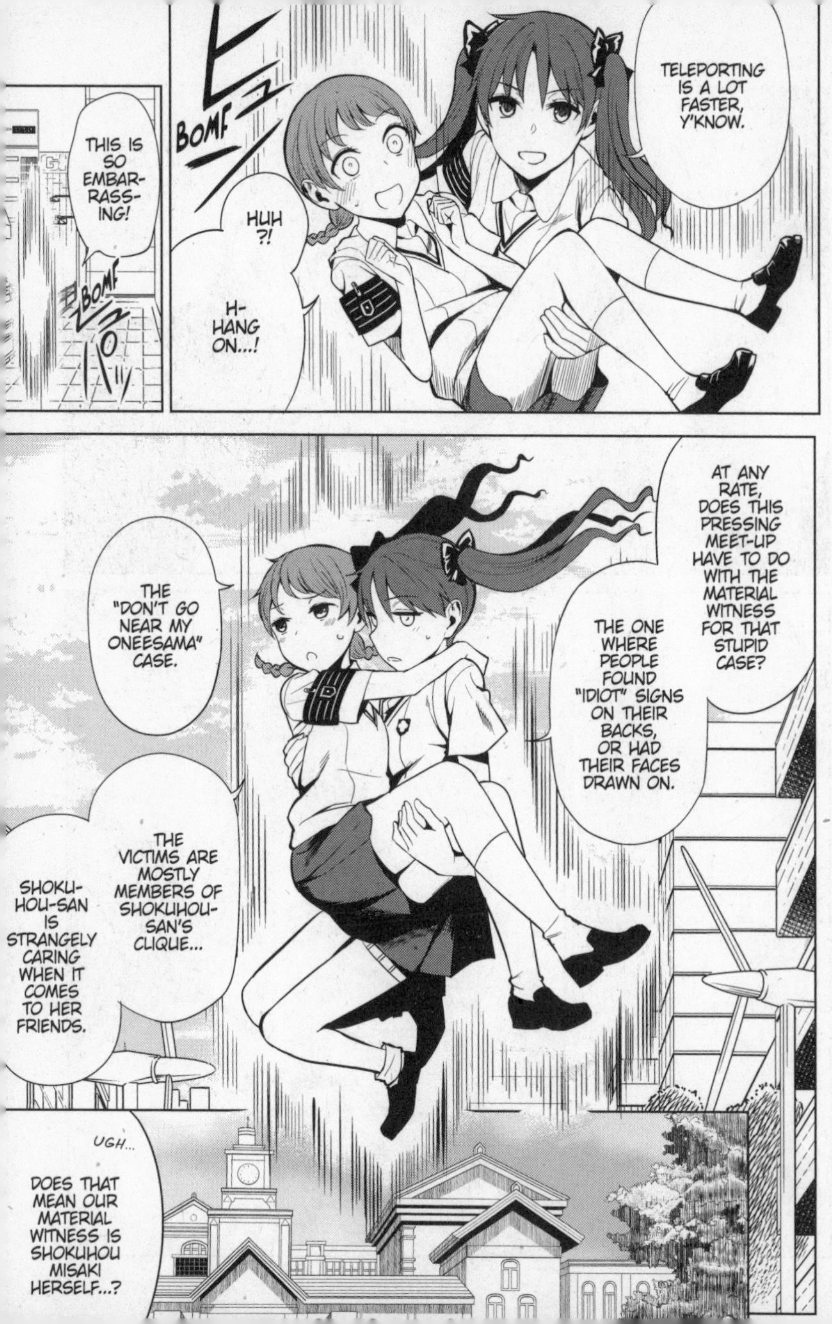
TELEPORTING IS A LOT FASTER, Y'KNOW.
BOMF
HUH?!
THIS IS SO EMBARRASSING!
H-HANG ON...!
BOMF
AT ANY RATE, DOES THIS PRESSING MEET-UP HAVE TO DO WITH THE MATERIAL WITNESS FOR THAT STUPID CASE?
THE ONE WHERE PEOPLE FOUND "IDIOT" SIGNS ON THEIR BACKS, OR HAD THEIR FACES DRAWN ON.
THE "DON'T GO NEAR MY ONEESAMA" CASE.
THE VICTIMS ARE MOSTLY MEMBERS OF SHOKUHOU-SAN'S CLIQUE...
SHOKUHOU-SAN IS STRANGELY CARING WHEN IT COMES TO HER FRIENDS.
UGH...
DOES THAT MEAN OUR MATERIAL WITNESS IS SHOKUHOU MISAKI HERSELF...?

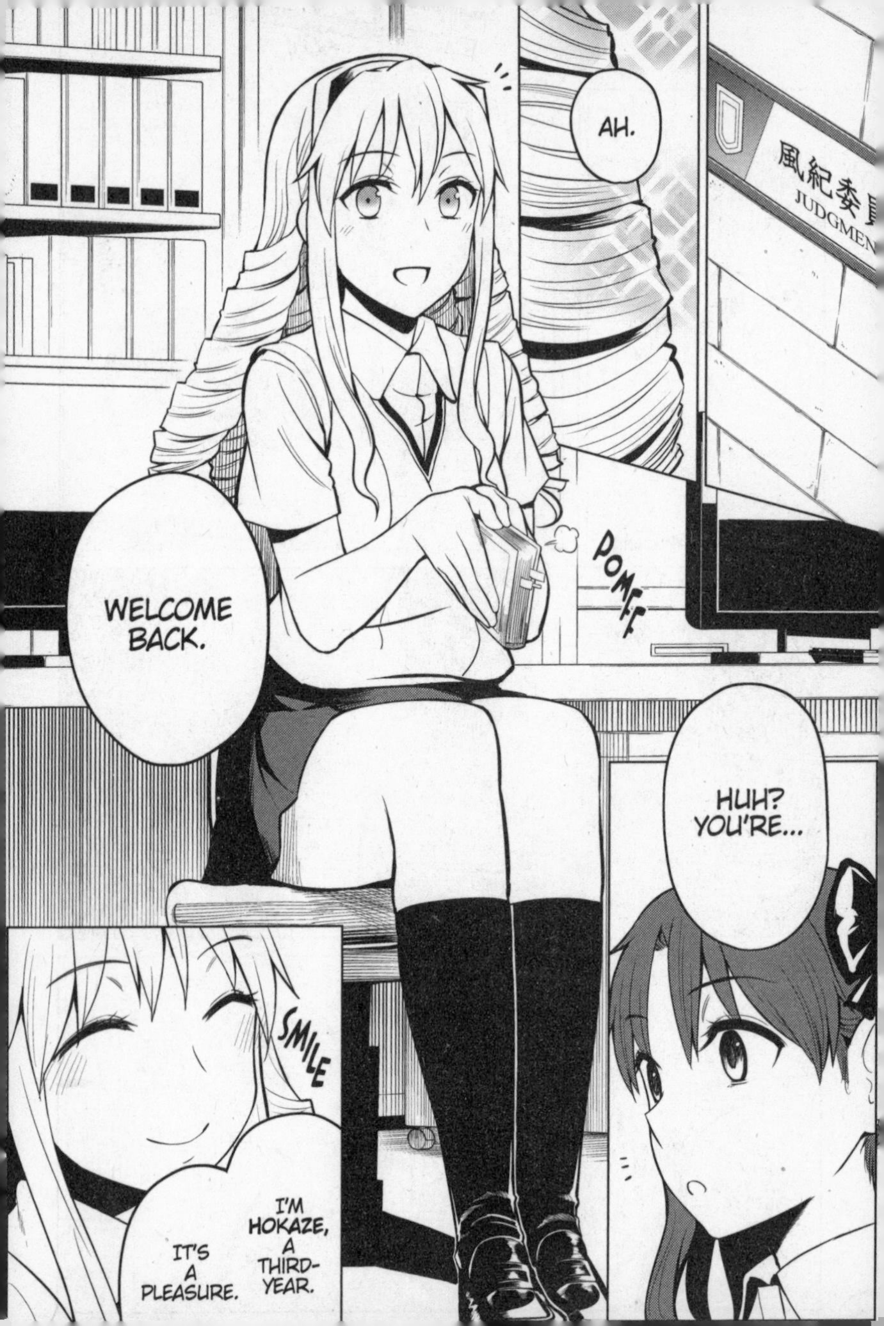
AH.
風紀委員
JUDGMEN
WELCOME BACK.
POMFF
HUH? YOU'RE...
SMILE
I'M HOKAZE, A THIRD-YEAR.
IT'S A PLEASURE.

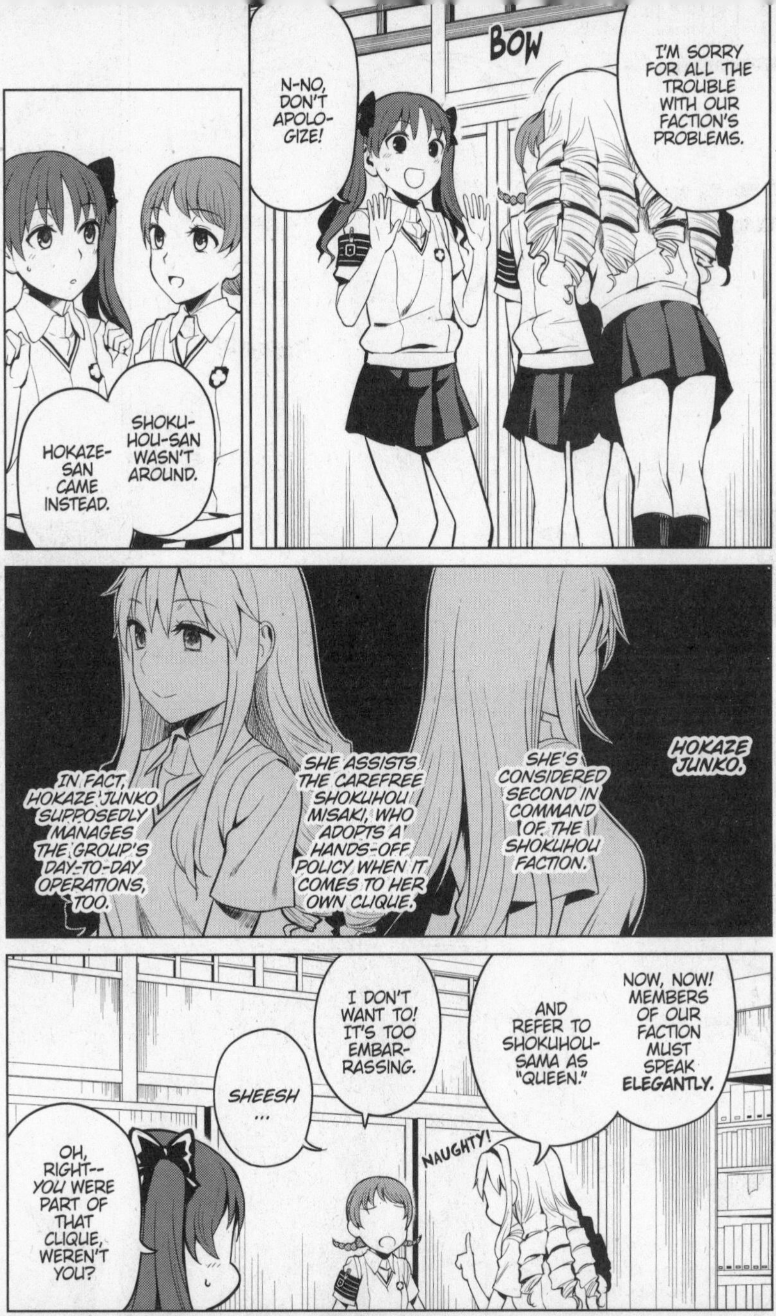
I'M SORRY FOR ALL THE TROUBLE WITH OUR FACTION'S PROBLEMS.
BOW
N-NO, DON'T APOLO-GIZE!
SHOKU-HOU-SAN WASN'T AROUND.
HOKAZE-SAN CAME INSTEAD.
HOKAZE JUNKO.
SHE'S CONSIDERED SECOND IN COMMAND OF THE SHOKUHOU FACTION.
SHE ASSISTS THE CAREFREE SHOKUHOU MISAKI, WHO ADOPTS A HANDS-OFF POLICY WHEN IT COMES TO HER OWN CLIQUE.
IN FACT, HOKAZE JUNKO SUPPOSEDLY MANAGES THE GROUP'S DAY-TO-DAY OPERATIONS, TOO.
NOW, NOW! MEMBERS OF OUR FACTION MUST SPEAK ELEGANTLY.
AND REFER TO SHOKUHOU-SAMA AS "QUEEN."
I DON'T WANT TO! IT'S TOO EMBAR-RASSING.
SHEESH ...
NAUGHTY!
OH, RIGHT-- YOU WERE PART OF THAT CLIQUE, WEREN'T YOU?

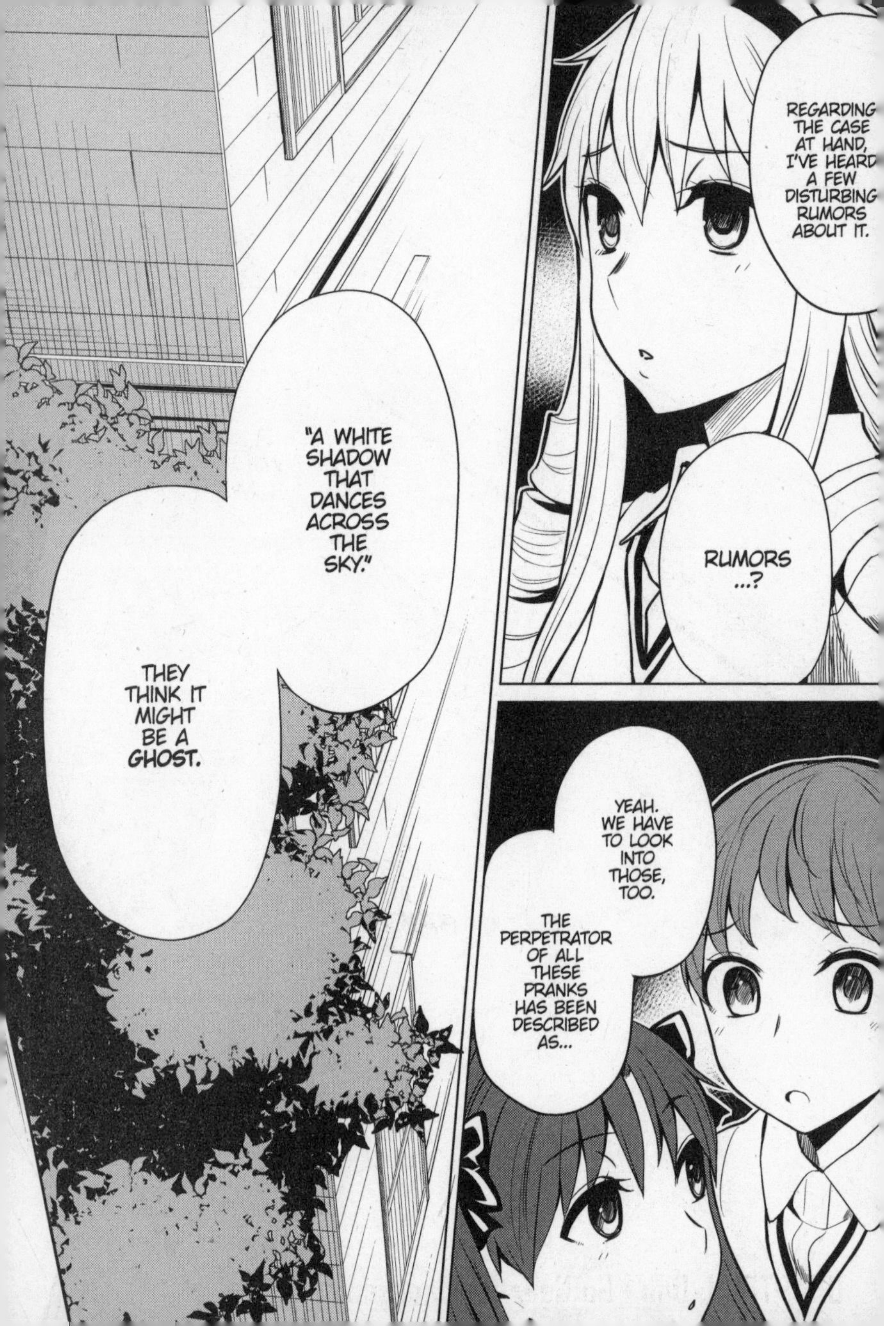
REGARDING THE CASE AT HAND, I'VE HEARD A FEW DISTURBING RUMORS ABOUT IT.
RUMORS ...?
YEAH. WE HAVE TO LOOK INTO THOSE, TOO.
THE PERPETRATOR OF ALL THESE PRANKS HAS BEEN DESCRIBED AS...
"A WHITE SHADOW THAT DANCES ACROSS THE SKY."
THEY THINK IT MIGHT BE A GHOST.

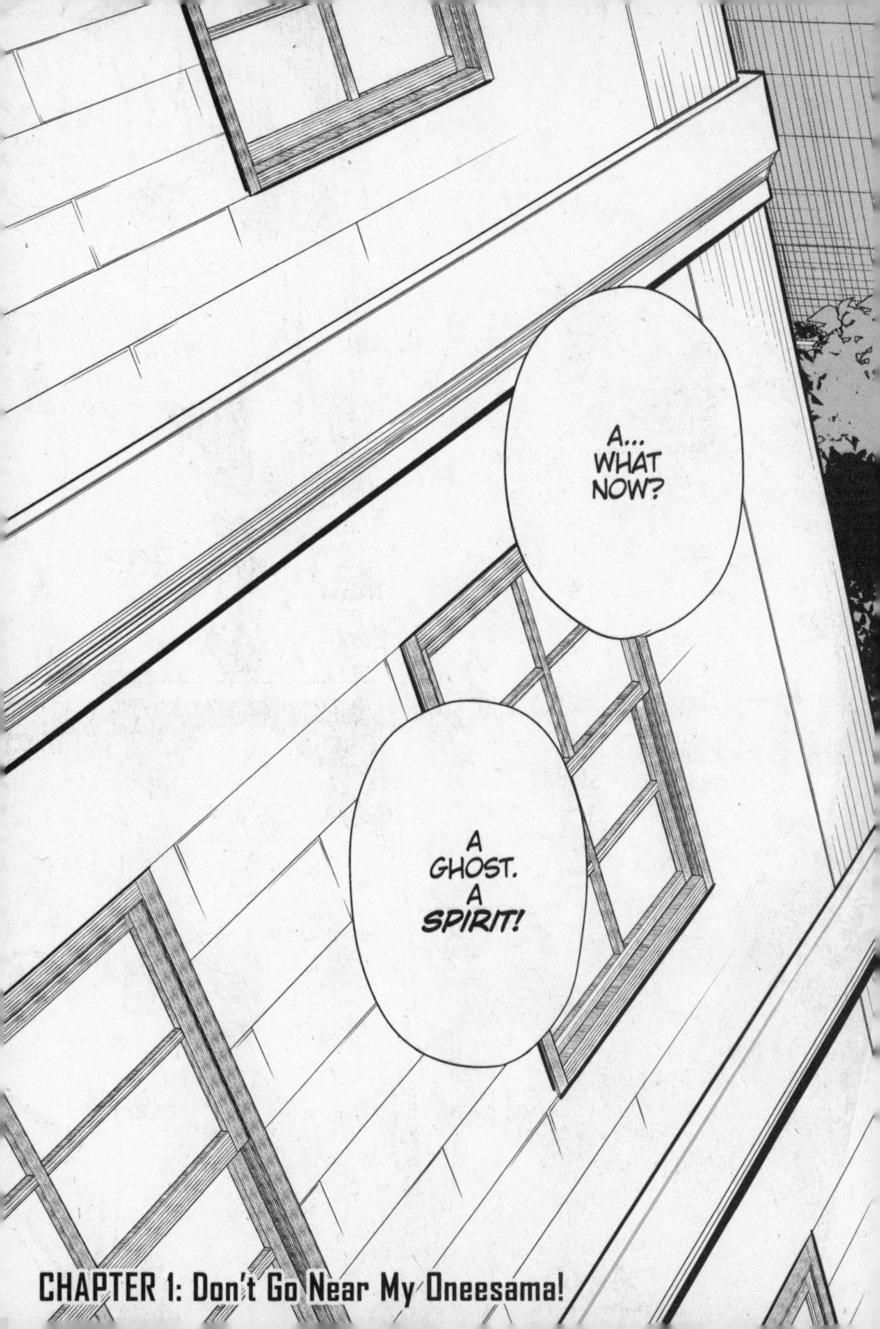
A... WHAT NOW?
A GHOST. A SPIRIT!

CHAPTER 1: Don't Go Near My Oneesama!

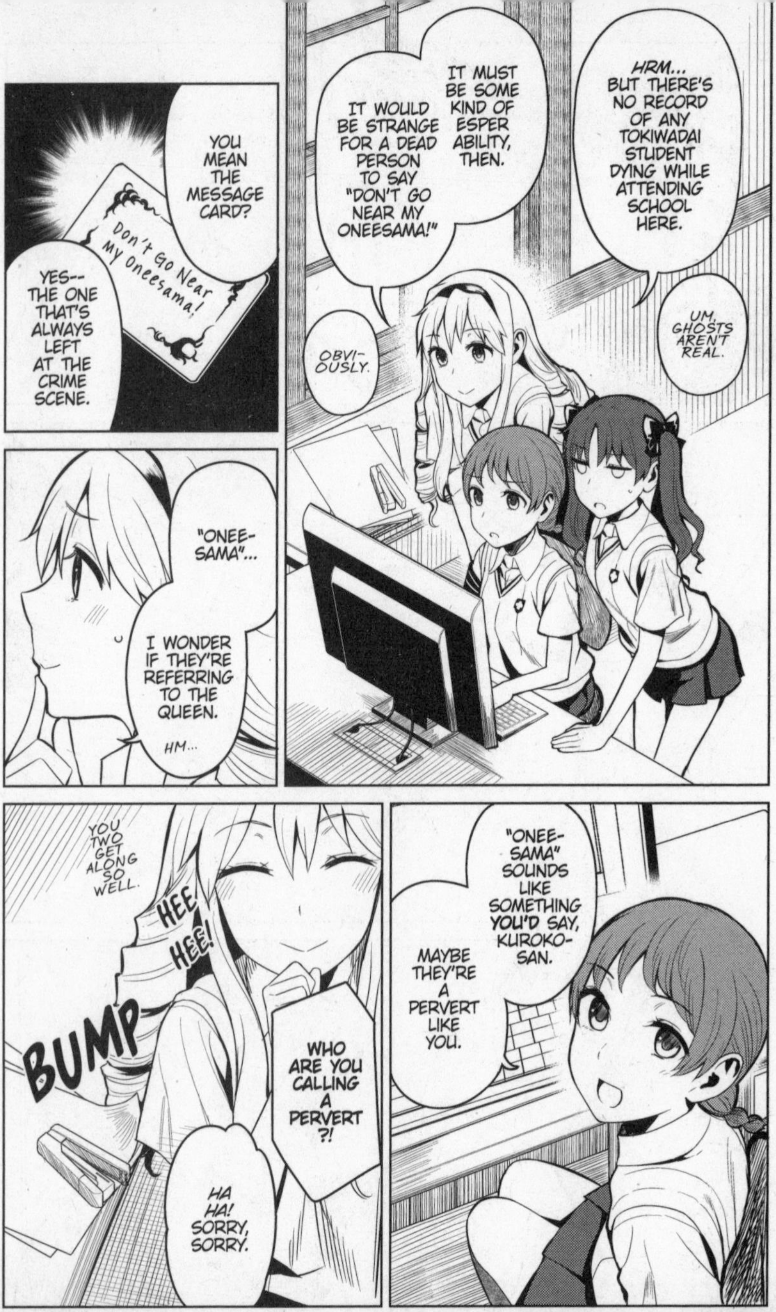
HRM... BUT THERE'S NO RECORD OF ANY TOKIWADAI STUDENT DYING WHILE ATTENDING SCHOOL HERE.
IT MUST BE SOME KIND OF ESPER ABILITY, THEN.
IT WOULD BE STRANGE FOR A DEAD PERSON TO SAY "DON'T GO NEAR MY ONEESAMA!"
UM, GHOSTS AREN'T REAL.
OBVI-OUSLY.
YOU MEAN THE MESSAGE CARD?
Don't Go Near my Oneesama!
YES-- THE ONE THAT'S ALWAYS LEFT AT THE CRIME SCENE.
"ONEE-SAMA"...
I WONDER IF THEY'RE REFERRING TO THE QUEEN.
HM...
"ONEE-SAMA" SOUNDS LIKE SOMETHING YOU'D SAY, KUROKO-SAN.
MAYBE THEY'RE A PERVERT LIKE YOU.
WHO ARE YOU CALLING A PERVERT?!
BUMP
HA HA! SORRY, SORRY.
YOU TWO GET ALONG SO WELL.
HEE HEE!

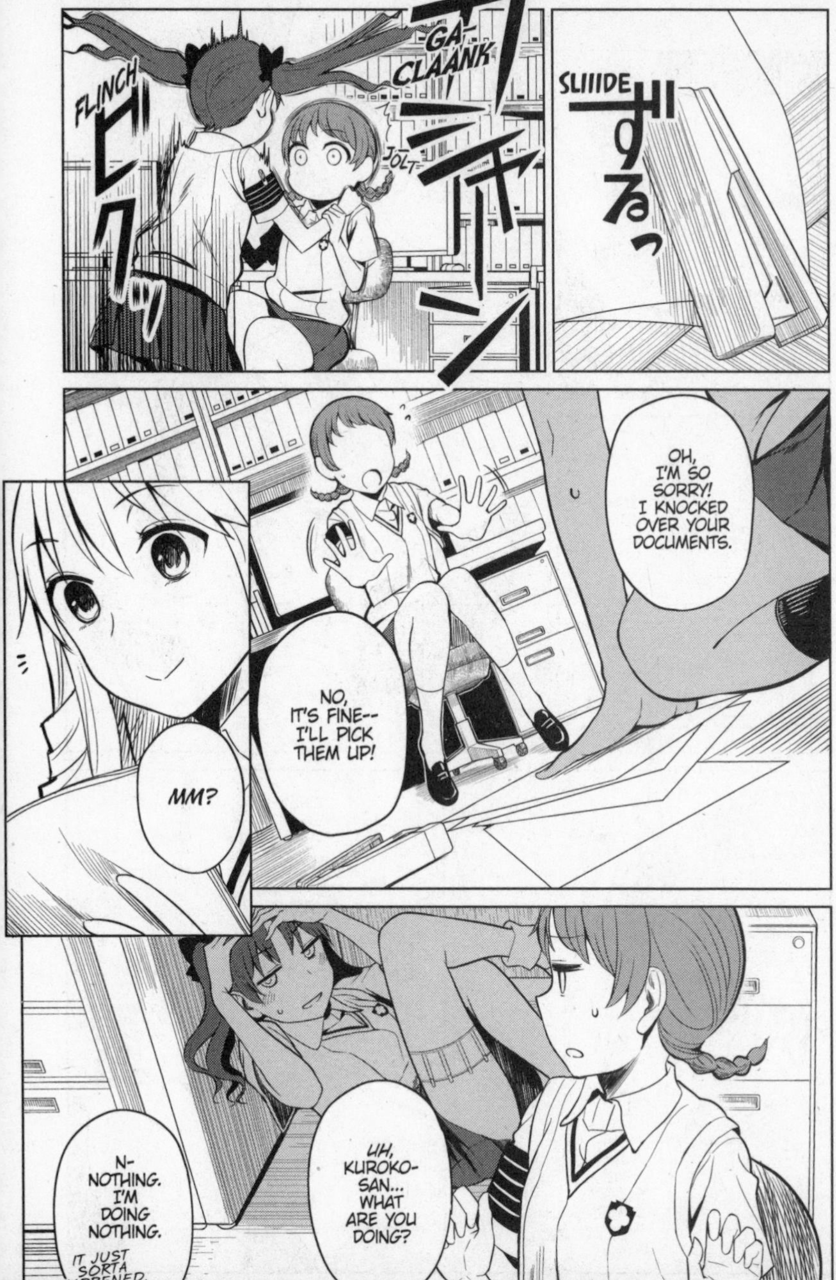
SLIIIDE
ずるっ
GA-CLAANK
ガシャーン
JOLT
FLINCH
ビクッ
OH, I'M SO SORRY! I KNOCKED OVER YOUR DOCUMENTS.
NO, IT'S FINE-- I'LL PICK THEM UP!
MM?
UH, KUROKO-SAN... WHAT ARE YOU DOING?
N-NOTHING. I'M DOING NOTHING.
IT JUST SORTA HAPPENED.

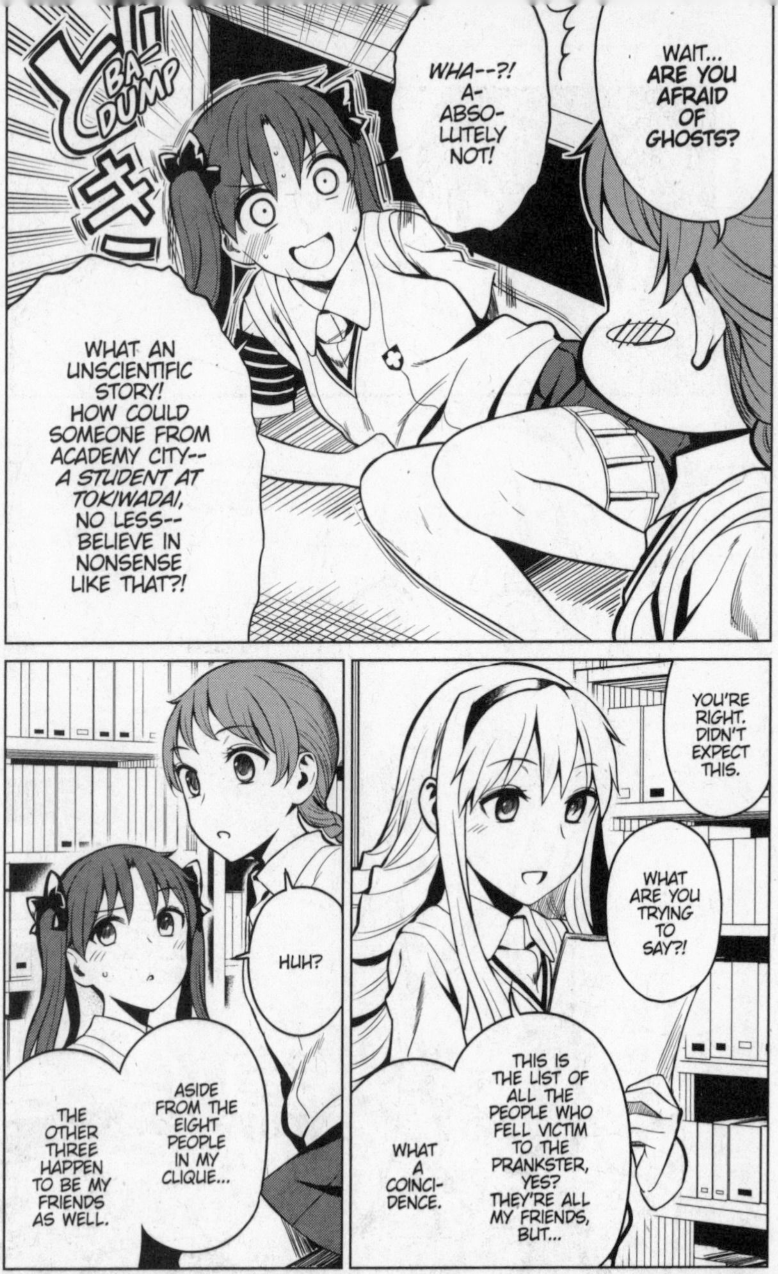
WAIT... ARE YOU AFRAID OF GHOSTS?
WHA--?! A- ABSO-LUTELY NOT!
BA-DUMP
WHAT AN UNSCIENTIFIC STORY! HOW COULD SOMEONE FROM ACADEMY CITY-- A STUDENT AT TOKIWADAI, NO LESS-- BELIEVE IN NONSENSE LIKE THAT?!
YOU'RE RIGHT. DIDN'T EXPECT THIS.
WHAT ARE YOU TRYING TO SAY?!
THIS IS THE LIST OF ALL THE PEOPLE WHO FELL VICTIM TO THE PRANKSTER, YES? THEY'RE ALL MY FRIENDS, BUT...
WHAT A COINCI-DENCE.
HUH?
ASIDE FROM THE EIGHT PEOPLE IN MY CLIQUE...
THE OTHER THREE HAPPEN TO BE MY FRIENDS AS WELL.

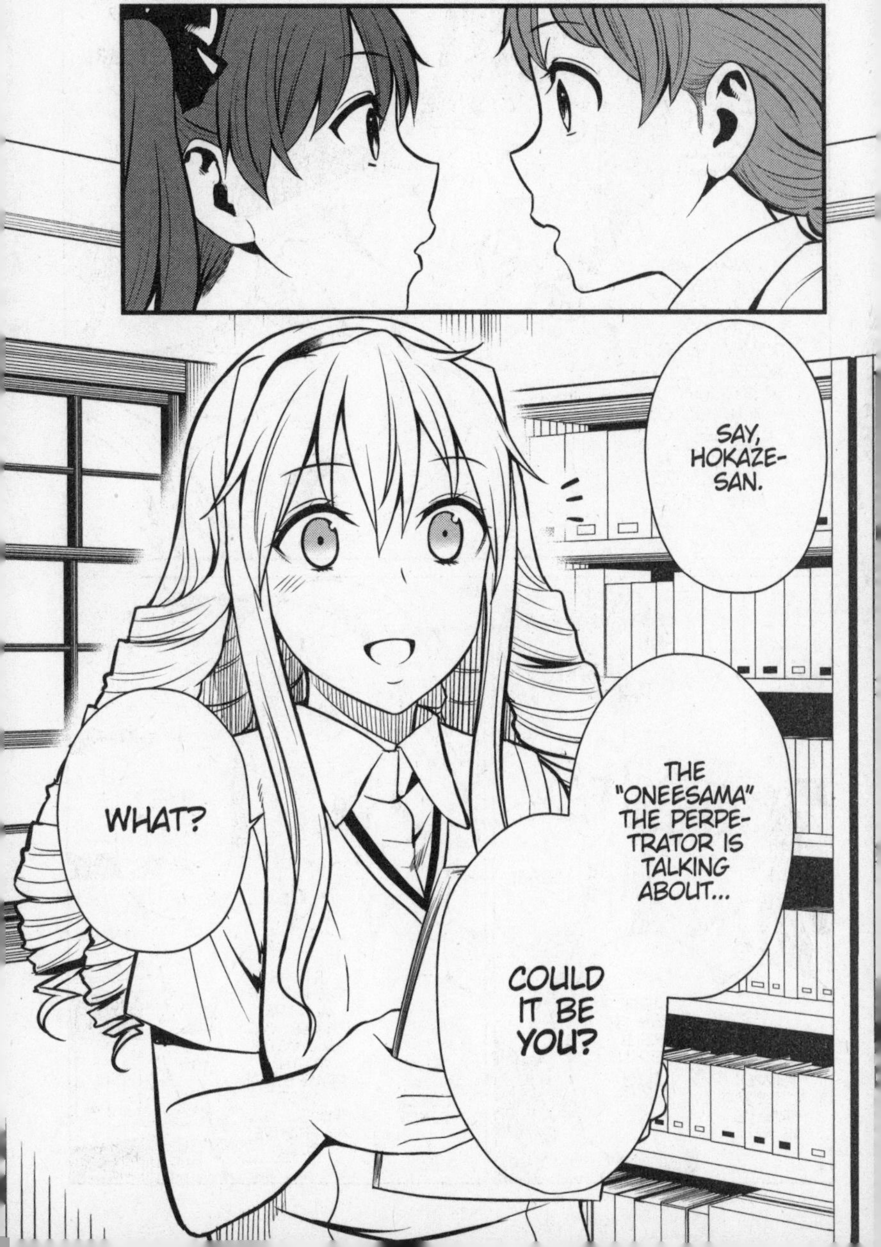
SAY, HOKAZE-SAN.
WHAT?
THE "ONEESAMA" THE PERPE-TRATOR IS TALKING ABOUT...
COULD IT BE YOU?

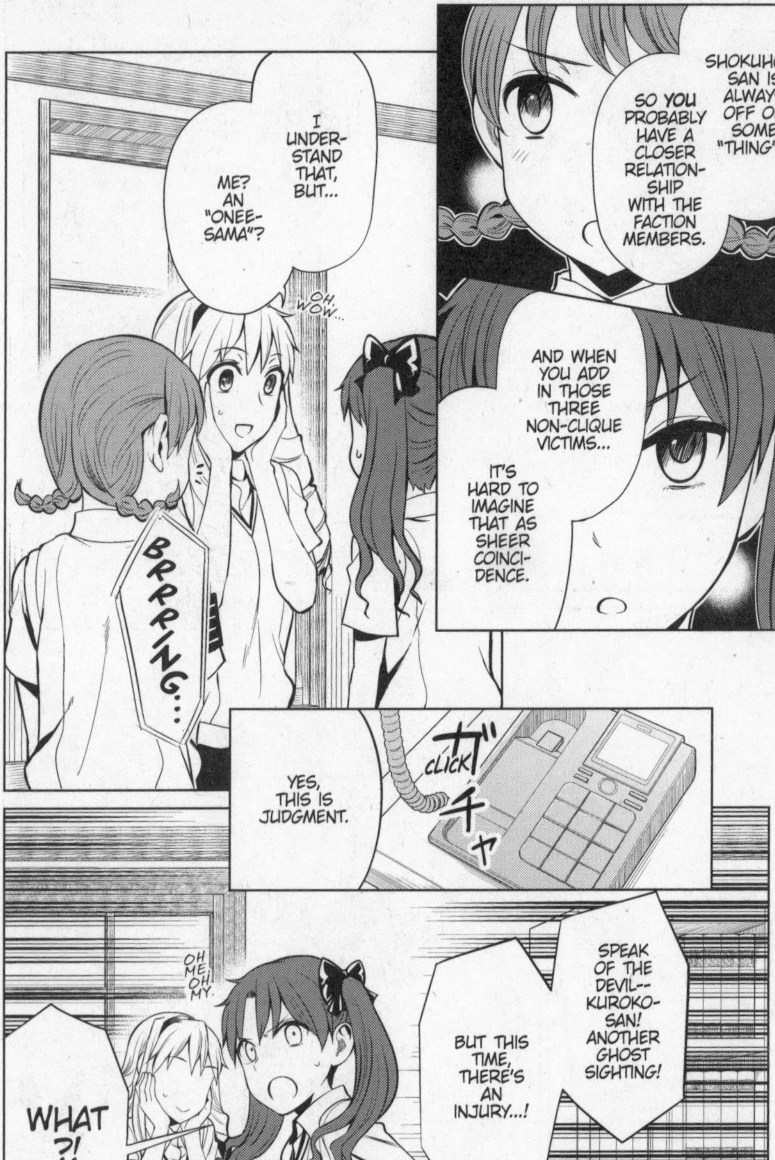
SHOKUHOU-SAN IS ALWAYS OFF ON SOME "THING"...
SO YOU PROBABLY HAVE A CLOSER RELATIONSHIP WITH THE FACTION MEMBERS.
AND WHEN YOU ADD IN THOSE THREE NON-CLIQUE VICTIMS...
IT'S HARD TO IMAGINE THAT AS SHEER COINCIDENCE.
I UNDERSTAND THAT, BUT...
ME? AN "ONEE-SAMA"?
OH, WOW...
BRRRING...
CLICK
ガチャ
YES, THIS IS JUDGMENT.
SPEAK OF THE DEVIL-- KUROKO-SAN! ANOTHER GHOST SIGHTING!
BUT THIS TIME, THERE'S AN INJURY...!
OH ME, OH MY.
WHAT?!

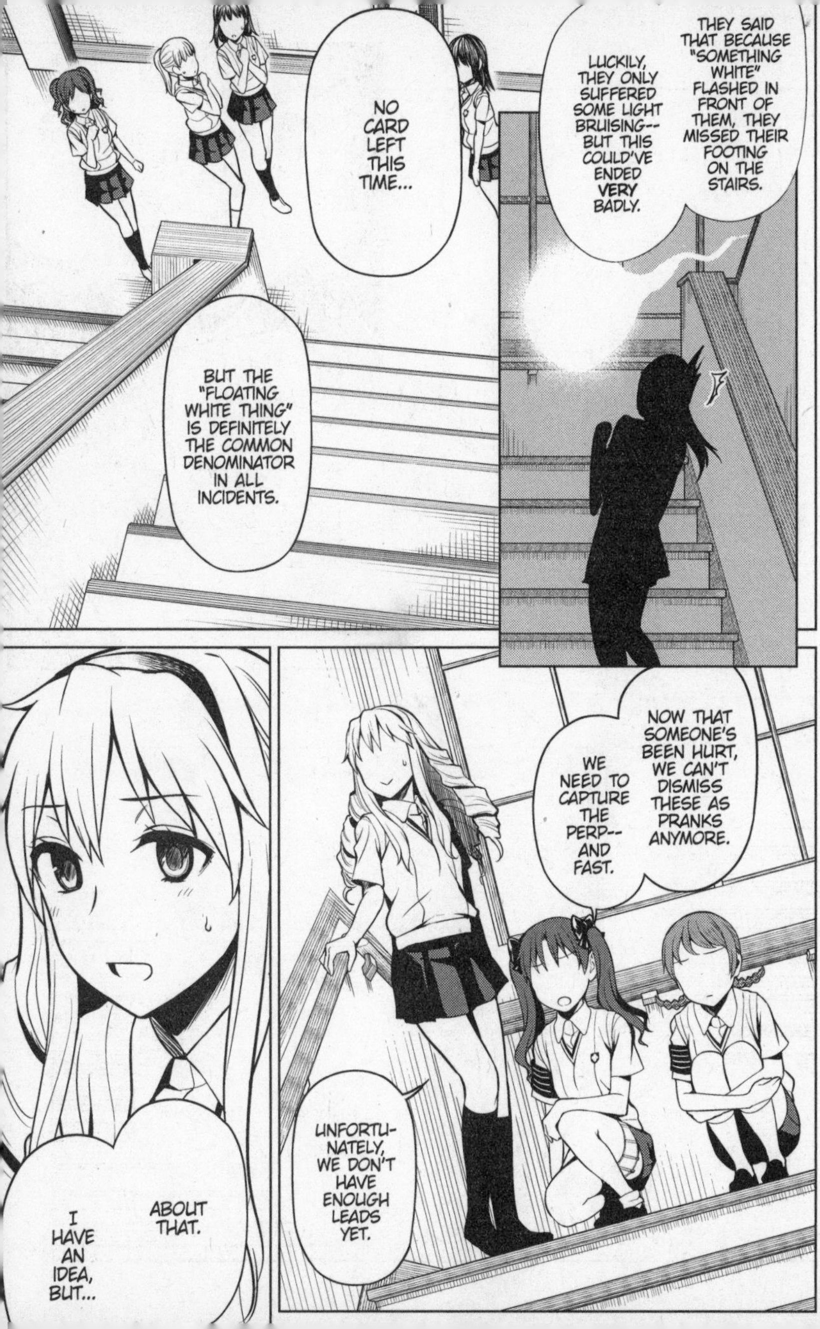
THEY SAID THAT BECAUSE "SOMETHING WHITE" FLASHED IN FRONT OF THEM, THEY MISSED THEIR FOOTING ON THE STAIRS.
LUCKILY, THEY ONLY SUFFERED SOME LIGHT BRUISING-- BUT THIS COULD'VE ENDED **VERY** BADLY.
NO CARD LEFT THIS TIME...
BUT THE "FLOATING WHITE THING" IS DEFINITELY THE COMMON DENOMINATOR IN ALL INCIDENTS.
NOW THAT SOMEONE'S BEEN HURT, WE CAN'T DISMISS THESE AS PRANKS ANYMORE.
WE NEED TO CAPTURE THE PERP-- AND FAST.
UNFORTU-NATELY, WE DON'T HAVE ENOUGH LEADS YET.
ABOUT THAT.
I HAVE AN IDEA, BUT...

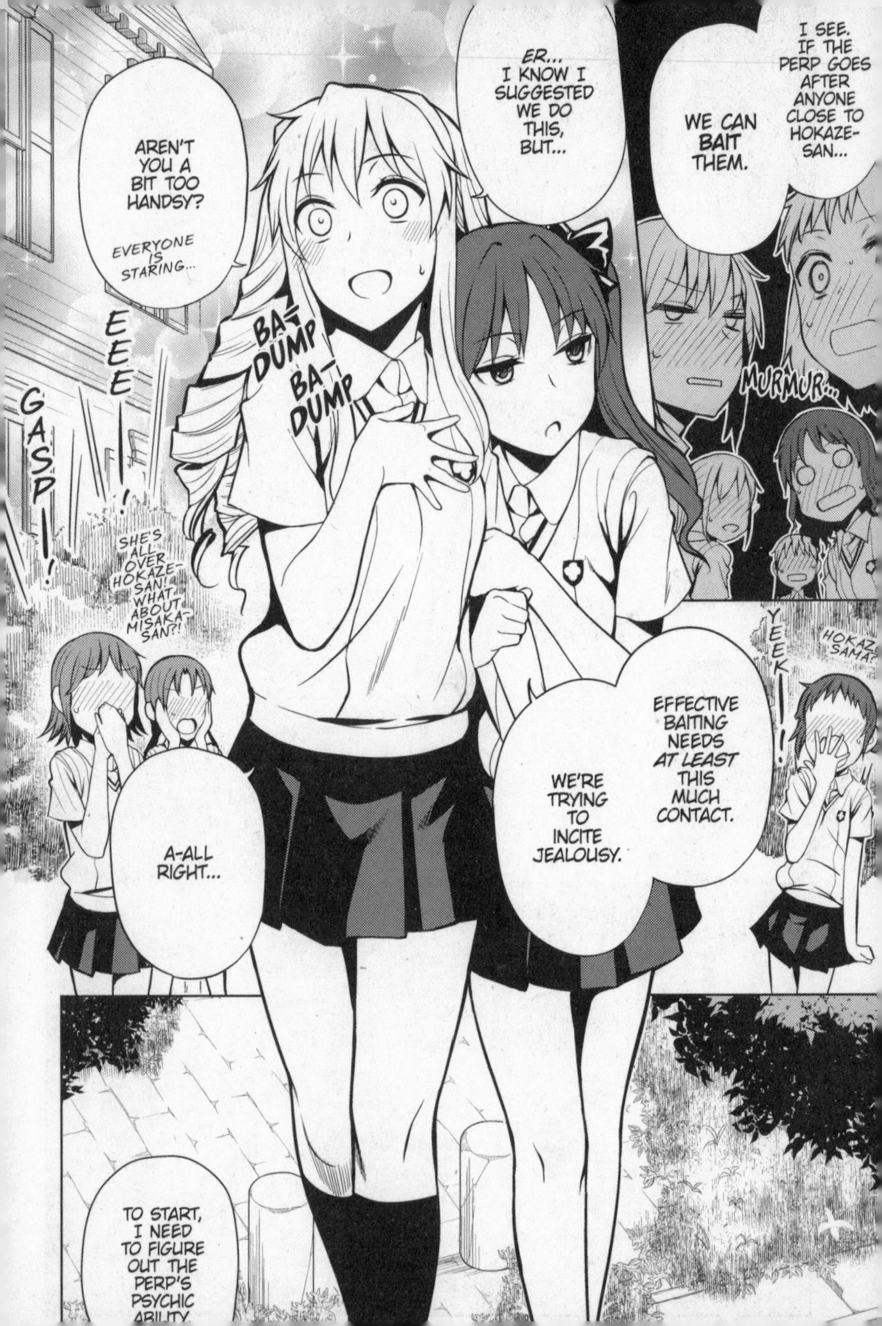
I SEE. IF THE PERP GOES AFTER ANYONE CLOSE TO HOKAZE-SAN...
WE CAN BAIT THEM.
MURMUR...
ER... I KNOW I SUGGESTED WE DO THIS, BUT...
AREN'T YOU A BIT TOO HANDSY?
EVERYONE IS STARING...
BA-DUMP
BA-DUMP
EEE!
GASP!
SHE'S ALL OVER HOKAZE-SAN! WHAT ABOUT MISAKA-SAN?!
HOKAZE-SAMA?
YEEK!
EFFECTIVE BAITING NEEDS AT LEAST THIS MUCH CONTACT.
WE'RE TRYING TO INCITE JEALOUSY.
A-ALL RIGHT...
TO START, I NEED TO FIGURE OUT THE PERP'S PSYCHIC ABILITY.

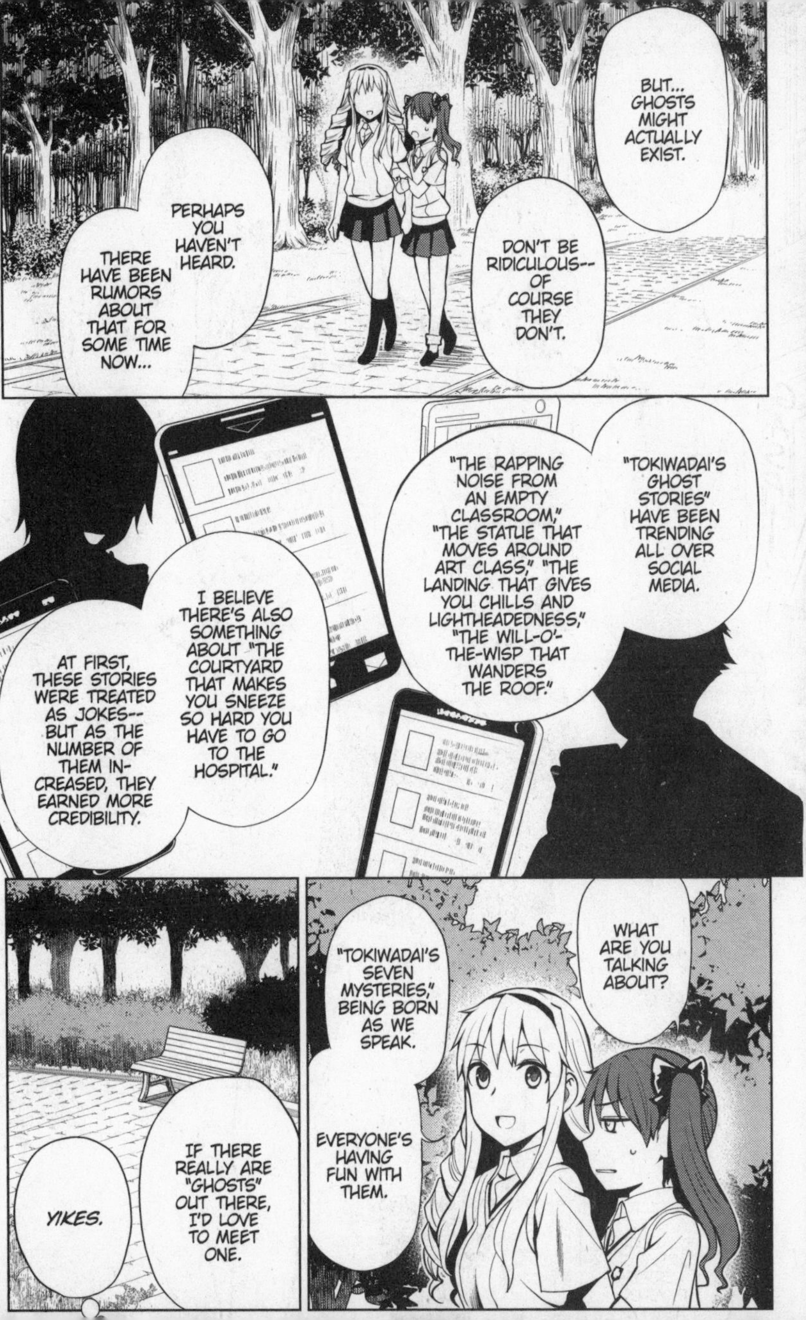
BUT... GHOSTS MIGHT ACTUALLY EXIST.
DON'T BE RIDICULOUS-- OF COURSE THEY DON'T.
PERHAPS YOU HAVEN'T HEARD.
THERE HAVE BEEN RUMORS ABOUT THAT FOR SOME TIME NOW...
"TOKIWADAI'S GHOST STORIES" HAVE BEEN TRENDING ALL OVER SOCIAL MEDIA.
"THE RAPPING NOISE FROM AN EMPTY CLASSROOM," "THE STATUE THAT MOVES AROUND ART CLASS," "THE LANDING THAT GIVES YOU CHILLS AND LIGHTHEADEDNESS," "THE WILL-O'-THE-WISP THAT WANDERS THE ROOF."
I BELIEVE THERE'S ALSO SOMETHING ABOUT "THE COURTYARD THAT MAKES YOU SNEEZE SO HARD YOU HAVE TO GO TO THE HOSPITAL."
AT FIRST, THESE STORIES WERE TREATED AS JOKES-- BUT AS THE NUMBER OF THEM IN-CREASED, THEY EARNED MORE CREDIBILITY.
WHAT ARE YOU TALKING ABOUT?
"TOKIWADAI'S SEVEN MYSTERIES," BEING BORN AS WE SPEAK.
EVERYONE'S HAVING FUN WITH THEM.
IF THERE REALLY ARE "GHOSTS" OUT THERE, I'D LOVE TO MEET ONE.
YIKES.

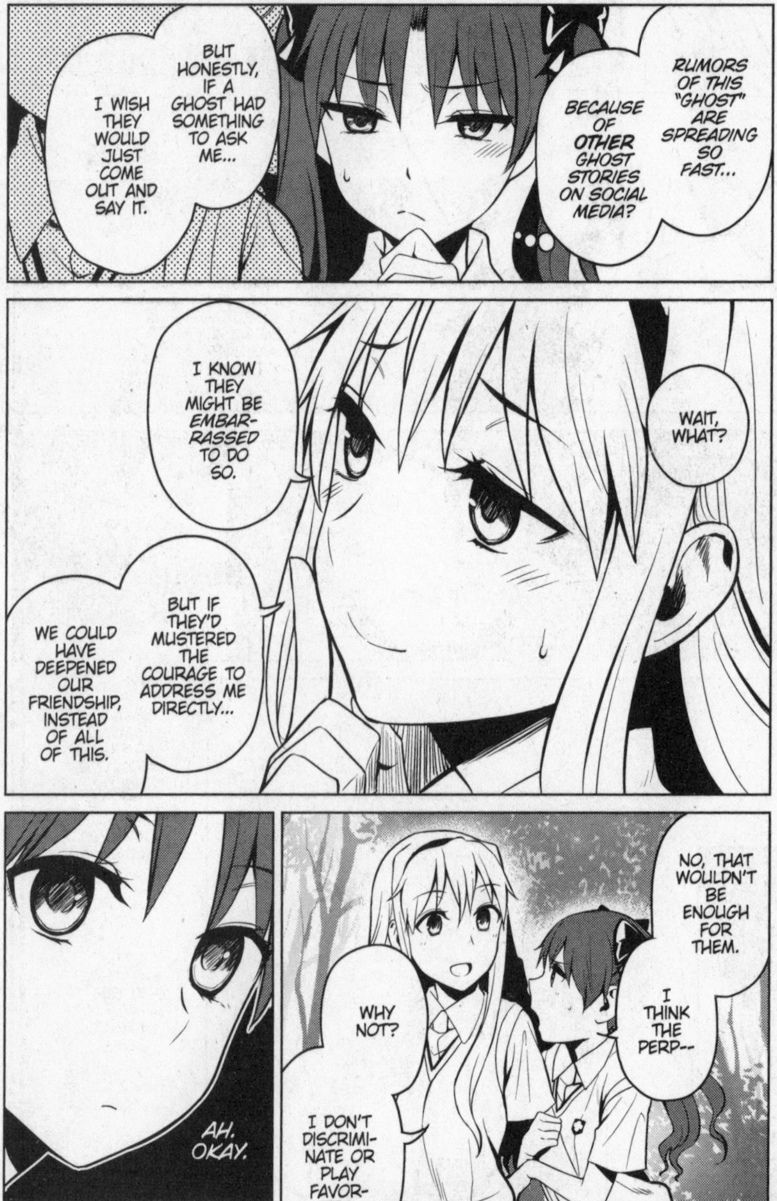
RUMORS OF THIS "GHOST" ARE SPREADING SO FAST...
BECAUSE OF OTHER GHOST STORIES ON SOCIAL MEDIA?
BUT HONESTLY, IF A GHOST HAD SOMETHING TO ASK ME...
I WISH THEY WOULD JUST COME OUT AND SAY IT.
WAIT, WHAT?
I KNOW THEY MIGHT BE EMBARRASSED TO DO SO.
BUT IF THEY'D MUSTERED THE COURAGE TO ADDRESS ME DIRECTLY...
WE COULD HAVE DEEPENED OUR FRIENDSHIP, INSTEAD OF ALL OF THIS.
NO, THAT WOULDN'T BE ENOUGH FOR THEM.
I THINK THE PERP--
WHY NOT?
I DON'T DISCRIMINATE OR PLAY FAVORITES.
AH. OKAY.

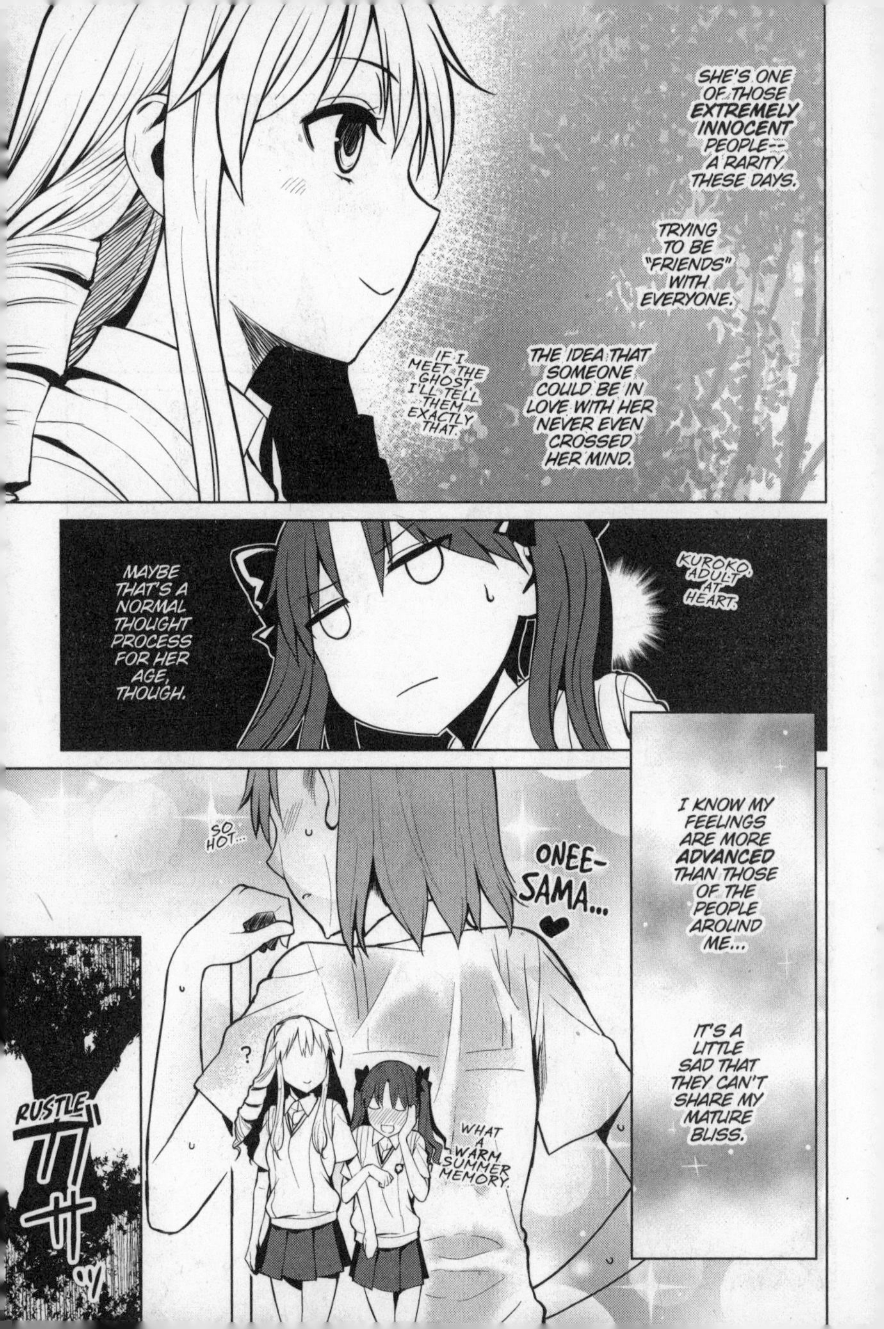
SHE'S ONE OF THOSE EXTREMELY INNOCENT PEOPLE-- A RARITY THESE DAYS.
TRYING TO BE "FRIENDS" WITH EVERYONE.
THE IDEA THAT SOMEONE COULD BE IN LOVE WITH HER NEVER EVEN CROSSED HER MIND.
IF I MEET THE GHOST, I'LL TELL THEM EXACTLY THAT.
KUROKO, ADULT AT HEART.
MAYBE THAT'S A NORMAL THOUGHT PROCESS FOR HER AGE, THOUGH.
I KNOW MY FEELINGS ARE MORE ADVANCED THAN THOSE OF THE PEOPLE AROUND ME...
IT'S A LITTLE SAD THAT THEY CAN'T SHARE MY MATURE BLISS.
ONEE-SAMA...
SO HOT...
?
WHAT A WARM SUMMER MEMORY.
RUSTLE

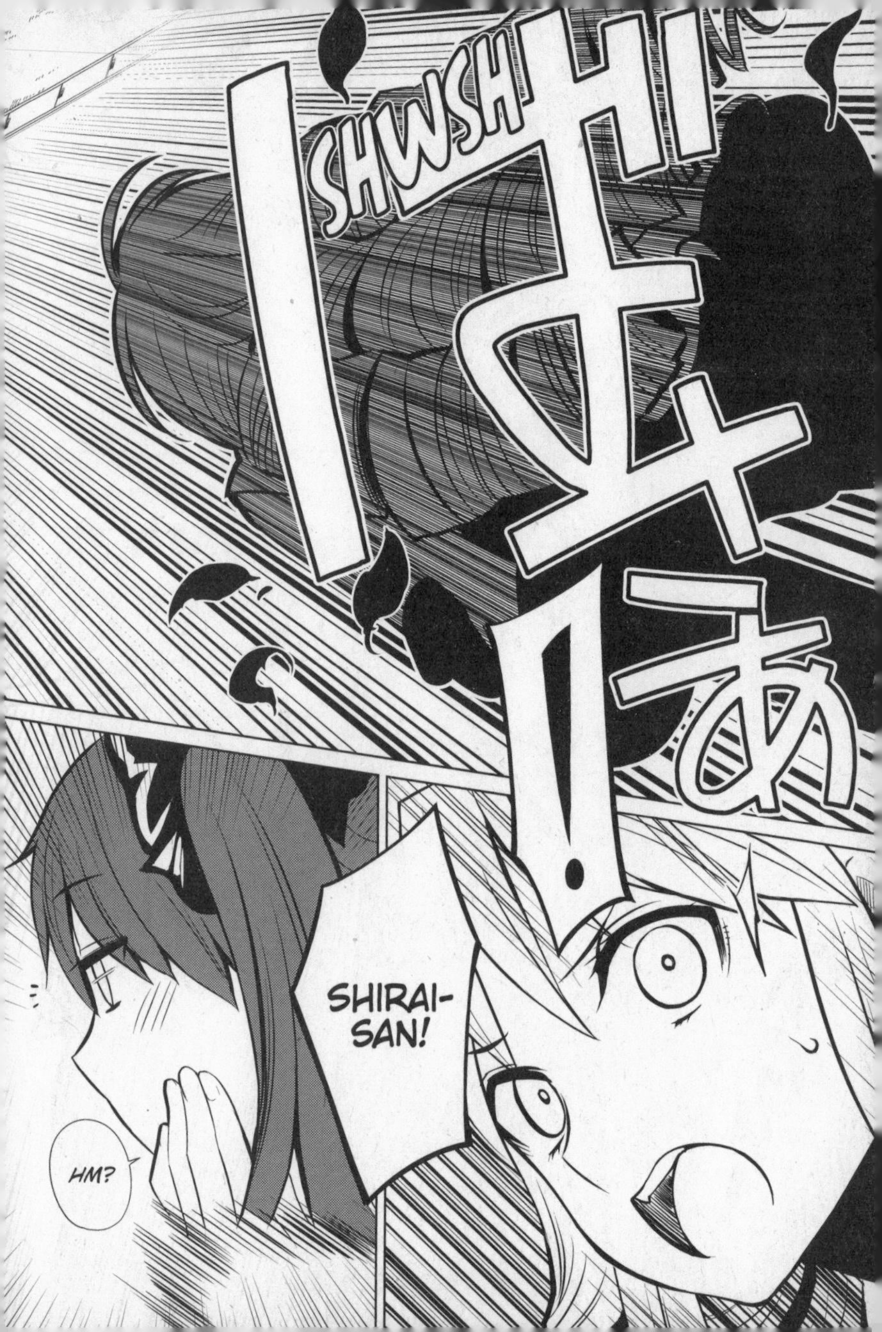
SHWSH
はあ!
SHIRAI-SAN!
HM?

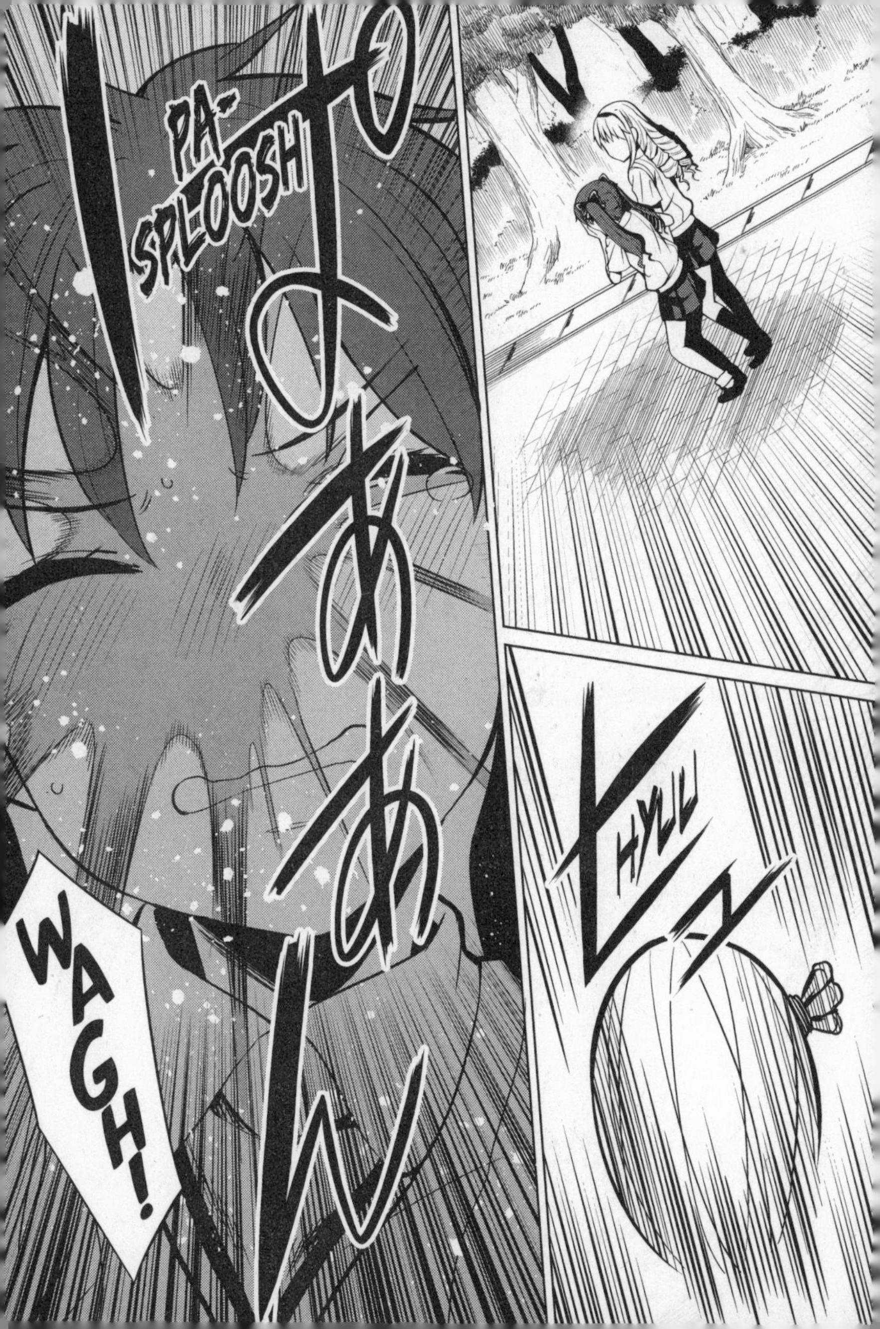
HYULL
PA-SPLOOSH
WAGH!

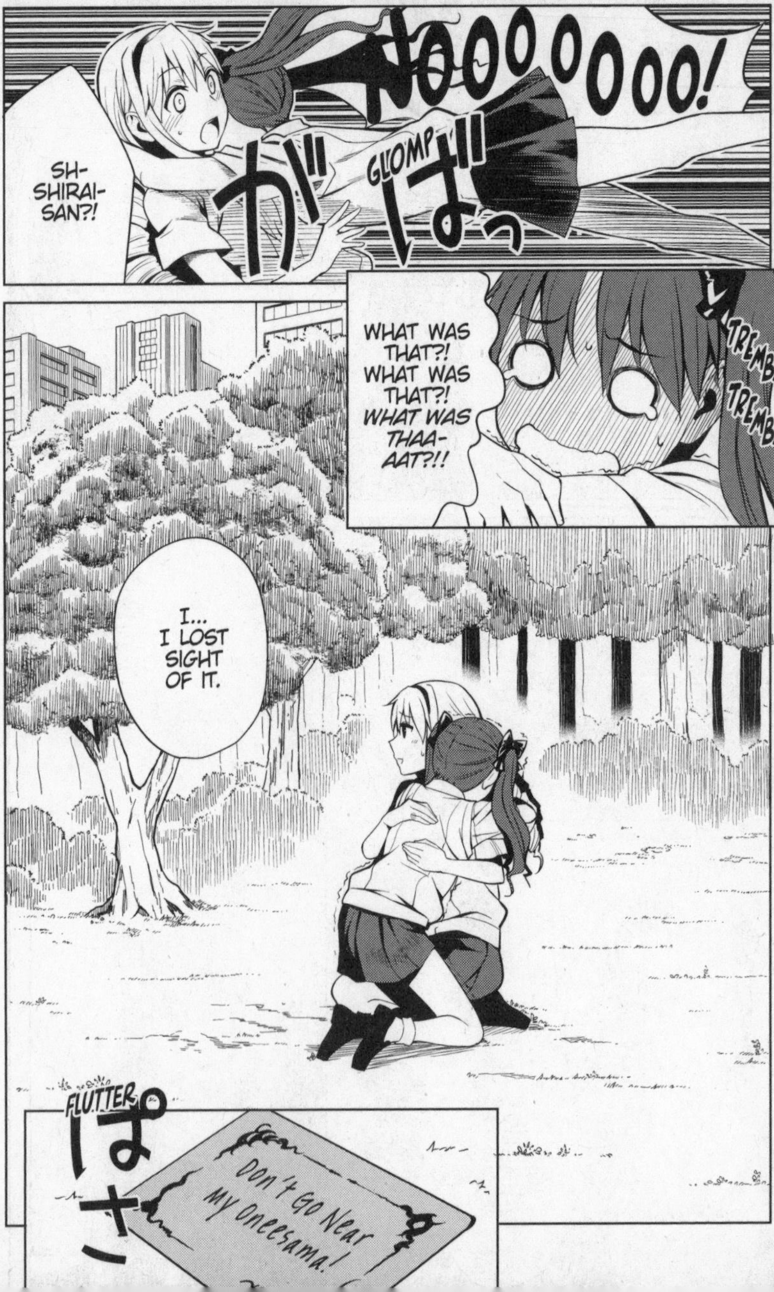
NOOOOOOOO!
がばっ
GLOMP
SH-SHIRAI-SAN?!
WHAT WAS THAT?! WHAT WAS THAT?! WHAT WAS THAA-AAT?!!
TREMBLE TREMBLE
I... I LOST SIGHT OF IT.
ぱさ
FLUTTER
Don't Go Near My Oneesama!

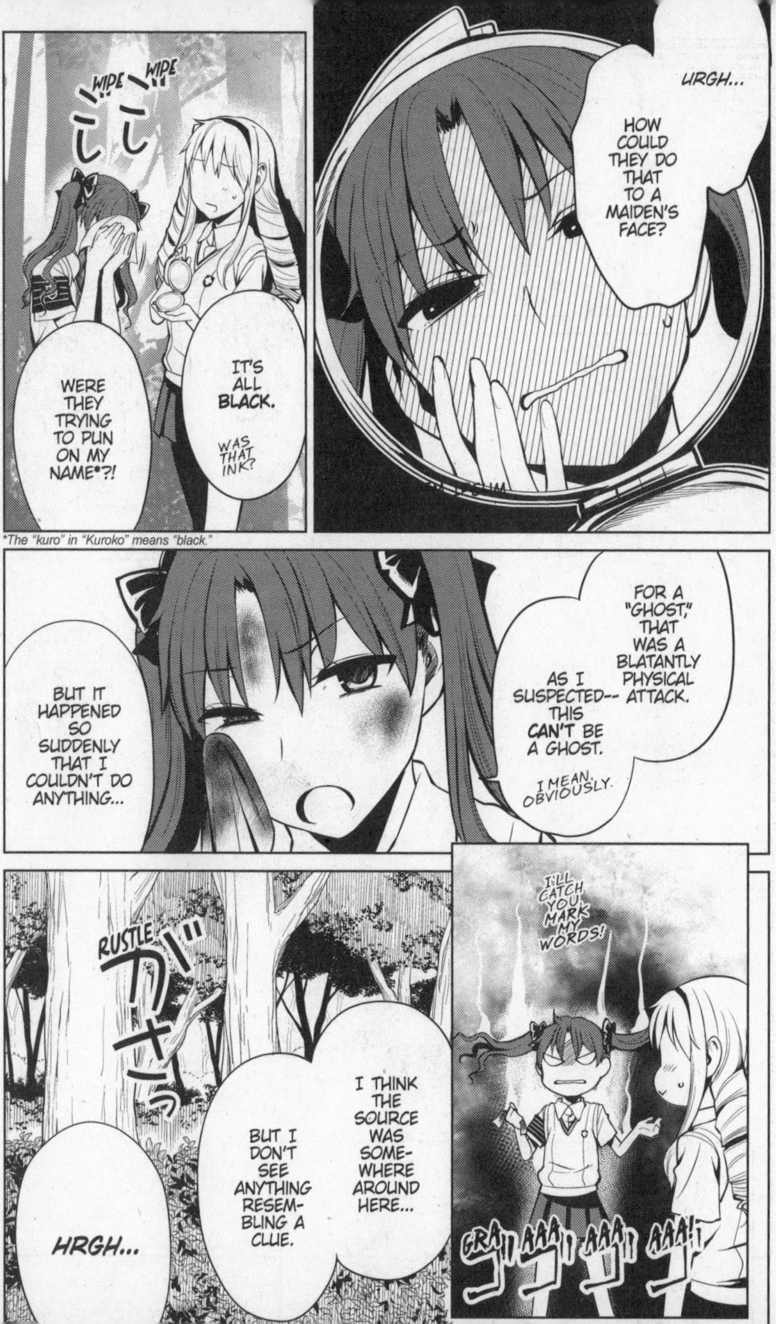
URGH...
HOW COULD THEY DO THAT TO A MAIDEN'S FACE?
WIPE WIPE
IT'S ALL BLACK.
WAS THAT INK?
WERE THEY TRYING TO PUN ON MY NAME*?!
FOR A "GHOST," THAT WAS A BLATANTLY PHYSICAL ATTACK.
AS I SUSPECTED-- THIS CAN'T BE A GHOST.
I MEAN, OBVIOUSLY.
BUT IT HAPPENED SO SUDDENLY THAT I COULDN'T DO ANYTHING...
RUSTLE
I THINK THE SOURCE WAS SOMEWHERE AROUND HERE...
BUT I DON'T SEE ANYTHING RESEMBLING A CLUE.
HRGH...
I'LL CATCH YOU, MARK MY WORDS!
GRAAAAAAAAAA!

*The "kuro" in "Kuroko" means "black."

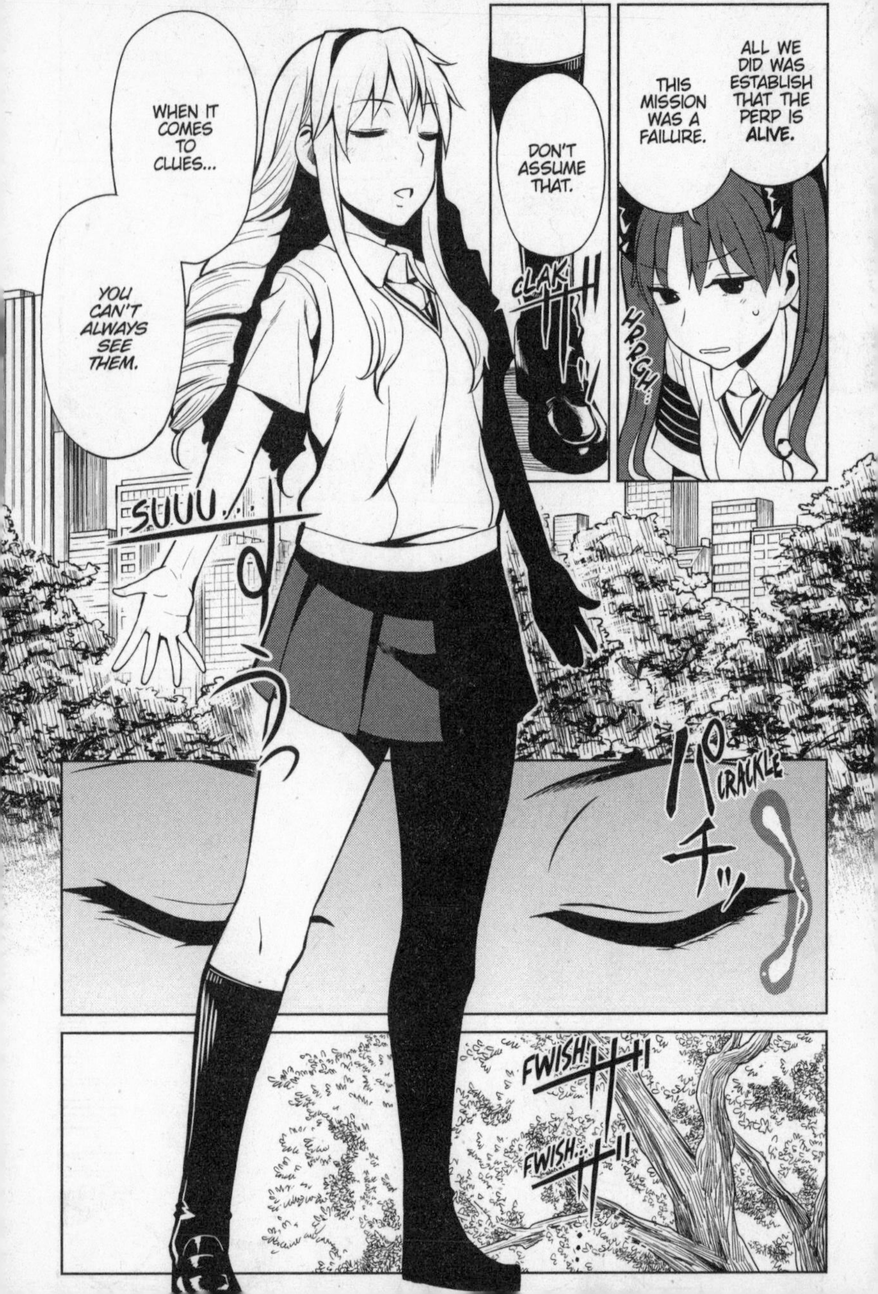
ALL WE DID WAS ESTABLISH THAT THE PERP IS ALIVE.
THIS MISSION WAS A FAILURE.
HRRGH...
DON'T ASSUME THAT.
CLAK
WHEN IT COMES TO CLUES...
YOU CAN'T ALWAYS SEE THEM.
SUUU...
パチッ
CRACKLE
FWISH
FWISH...

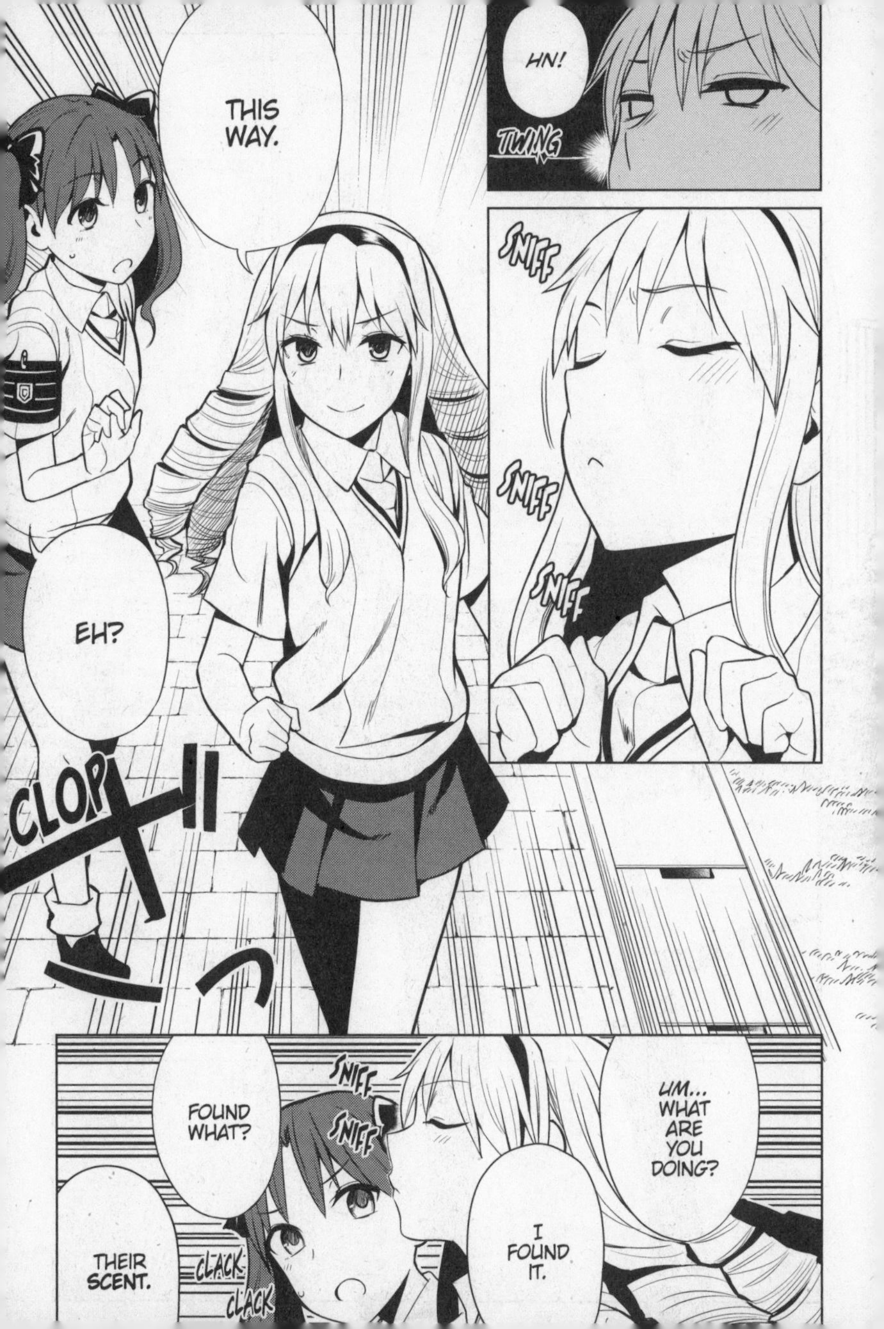
HN!
TWING
THIS WAY.
SNIFF
SNIFF
SNIFF
EH?
CLOP
UM... WHAT ARE YOU DOING?
SNIFF
SNIFF
I FOUND IT.
FOUND WHAT?
THEIR SCENT.
CLACK
CLACK

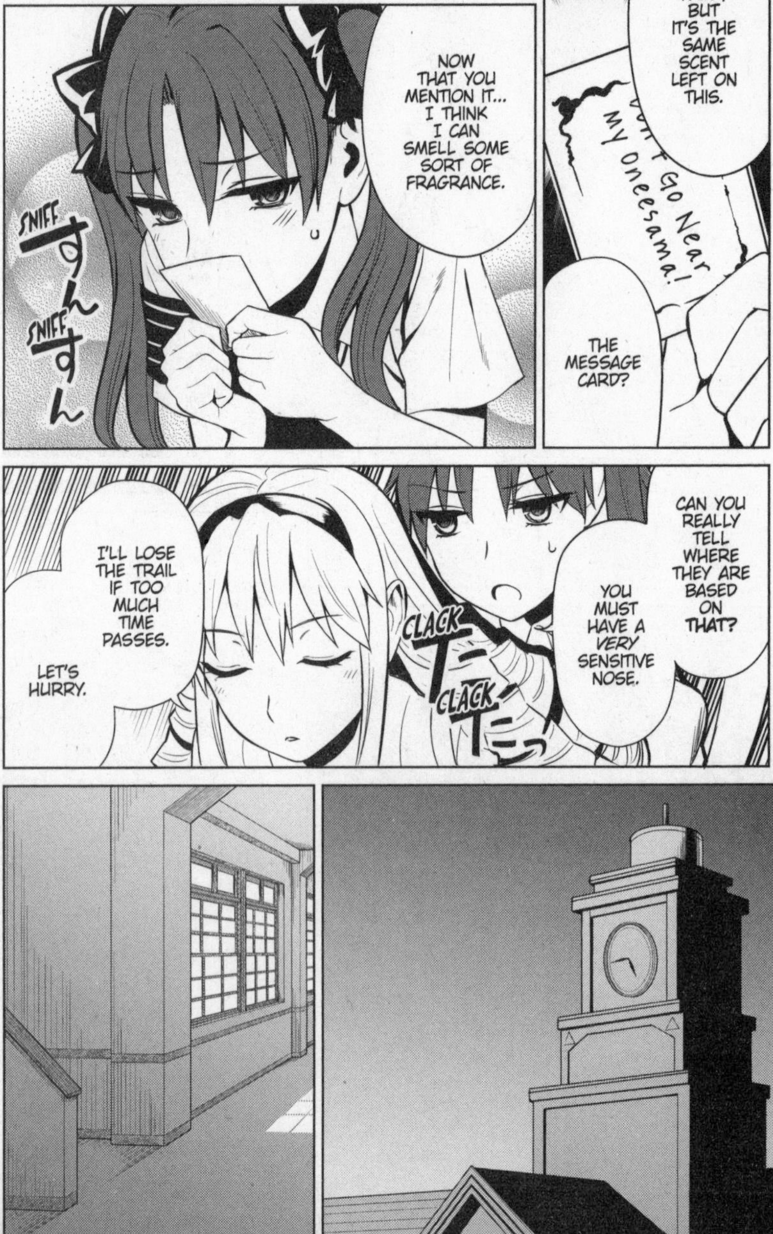
IT'S FAINT, BUT IT'S THE SAME SCENT LEFT ON THIS.
Go Near My Oneesama!
THE MESSAGE CARD?
NOW THAT YOU MENTION IT... I THINK I CAN SMELL SOME SORT OF FRAGRANCE.
SNIFF すん
SNIFF すん
CAN YOU REALLY TELL WHERE THEY ARE BASED ON THAT?
YOU MUST HAVE A VERY SENSITIVE NOSE.
CLACK
CLACK
I'LL LOSE THE TRAIL IF TOO MUCH TIME PASSES.
LET'S HURRY.

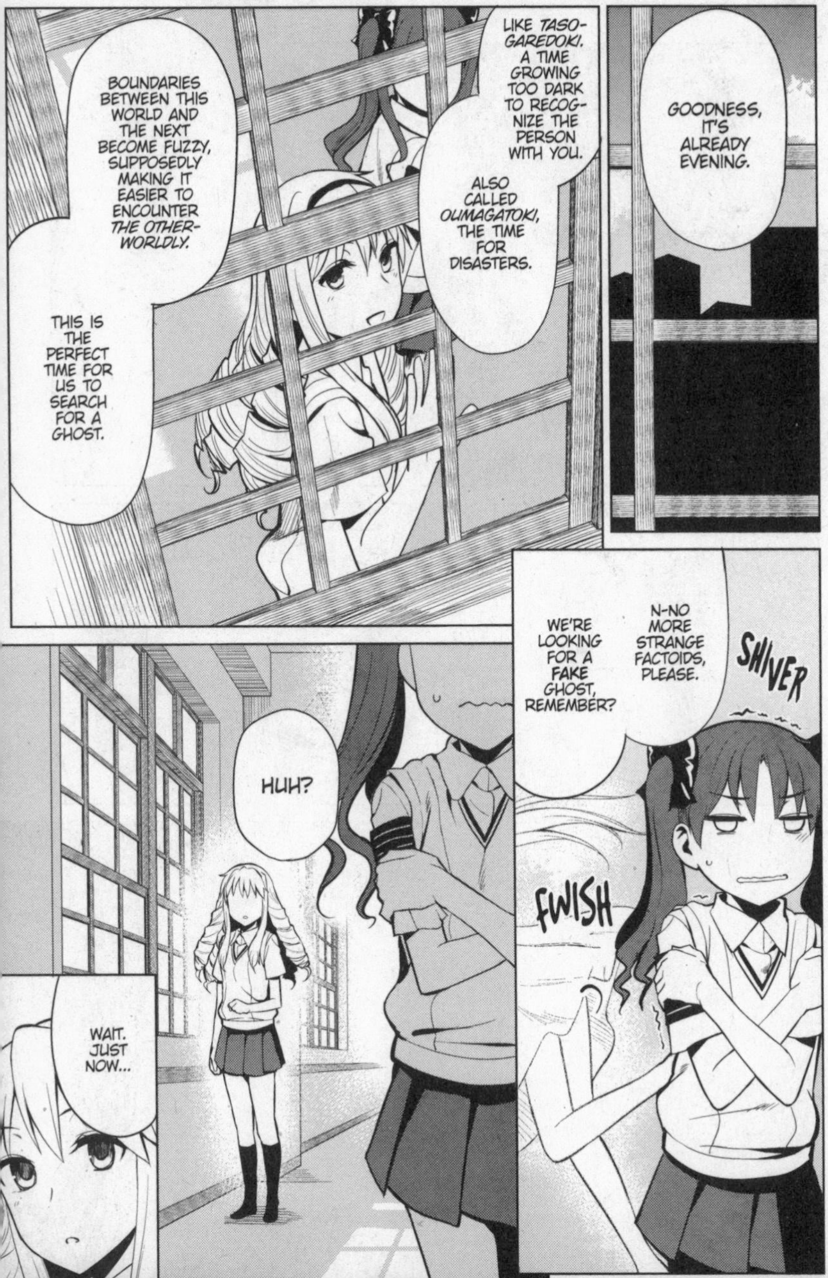
GOODNESS, IT'S ALREADY EVENING.
LIKE TASO-GAREDOKI. A TIME GROWING TOO DARK TO RECOG-NIZE THE PERSON WITH YOU.
ALSO CALLED OUMAGATOKI, THE TIME FOR DISASTERS.
BOUNDARIES BETWEEN THIS WORLD AND THE NEXT BECOME FUZZY, SUPPOSEDLY MAKING IT EASIER TO ENCOUNTER THE OTHER-WORLDLY.
THIS IS THE PERFECT TIME FOR US TO SEARCH FOR A GHOST.
SHIVER
N-NO MORE STRANGE FACTOIDS, PLEASE.
WE'RE LOOKING FOR A FAKE GHOST, REMEMBER?
FWISH
HUH?
WAIT. JUST NOW...

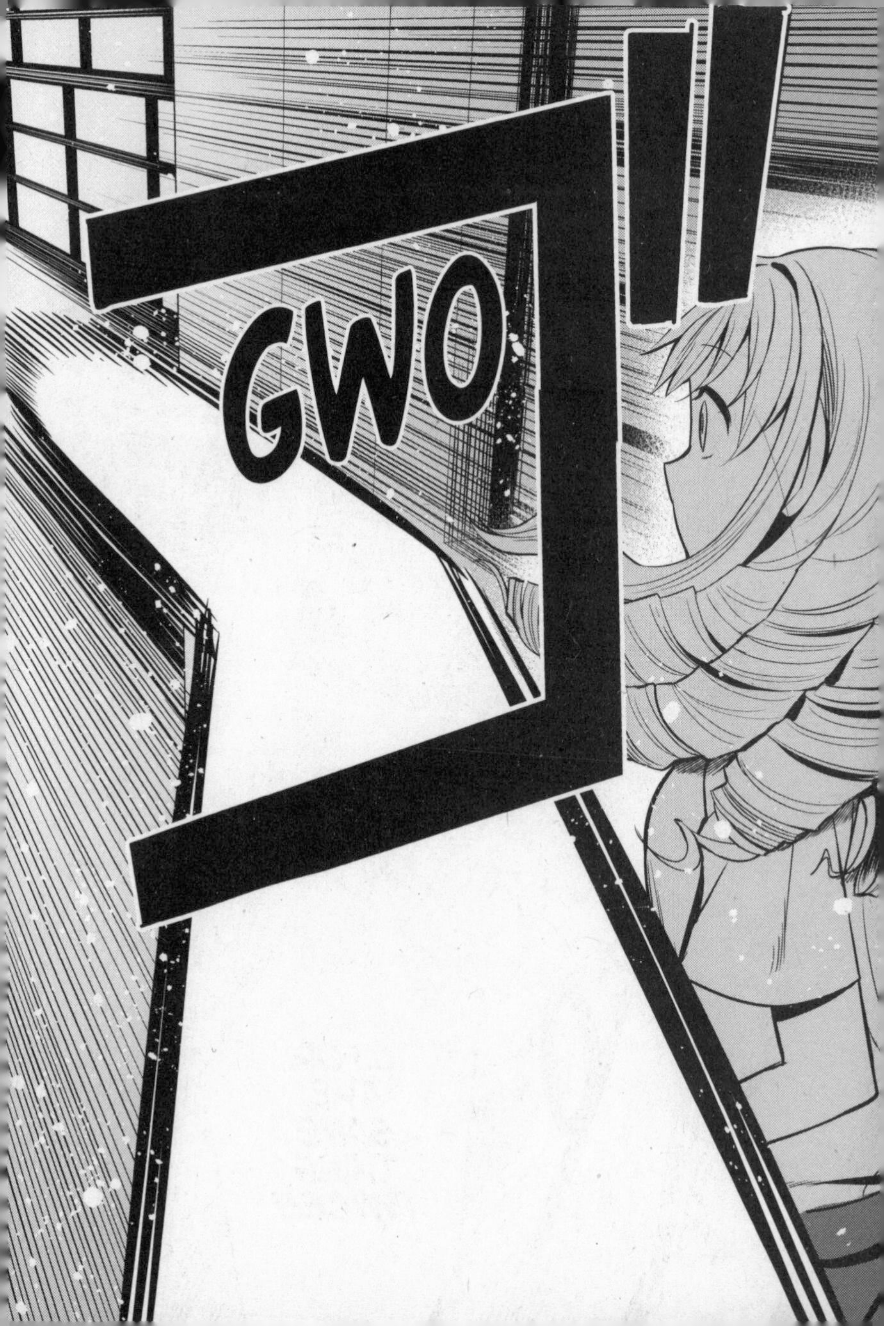
GWO!!

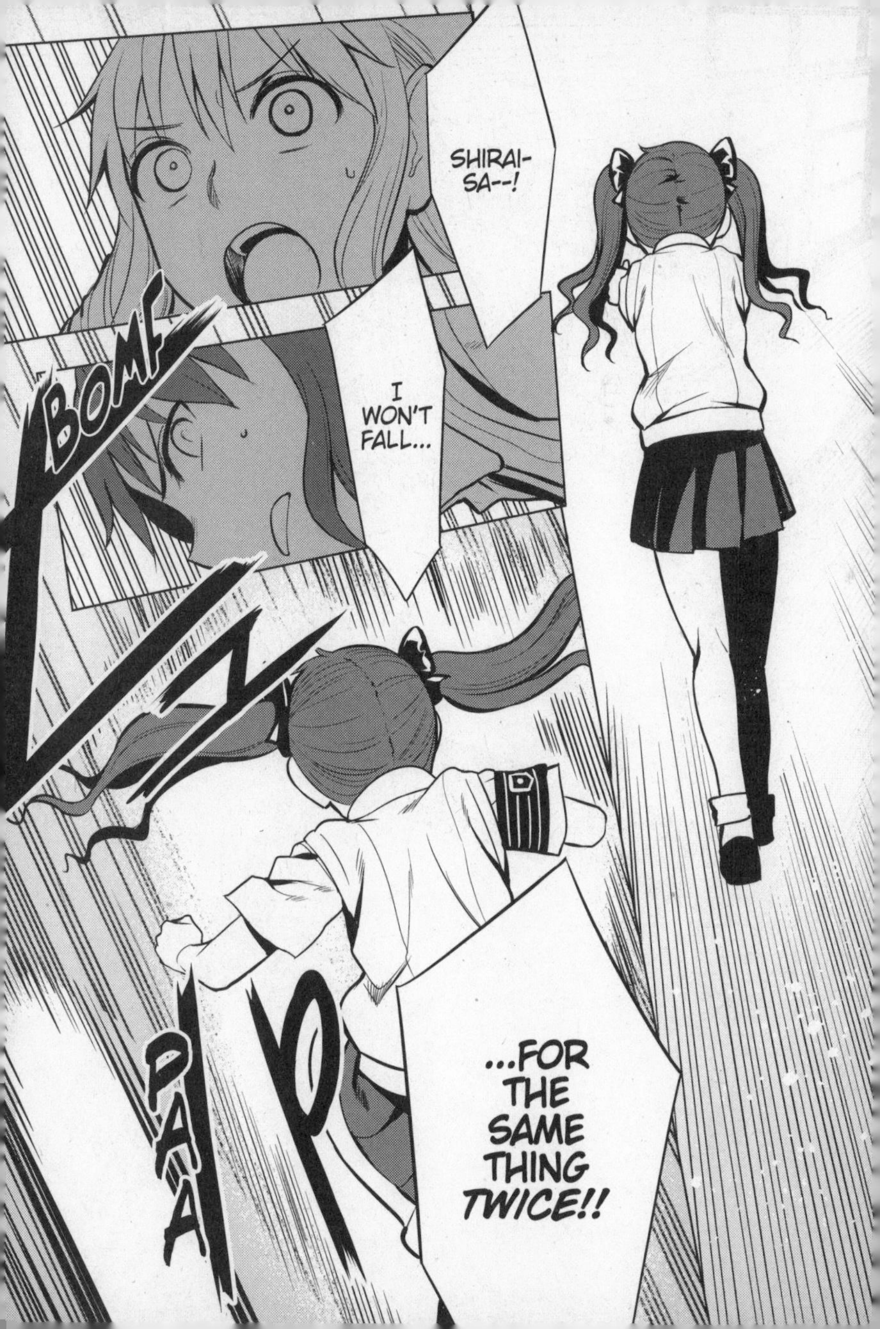
SHIRAI-
SA--!
BOMF
I
WON'T
FALL...
PAAA
...FOR
THE
SAME
THING
TWICE!!

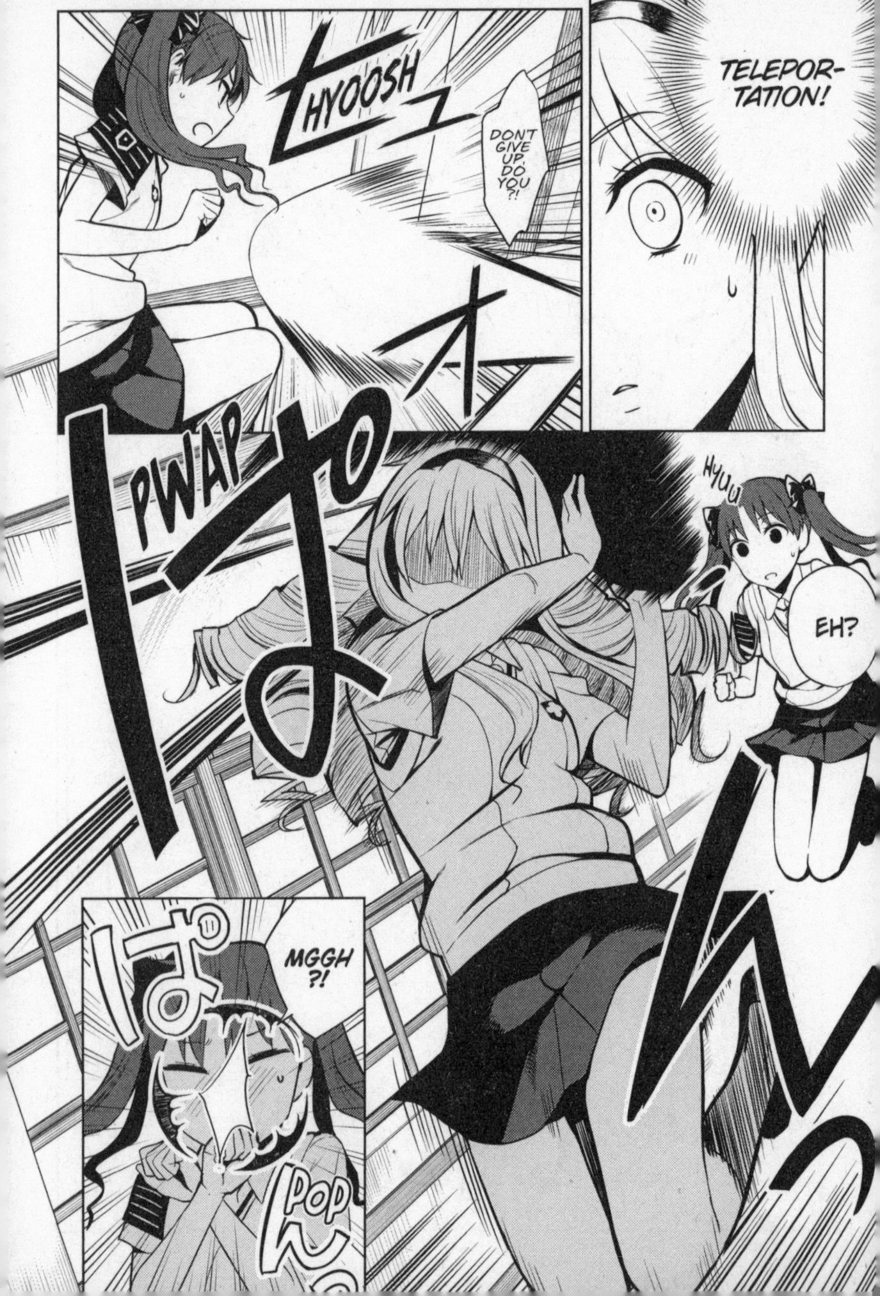
TELEPOR-
TATION!
DON'T GIVE UP, DO YOU?!
HYOOSH
PWAP
HYUU
EH?
MGGH ?!
POP

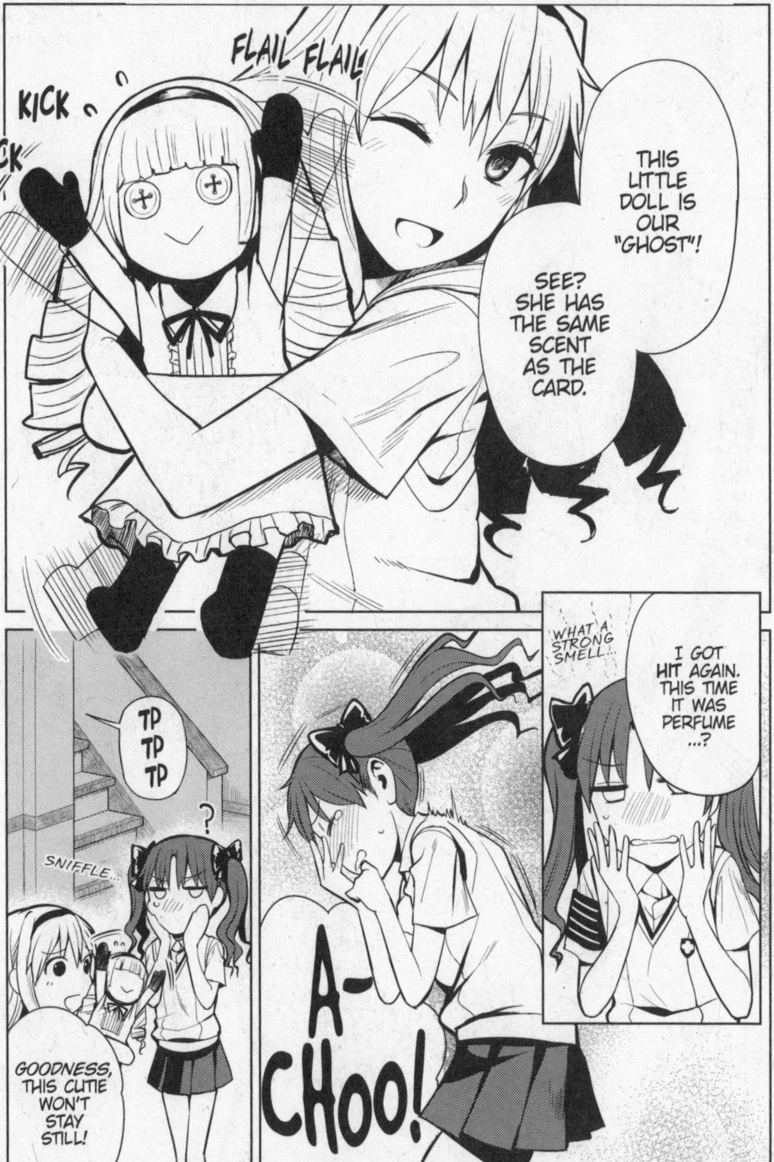
THIS LITTLE DOLL IS OUR "GHOST"!
SEE? SHE HAS THE SAME SCENT AS THE CARD.
FLAIL FLAIL!
KICK
KICK
I GOT HIT AGAIN. THIS TIME IT WAS PERFUME ...?
WHAT A STRONG SMELL...
A-CHOO!
TP TP TP
?
SNIFFLE...
GOODNESS, THIS CUTIE WON'T STAY STILL!

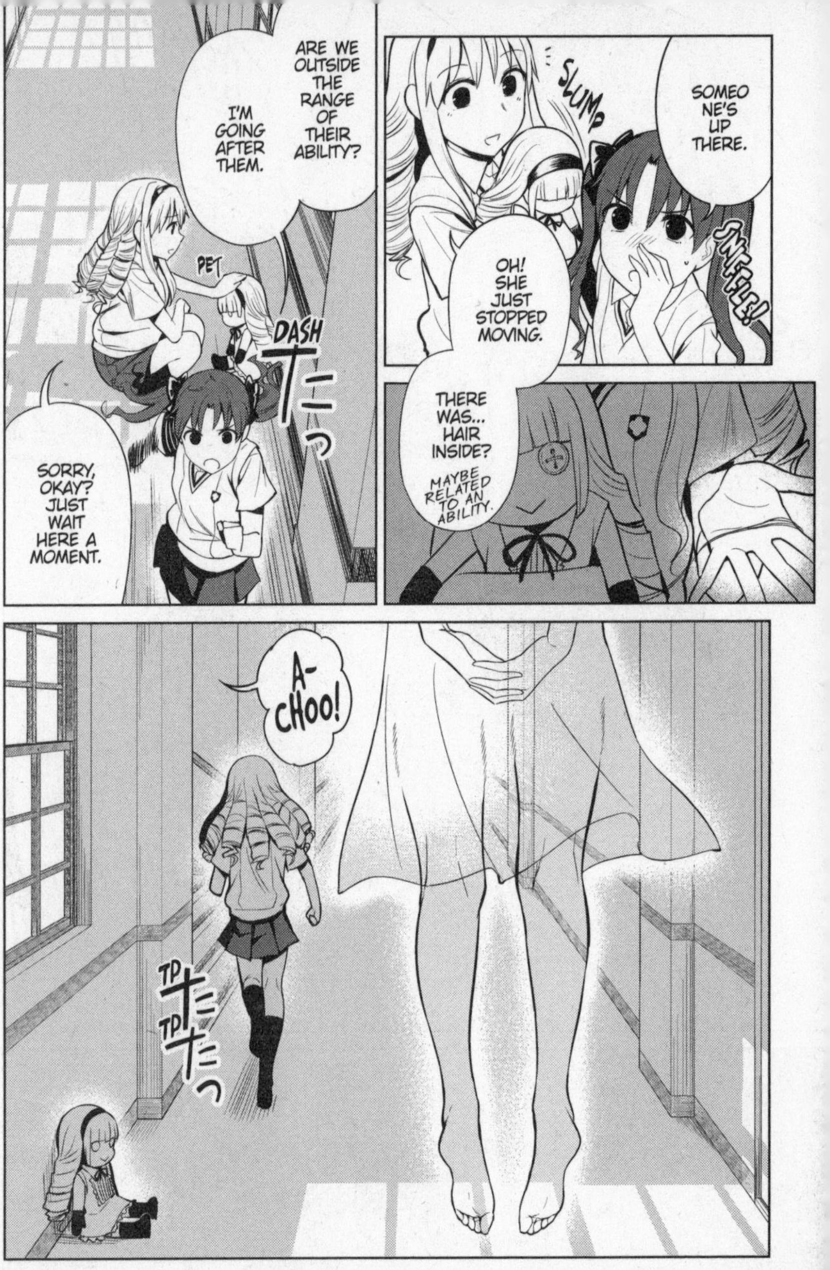
SOMEONE'S UP THERE.
SLUMP
SNIFFLE!
OH! SHE JUST STOPPED MOVING.
THERE WAS... HAIR INSIDE?
MAYBE RELATED TO AN ABILITY.
ARE WE OUTSIDE THE RANGE OF THEIR ABILITY?
I'M GOING AFTER THEM.
PET
DASH
SORRY, OKAY? JUST WAIT HERE A MOMENT.
A-CHOO!
TP
TP

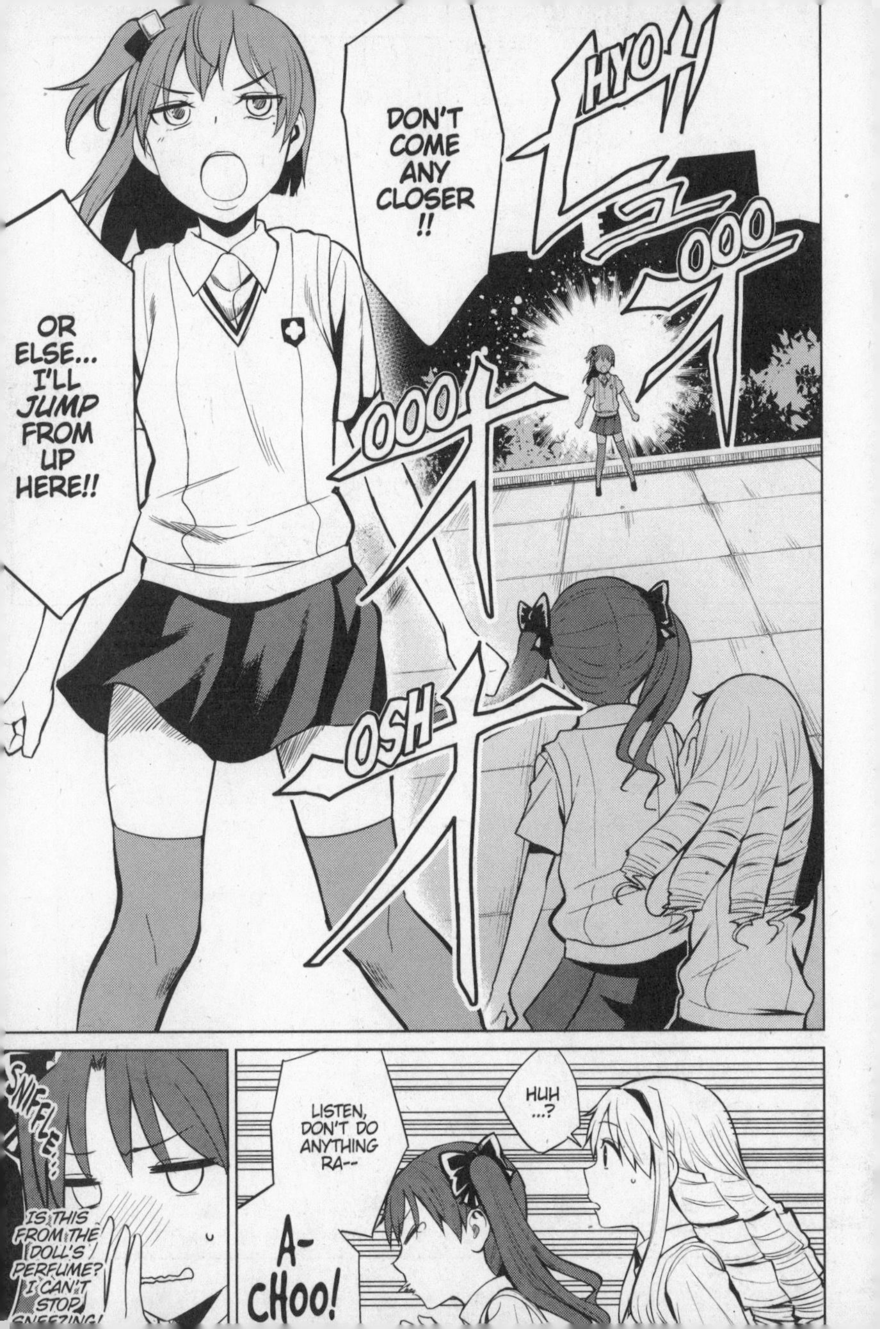
HYOH
DON'T COME ANY CLOSER !!
OR ELSE... I'LL JUMP FROM UP HERE!!
OOO
OOO
OSH
HUH ...?
LISTEN, DON'T DO ANYTHING RA--
SNIFFLE...
IS THIS FROM THE DOLL'S PERFUME? I CAN'T STOP SNEEZING!
A-CHOO!

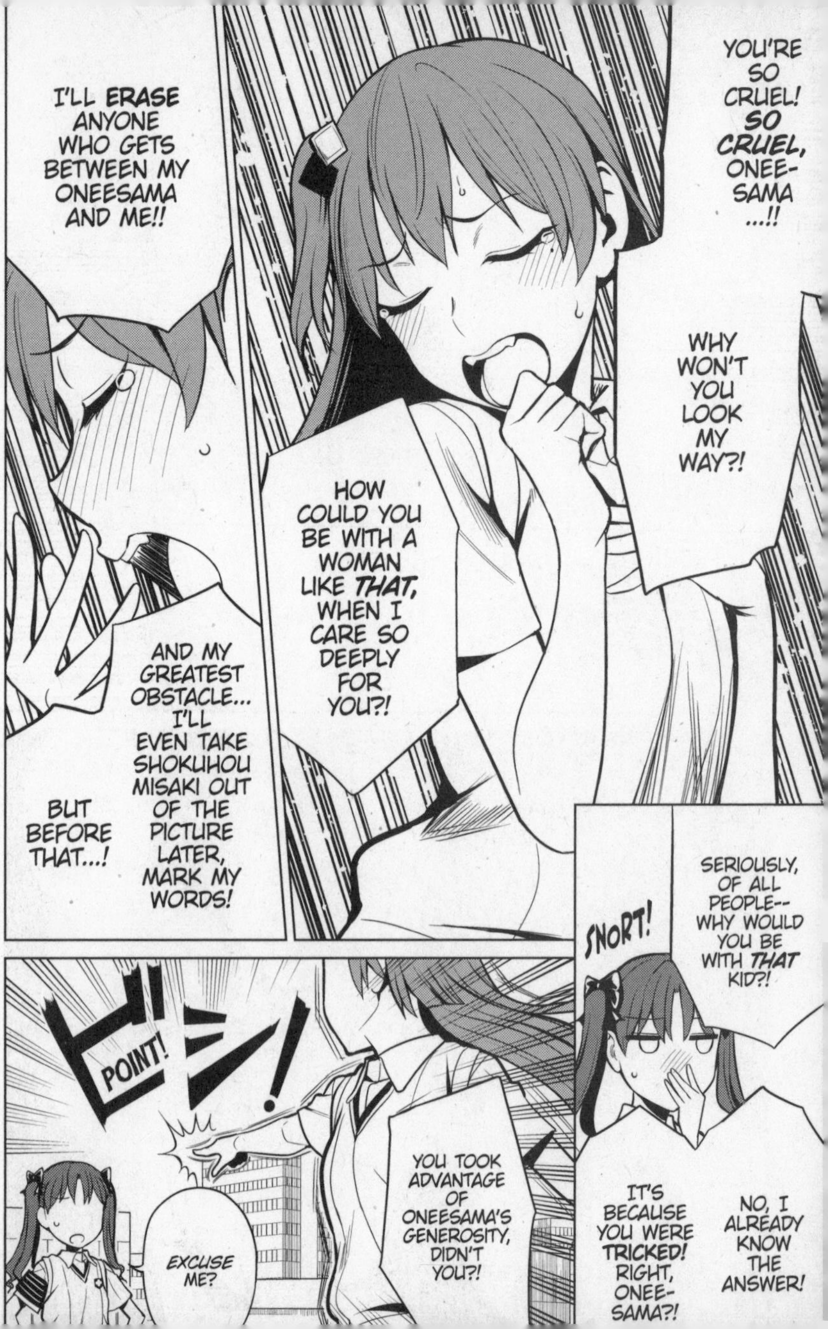
YOU'RE SO CRUEL! SO CRUEL, ONEE-SAMA ...!!
WHY WON'T YOU LOOK MY WAY?!
HOW COULD YOU BE WITH A WOMAN LIKE THAT, WHEN I CARE SO DEEPLY FOR YOU?!
I'LL ERASE ANYONE WHO GETS BETWEEN MY ONEESAMA AND ME!!
AND MY GREATEST OBSTACLE... I'LL EVEN TAKE SHOKUHOU MISAKI OUT OF THE PICTURE LATER, MARK MY WORDS!
BUT BEFORE THAT...!
SERIOUSLY, OF ALL PEOPLE-- WHY WOULD YOU BE WITH THAT KID?!
SNORT!
NO, I ALREADY KNOW THE ANSWER!
IT'S BECAUSE YOU WERE TRICKED! RIGHT, ONEE-SAMA?!
YOU TOOK ADVANTAGE OF ONEESAMA'S GENEROSITY, DIDN'T YOU?!
POINT!
EXCUSE ME?

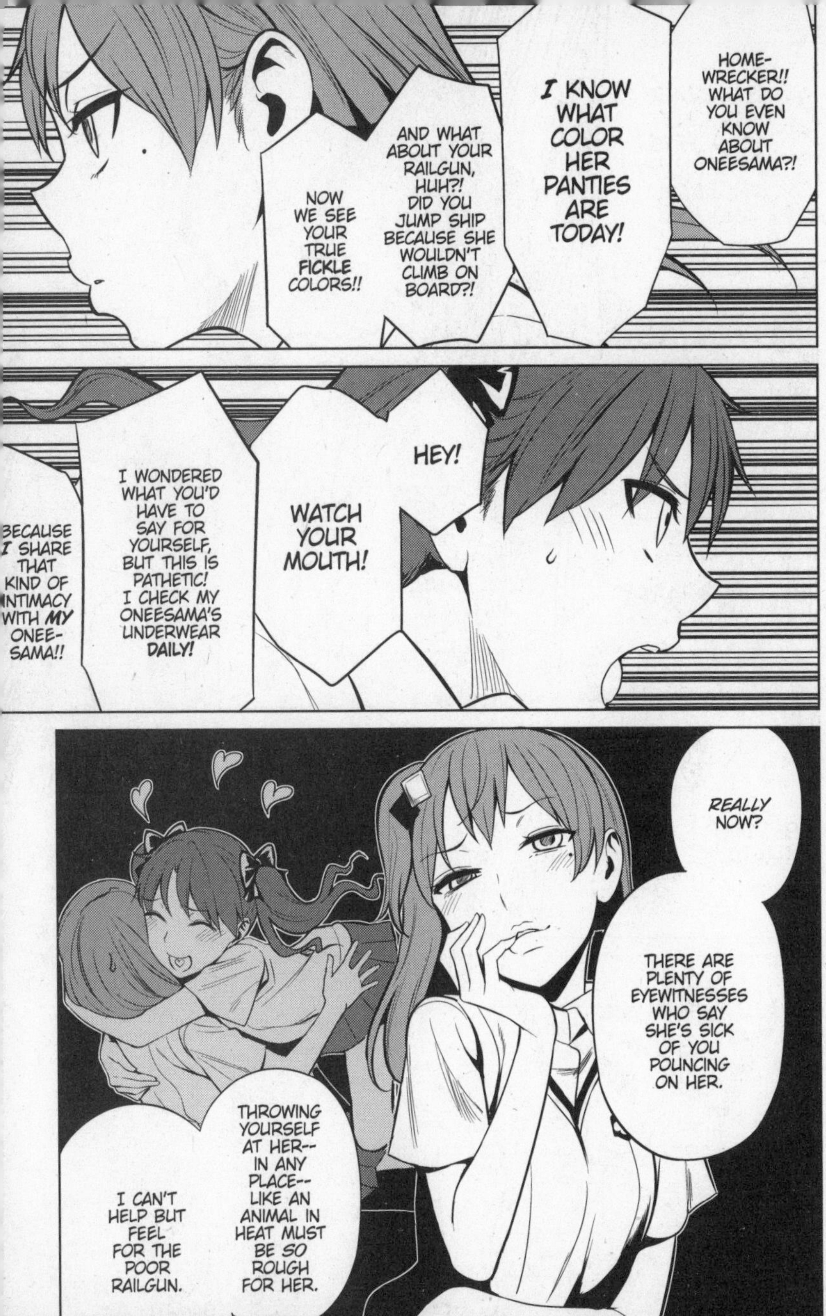
HOME-WRECKER!! WHAT DO YOU EVEN KNOW ABOUT ONEESAMA?!
I KNOW WHAT COLOR HER PANTIES ARE TODAY!
AND WHAT ABOUT YOUR RAILGUN, HUH?! DID YOU JUMP SHIP BECAUSE SHE WOULDN'T CLIMB ON BOARD?!
NOW WE SEE YOUR TRUE FICKLE COLORS!!
HEY!
WATCH YOUR MOUTH!
I WONDERED WHAT YOU'D HAVE TO SAY FOR YOURSELF, BUT THIS IS PATHETIC! I CHECK MY ONEESAMA'S UNDERWEAR DAILY!
BECAUSE I SHARE THAT KIND OF INTIMACY WITH MY ONEE-SAMA!!
REALLY NOW?
THERE ARE PLENTY OF EYEWITNESSES WHO SAY SHE'S SICK OF YOU POUNCING ON HER.
THROWING YOURSELF AT HER-- IN ANY PLACE-- LIKE AN ANIMAL IN HEAT MUST BE SO ROUGH FOR HER.
I CAN'T HELP BUT FEEL FOR THE POOR RAILGUN.

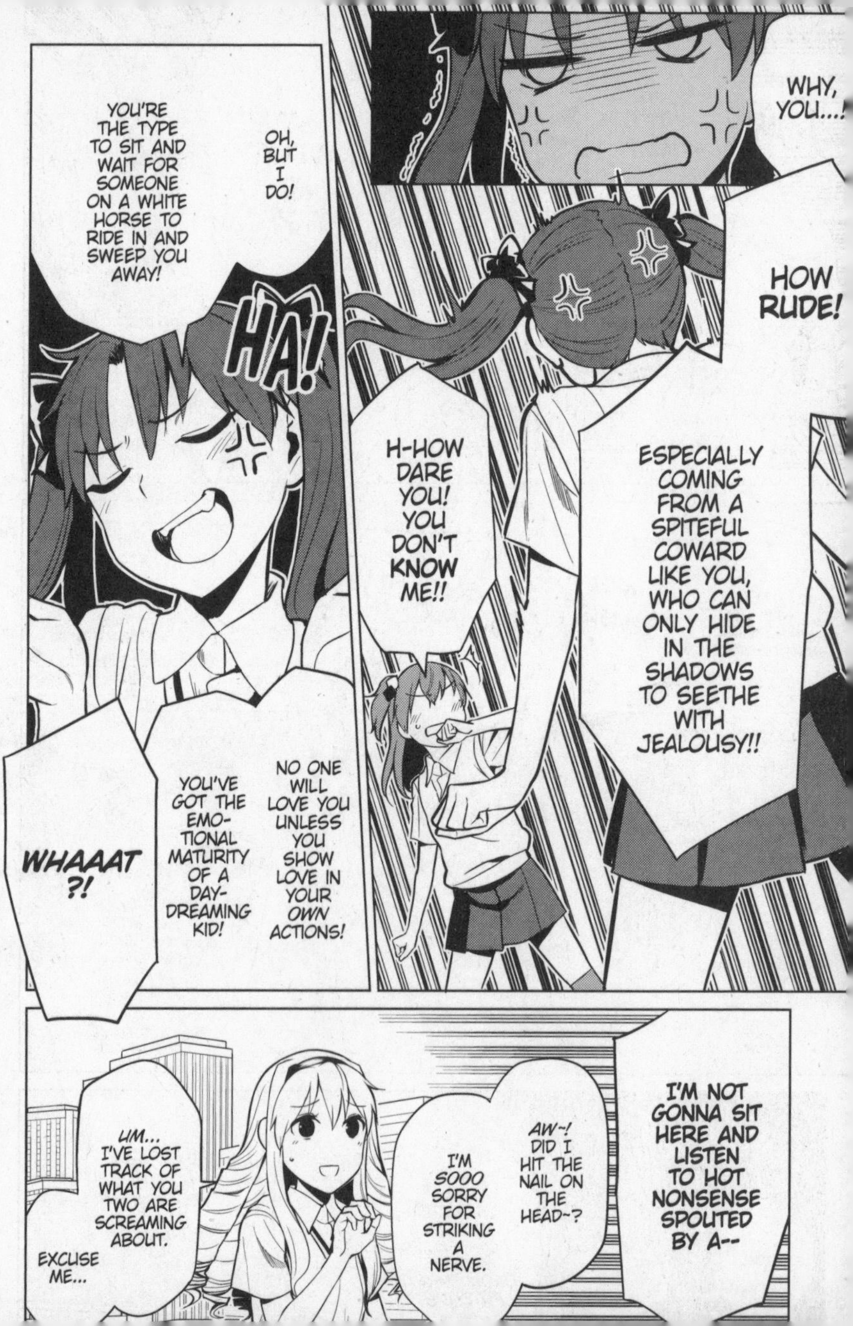
WHY, YOU...!
HOW RUDE!
ESPECIALLY COMING FROM A SPITEFUL COWARD LIKE YOU, WHO CAN ONLY HIDE IN THE SHADOWS TO SEETHE WITH JEALOUSY!!
H-HOW DARE YOU! YOU DON'T KNOW ME!!
OH, BUT I DO!
YOU'RE THE TYPE TO SIT AND WAIT FOR SOMEONE ON A WHITE HORSE TO RIDE IN AND SWEEP YOU AWAY!
HA!
NO ONE WILL LOVE YOU UNLESS YOU SHOW LOVE IN YOUR OWN ACTIONS!
YOU'VE GOT THE EMOTIONAL MATURITY OF A DAYDREAMING KID!
WHAAAT?!
I'M NOT GONNA SIT HERE AND LISTEN TO HOT NONSENSE SPOUTED BY A--
AW~! DID I HIT THE NAIL ON THE HEAD~?
I'M SOOO SORRY FOR STRIKING A NERVE.
UM... I'VE LOST TRACK OF WHAT YOU TWO ARE SCREAMING ABOUT.
EXCUSE ME...

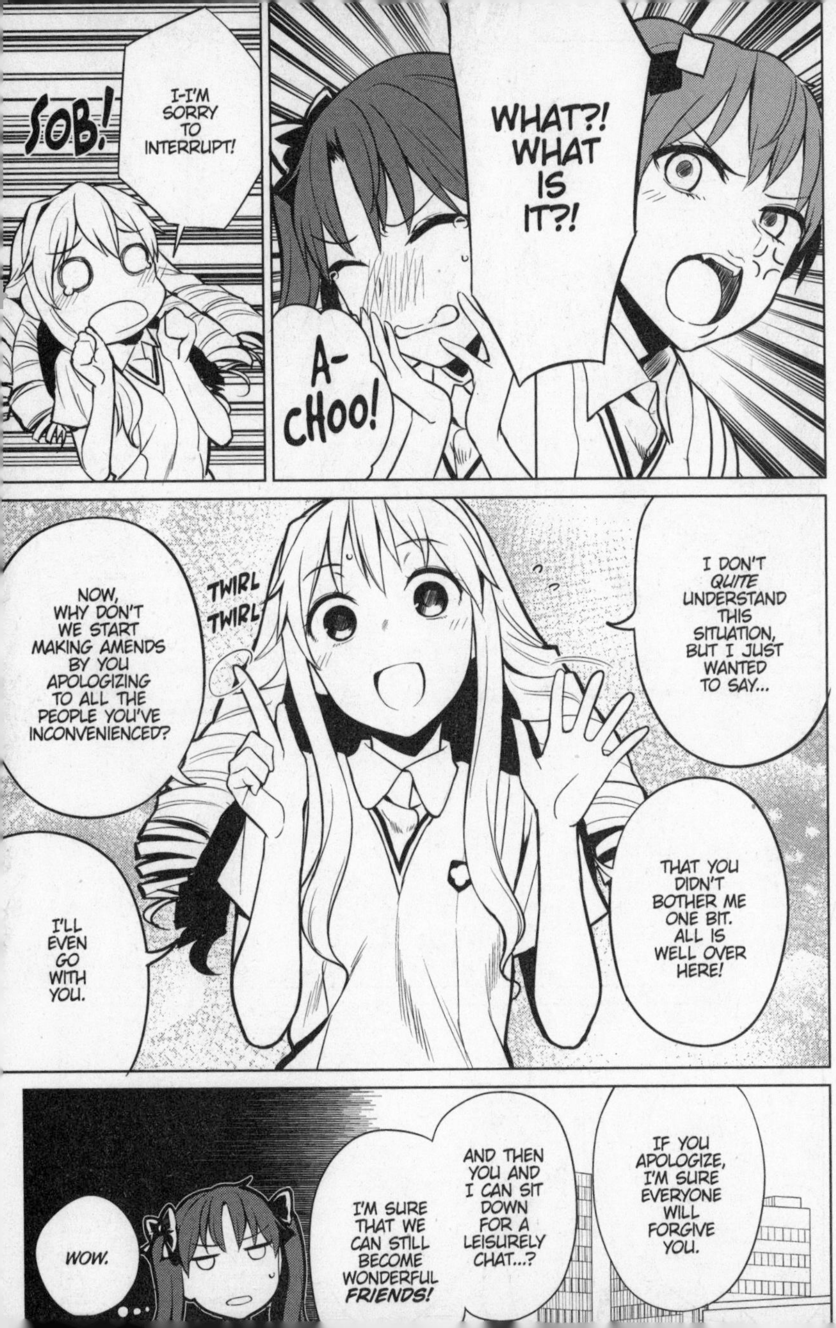
WHAT?! WHAT IS IT?!
A-CHOO!
SOB!
I-I'M SORRY TO INTERRUPT!
I DON'T *QUITE* UNDERSTAND THIS SITUATION, BUT I JUST WANTED TO SAY...
THAT YOU DIDN'T BOTHER ME ONE BIT. ALL IS WELL OVER HERE!
TWIRL TWIRL
NOW, WHY DON'T WE START MAKING AMENDS BY YOU APOLOGIZING TO ALL THE PEOPLE YOU'VE INCONVENIENCED?
I'LL EVEN GO WITH YOU.
IF YOU APOLOGIZE, I'M SURE EVERYONE WILL FORGIVE YOU.
AND THEN YOU AND I CAN SIT DOWN FOR A LEISURELY CHAT...?
I'M SURE THAT WE CAN STILL BECOME WONDERFUL ***FRIENDS!***
WOW.

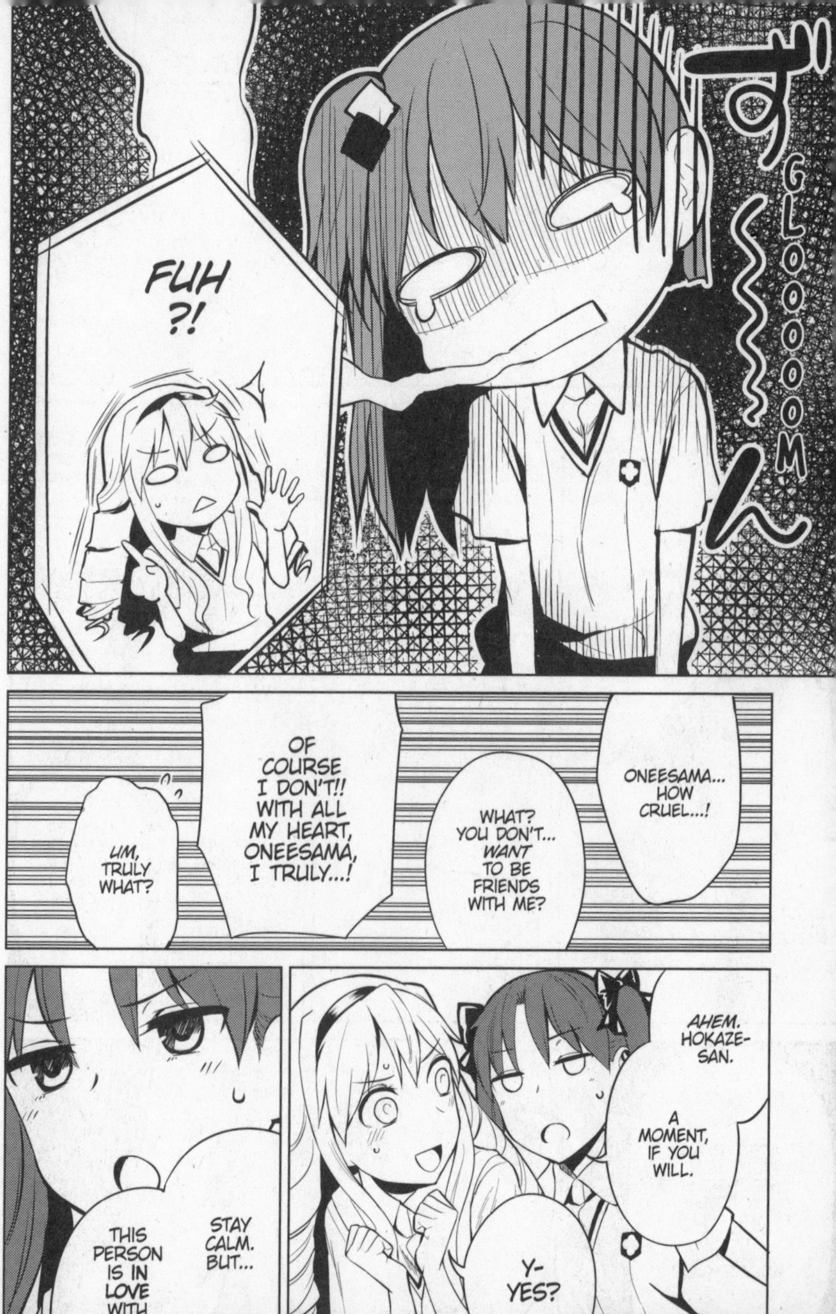
ずーん
GLOOOOOM
FUH ?!
ONEESAMA... HOW CRUEL...!
WHAT? YOU DON'T... WANT TO BE FRIENDS WITH ME?
OF COURSE I DON'T!! WITH ALL MY HEART, ONEESAMA, I TRULY...!
UM, TRULY WHAT?
AHEM. HOKAZE-SAN.
A MOMENT, IF YOU WILL.
Y-YES?
STAY CALM. BUT...
THIS PERSON IS IN LOVE WITH

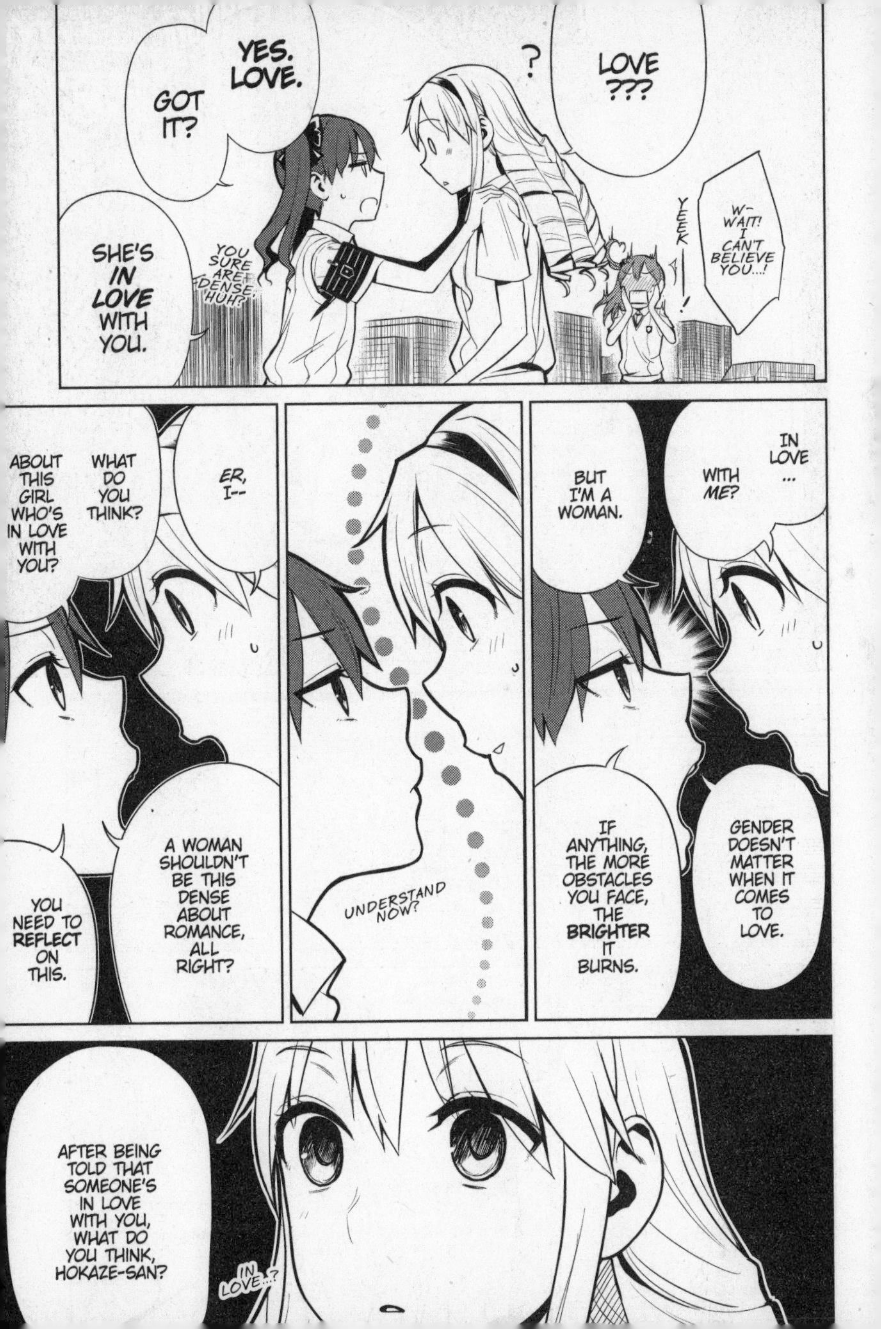
LOVE???
?
YES. LOVE.
GOT IT?
W-WAIT! I CAN'T BELIEVE YOU...!
YEEK—!
SHE'S IN LOVE WITH YOU.
YOU SURE ARE DENSE, HUH?
IN LOVE...
WITH ME?
BUT I'M A WOMAN.
GENDER DOESN'T MATTER WHEN IT COMES TO LOVE.
IF ANYTHING, THE MORE OBSTACLES YOU FACE, THE BRIGHTER IT BURNS.
UNDERSTAND NOW?
ER, I--
WHAT DO YOU THINK
ABOUT THIS GIRL WHO'S IN LOVE WITH YOU?
A WOMAN SHOULDN'T BE THIS DENSE ABOUT ROMANCE, ALL RIGHT?
YOU NEED TO REFLECT ON THIS.
AFTER BEING TOLD THAT SOMEONE'S IN LOVE WITH YOU, WHAT DO YOU THINK, HOKAZE-SAN?
IN LOVE...?

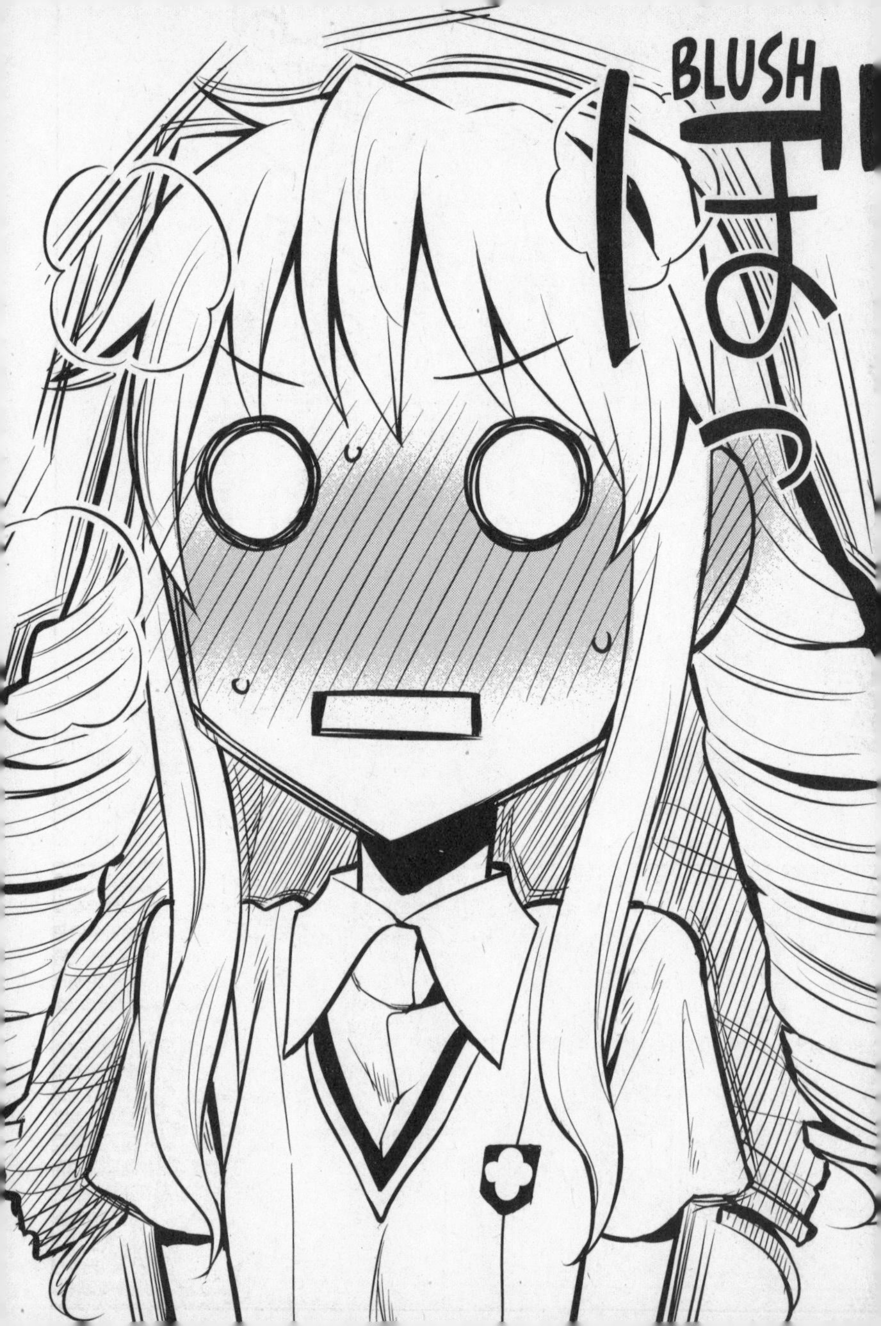
BLUSH
ぼっ

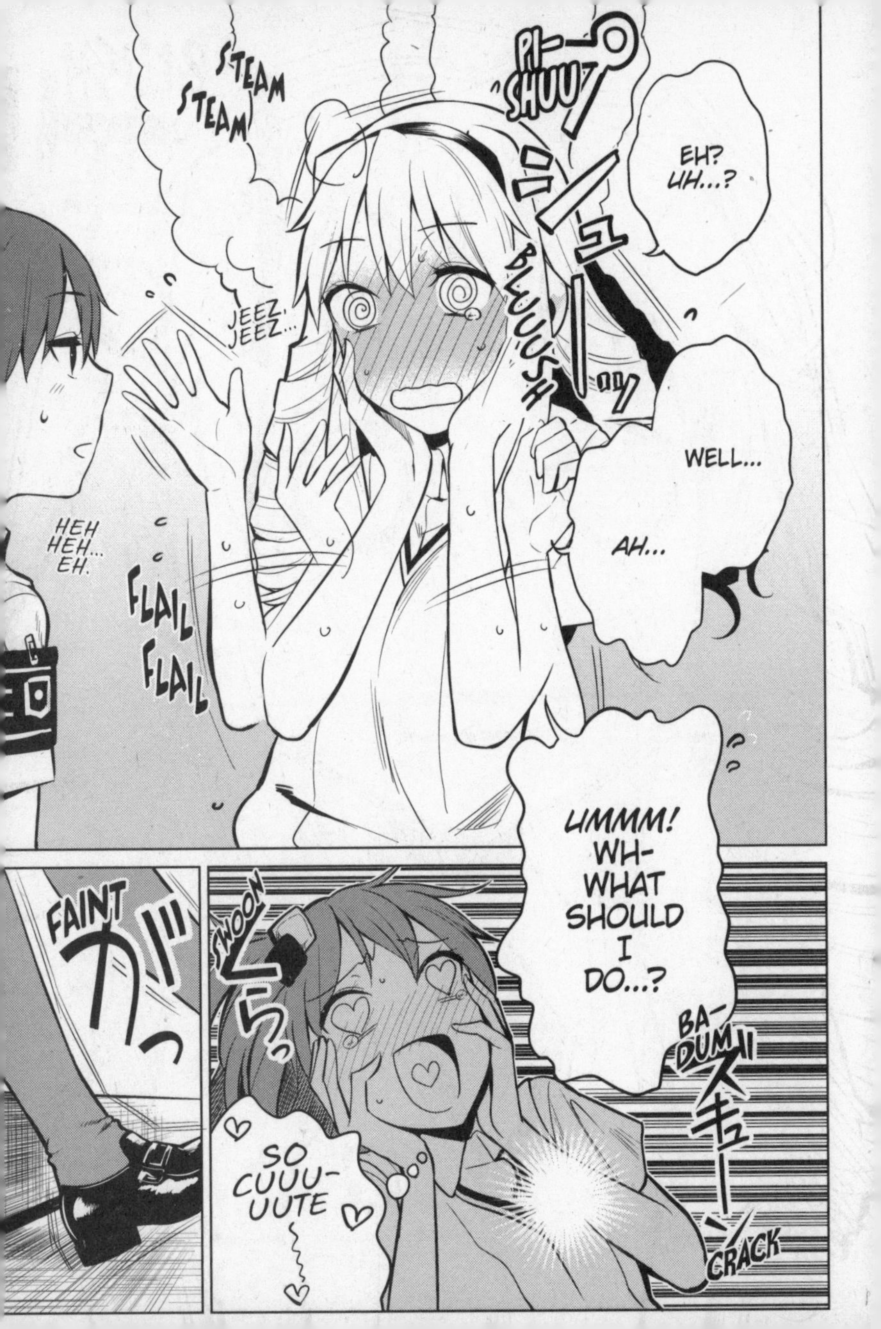
EH? UH...?
PI-SHUU
STEAM STEAM
BLUUUSH
WELL...
AH...
JEEZ, JEEZ...
HEH HEH... EH.
FLAIL FLAIL
UMMM! WH-WHAT SHOULD I DO...?
BA-DUM
CRACK
SWOON
SO CUUUU-UUTE
FAINT

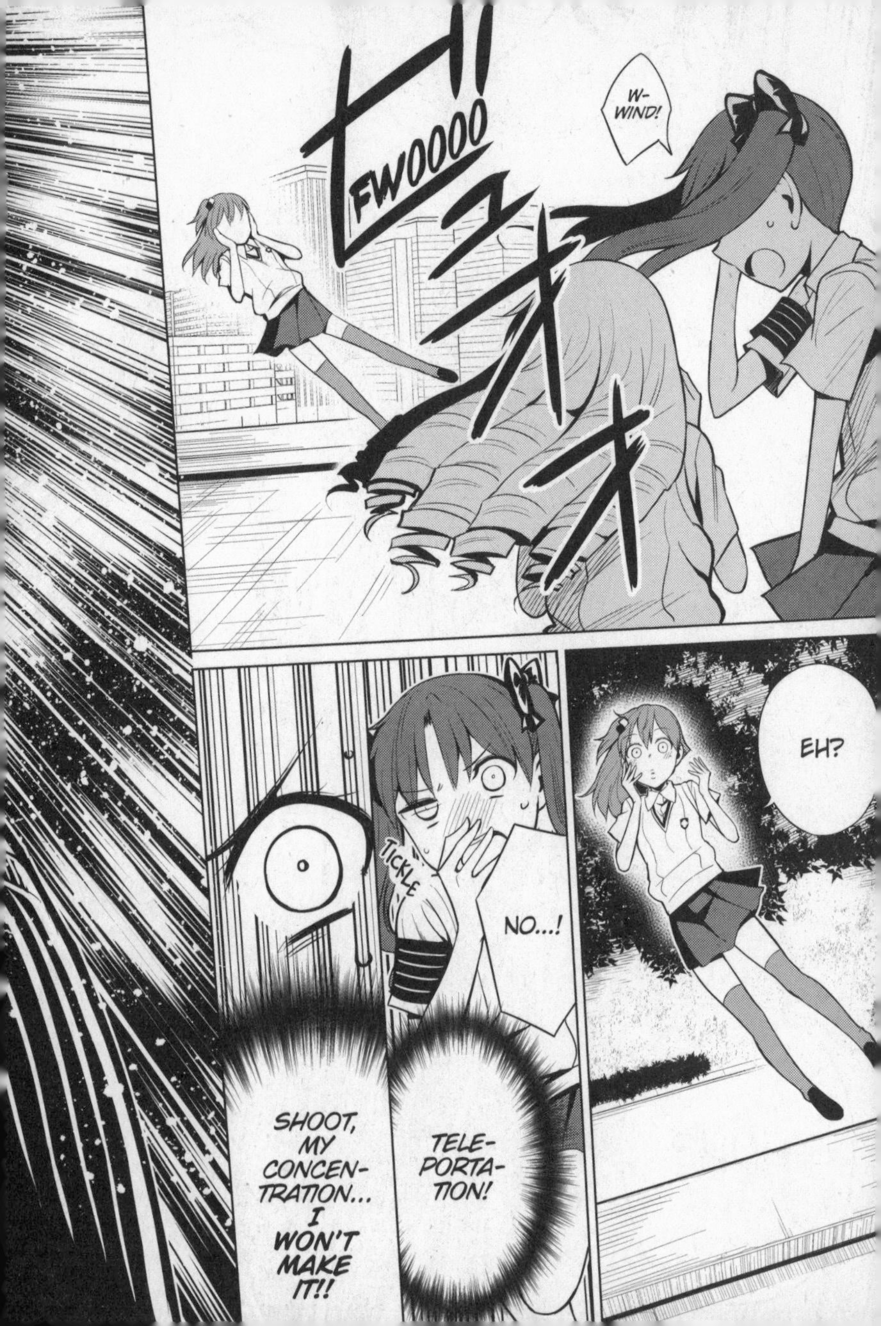
W-
WIND!
FWOOOO
EH?
NO...!
TICKLE
TELE-
PORTA-
TION!
SHOOT,
MY
CONCEN-
TRATION...
I
WON'T
MAKE
IT!!

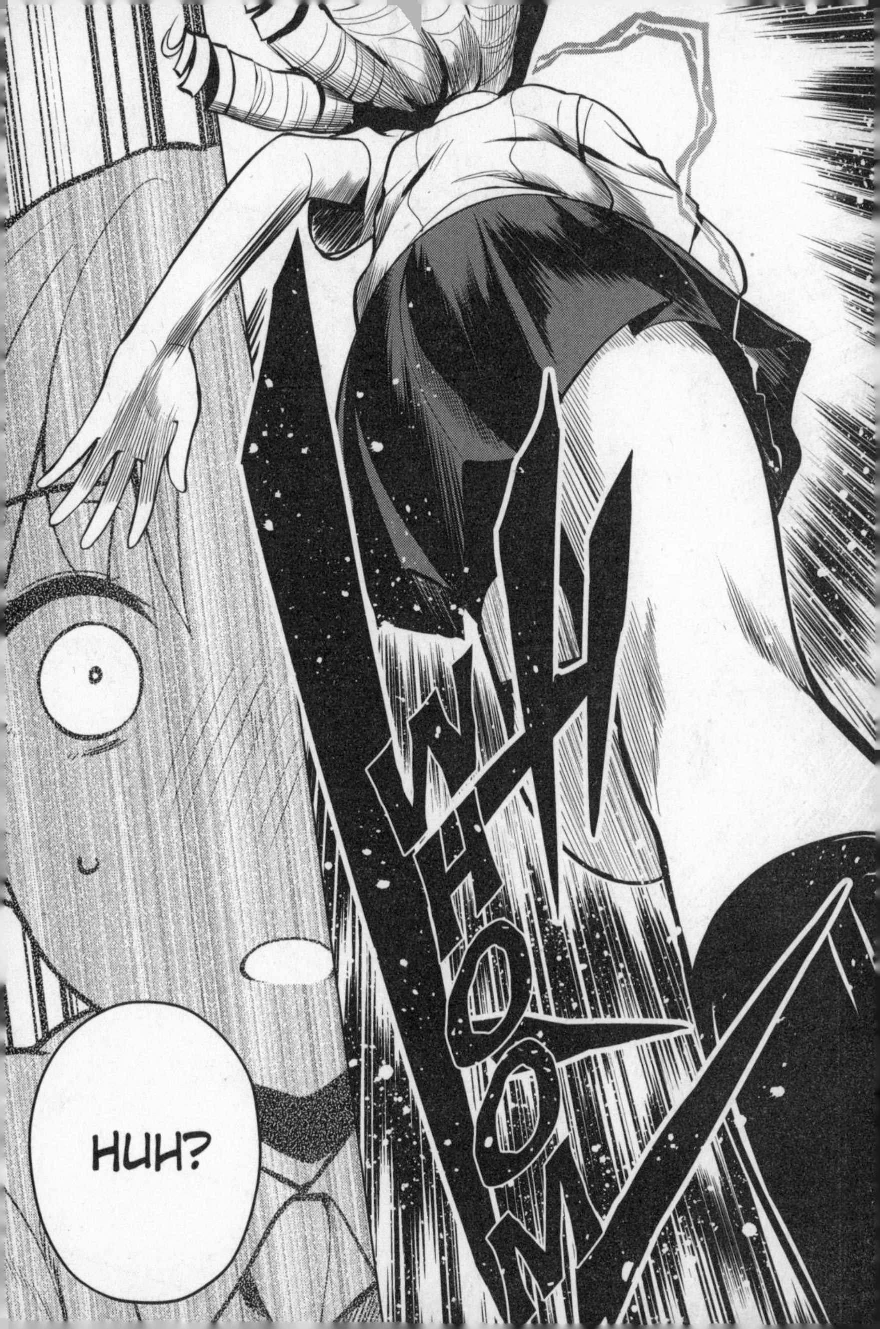
WHOOM
HUH?

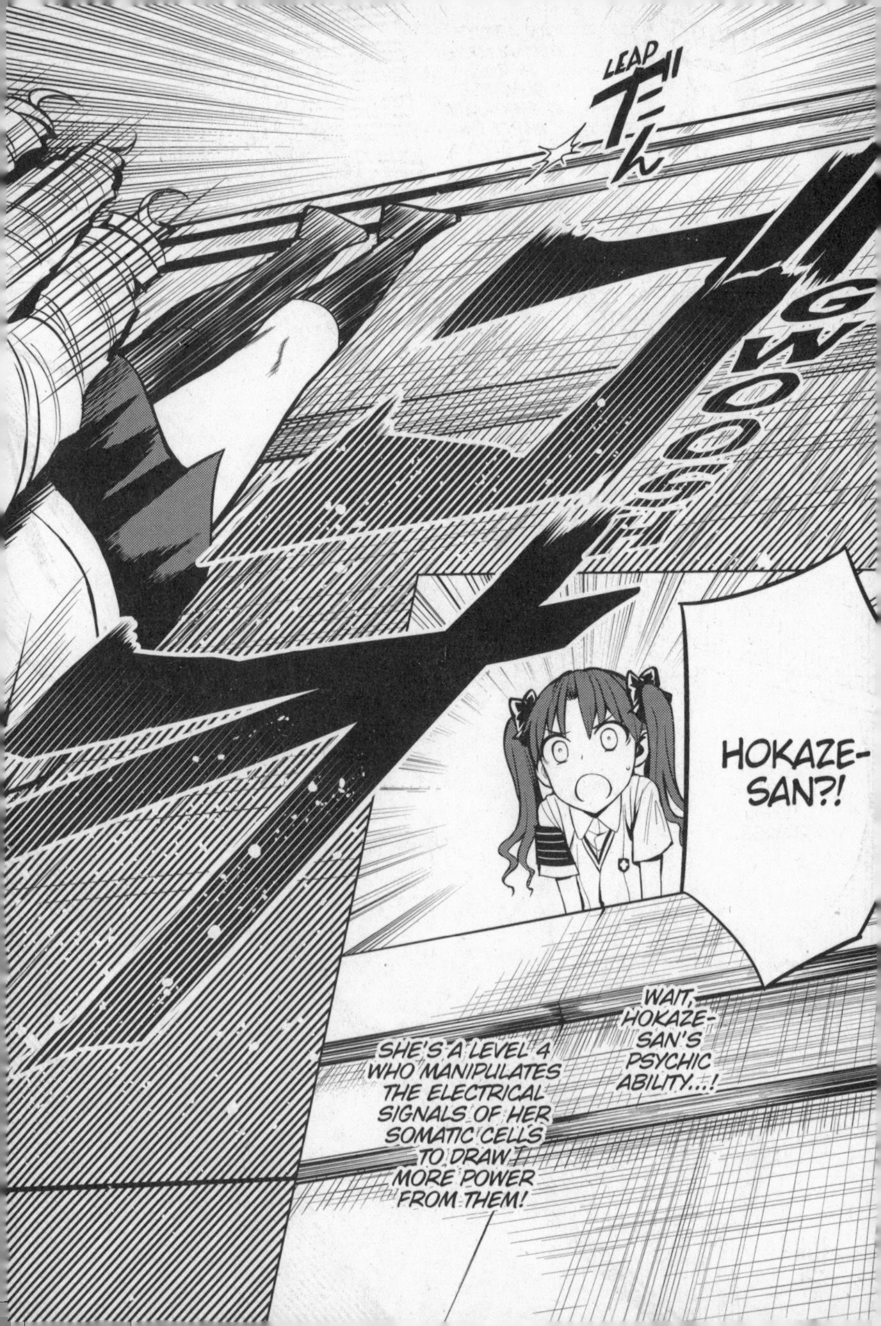
LEAP
ダーん
GWOOOSH
HOKAZE-SAN?!
WAIT, HOKAZE-SAN'S PSYCHIC ABILITY...!
SHE'S A LEVEL 4 WHO MANIPULATES THE ELECTRICAL SIGNALS OF HER SOMATIC CELLS TO DRAW MORE POWER FROM THEM!

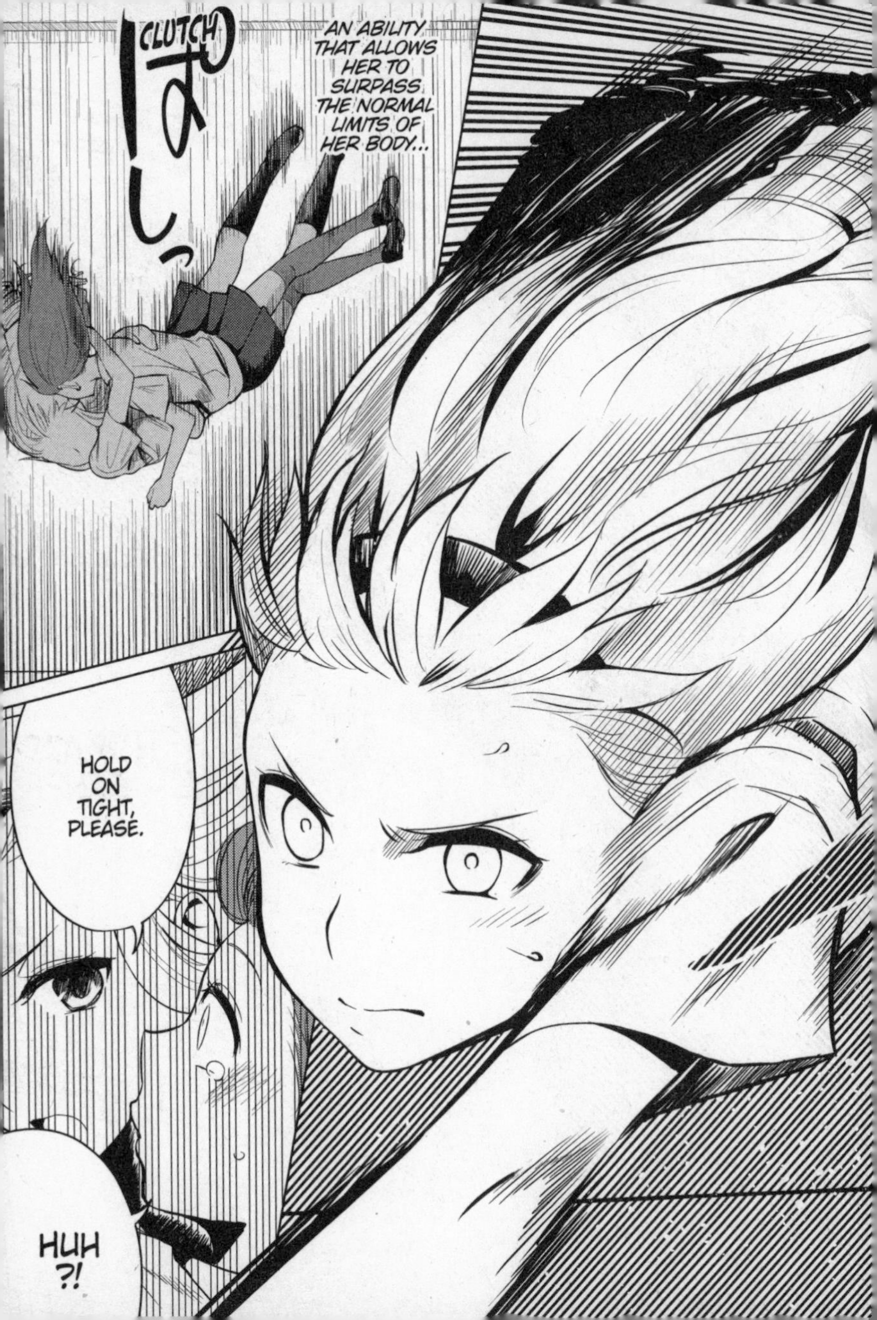
AN ABILITY THAT ALLOWS HER TO SURPASS THE NORMAL LIMITS OF HER BODY...
CLUTCH
ぱしっ
HOLD ON TIGHT, PLEASE.
HUH ?!

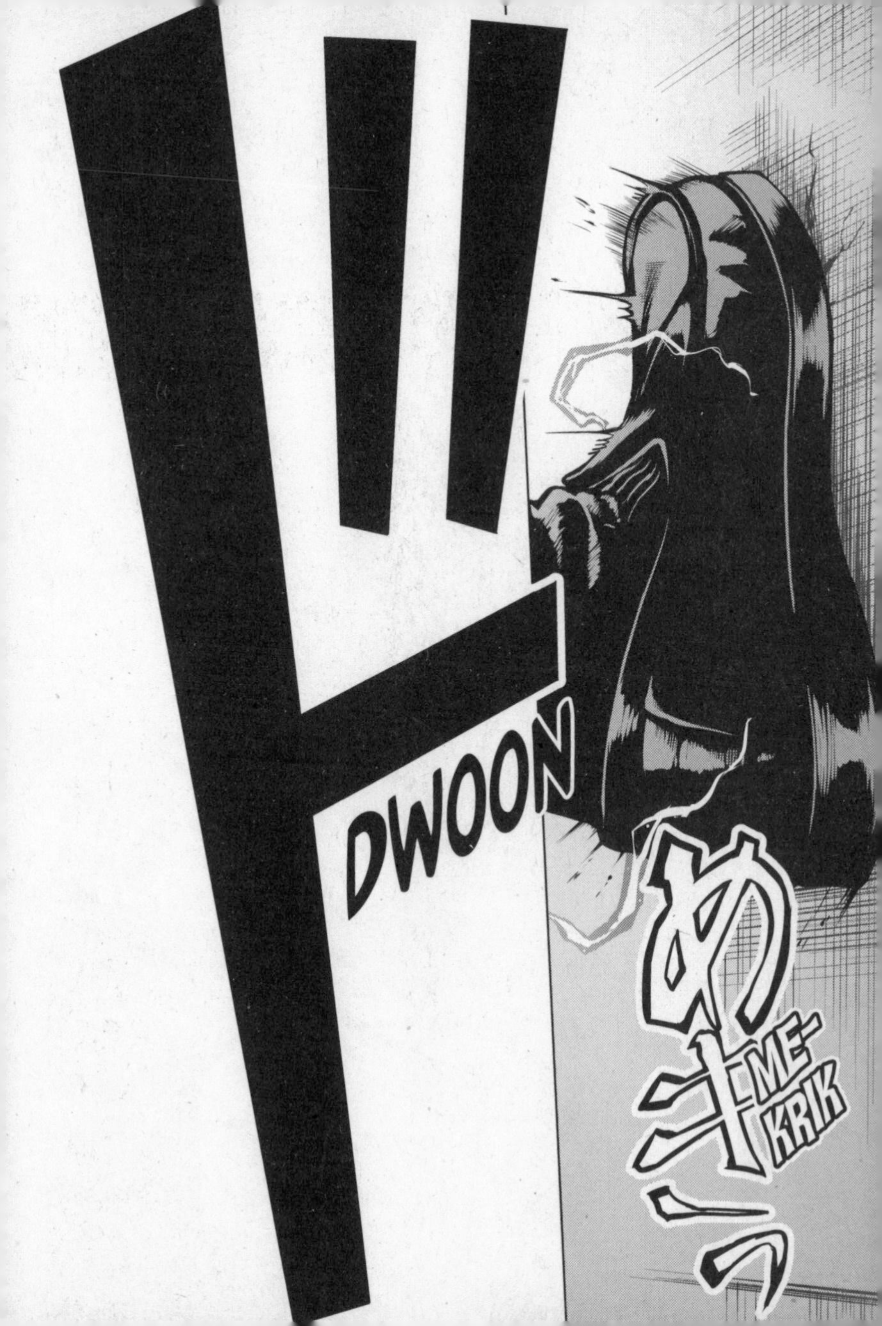
DWOON
ME-
KRIK

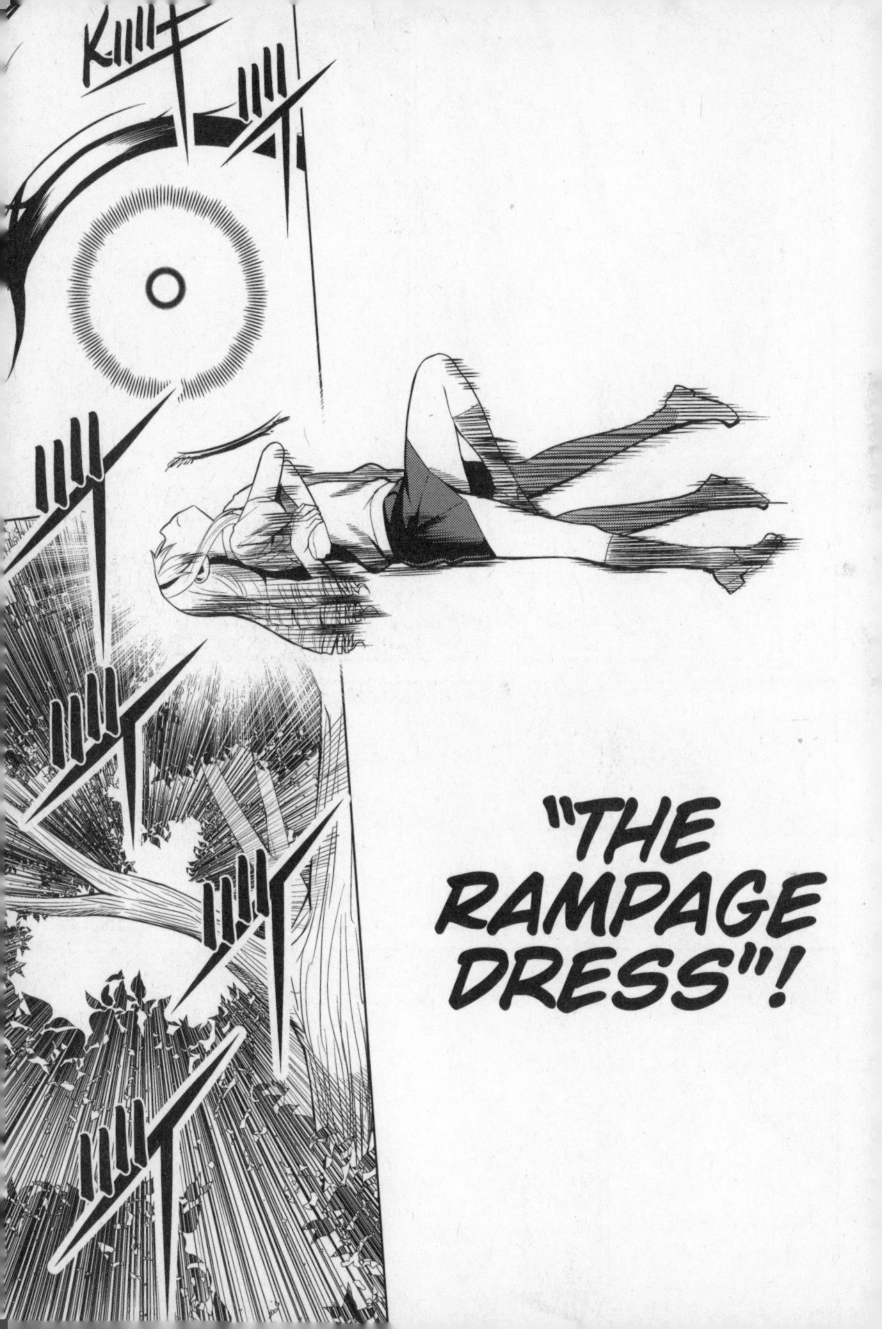
"THE RAMPAGE DRESS"!

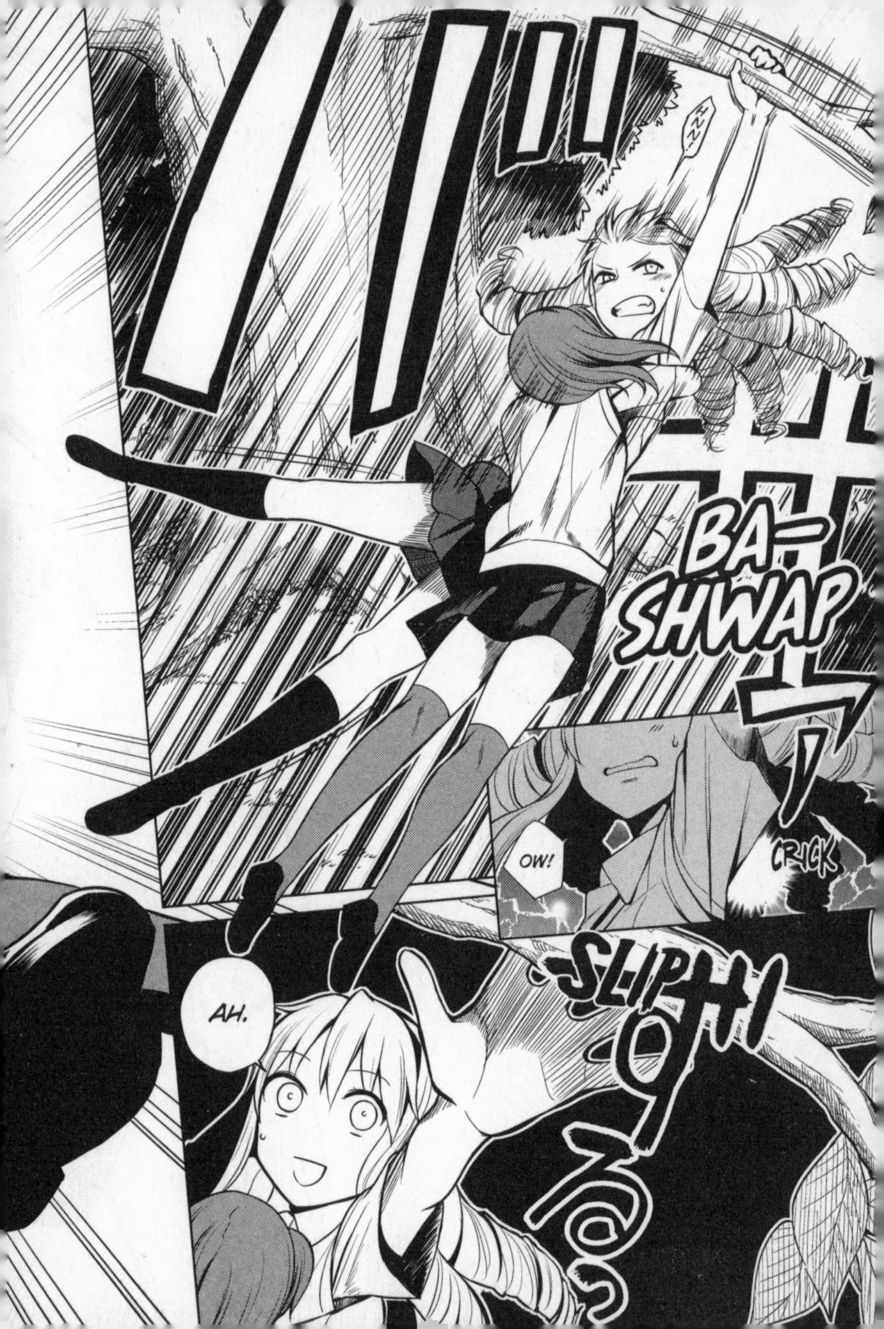
BA-SHWAP
OW!
CRICK
SLIP
AH.

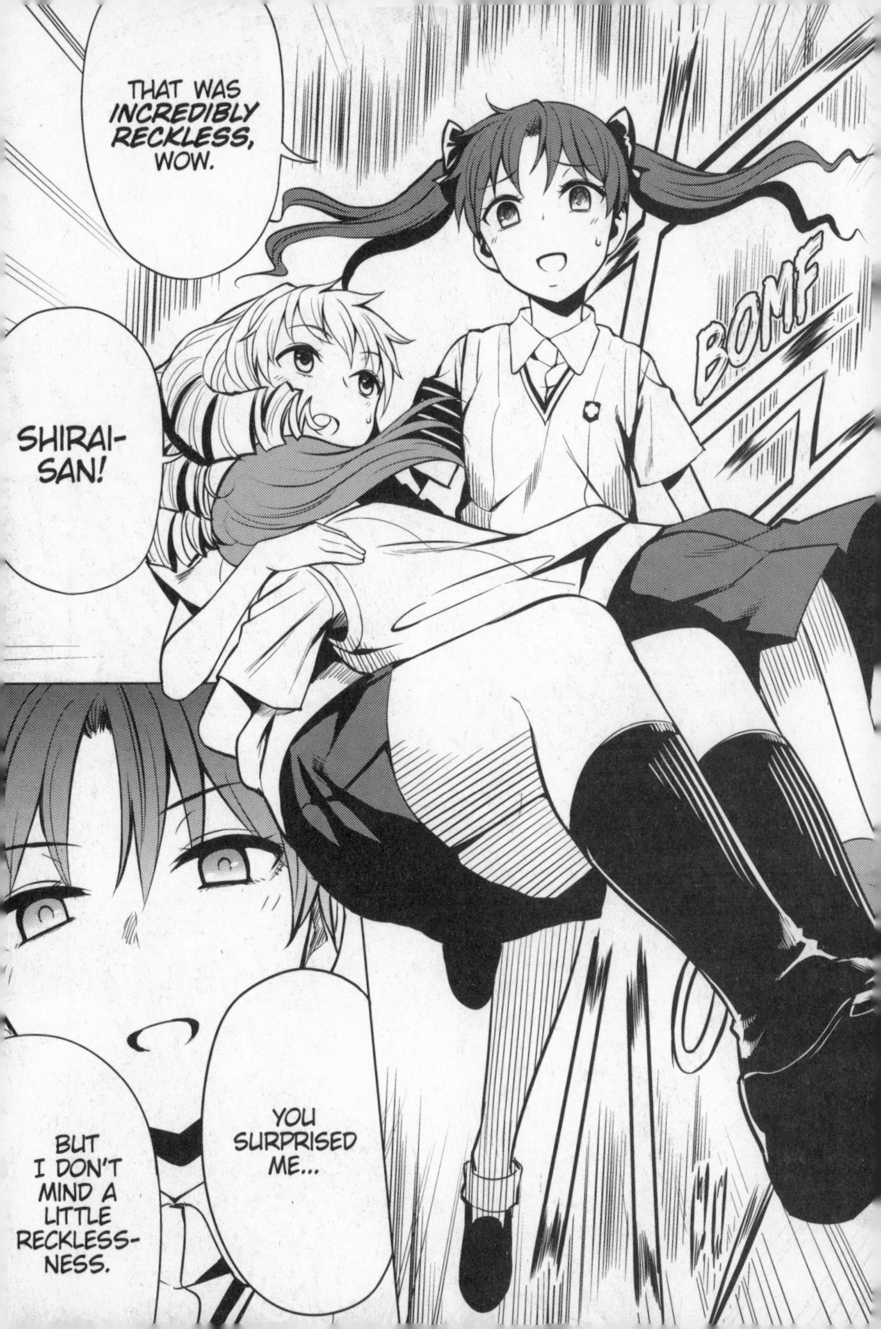

BOMF
THAT WAS INCREDIBLY RECKLESS, WOW.
SHIRAI-SAN!
YOU SURPRISED ME...
BUT I DON'T MIND A LITTLE RECKLESS-NESS.

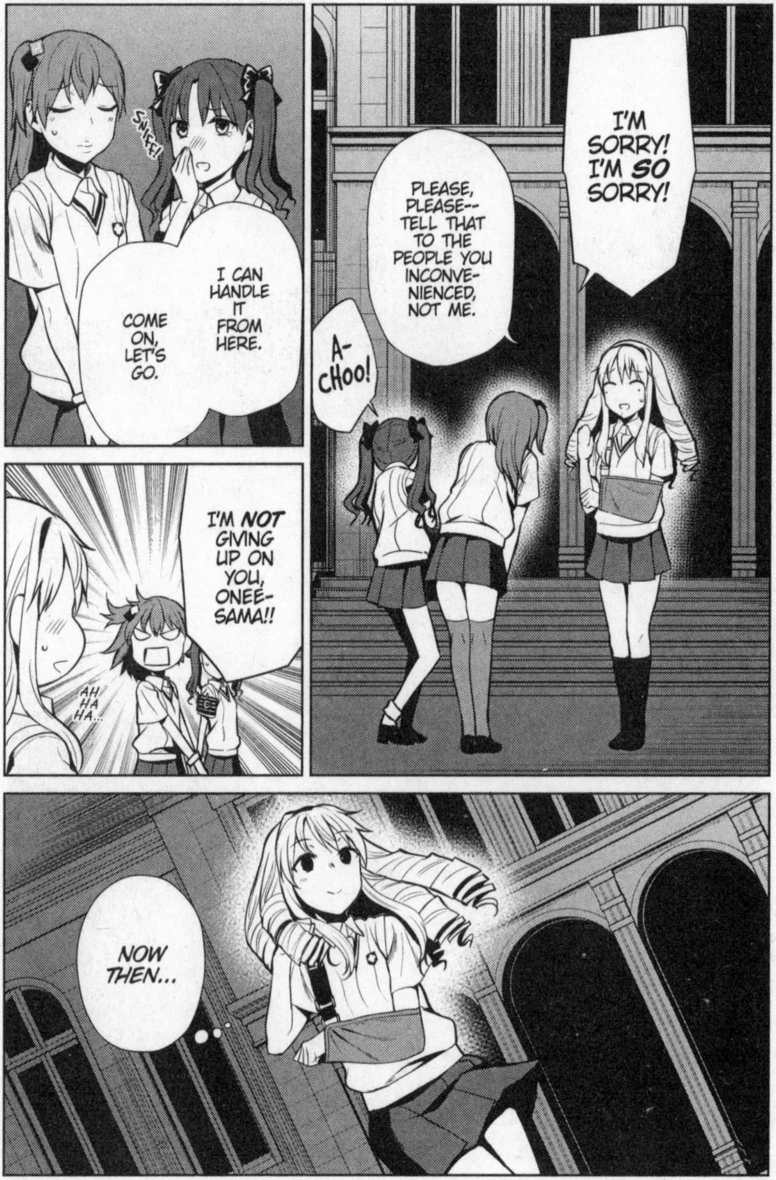
I'M SORRY! I'M SO SORRY!
PLEASE, PLEASE-- TELL THAT TO THE PEOPLE YOU INCONVENIENCED, NOT ME.
A-CHOO!
SNIFF!
I CAN HANDLE IT FROM HERE.
COME ON, LET'S GO.
I'M NOT GIVING UP ON YOU, ONEE-SAMA!!
AH HA HA...
NOW THEN...

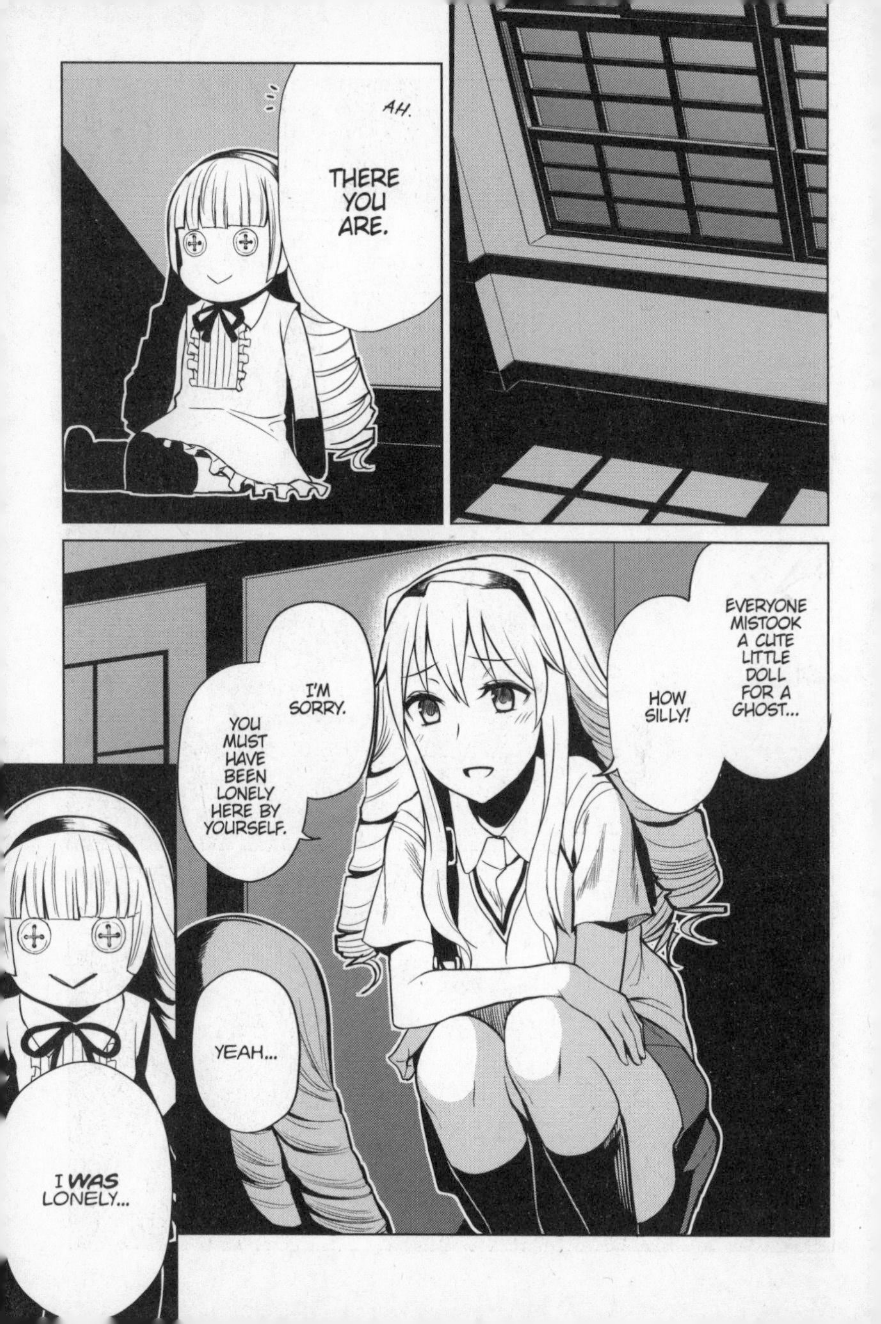

AH.
THERE YOU ARE.
EVERYONE MISTOOK A CUTE LITTLE DOLL FOR A GHOST...
HOW SILLY!
I'M SORRY.
YOU MUST HAVE BEEN LONELY HERE BY YOURSELF.
YEAH...
I WAS LONELY...

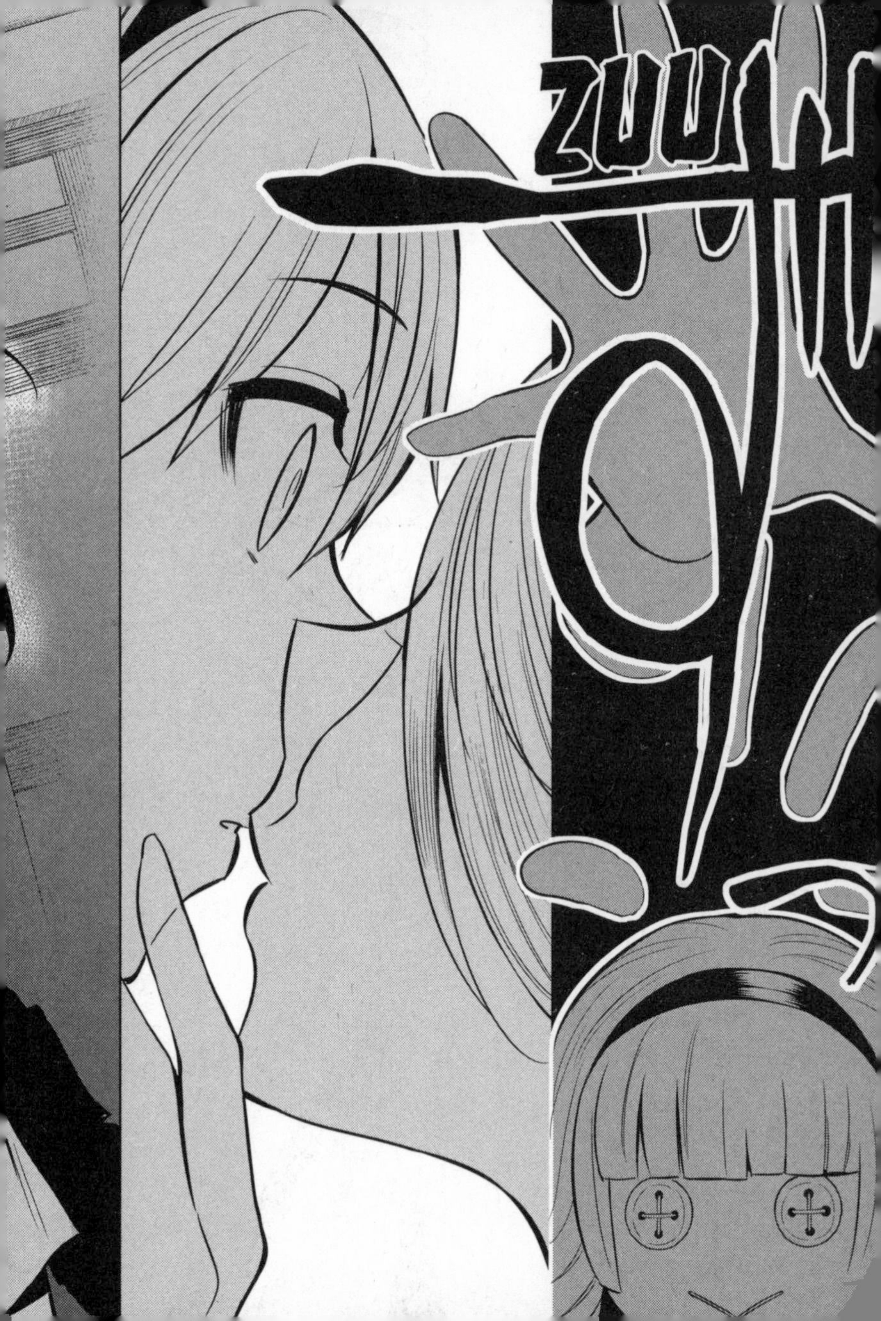
ZUU

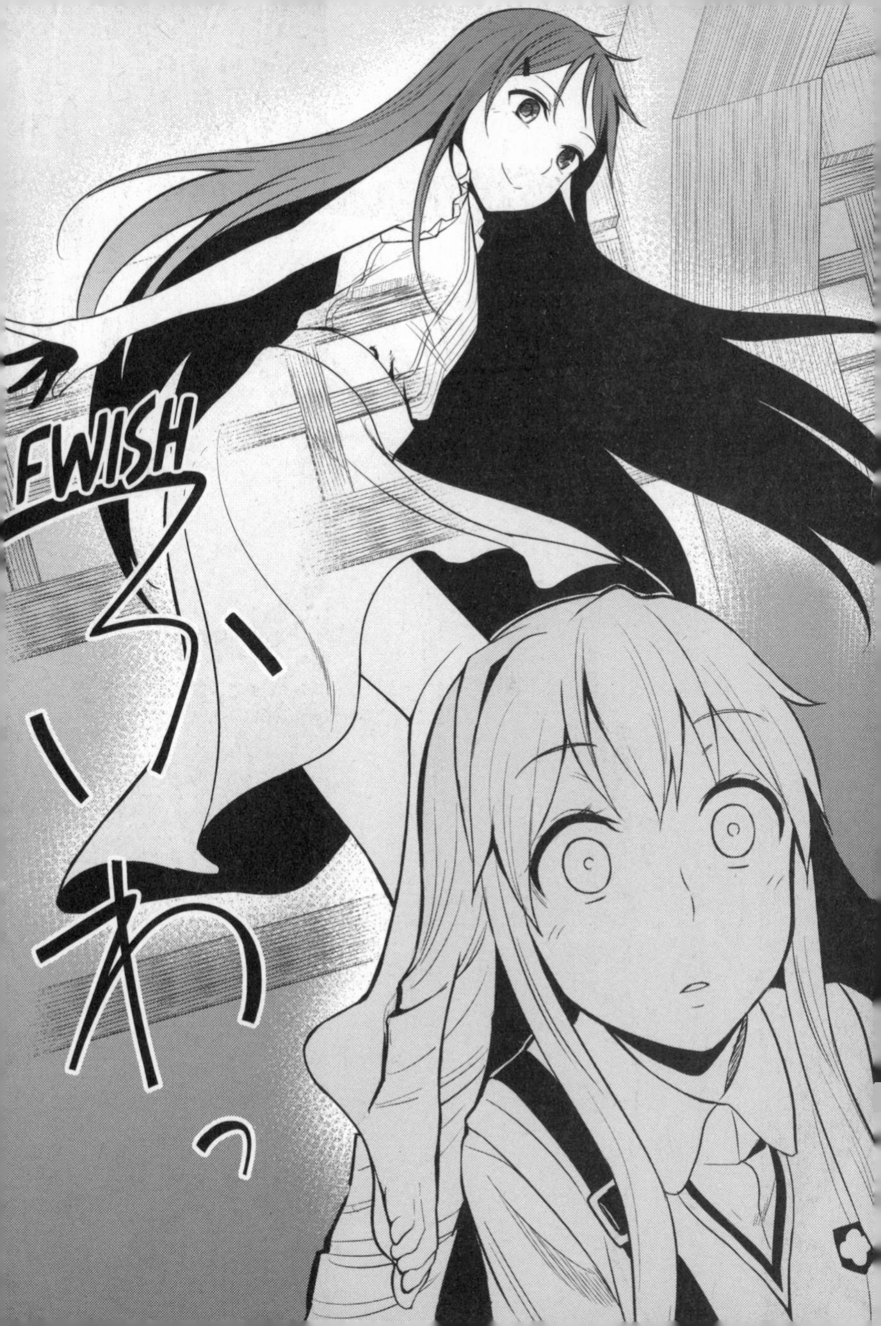

FWISH
ふぃーわっ

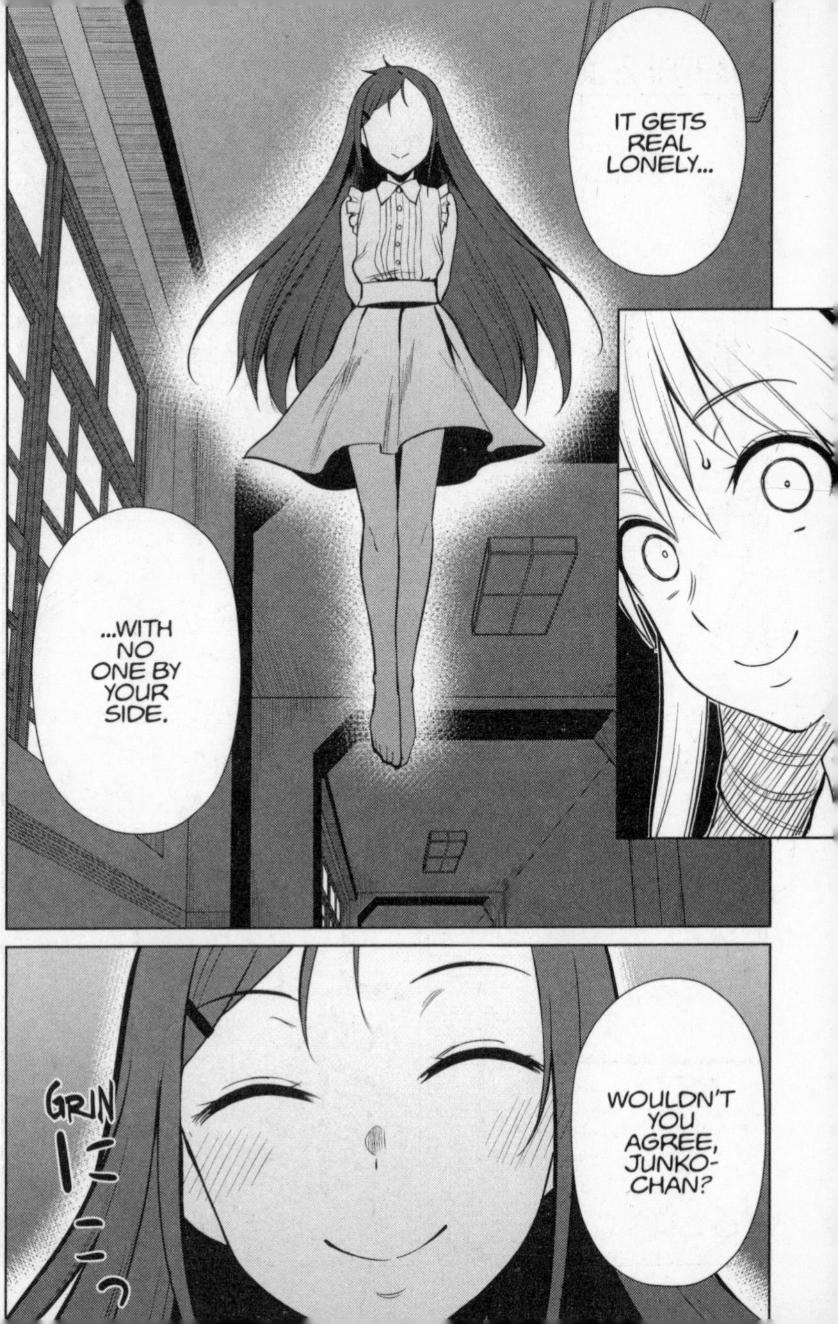
IT GETS REAL LONELY...
...WITH NO ONE BY YOUR SIDE.
WOULDN'T YOU AGREE, JUNKO-CHAN?
GRIN

CHAPTER 2: Just Who Are You, Exactly?

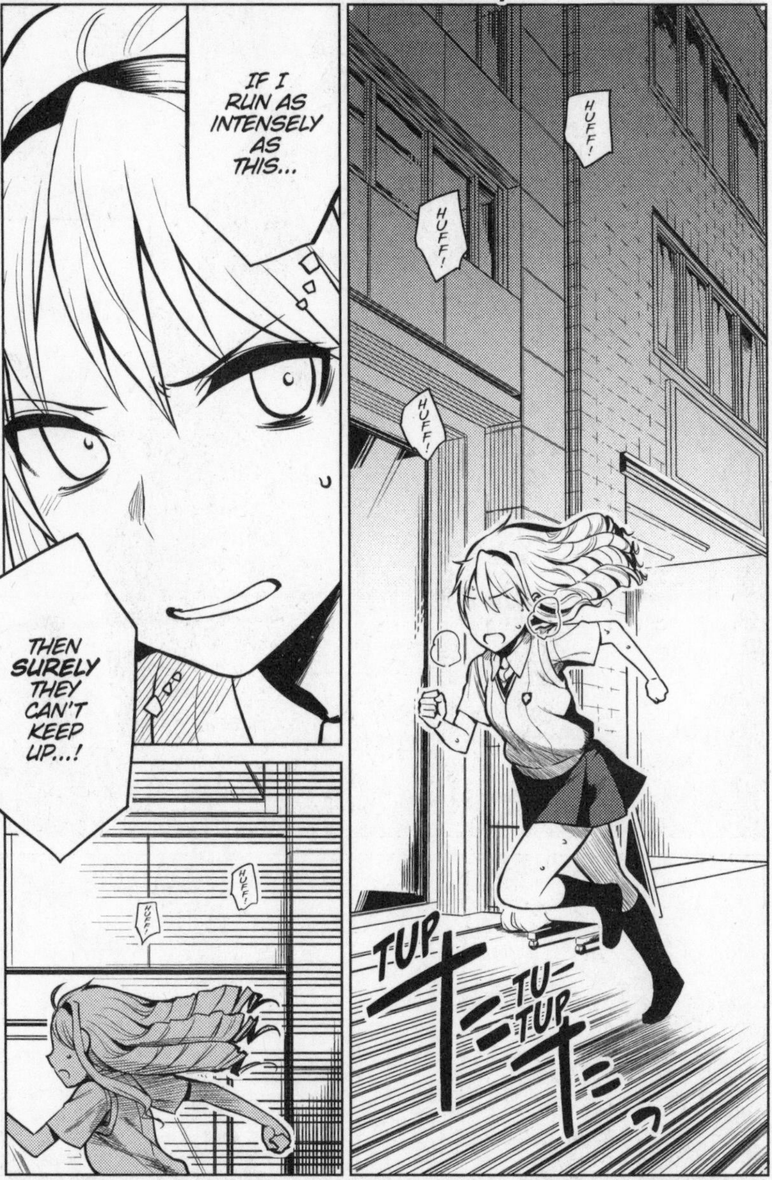
HUFF!
HUFF!
HUFF!
TUP
TU TUP
IF I RUN AS INTENSELY AS THIS...
THEN SURELY THEY CAN'T KEEP UP...!
HUFF!
HUFF!

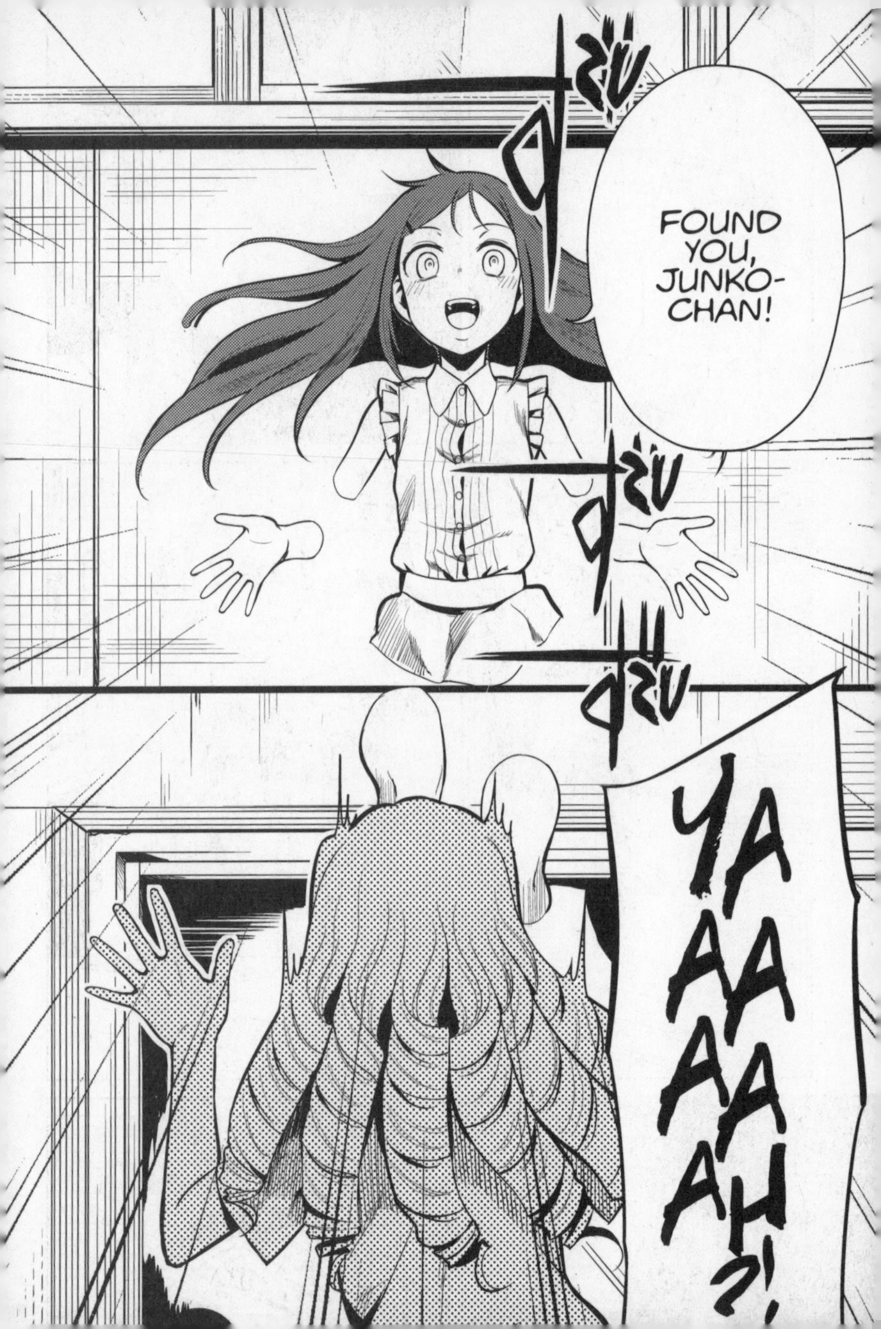
FOUND YOU, JUNKO-CHAN!
YAAAAAAH?!

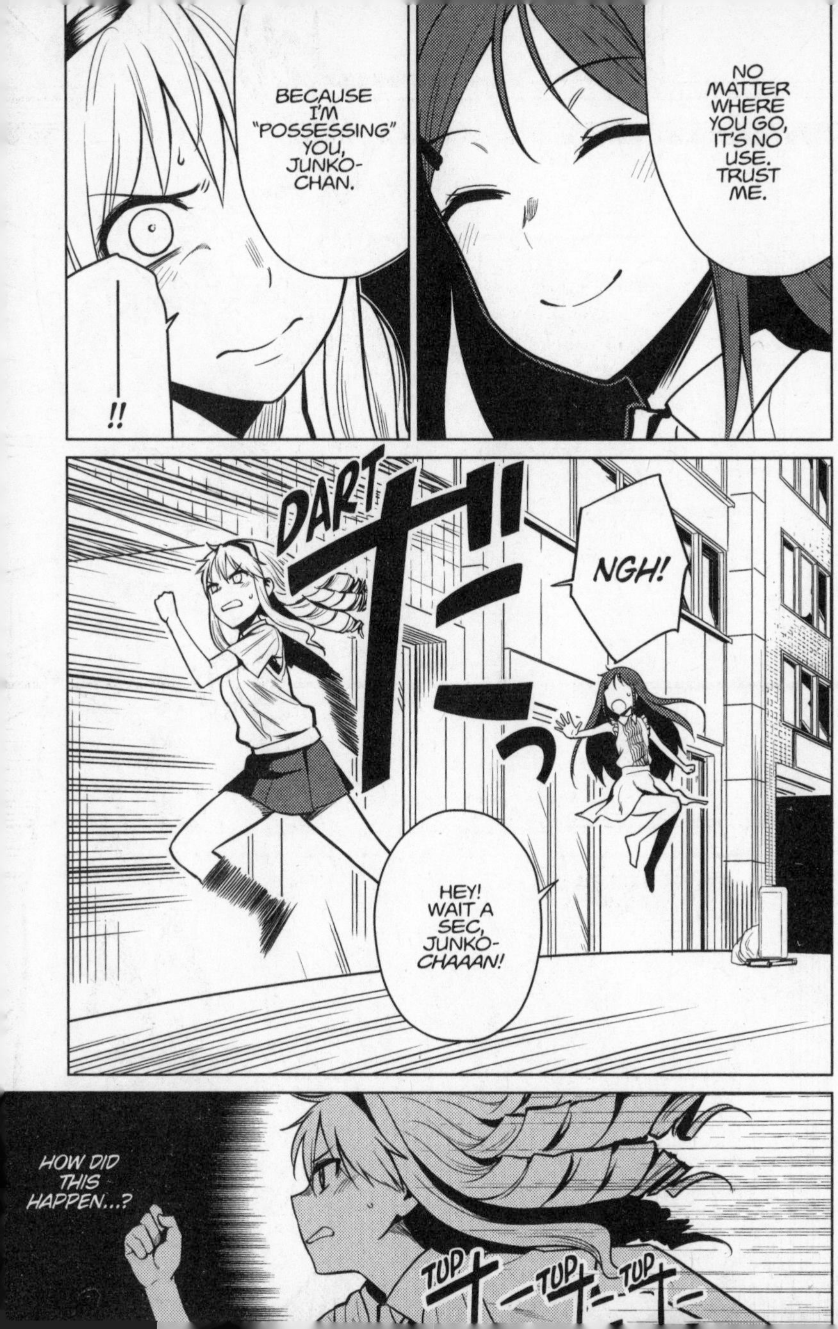
NO MATTER WHERE YOU GO, IT'S NO USE. TRUST ME.
BECAUSE I'M "POSSESSING" YOU, JUNKO-CHAN.
!!
DART
NGH!
HEY! WAIT A SEC, JUNKO-CHAAAN!
HOW DID THIS HAPPEN...?
TUP
TUP
TUP

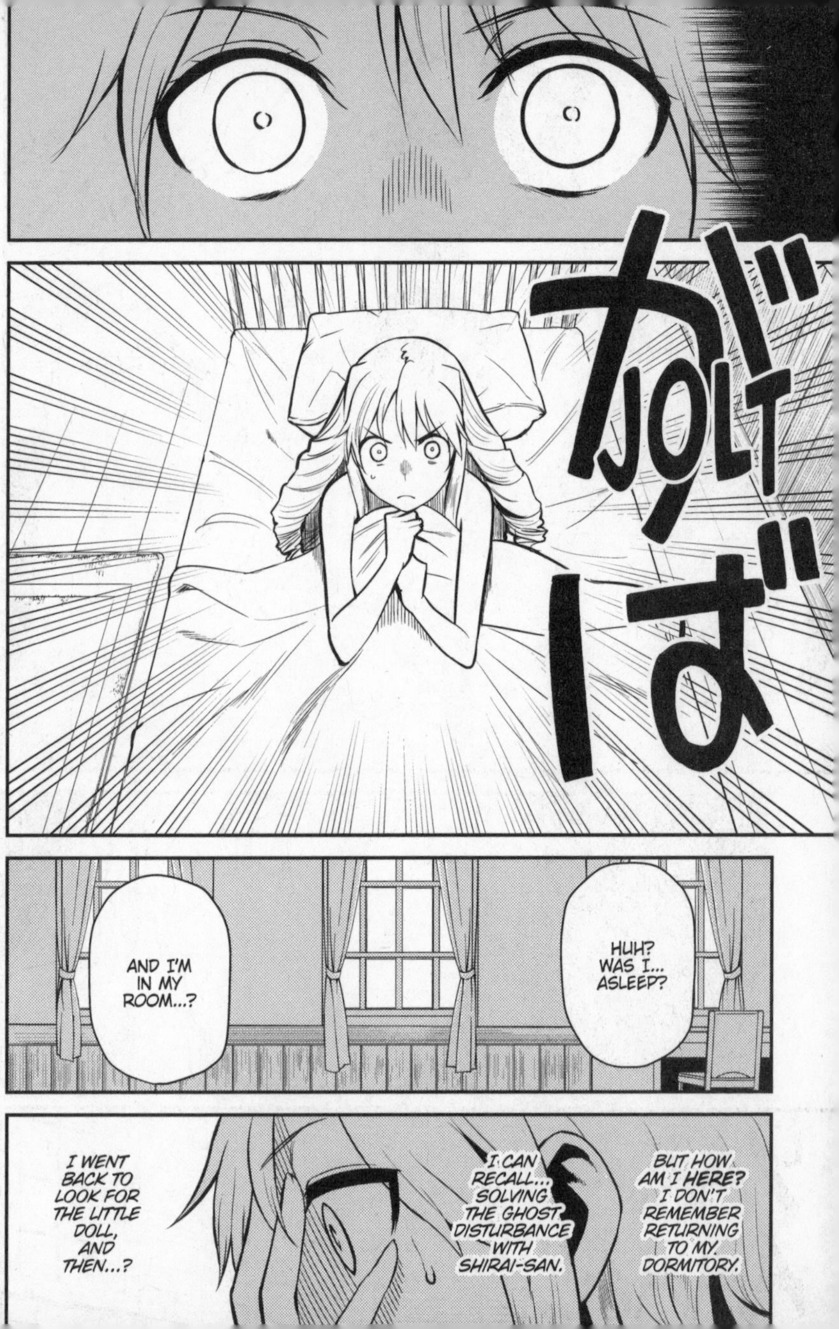

JOLT
HUH? WAS I... ASLEEP?
AND I'M IN MY ROOM...?
BUT HOW AM I HERE? I DON'T REMEMBER RETURNING TO MY DORMITORY.
I CAN RECALL... SOLVING THE GHOST DISTURBANCE WITH SHIRAI-SAN.
I WENT BACK TO LOOK FOR THE LITTLE DOLL, AND THEN...?

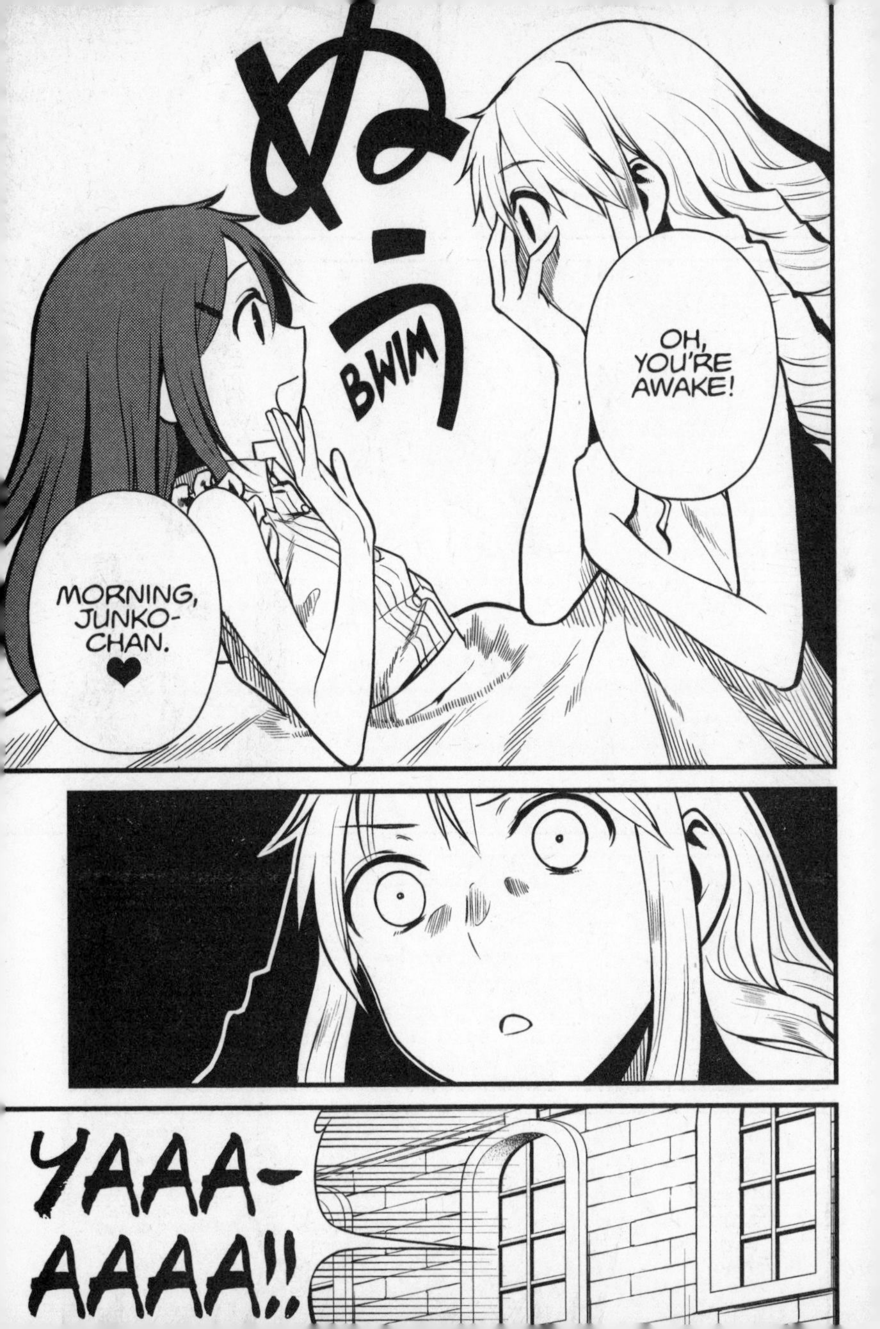
OH, YOU'RE AWAKE!
BWIM
MORNING, JUNKO-CHAN. ♥
YAAA-AAAA!!

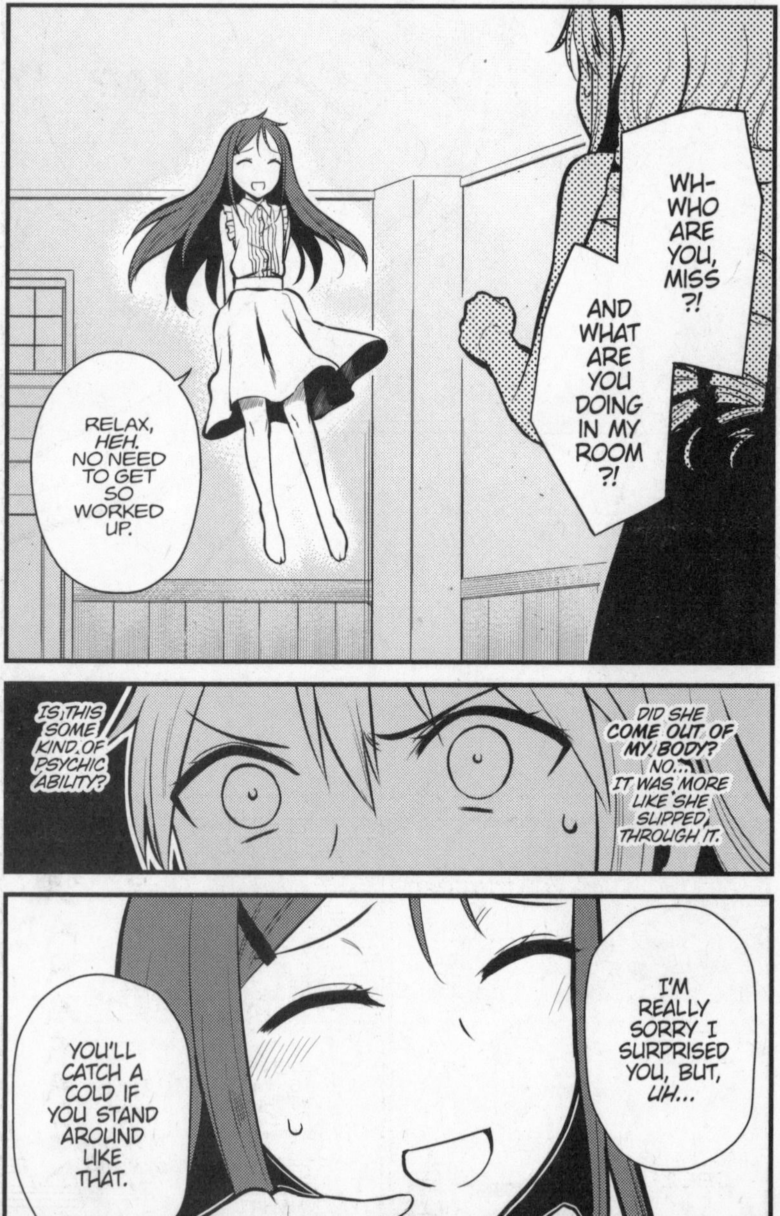
WH-WHO ARE YOU, MISS ?!
AND WHAT ARE YOU DOING IN MY ROOM ?!
RELAX, HEH. NO NEED TO GET SO WORKED UP.
DID SHE COME OUT OF MY BODY? NO... IT WAS MORE LIKE SHE SLIPPED THROUGH IT.
IS THIS SOME KIND OF PSYCHIC ABILITY?
I'M REALLY SORRY I SURPRISED YOU, BUT, UH...
YOU'LL CATCH A COLD IF YOU STAND AROUND LIKE THAT.

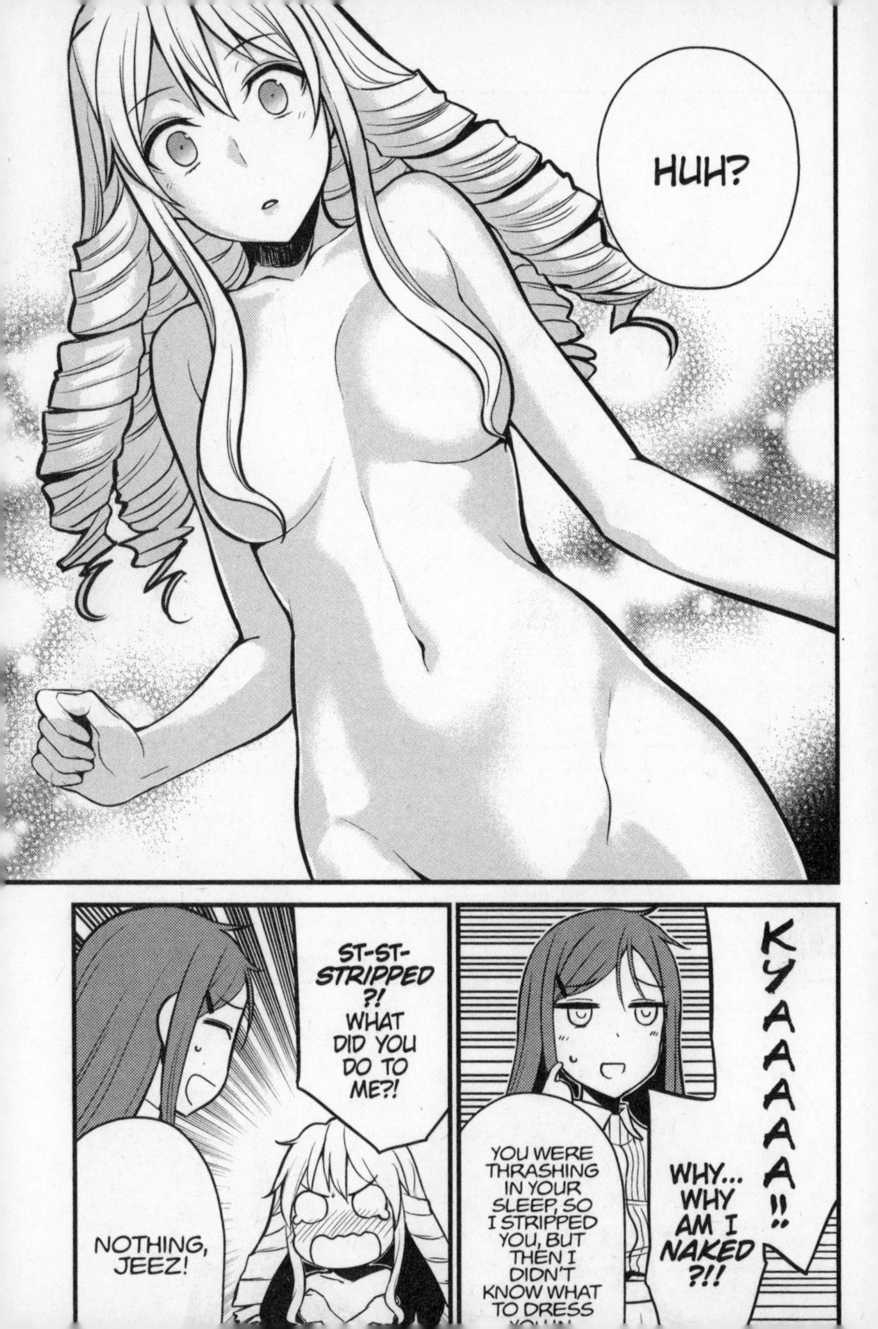
HUH?
KYAAAAA!!
WHY... WHY AM I NAKED?!!
YOU WERE THRASHING IN YOUR SLEEP, SO I STRIPPED YOU, BUT THEN I DIDN'T KNOW WHAT TO DRESS
ST-ST-STRIPPED?! WHAT DID YOU DO TO ME?!
NOTHING, JEEZ!

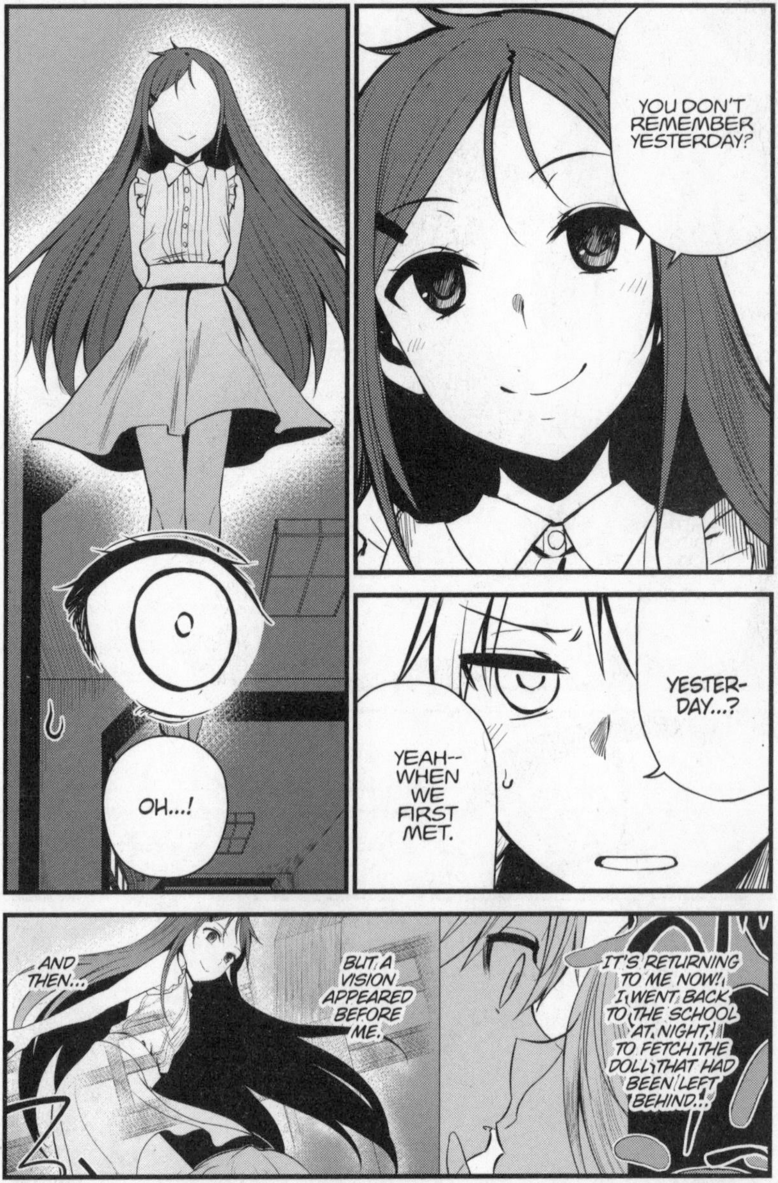
YOU DON'T REMEMBER YESTERDAY?
OH...!
YESTER-DAY...?
YEAH-- WHEN WE FIRST MET.
IT'S RETURNING TO ME NOW! I WENT BACK TO THE SCHOOL AT NIGHT, TO FETCH THE DOLL THAT HAD BEEN LEFT BEHIND...
BUT A VISION APPEARED BEFORE ME.
AND THEN...

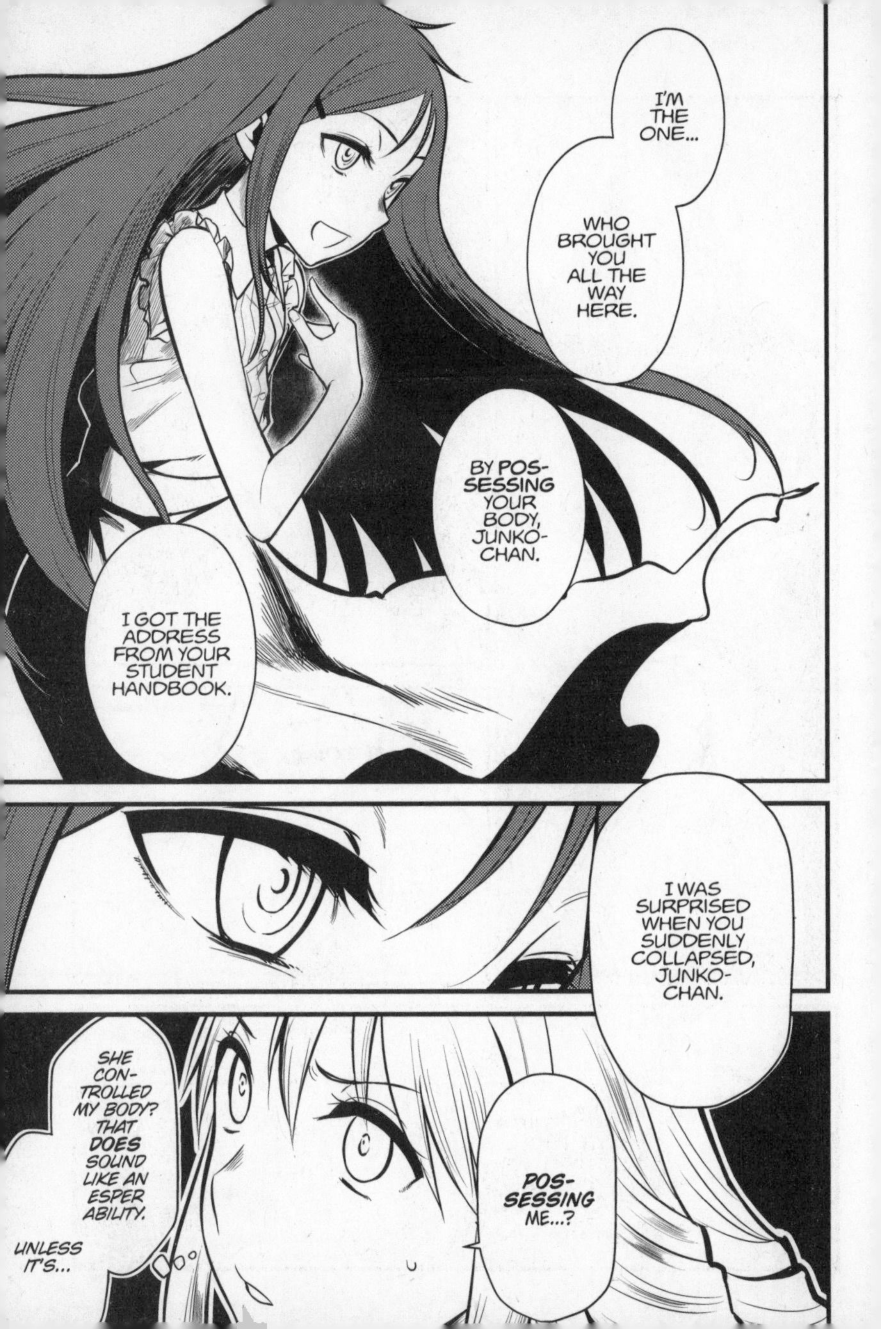
I'M THE ONE...
WHO BROUGHT YOU ALL THE WAY HERE.
BY POS-SESSING YOUR BODY, JUNKO-CHAN.
I GOT THE ADDRESS FROM YOUR STUDENT HANDBOOK.
I WAS SURPRISED WHEN YOU SUDDENLY COLLAPSED, JUNKO-CHAN.
POS-SESSING ME...?
SHE CON-TROLLED MY BODY? THAT DOES SOUND LIKE AN ESPER ABILITY.
UNLESS IT'S...

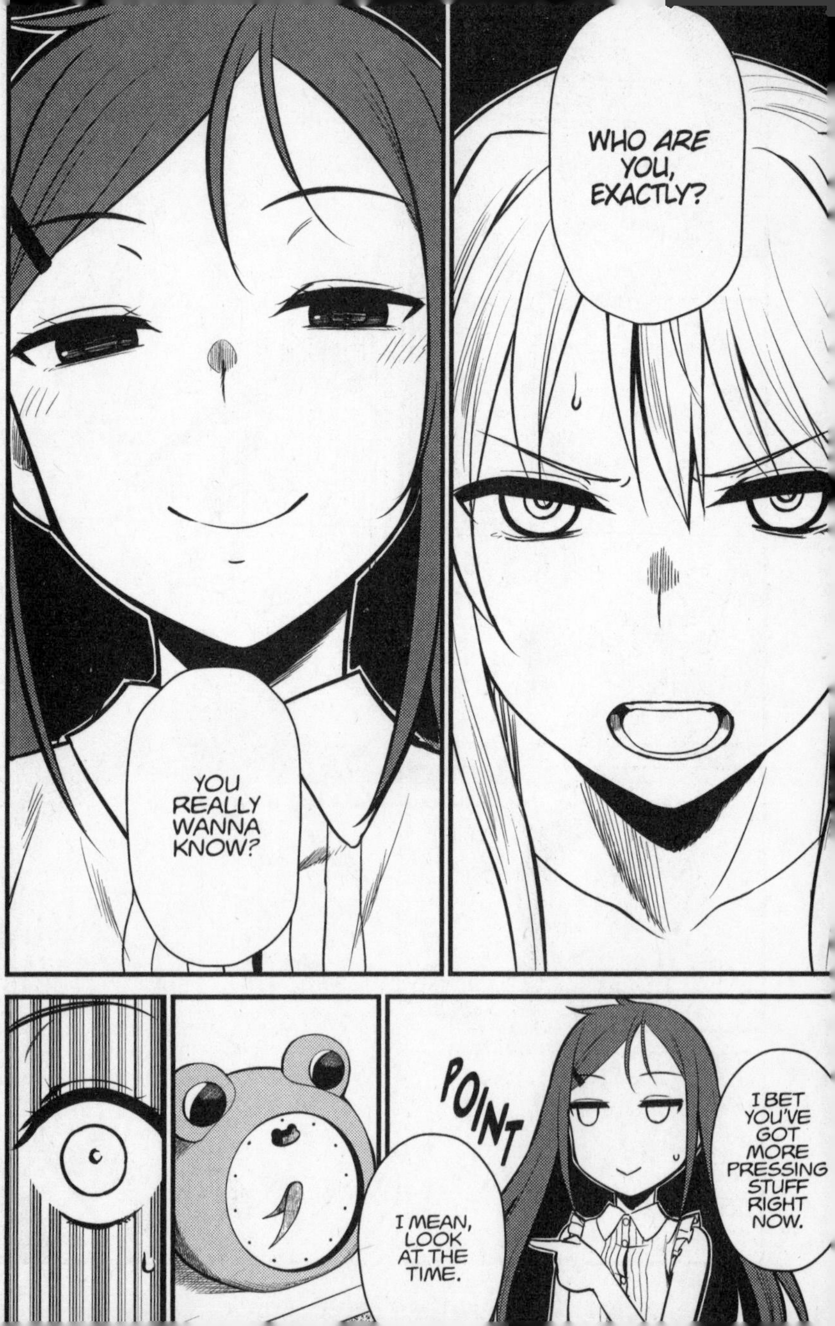
WHO ARE YOU, EXACTLY?
YOU REALLY WANNA KNOW?
I BET YOU'VE GOT MORE PRESSING STUFF RIGHT NOW.
POINT
I MEAN, LOOK AT THE TIME.

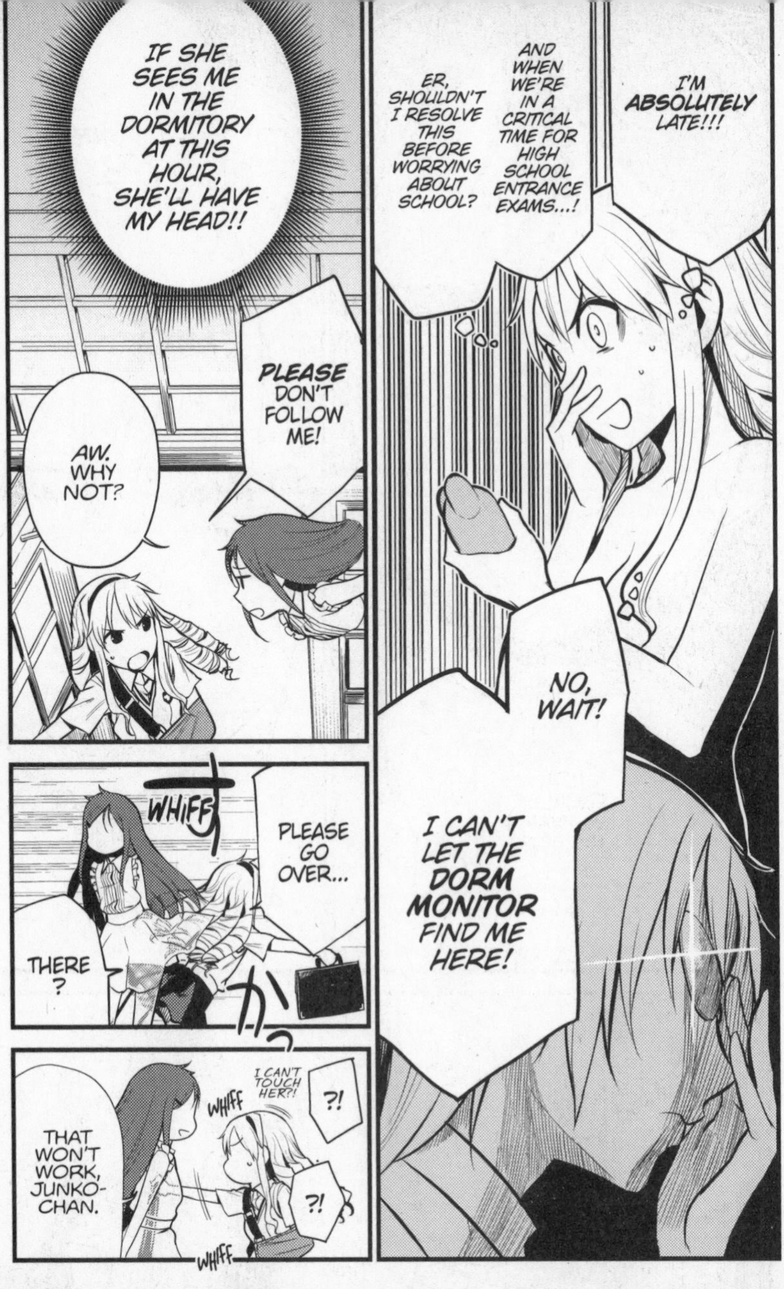
I'M ABSOLUTELY LATE!!!
AND WHEN WE'RE IN A CRITICAL TIME FOR HIGH SCHOOL ENTRANCE EXAMS...!
ER, SHOULDN'T I RESOLVE THIS BEFORE WORRYING ABOUT SCHOOL?
NO, WAIT!
I CAN'T LET THE DORM MONITOR FIND ME HERE!
IF SHE SEES ME IN THE DORMITORY AT THIS HOUR, SHE'LL HAVE MY HEAD!!
PLEASE DON'T FOLLOW ME!
AW. WHY NOT?
WHIFF
PLEASE GO OVER...
THERE?
?!
I CAN'T TOUCH HER?!
WHIFF
?!
THAT WON'T WORK, JUNKO-CHAN.
WHIFF

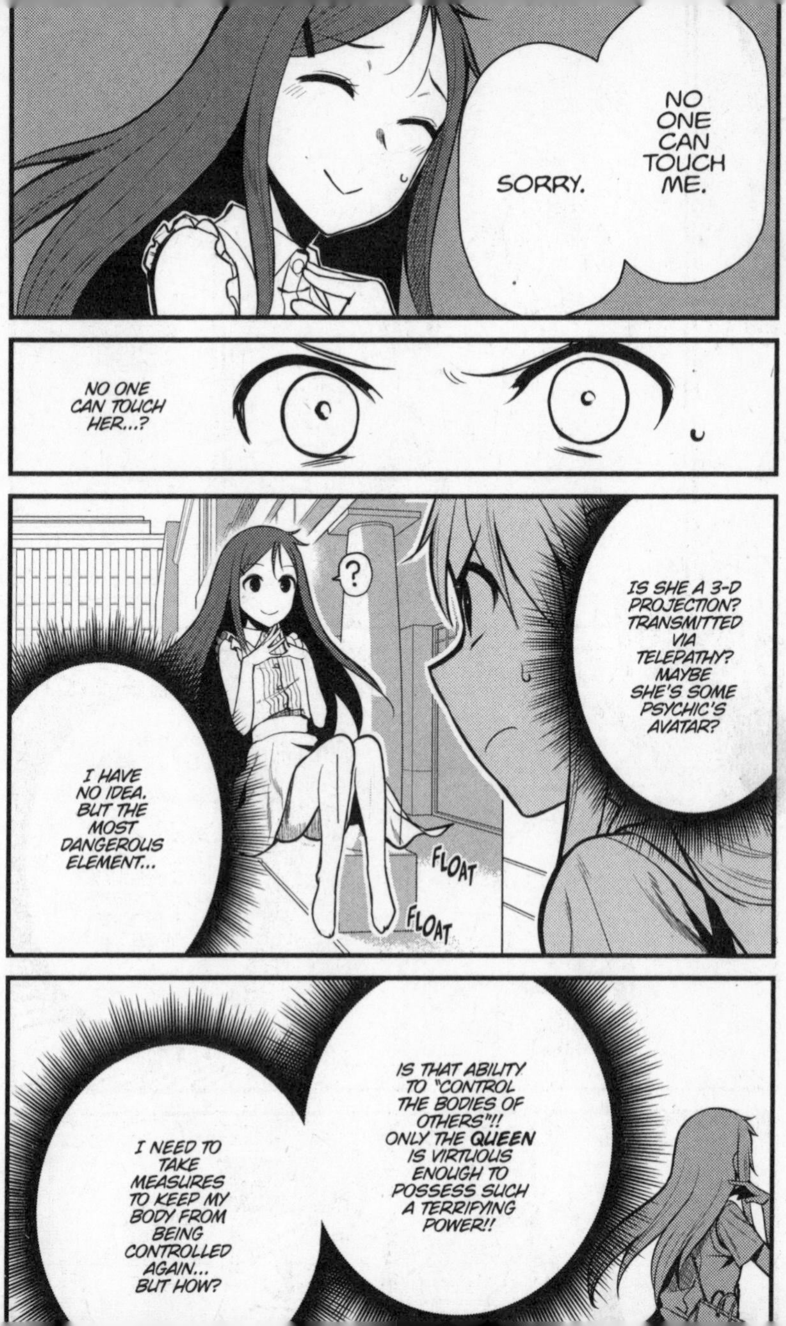
NO ONE CAN TOUCH ME.
SORRY.
NO ONE CAN TOUCH HER...?
?
IS SHE A 3-D PROJECTION? TRANSMITTED VIA TELEPATHY? MAYBE SHE'S SOME PSYCHIC'S AVATAR?
I HAVE NO IDEA. BUT THE MOST DANGEROUS ELEMENT...
FLOAT
FLOAT
IS THAT ABILITY TO "CONTROL THE BODIES OF OTHERS"!! ONLY THE QUEEN IS VIRTUOUS ENOUGH TO POSSESS SUCH A TERRIFYING POWER!!
I NEED TO TAKE MEASURES TO KEEP MY BODY FROM BEING CONTROLLED AGAIN... BUT HOW?

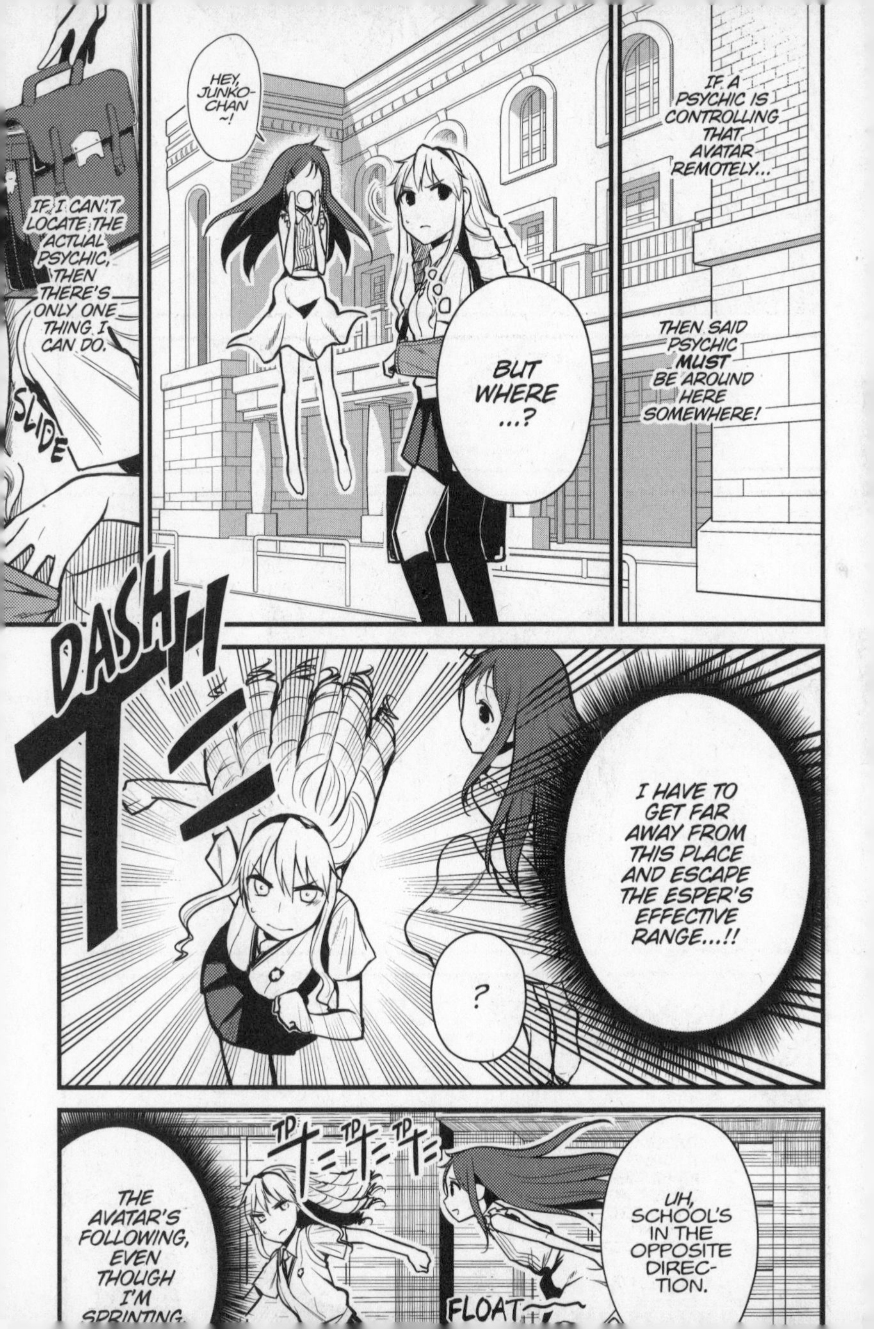
IF A PSYCHIC IS CONTROLLING THAT AVATAR REMOTELY...
THEN SAID PSYCHIC MUST BE AROUND HERE SOMEWHERE!
HEY, JUNKO-CHAN ~!
BUT WHERE ...?
IF I CAN'T LOCATE THE ACTUAL PSYCHIC, THEN THERE'S ONLY ONE THING I CAN DO.
SLIDE
DASH-!
I HAVE TO GET FAR AWAY FROM THIS PLACE AND ESCAPE THE ESPER'S EFFECTIVE RANGE...!!
?
TP TP TP
UH, SCHOOL'S IN THE OPPOSITE DIRECTION.
FLOAT
THE AVATAR'S FOLLOWING, EVEN THOUGH I'M SPRINTING

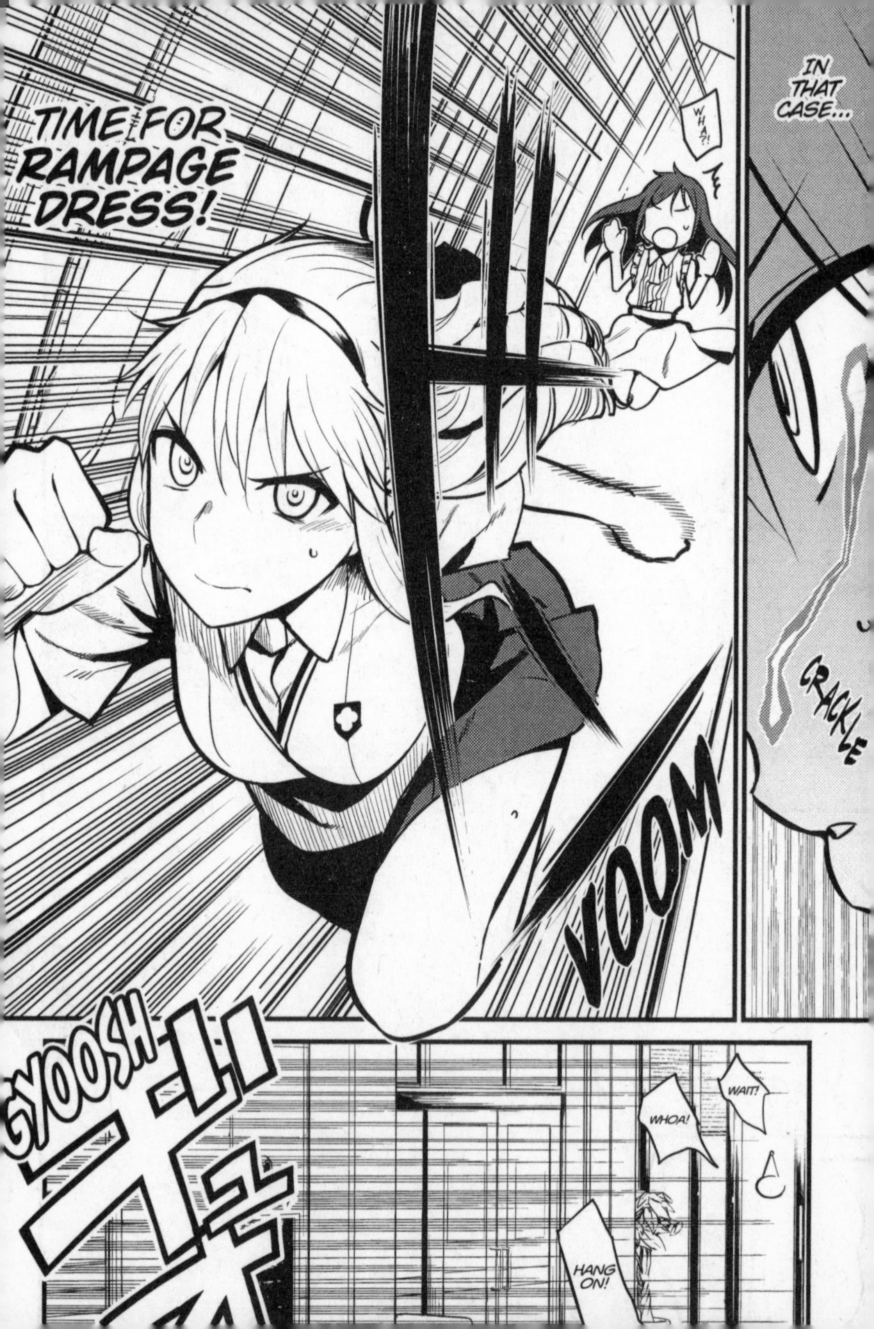

IN THAT CASE...
WHA?!
TIME FOR RAMPAGE DRESS!
CRACKLE
VOOM
WAIT!
WHOA!
HANG ON!
GYOOSH

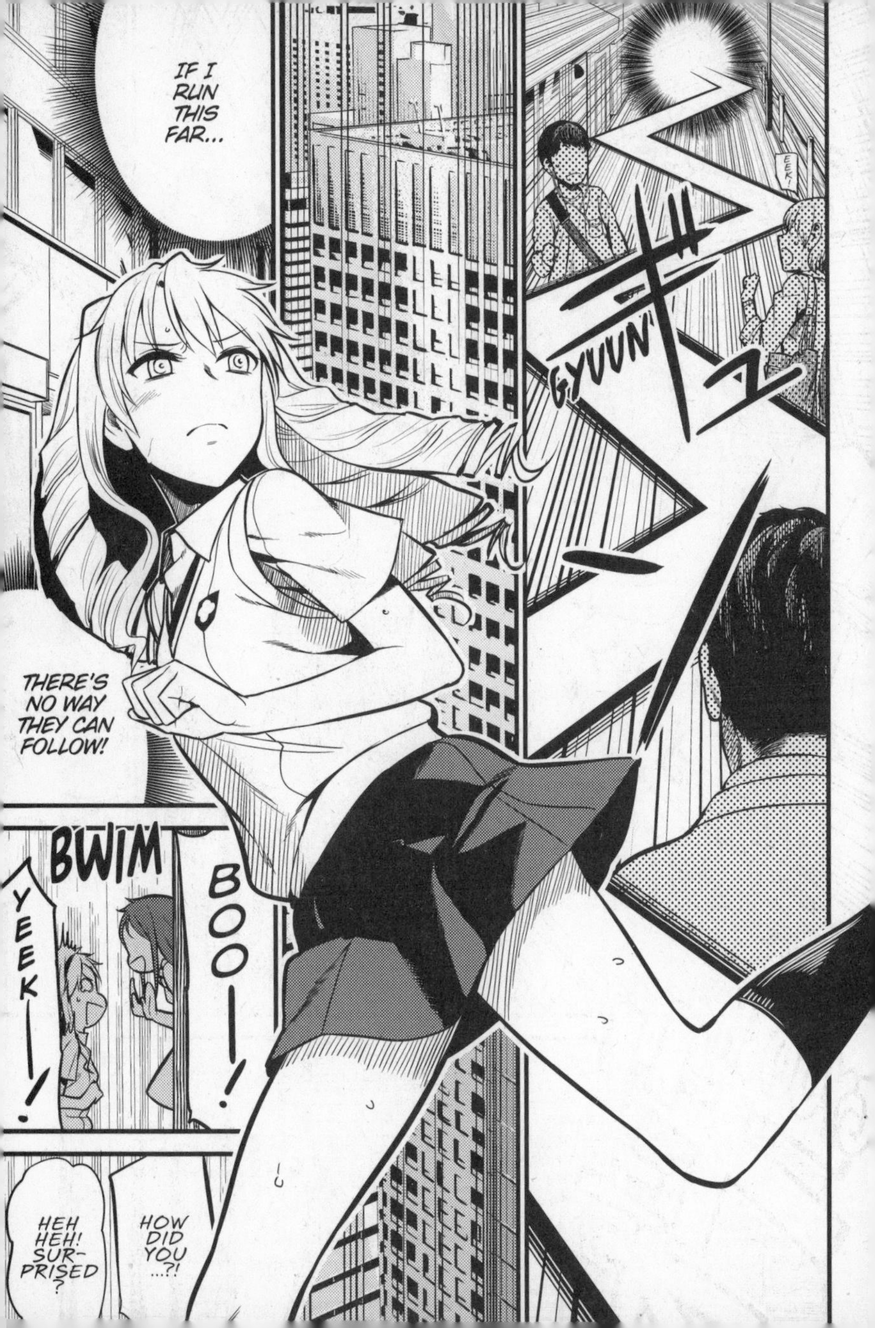

EEK!
GYUUN
IF I RUN THIS FAR...
THERE'S NO WAY THEY CAN FOLLOW!
BWIM
BOO—!
YEEK—!
HOW DID YOU ...?!
HEH HEH! SURPRISED?

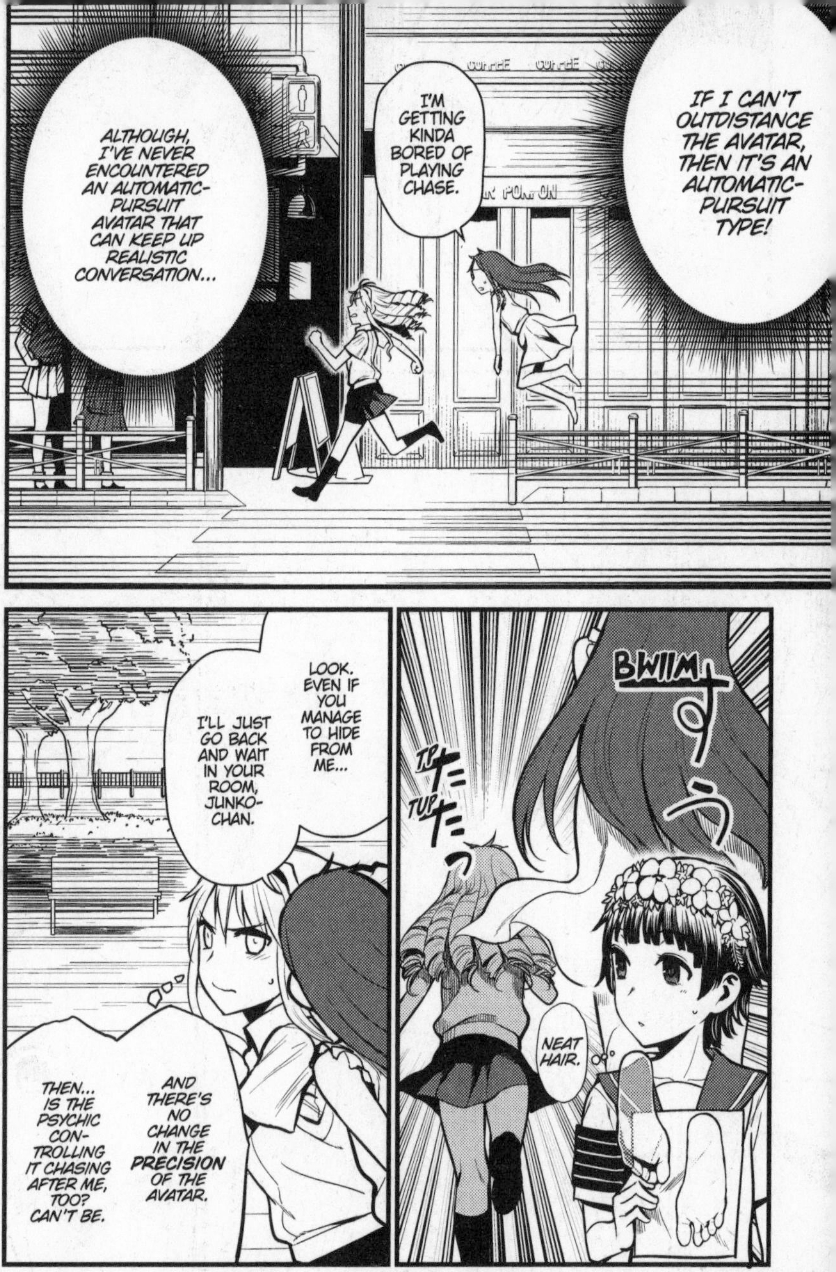

IF I CAN'T OUTDISTANCE THE AVATAR, THEN IT'S AN AUTOMATIC-PURSUIT TYPE!
I'M GETTING KINDA BORED OF PLAYING CHASE.
ALTHOUGH, I'VE NEVER ENCOUNTERED AN AUTOMATIC-PURSUIT AVATAR THAT CAN KEEP UP REALISTIC CONVERSATION...
BWIIM
TP
TUP
NEAT HAIR.
LOOK. EVEN IF YOU MANAGE TO HIDE FROM ME...
I'LL JUST GO BACK AND WAIT IN YOUR ROOM, JUNKO-CHAN.
AND THERE'S NO CHANGE IN THE PRECISION OF THE AVATAR.
THEN... IS THE PSYCHIC CON-TROLLING IT CHASING AFTER ME, TOO? CAN'T BE.

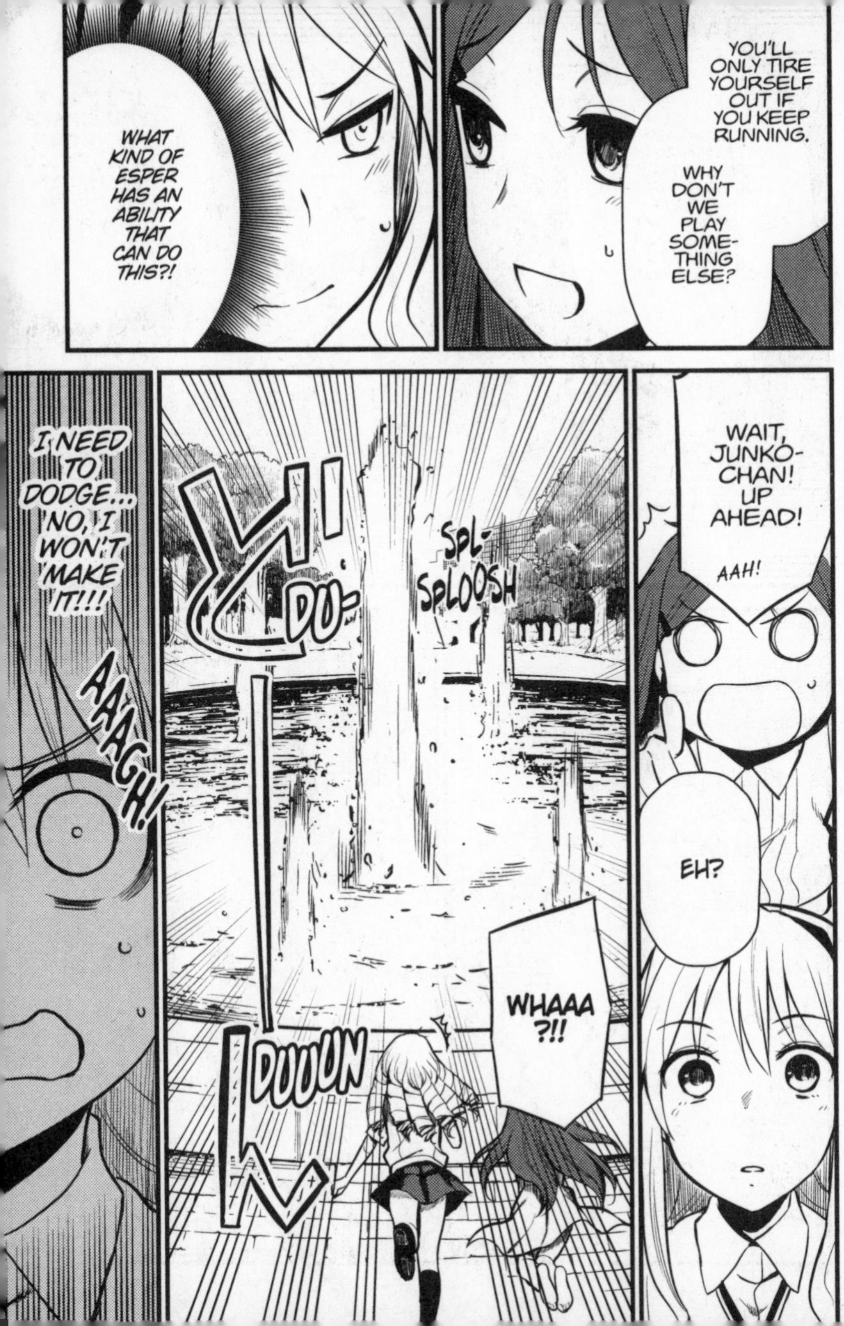
YOU'LL ONLY TIRE YOURSELF OUT IF YOU KEEP RUNNING.
WHY DON'T WE PLAY SOME-THING ELSE?
WHAT KIND OF ESPER HAS AN ABILITY THAT CAN DO THIS?!
WAIT, JUNKO-CHAN! UP AHEAD!
AAH!
EH?
SPL-SPLOOSH
DU-DUUUN
WHAAA?!!
I NEED TO DODGE... NO, I WON'T MAKE IT!!!
AAAGH!

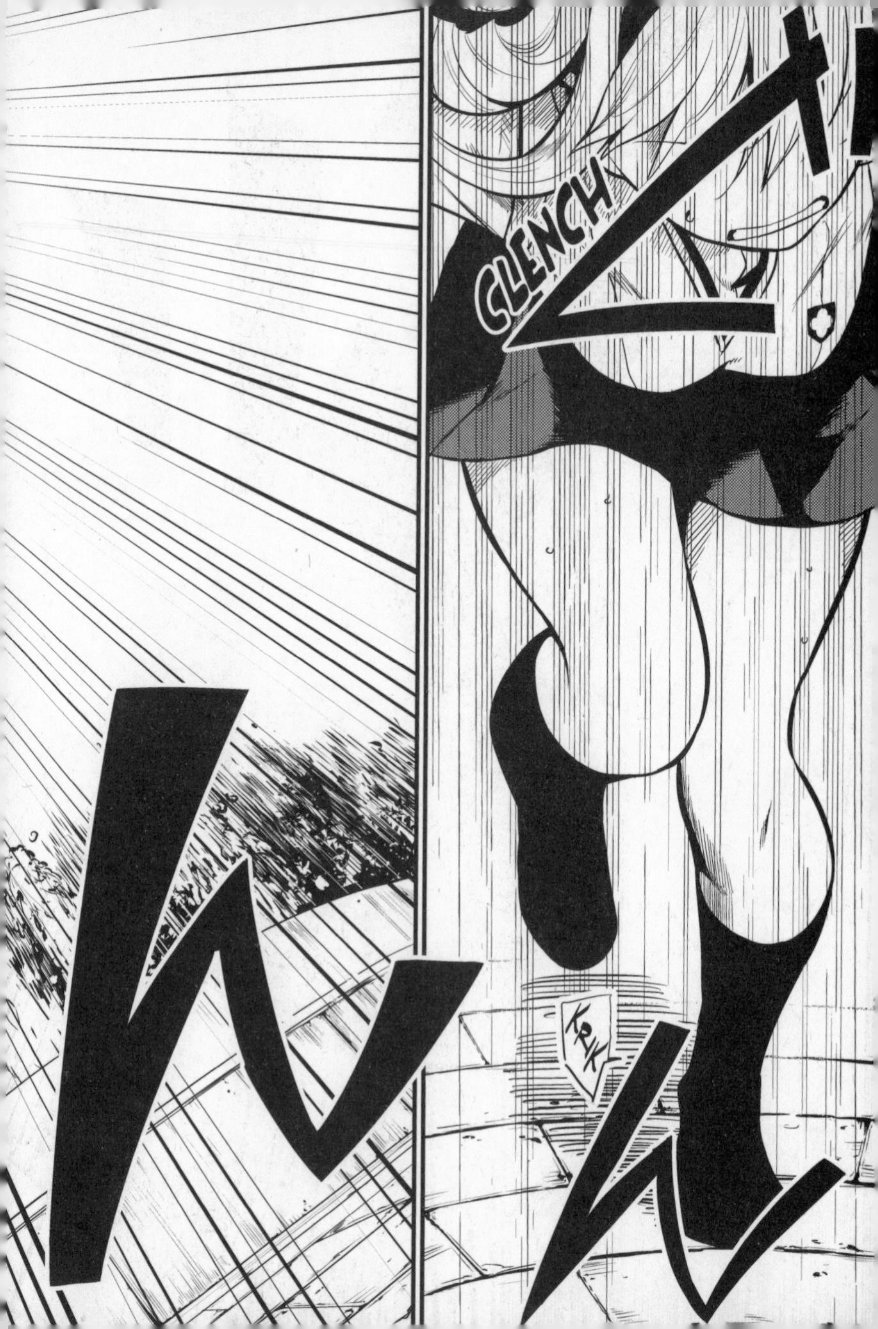
CLENCH
KRIK

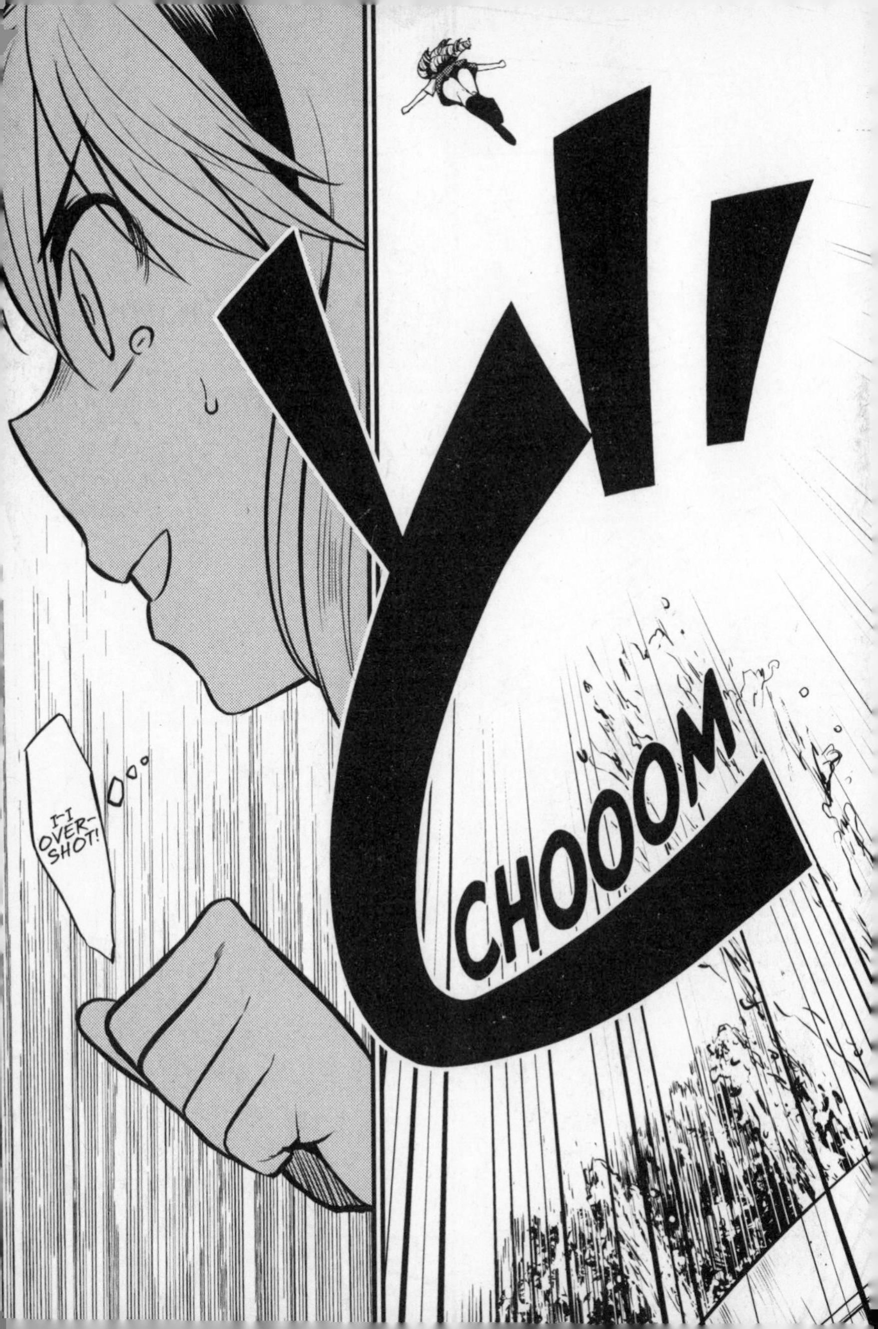
CHOOOM
I-I OVER-SHOT!

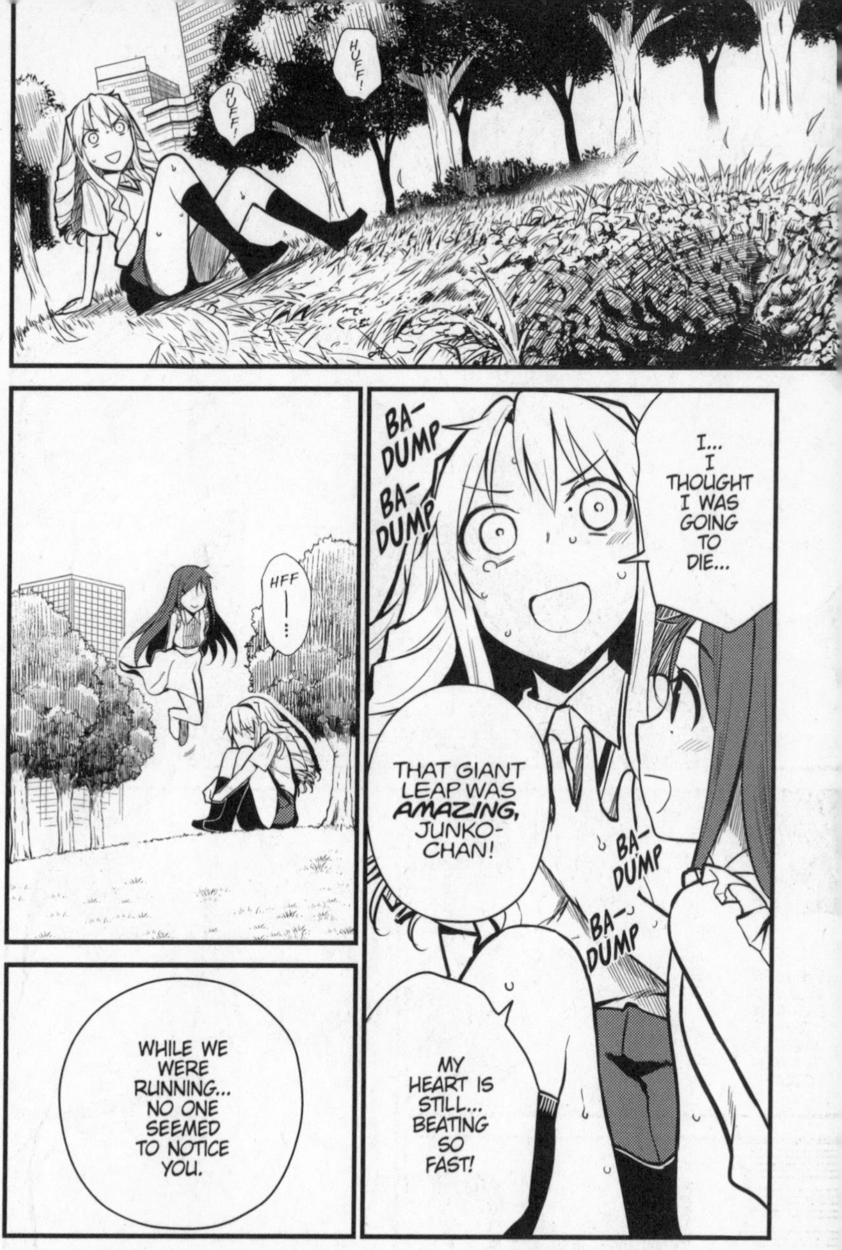
HUFF!
HUFF!
BA-DUMP
BA-DUMP
I... I THOUGHT I WAS GOING TO DIE...
THAT GIANT LEAP WAS *AMAZING*, JUNKO-CHAN!
BA-DUMP
BA-DUMP
MY HEART IS STILL... BEATING SO FAST!
HFF...!
WHILE WE WERE RUNNING... NO ONE SEEMED TO NOTICE YOU.

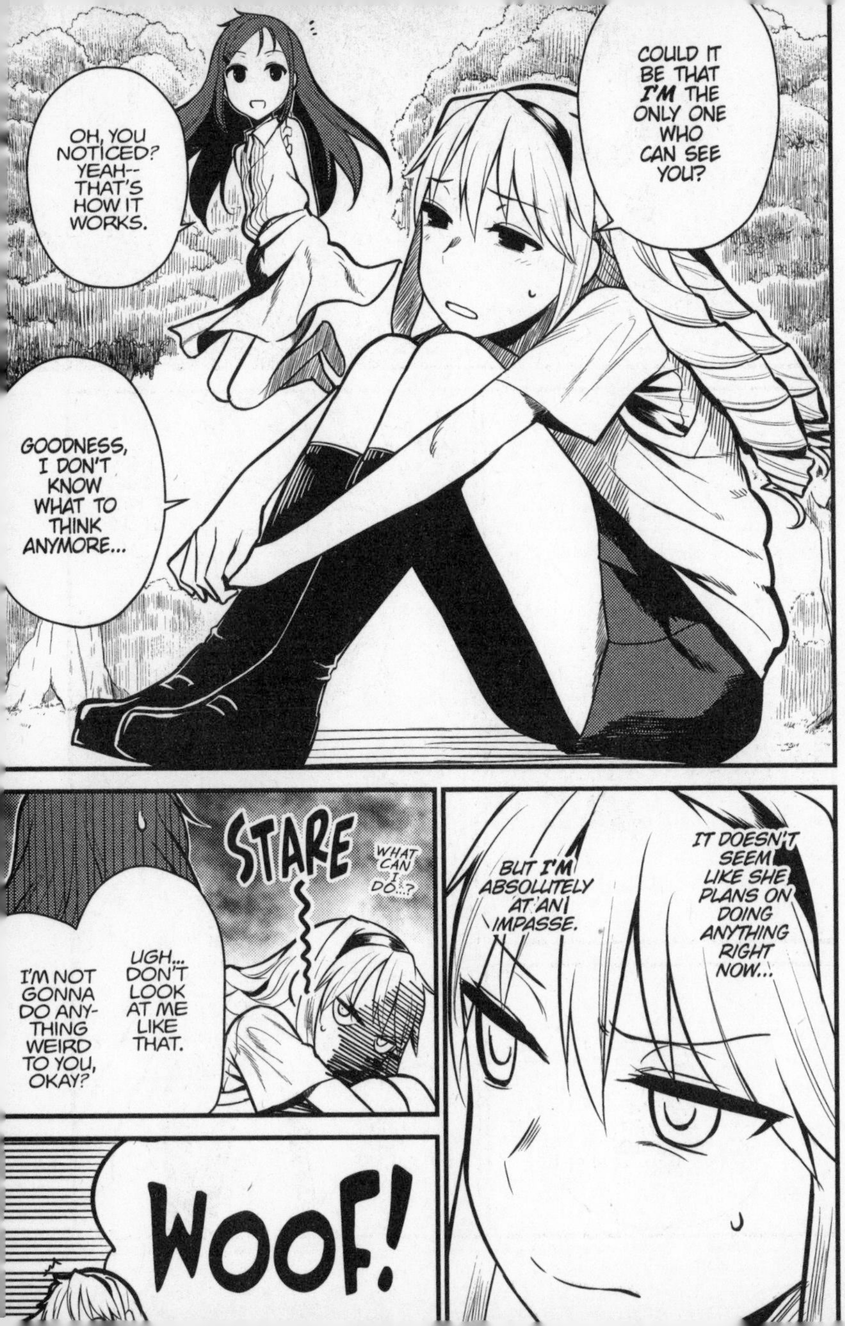
COULD IT BE THAT *I'M* THE ONLY ONE WHO CAN SEE YOU?
OH, YOU NOTICED? YEAH-- THAT'S HOW IT WORKS.
GOODNESS, I DON'T KNOW WHAT TO THINK ANYMORE...
IT DOESN'T SEEM LIKE SHE PLANS ON DOING ANYTHING RIGHT NOW...
BUT I'M ABSOLUTELY AT AN IMPASSE.
STARE
WHAT CAN I DO...?
UGH... DON'T LOOK AT ME LIKE THAT.
I'M NOT GONNA DO ANY-THING WEIRD TO YOU, OKAY?
WOOF!

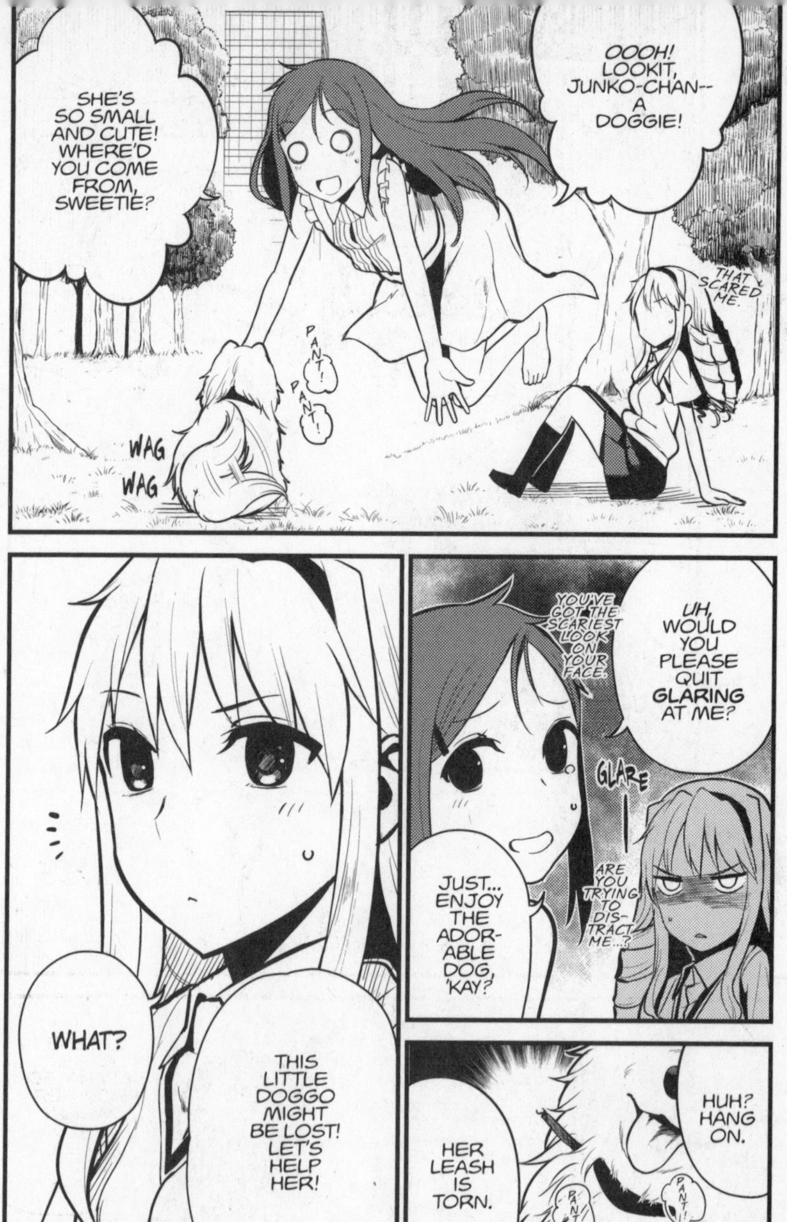
OOOH! LOOKIT, JUNKO-CHAN-- A DOGGIE!
SHE'S SO SMALL AND CUTE! WHERE'D YOU COME FROM, SWEETIE?
THAT SCARED ME.
PANT! PANT!
WAG WAG
UH, WOULD YOU PLEASE QUIT GLARING AT ME?
YOU'VE GOT THE SCARIEST LOOK ON YOUR FACE.
GLARE
ARE YOU TRYING TO DISTRACT ME...?
JUST... ENJOY THE ADORABLE DOG, 'KAY?
WHAT?
THIS LITTLE DOGGO MIGHT BE LOST! LET'S HELP HER!
HUH? HANG ON.
HER LEASH IS TORN.
PANT! PANT!

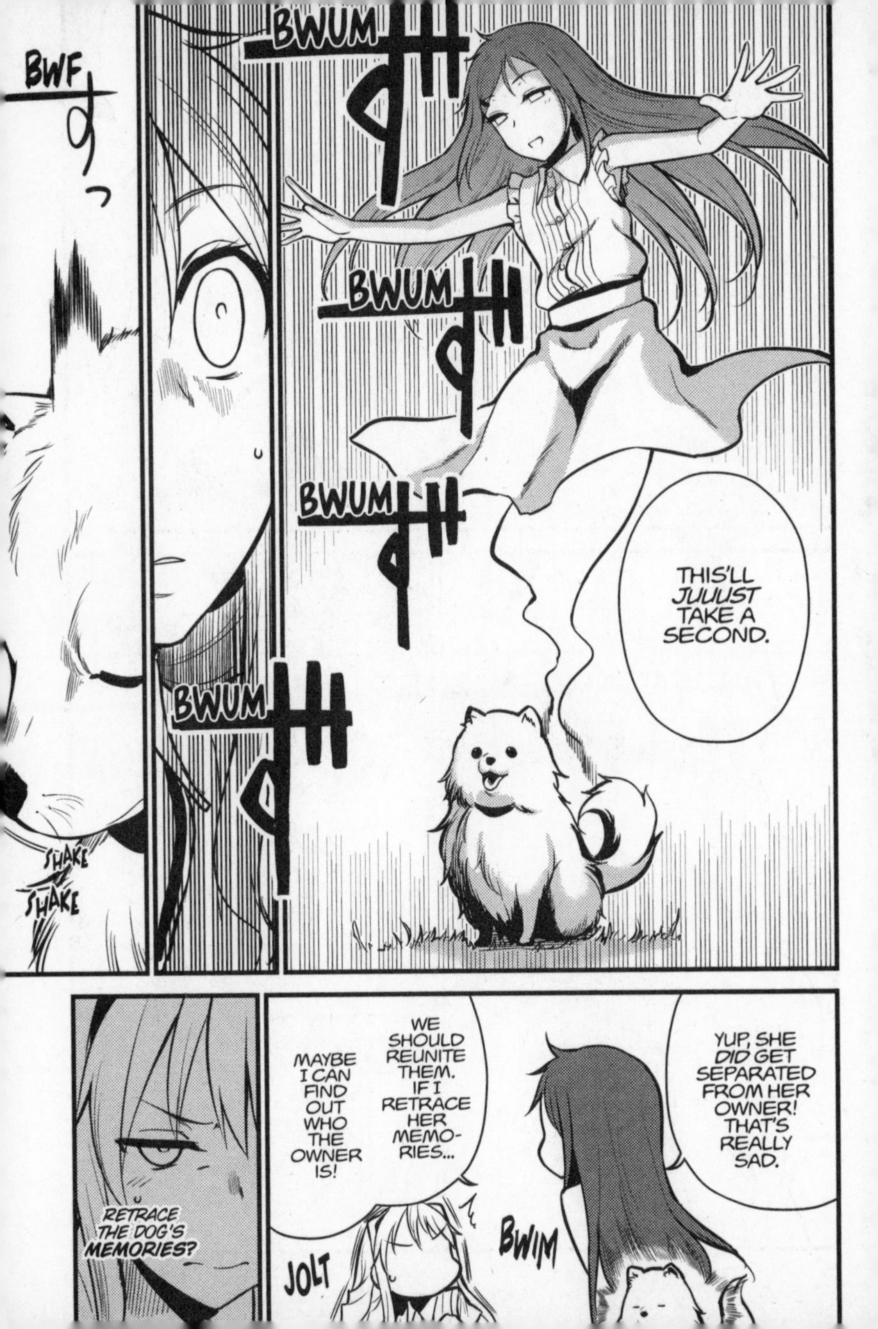
BWUM
BWUM
BWUM
BWUM
THIS'LL JUUUST TAKE A SECOND.
BWF
すっ
SHAKE SHAKE
YUP, SHE DID GET SEPARATED FROM HER OWNER! THAT'S REALLY SAD.
BWIM
WE SHOULD REUNITE THEM. IF I RETRACE HER MEMORIES...
MAYBE I CAN FIND OUT WHO THE OWNER IS!
JOLT
RETRACE THE DOG'S MEMORIES?

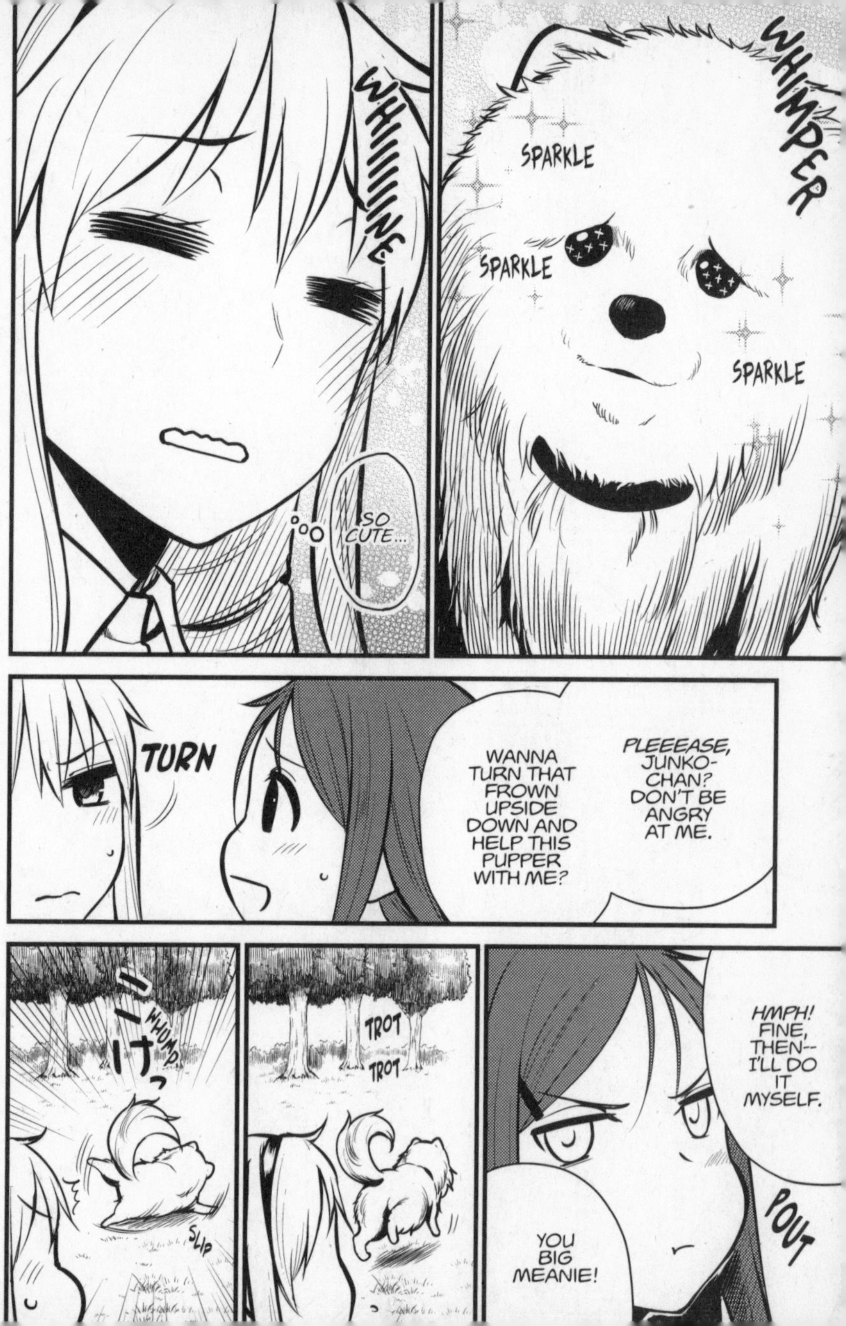
WHIMPER
SPARKLE
SPARKLE
SPARKLE
WHIIIIIINE
SO CUTE...
PLEEEASE, JUNKO-CHAN? DON'T BE ANGRY AT ME.
WANNA TURN THAT FROWN UPSIDE DOWN AND HELP THIS PUPPER WITH ME?
TURN
HMPH! FINE, THEN-- I'LL DO IT MYSELF.
POUT
YOU BIG MEANIE!
TROT
TROT
WHUMP
けっ
SLIP

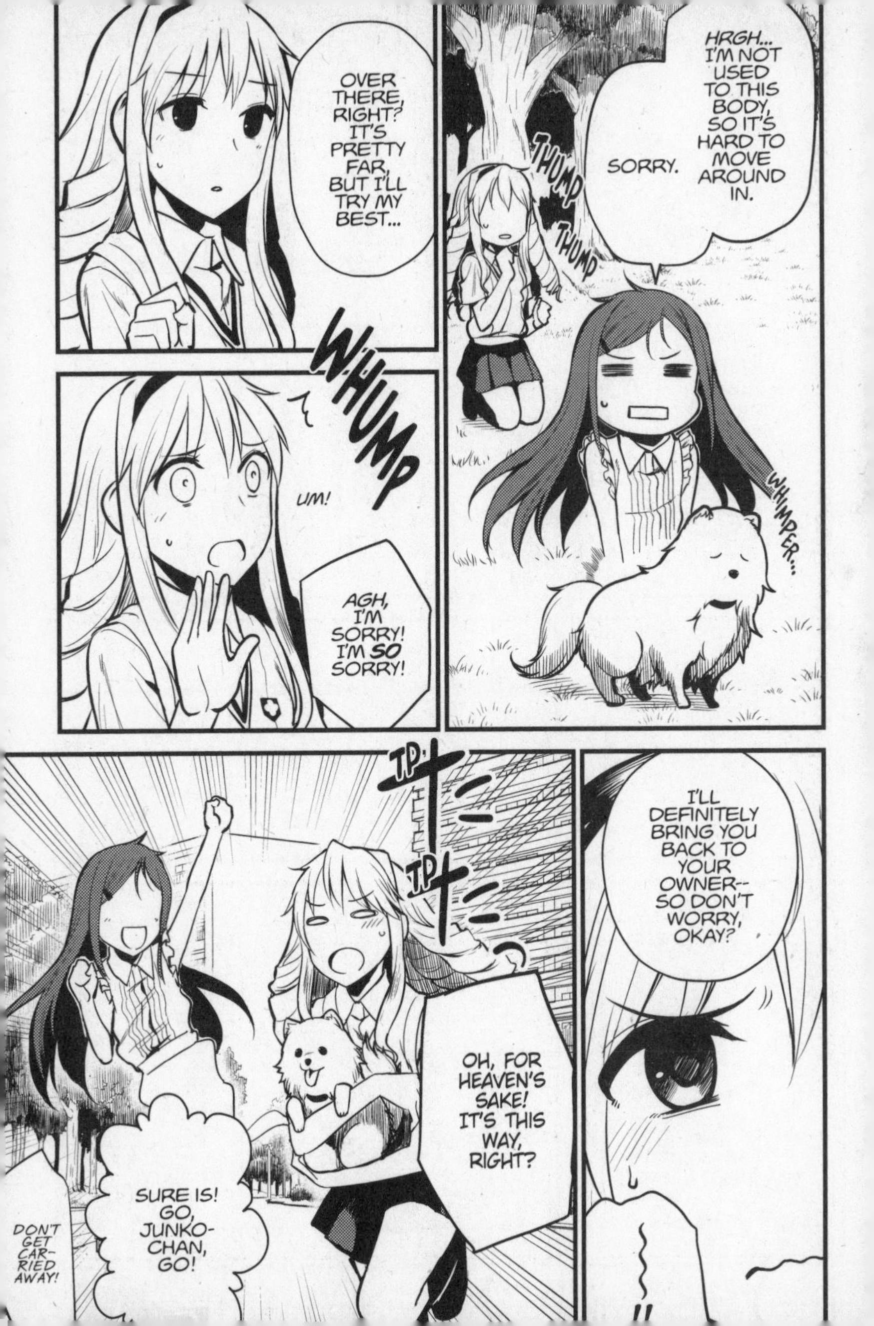
HRGH... I'M NOT USED TO THIS BODY, SO IT'S HARD TO MOVE AROUND IN.
SORRY.
THUMP THUMP
OVER THERE, RIGHT? IT'S PRETTY FAR, BUT I'LL TRY MY BEST...
WHIMPER...
WHUMP
UM!
AGH, I'M SORRY! I'M SO SORRY!
I'LL DEFINITELY BRING YOU BACK TO YOUR OWNER-- SO DON'T WORRY, OKAY?
TP TP
OH, FOR HEAVEN'S SAKE! IT'S THIS WAY, RIGHT?
SURE IS! GO, JUNKO-CHAN, GO!
DON'T GET CAR-RIED AWAY!

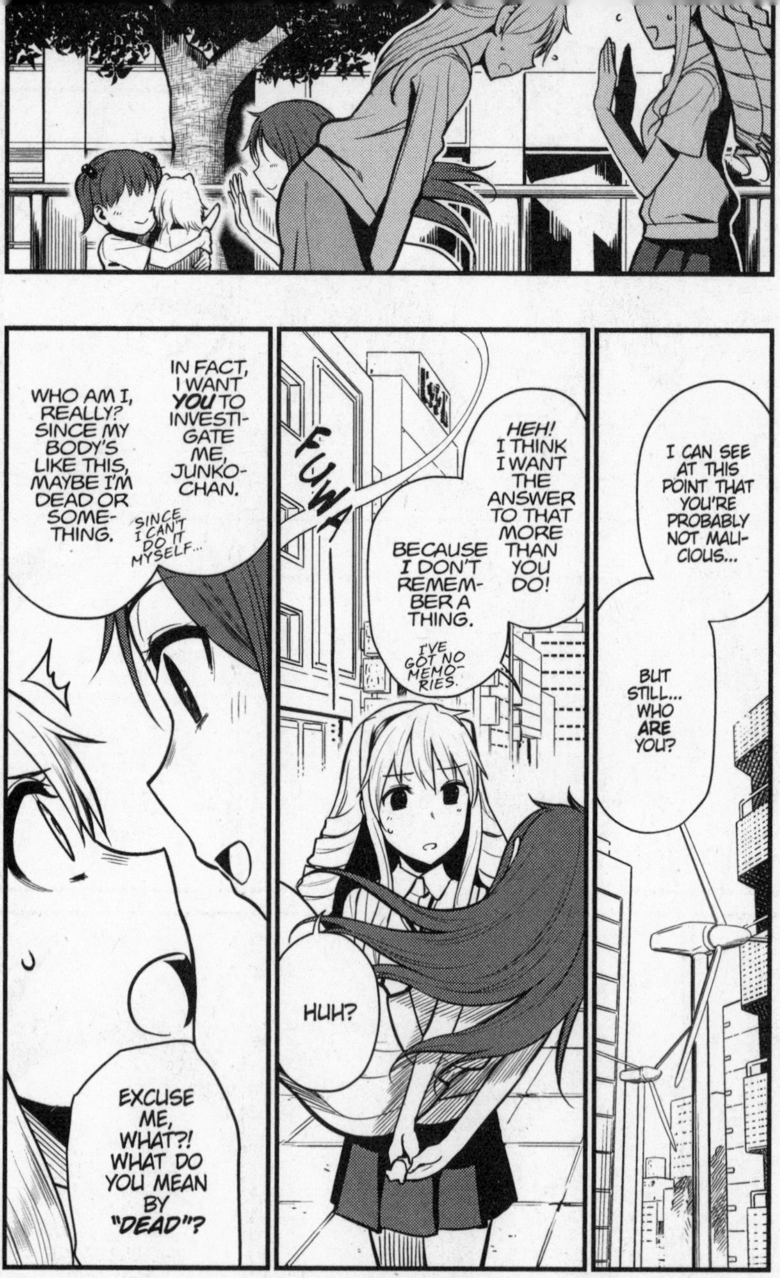
I CAN SEE AT THIS POINT THAT YOU'RE PROBABLY NOT MALICIOUS...
BUT STILL... WHO *ARE* YOU?
HUH?
HEH! I THINK I WANT THE ANSWER TO THAT MORE THAN YOU DO!
BECAUSE I DON'T REMEMBER A THING.
I'VE GOT NO MEMORIES.
FUWA
IN FACT, I WANT **YOU** TO INVESTIGATE ME, JUNKO-CHAN.
SINCE I CAN'T DO IT MYSELF...
WHO AM I, REALLY? SINCE MY BODY'S LIKE THIS, MAYBE I'M DEAD OR SOMETHING.
EXCUSE ME, WHAT?! WHAT DO YOU MEAN BY "DEAD"?

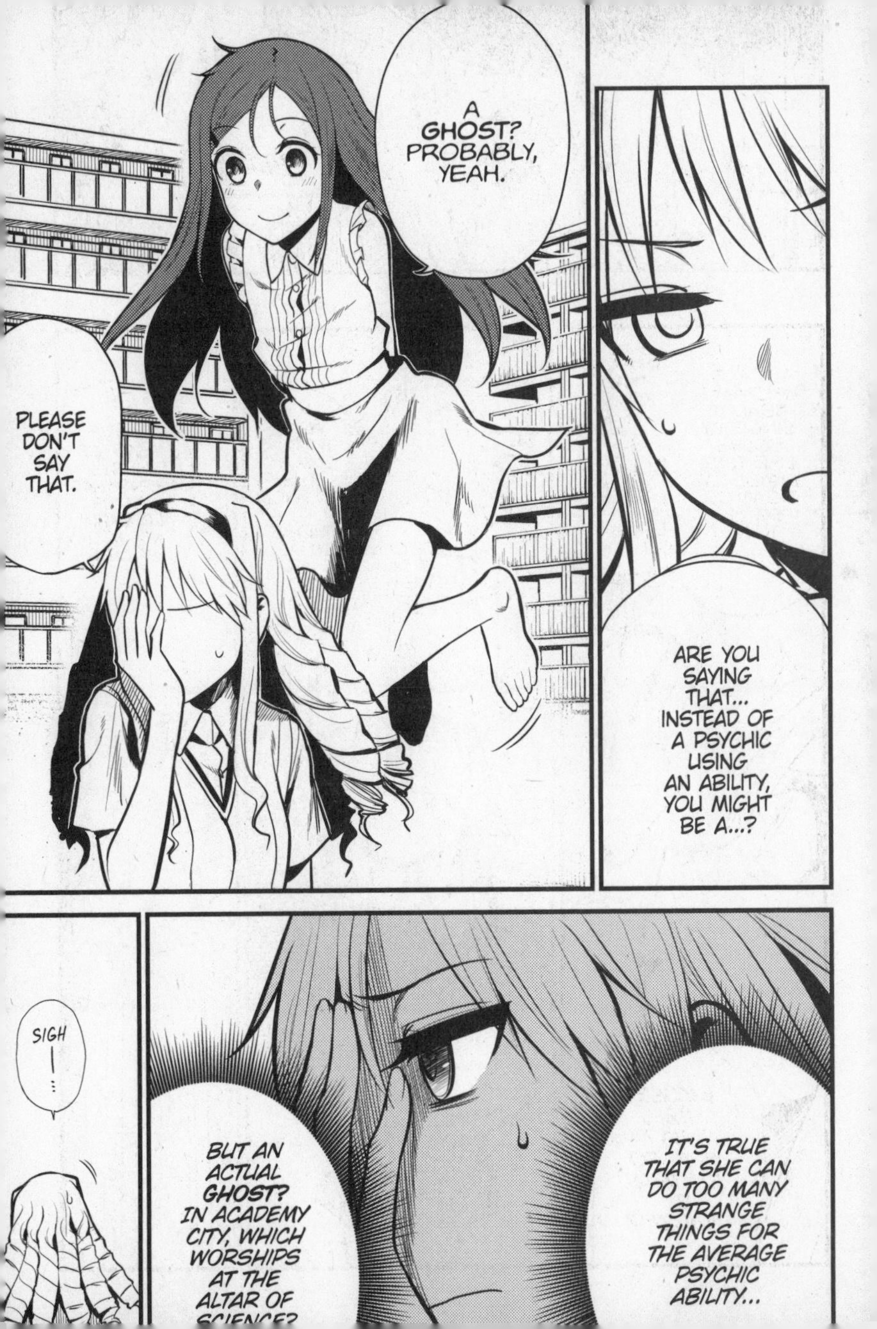
ARE YOU SAYING THAT... INSTEAD OF A PSYCHIC USING AN ABILITY, YOU MIGHT BE A...?
A GHOST? PROBABLY, YEAH.
PLEASE DON'T SAY THAT.
IT'S TRUE THAT SHE CAN DO TOO MANY STRANGE THINGS FOR THE AVERAGE PSYCHIC ABILITY...
BUT AN ACTUAL GHOST? IN ACADEMY CITY, WHICH WORSHIPS AT THE ALTAR OF
SIGH

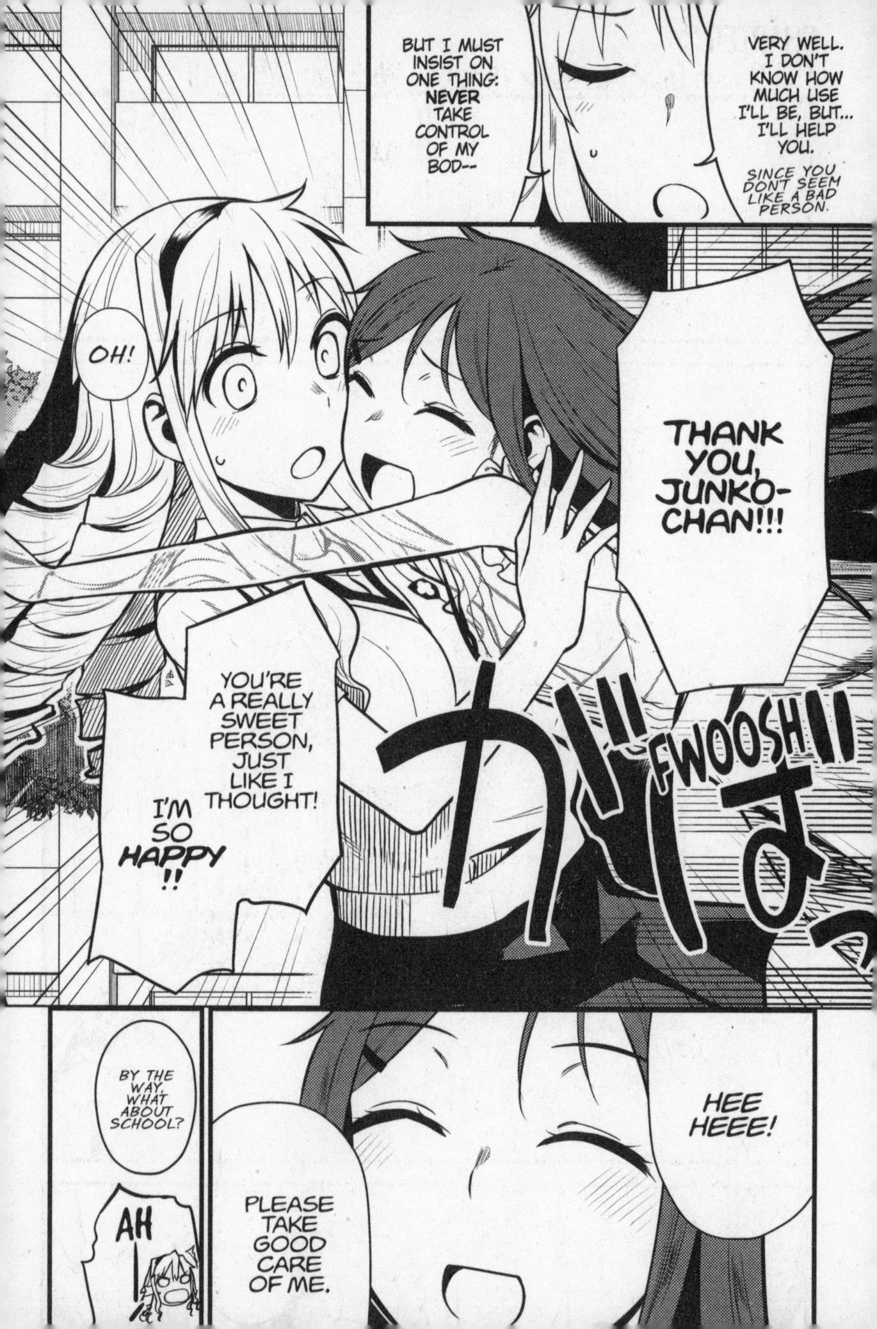

VERY WELL. I DON'T KNOW HOW MUCH USE I'LL BE, BUT... I'LL HELP YOU.
SINCE YOU DON'T SEEM LIKE A BAD PERSON.
BUT I MUST INSIST ON ONE THING: NEVER TAKE CONTROL OF MY BOD--
THANK YOU, JUNKO-CHAN!!!
OH!
FWOOSH!!
YOU'RE A REALLY SWEET PERSON, JUST LIKE I THOUGHT!
I'M SO HAPPY!!
HEE HEEE!
PLEASE TAKE GOOD CARE OF ME.
BY THE WAY, WHAT ABOUT SCHOOL?
AH

CHAPTER 3:
The Queen Ought to Have That Bag With Her, After All

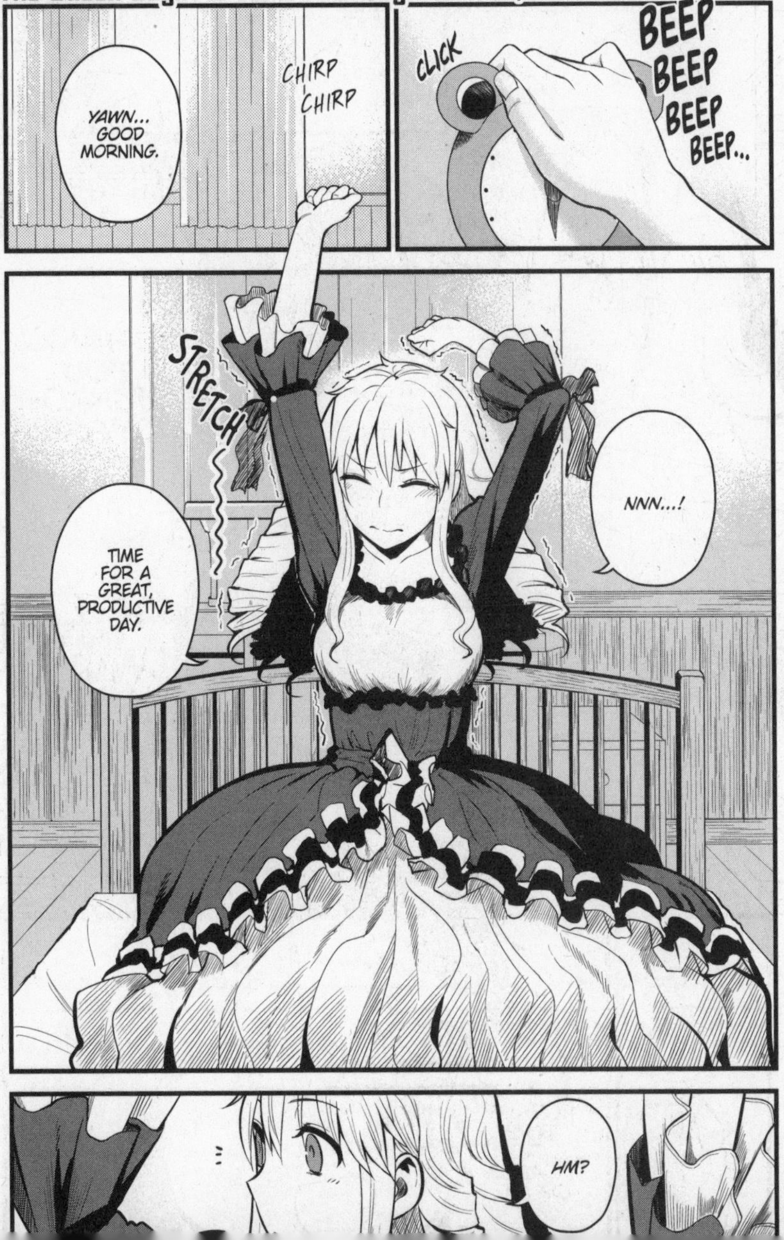

BEEP BEEP BEEP BEEP...
CLICK
CHIRP CHIRP
YAWN... GOOD MORNING.
NNN...!
STRETCH
TIME FOR A GREAT, PRODUCTIVE DAY.
HM?

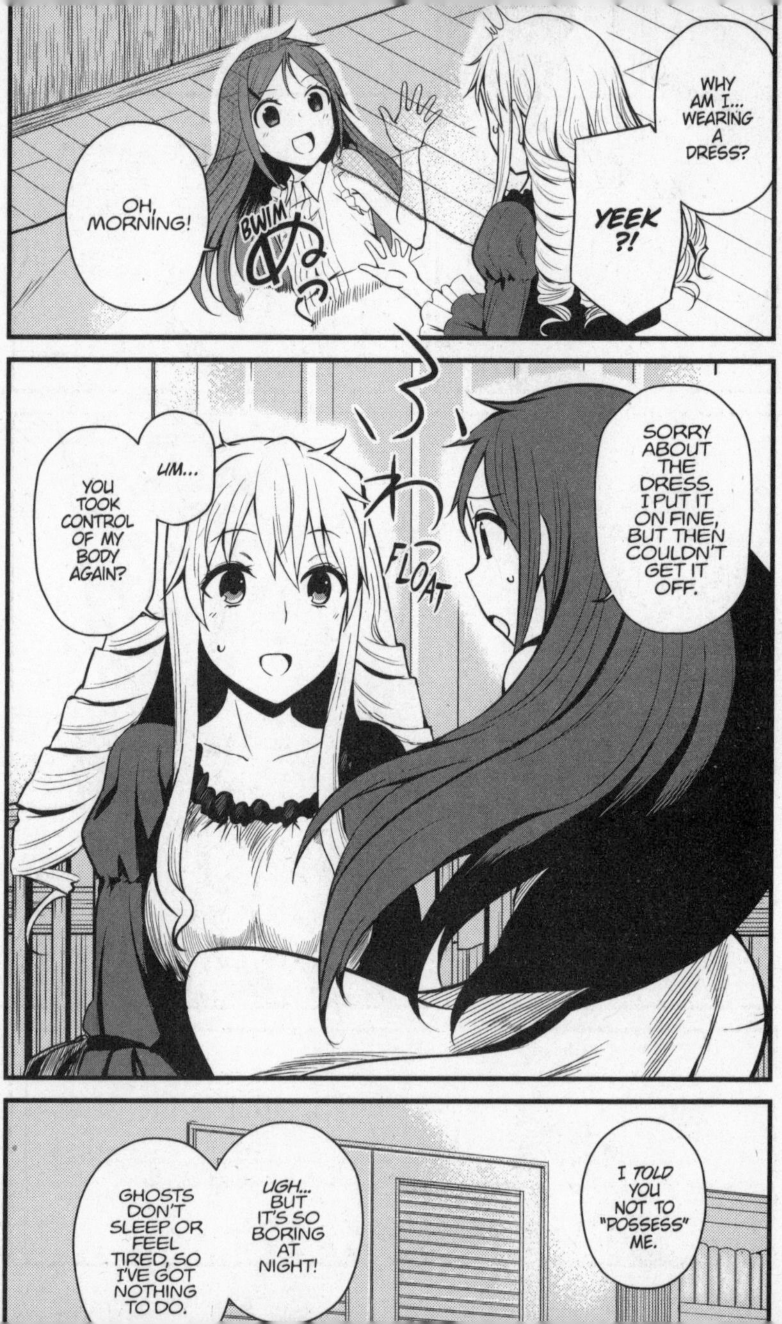
WHY AM I... WEARING A DRESS?
YEEK ?!
BWIM
OH, MORNING!
SORRY ABOUT THE DRESS. I PUT IT ON FINE, BUT THEN COULDN'T GET IT OFF.
FLOAT
UM... YOU TOOK CONTROL OF MY BODY AGAIN?
I *TOLD* YOU NOT TO "POSSESS" ME.
UGH... BUT IT'S SO BORING AT NIGHT!
GHOSTS DON'T SLEEP OR FEEL TIRED, SO I'VE GOT NOTHING TO DO.

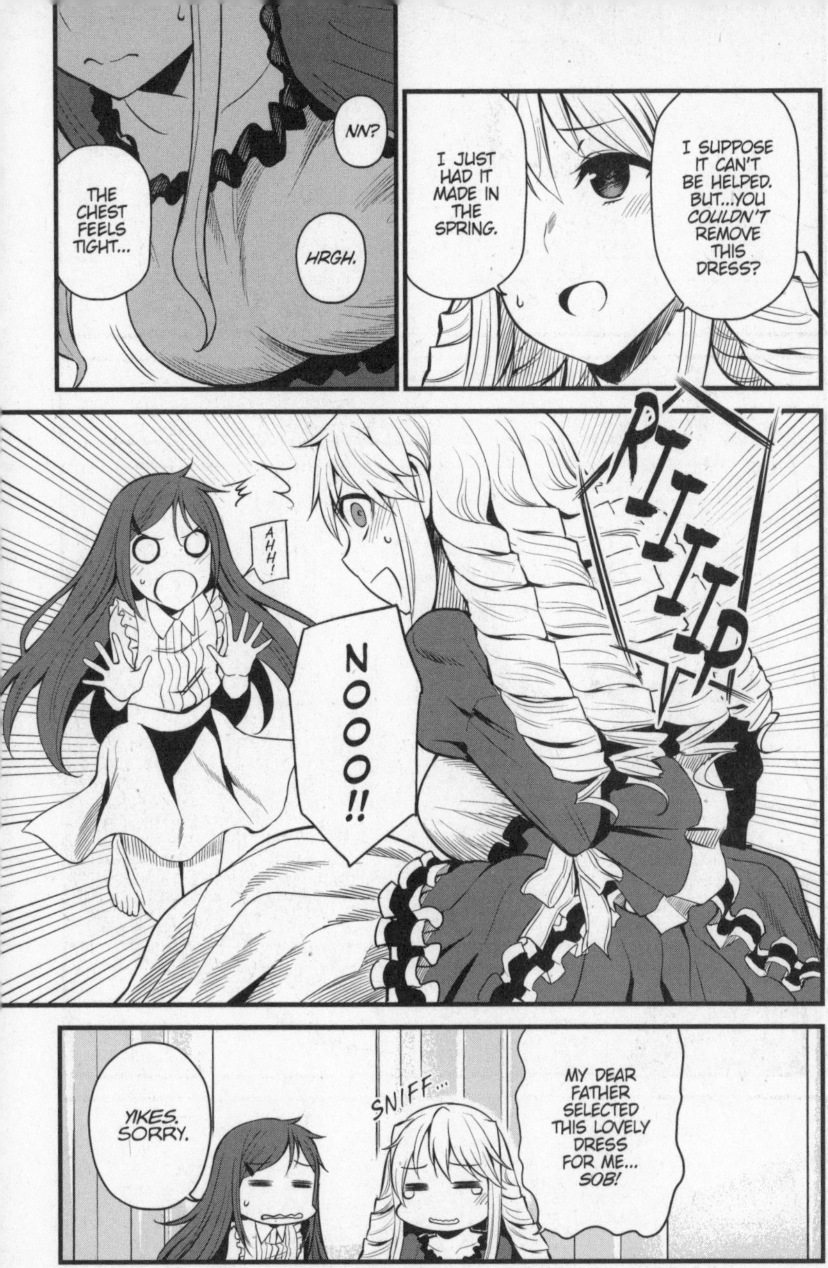
I SUPPOSE IT CAN'T BE HELPED. BUT...YOU COULDN'T REMOVE THIS DRESS?
I JUST HAD IT MADE IN THE SPRING.
NN?
HRGH.
THE CHEST FEELS TIGHT...
RIIIIP
AHH!
NOOOO!!
MY DEAR FATHER SELECTED THIS LOVELY DRESS FOR ME... SOB!
SNIFF...
YIKES. SORRY.

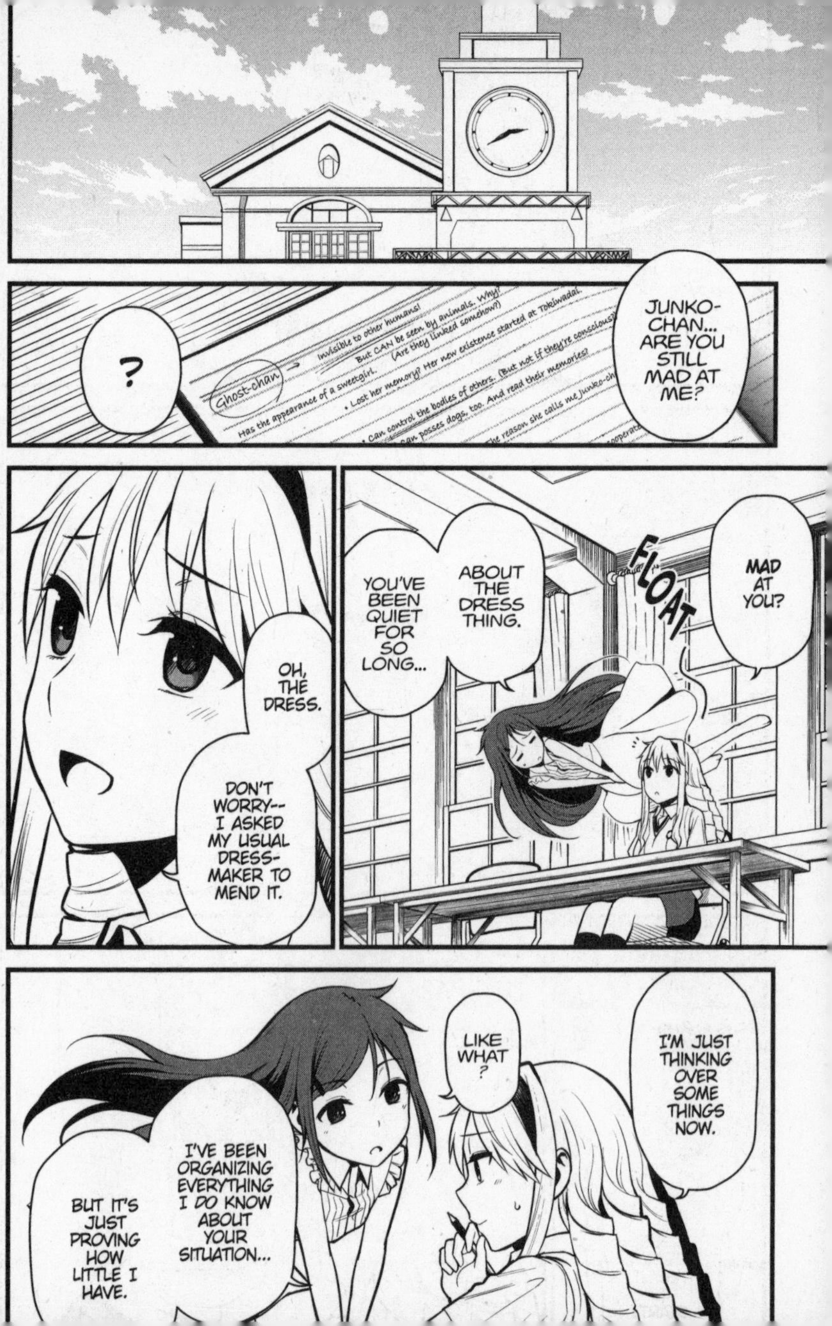

Ghost-chan
Invisible to other humans!
But CAN be seen by animals. Why?
(Are they linked somehow?)
Has the appearance of a sweetgirl.
• Lost her memory? Her new existence started at Tokiwadai.
• Can control the bodies of others. (But not if they're conscious?)
posses dogs, too. And read their memories?
reason she calls me
JUNKO-CHAN... ARE YOU STILL MAD AT ME?
?
MAD AT YOU?
FLOAT
ABOUT THE DRESS THING.
YOU'VE BEEN QUIET FOR SO LONG...
OH, THE DRESS.
DON'T WORRY-- I ASKED MY USUAL DRESS-MAKER TO MEND IT.
I'M JUST THINKING OVER SOME THINGS NOW.
LIKE WHAT?
I'VE BEEN ORGANIZING EVERYTHING I DO KNOW ABOUT YOUR SITUATION...
BUT IT'S JUST PROVING HOW LITTLE I HAVE.

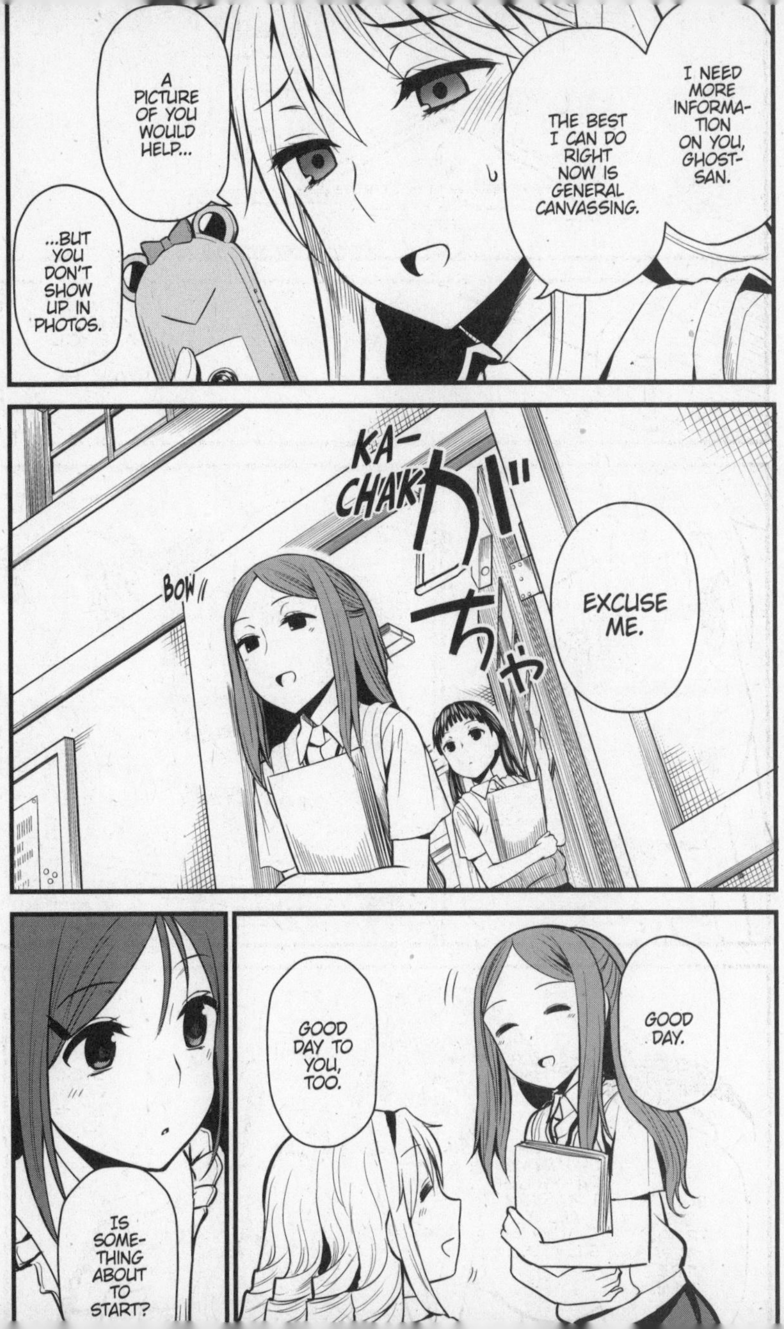
I NEED MORE INFORMATION ON YOU, GHOST-SAN.
THE BEST I CAN DO RIGHT NOW IS GENERAL CANVASSING.
A PICTURE OF YOU WOULD HELP...
...BUT YOU DON'T SHOW UP IN PHOTOS.
KA-CHA'K
がちゃ
EXCUSE ME.
BOW
GOOD DAY.
GOOD DAY TO YOU, TOO.
IS SOMETHING ABOUT TO START?

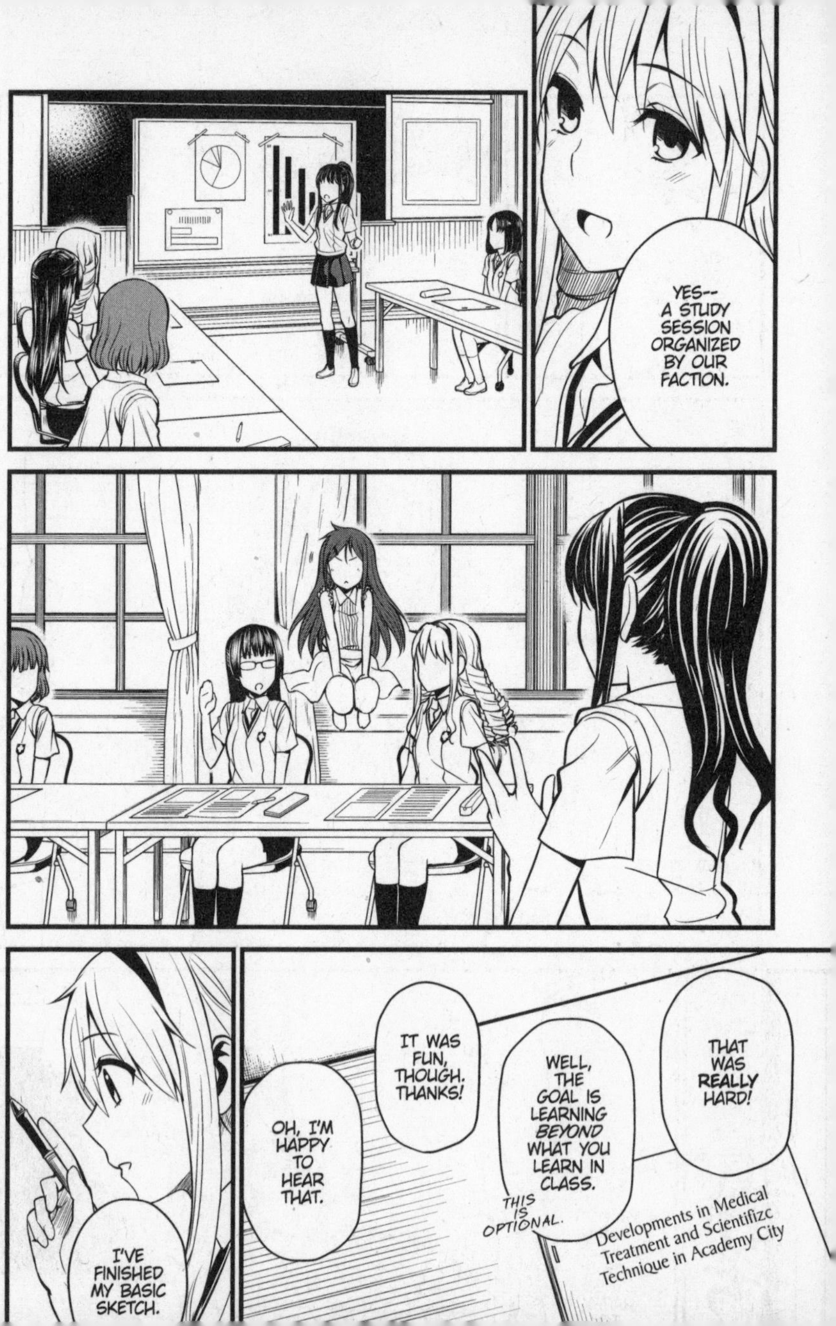
YES-- A STUDY SESSION ORGANIZED BY OUR FACTION.
THAT WAS REALLY HARD!
WELL, THE GOAL IS LEARNING BEYOND WHAT YOU LEARN IN CLASS.
THIS IS OPTIONAL.
IT WAS FUN, THOUGH. THANKS!
OH, I'M HAPPY TO HEAR THAT.
Developments in Medical Treatment and Scientifizc Technique in Academy City
I'VE FINISHED MY BASIC SKETCH.

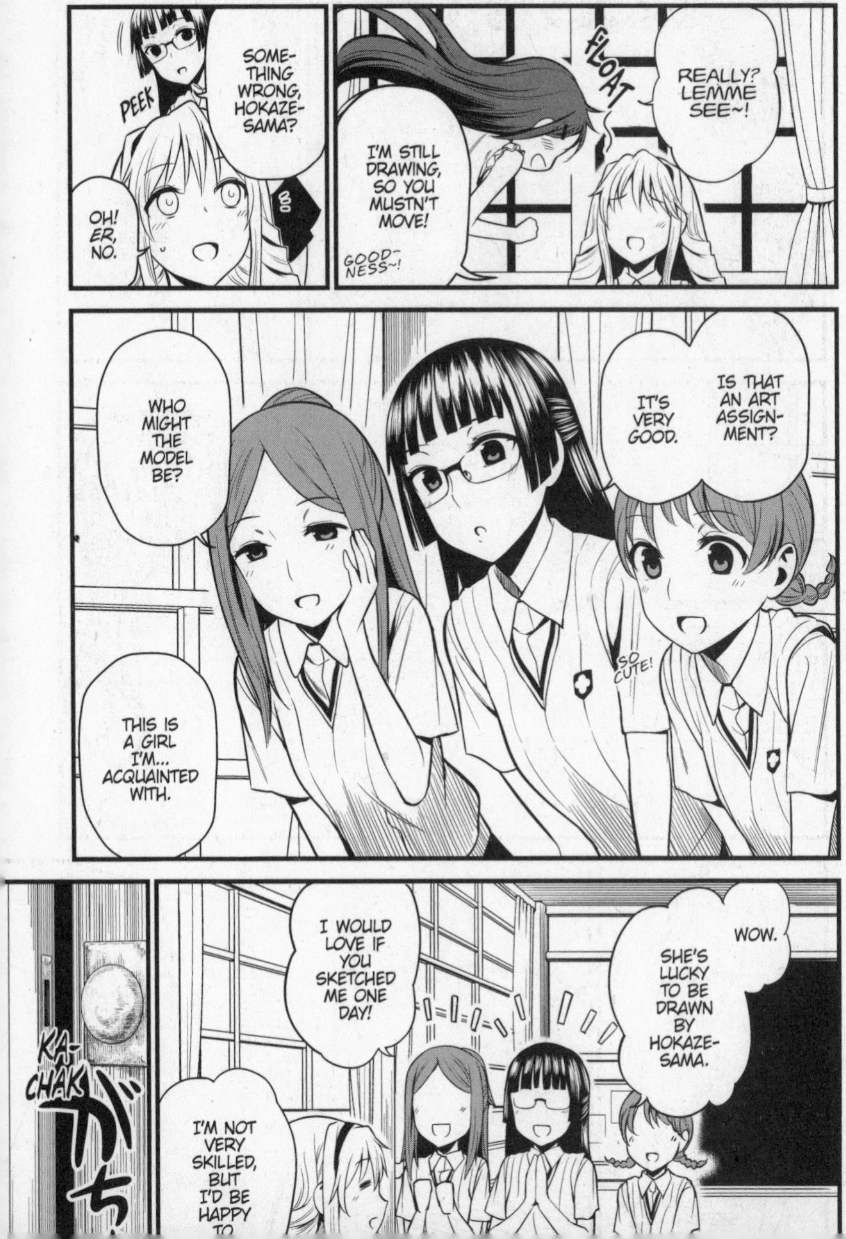
REALLY? LEMME SEE~!
FLOAT
I'M STILL DRAWING, SO YOU MUSTN'T MOVE!
GOOD-NESS~!
SOME-THING WRONG, HOKAZE-SAMA?
PEEK
OH! ER, NO.
IS THAT AN ART ASSIGN-MENT?
IT'S VERY GOOD.
SO CUTE!
WHO MIGHT THE MODEL BE?
THIS IS A GIRL I'M... ACQUAINTED WITH.
WOW.
SHE'S LUCKY TO BE DRAWN BY HOKAZE-SAMA.
I WOULD LOVE IF YOU SKETCHED ME ONE DAY!
I'M NOT VERY SKILLED, BUT I'D BE HAPPY TO
KA-CHAK

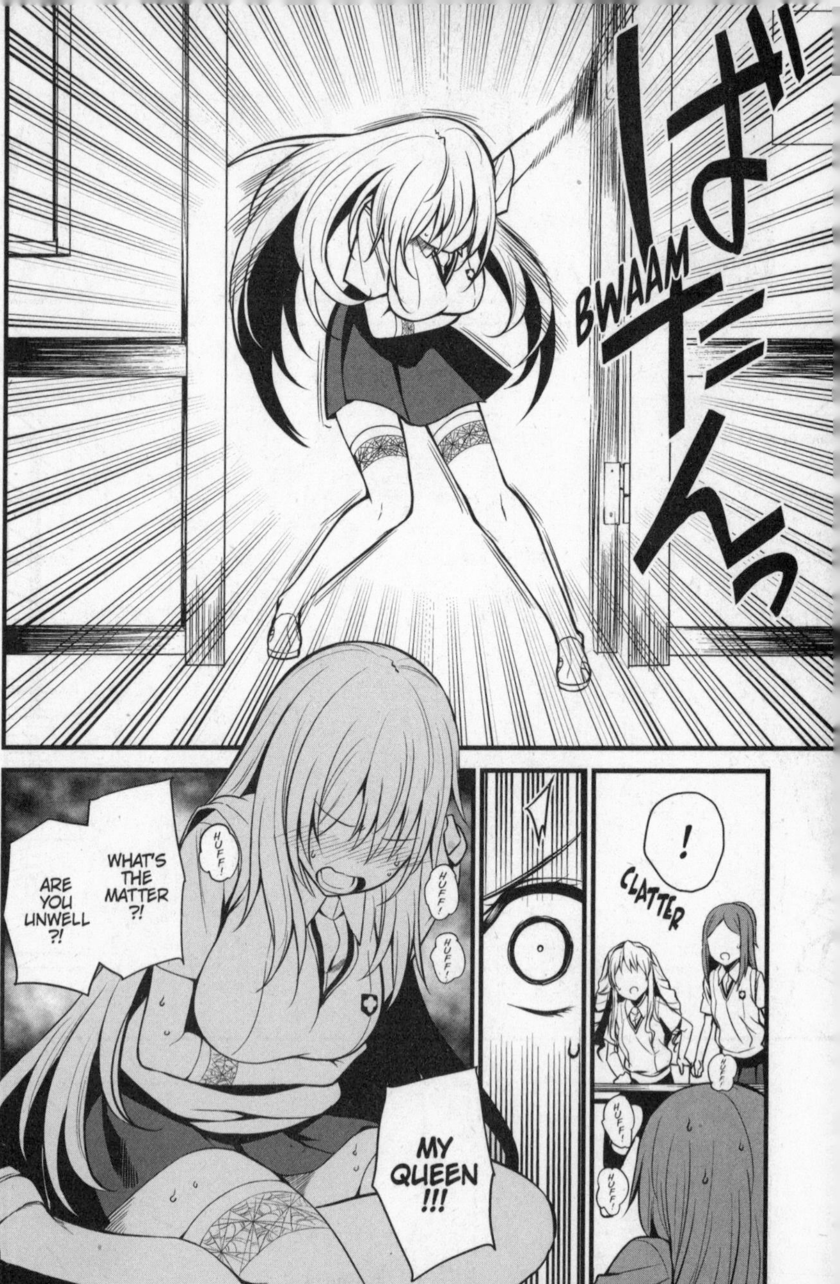
ばたんっ
BWAAM
!
CLATTER
HUFF!
HUFF!
HUFF!
HUFF!
HUFF!
MY QUEEN!!!
WHAT'S THE MATTER?!
ARE YOU UNWELL?!

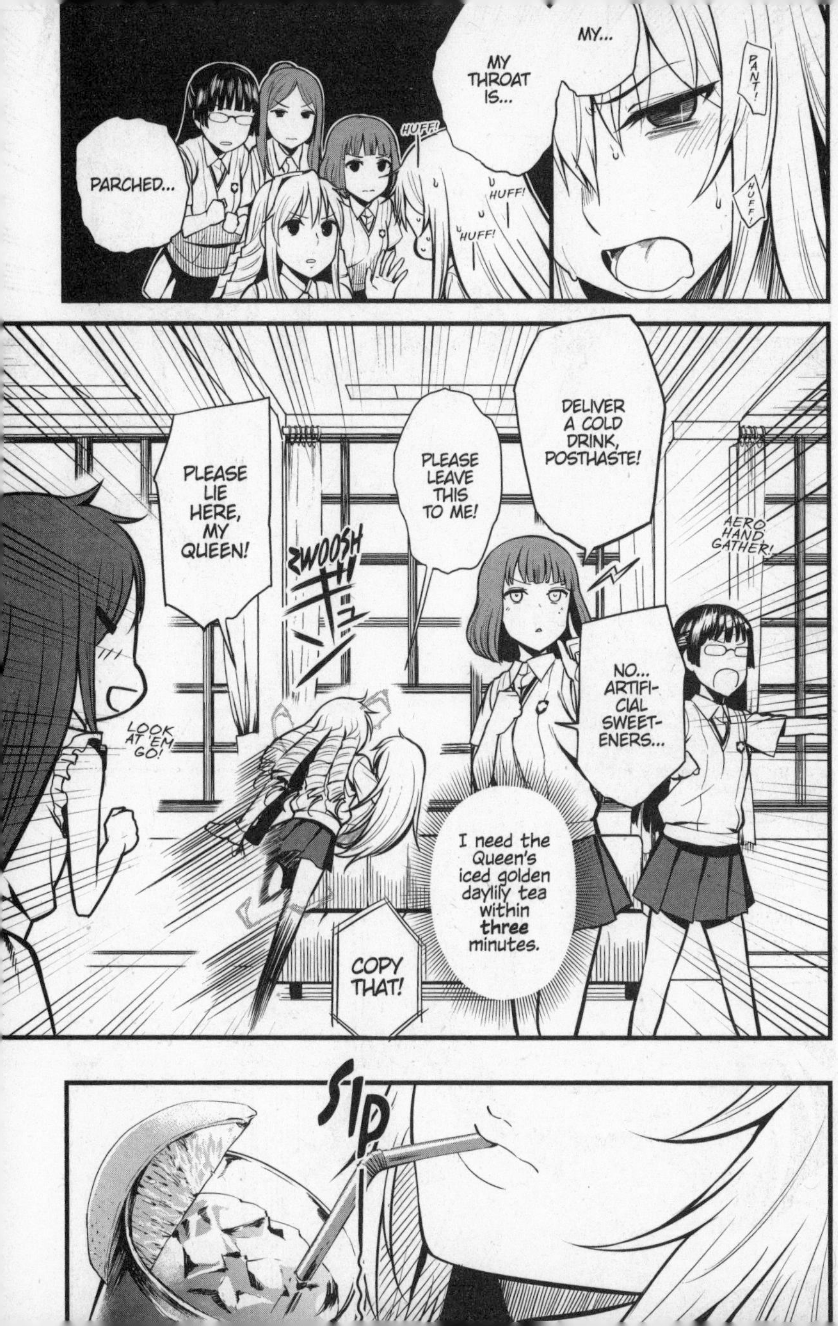
MY...
MY THROAT IS...
PANT!
HUFF!
HUFF!
HUFF!
HUFF!
PARCHED...
DELIVER A COLD DRINK, POSTHASTE!
AERO HAND GATHER!
PLEASE LEAVE THIS TO ME!
PLEASE LIE HERE, MY QUEEN!
ZWOOSH
ギュ
NO... ARTIFI-CIAL SWEET-ENERS...
I need the Queen's iced golden daylily tea within **three** minutes.
COPY THAT!
LOOK AT 'EM GO!
SIP!

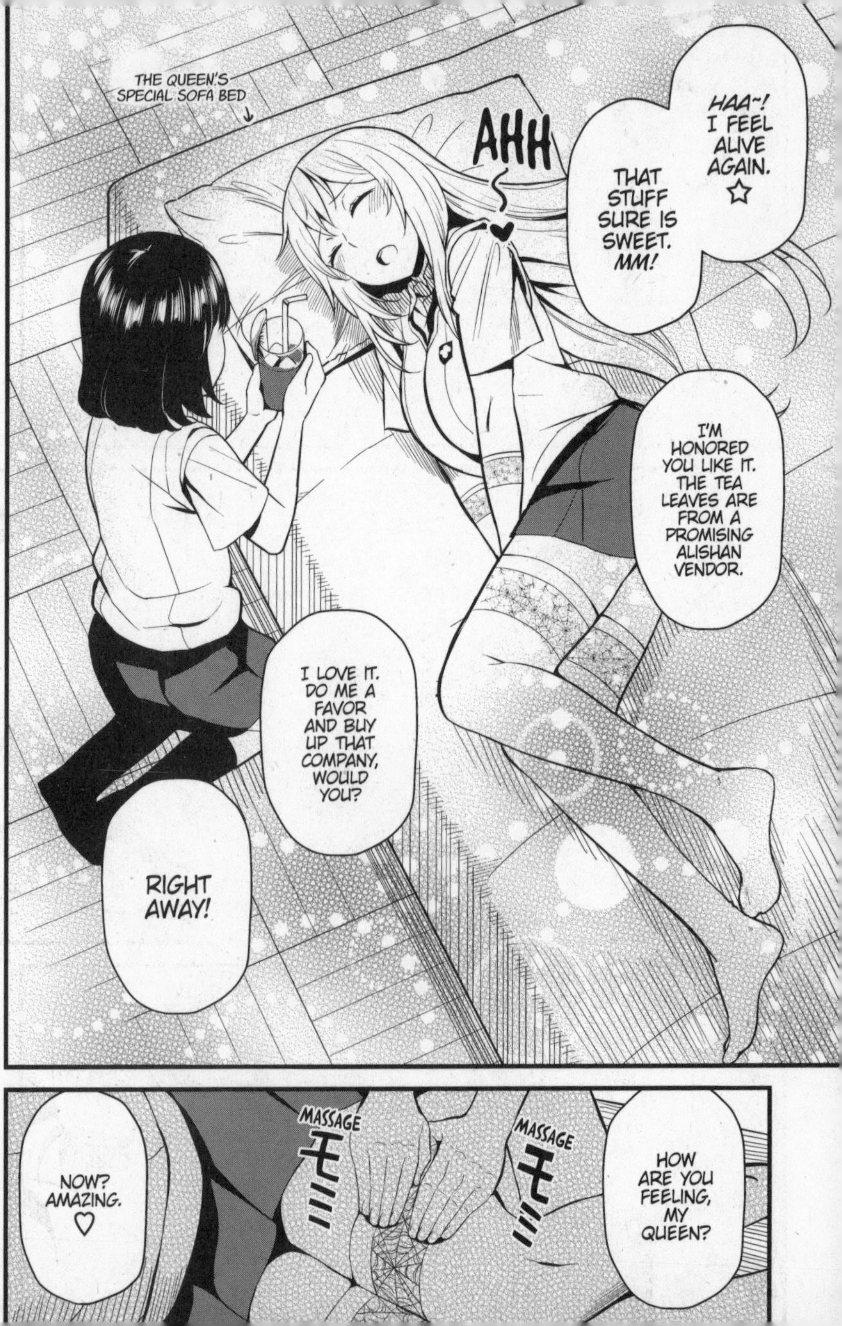
HAA~! I FEEL ALIVE AGAIN. ☆
THAT STUFF SURE IS SWEET. MM!
AHH
THE QUEEN'S SPECIAL SOFA BED
I'M HONORED YOU LIKE IT. THE TEA LEAVES ARE FROM A PROMISING ALISHAN VENDOR.
I LOVE IT. DO ME A FAVOR AND BUY UP THAT COMPANY, WOULD YOU?
RIGHT AWAY!
HOW ARE YOU FEELING, MY QUEEN?
MASSAGE
モミ
MASSAGE
モミ
NOW? AMAZING. ♡

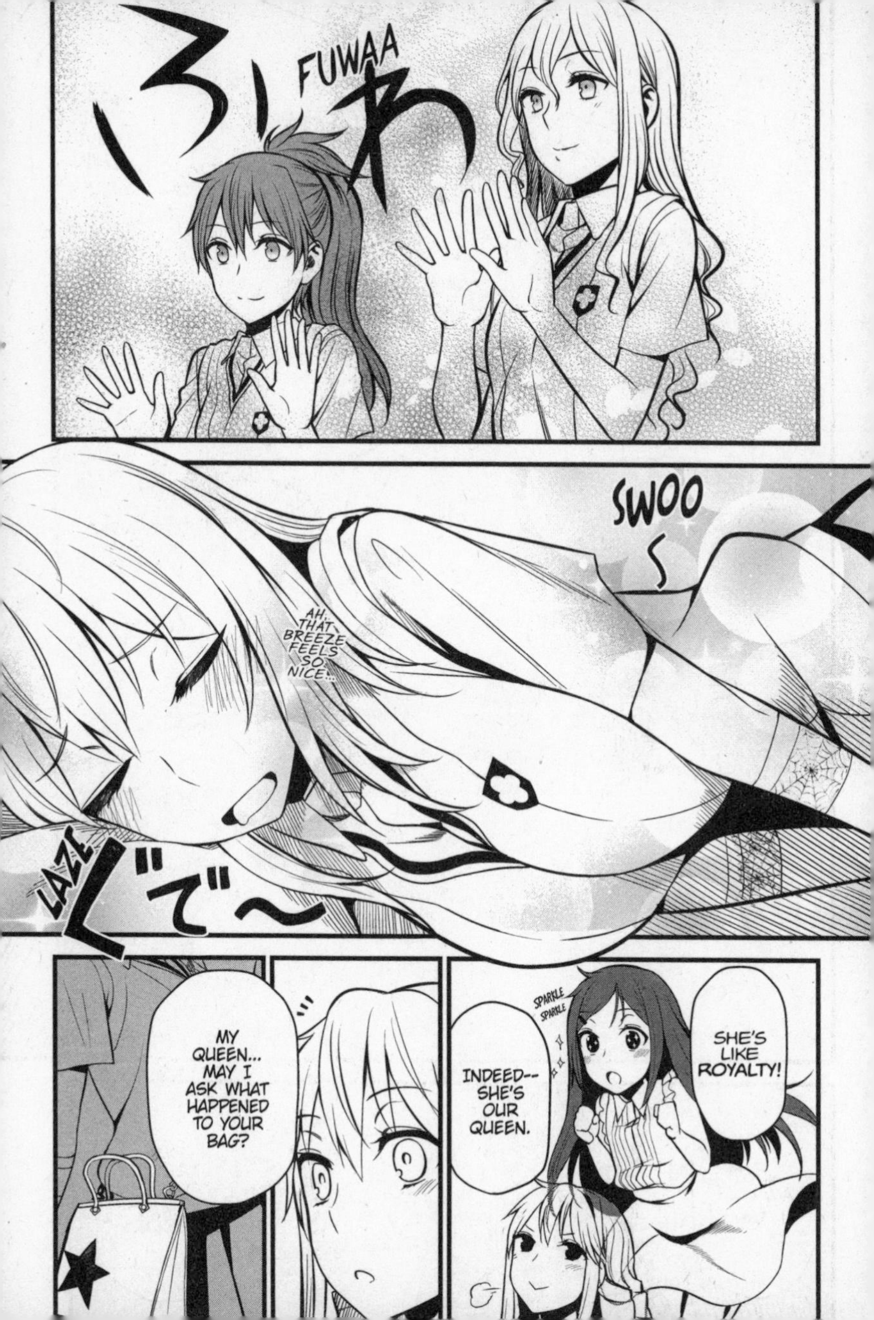
ふわ
FUWAA
SWOO
AH, THAT BREEZE FEELS SO NICE...
ぐで～
LAZE
SPARKLE SPARKLE
SHE'S LIKE ROYALTY!
INDEED-- SHE'S OUR QUEEN.
MY QUEEN... MAY I ASK WHAT HAPPENED TO YOUR BAG?

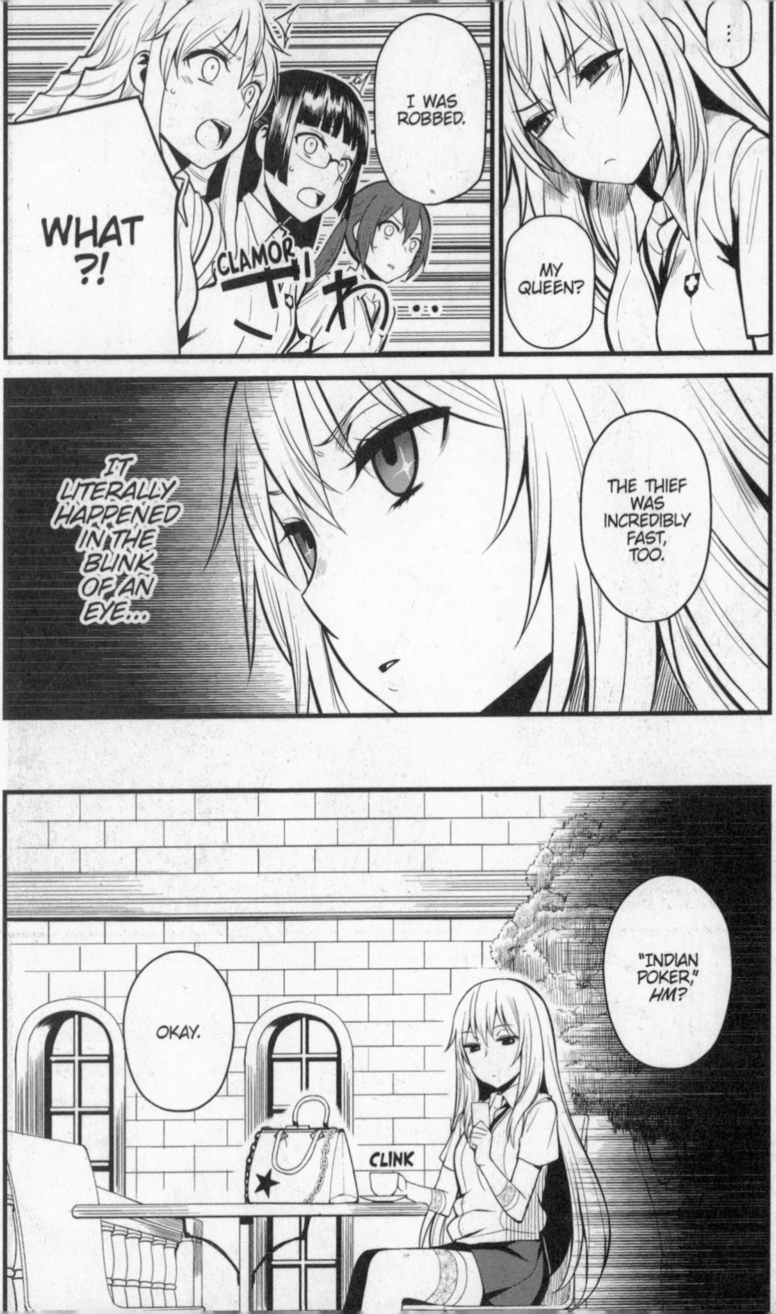
...
MY QUEEN?
I WAS ROBBED.
WHAT?!
CLAMOR
THE THIEF WAS INCREDIBLY FAST, TOO.
IT LITERALLY HAPPENED IN THE BLINK OF AN EYE...
"INDIAN POKER," HM?
OKAY.
CLINK

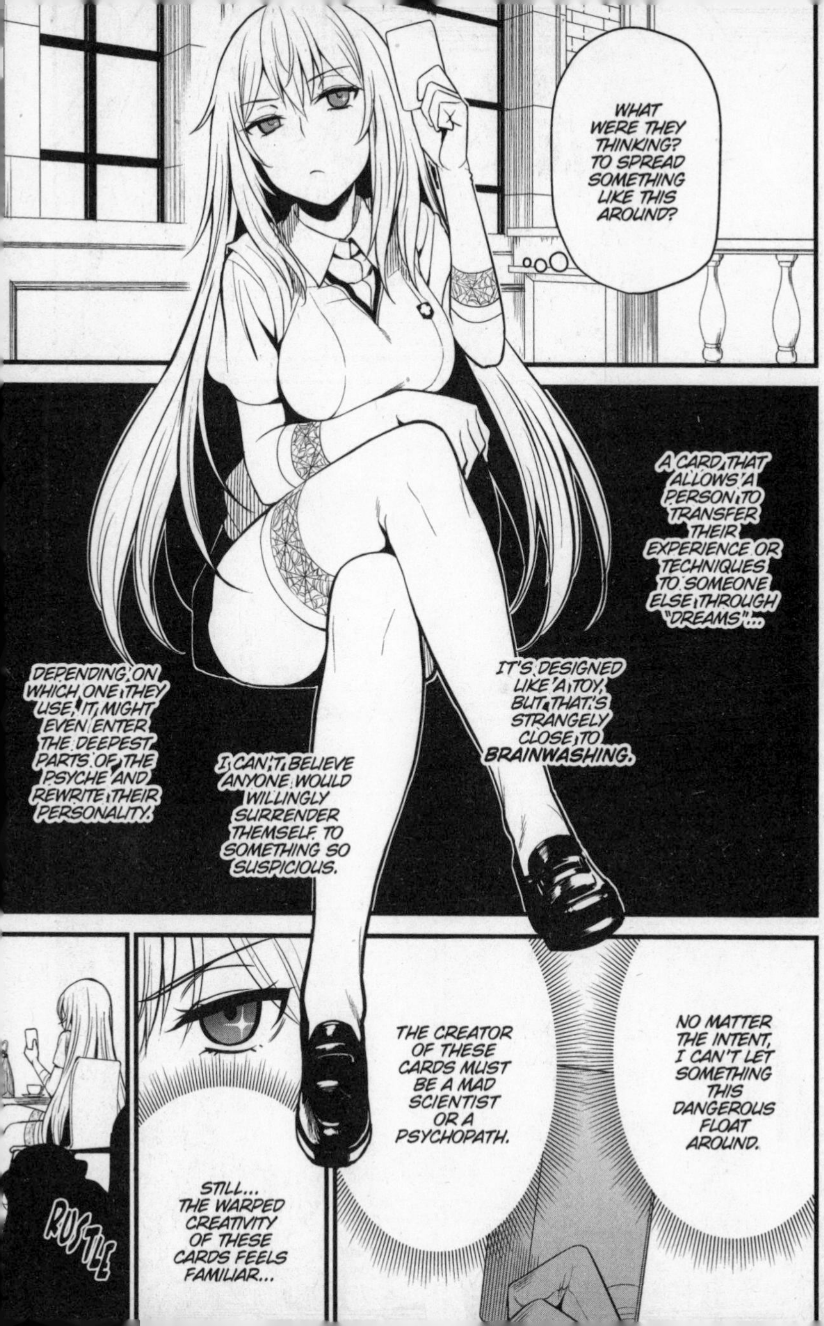
WHAT WERE THEY THINKING? TO SPREAD SOMETHING LIKE THIS AROUND?
A CARD THAT ALLOWS A PERSON TO TRANSFER THEIR EXPERIENCE OR TECHNIQUES TO SOMEONE ELSE THROUGH "DREAMS"...
IT'S DESIGNED LIKE A TOY, BUT THAT'S STRANGELY CLOSE TO BRAINWASHING.
I CAN'T BELIEVE ANYONE WOULD WILLINGLY SURRENDER THEMSELF TO SOMETHING SO SUSPICIOUS.
DEPENDING ON WHICH ONE THEY USE, IT MIGHT EVEN ENTER THE DEEPEST PARTS OF THE PSYCHE AND REWRITE THEIR PERSONALITY.
NO MATTER THE INTENT, I CAN'T LET SOMETHING THIS DANGEROUS FLOAT AROUND.
THE CREATOR OF THESE CARDS MUST BE A MAD SCIENTIST OR A PSYCHOPATH.
STILL... THE WARPED CREATIVITY OF THESE CARDS FEELS FAMILIAR...
RUSTLE

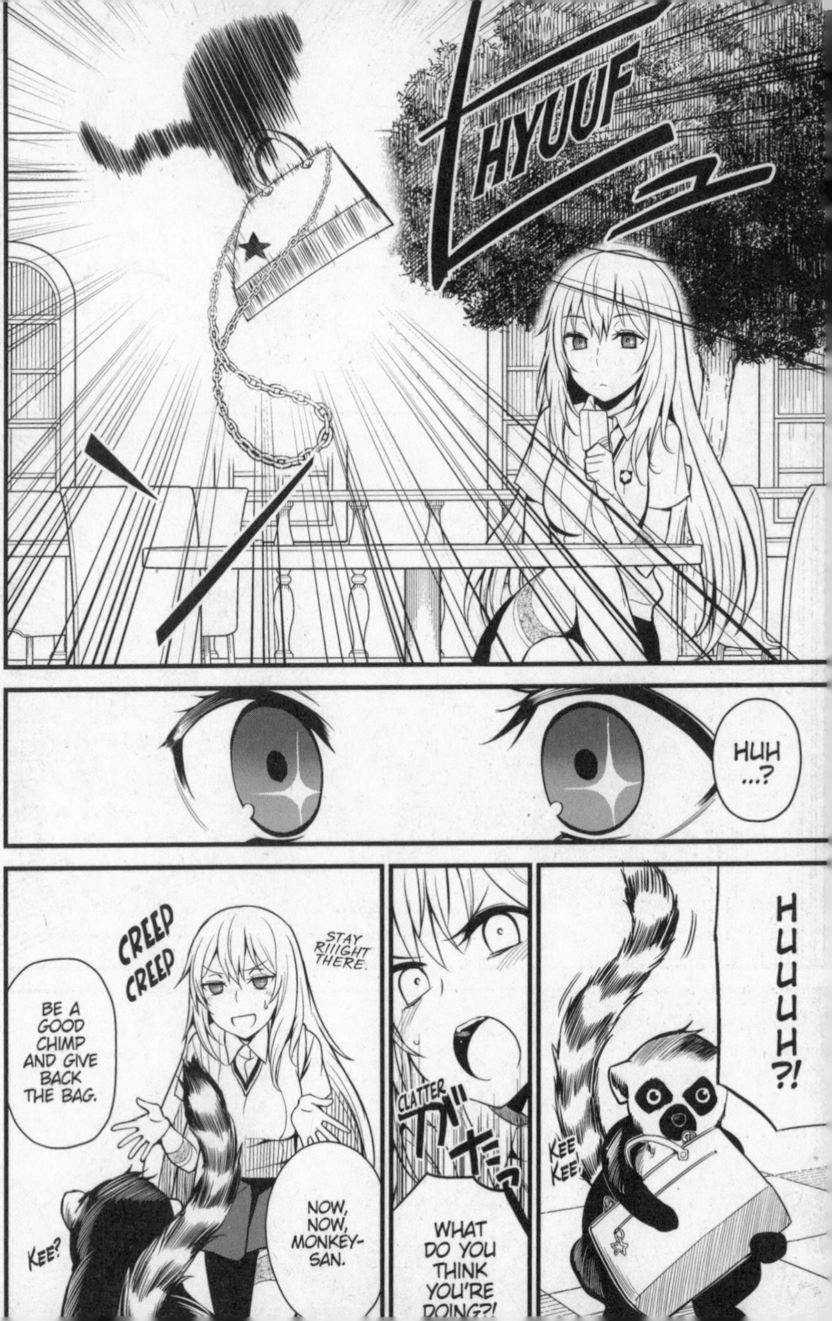
HYUUF
HUH ...?
HUUUH?!
KEE KEE
CLATTER
WHAT DO YOU THINK YOU'RE DOING?!
STAY RIIIGHT THERE.
CREEP CREEP
BE A GOOD CHIMP AND GIVE BACK THE BAG.
NOW, NOW, MONKEY-SAN.
KEE?

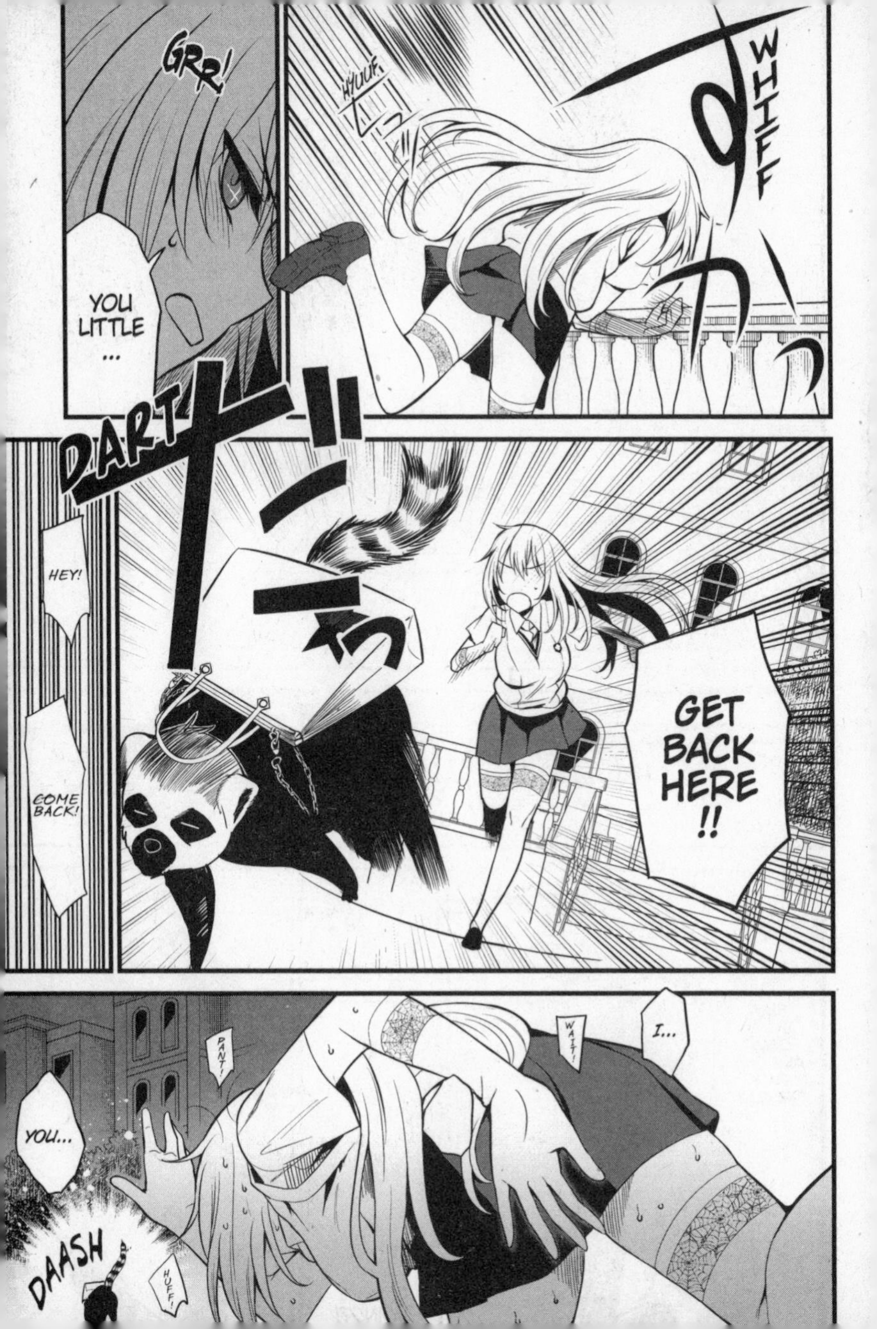
WHIFF
HYUUF!
GRR!
YOU LITTLE ...
DART
GET BACK HERE!!
HEY!
COME BACK!
I...
WAIT!
PANT!
YOU...
HUFF!
DAASH

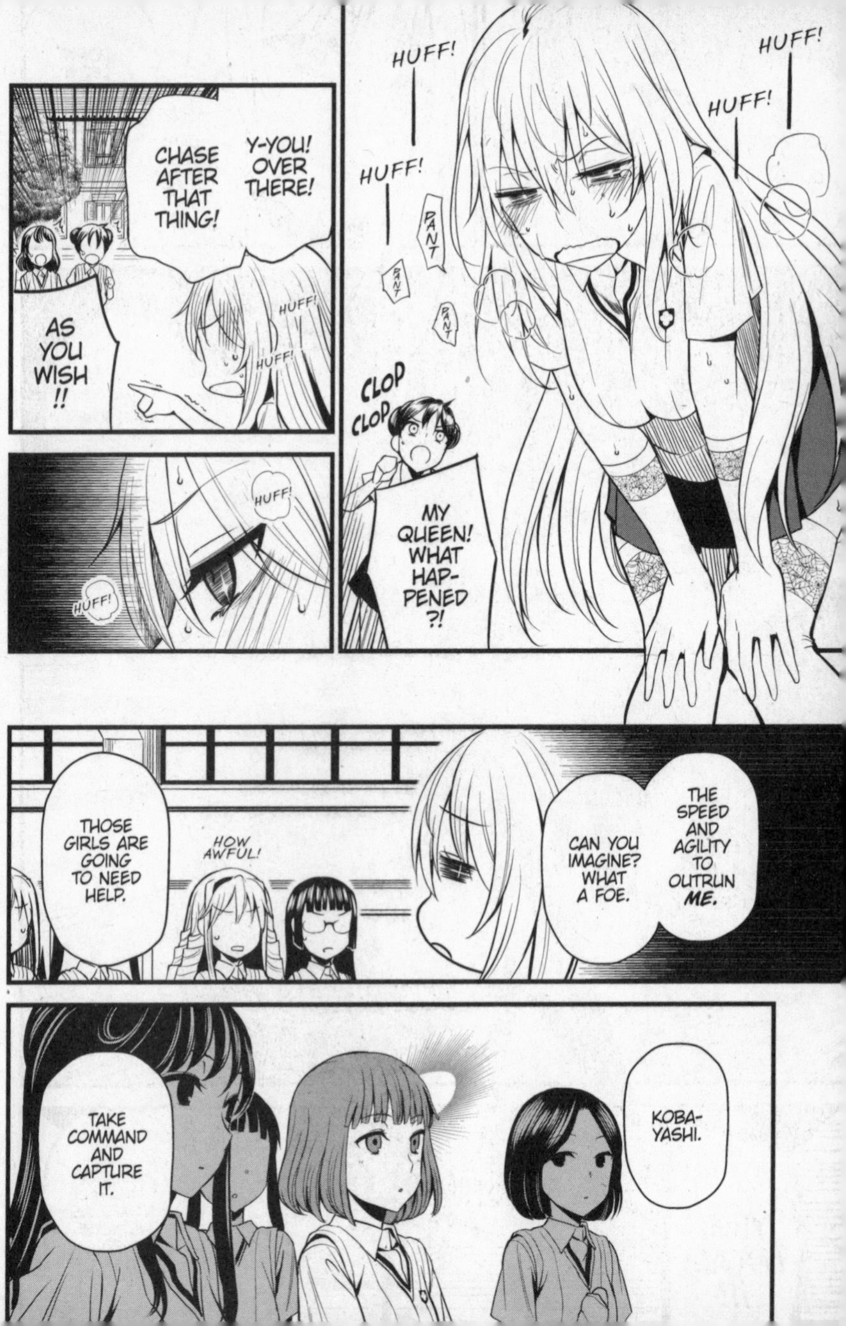
HUFF!
HUFF!
HUFF!
HUFF!
PANT
PANT
PANT
CLOP CLOP
MY QUEEN! WHAT HAPPENED?!
Y-YOU! OVER THERE!
CHASE AFTER THAT THING!
HUFF!
HUFF!
AS YOU WISH!!
HUFF!
HUFF!
THE SPEED AND AGILITY TO OUTRUN ME.
CAN YOU IMAGINE? WHAT A FOE.
HOW AWFUL!
THOSE GIRLS ARE GOING TO NEED HELP.
KOBAYASHI.
TAKE COMMAND AND CAPTURE IT.

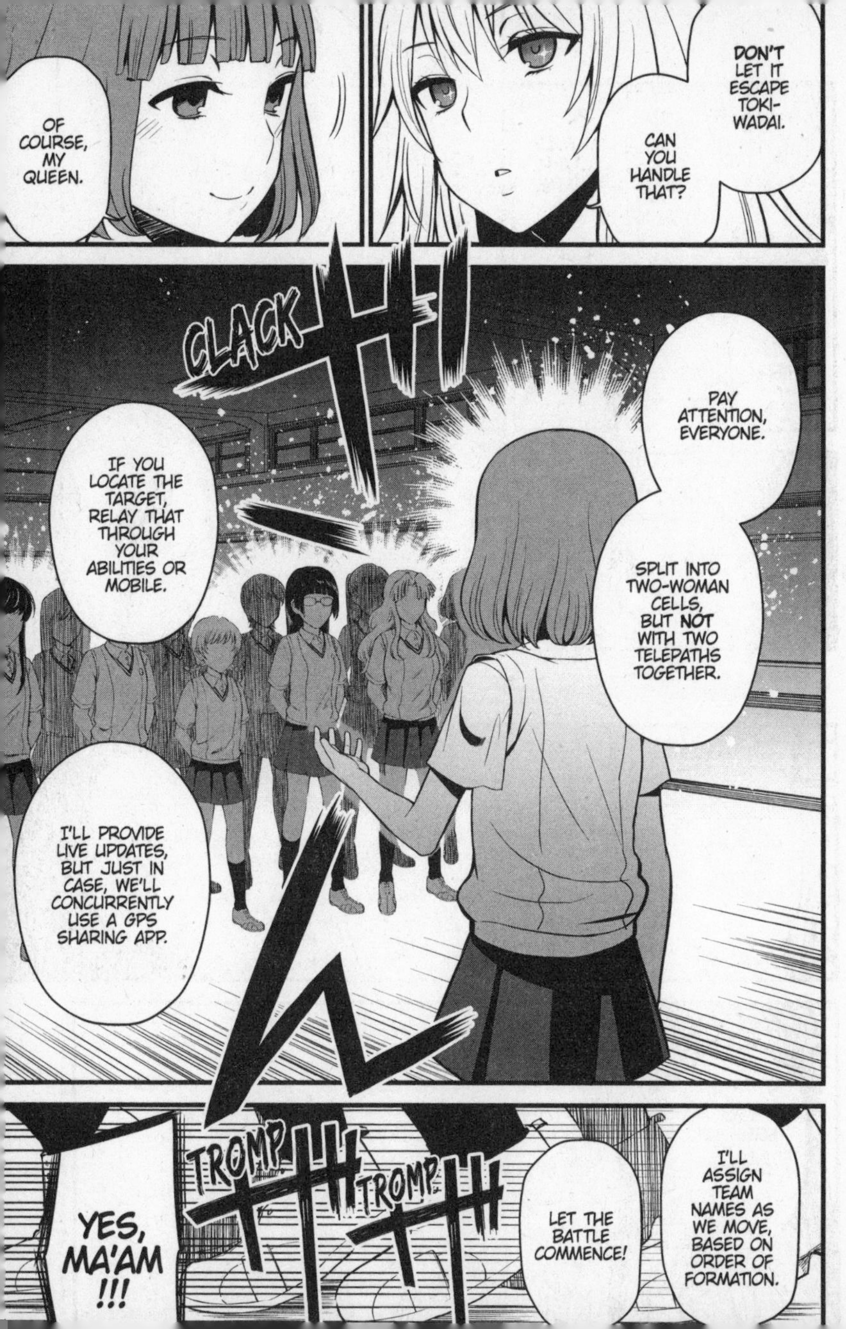
DON'T LET IT ESCAPE TOKI-WADAI.
CAN YOU HANDLE THAT?
OF COURSE, MY QUEEN.
CLACK
PAY ATTENTION, EVERYONE.
SPLIT INTO TWO-WOMAN CELLS, BUT NOT WITH TWO TELEPATHS TOGETHER.
IF YOU LOCATE THE TARGET, RELAY THAT THROUGH YOUR ABILITIES OR MOBILE.
I'LL PROVIDE LIVE UPDATES, BUT JUST IN CASE, WE'LL CONCURRENTLY USE A GPS SHARING APP.
I'LL ASSIGN TEAM NAMES AS WE MOVE, BASED ON ORDER OF FORMATION.
LET THE BATTLE COMMENCE!
TROMP
TROMP
YES, MA'AM!!!

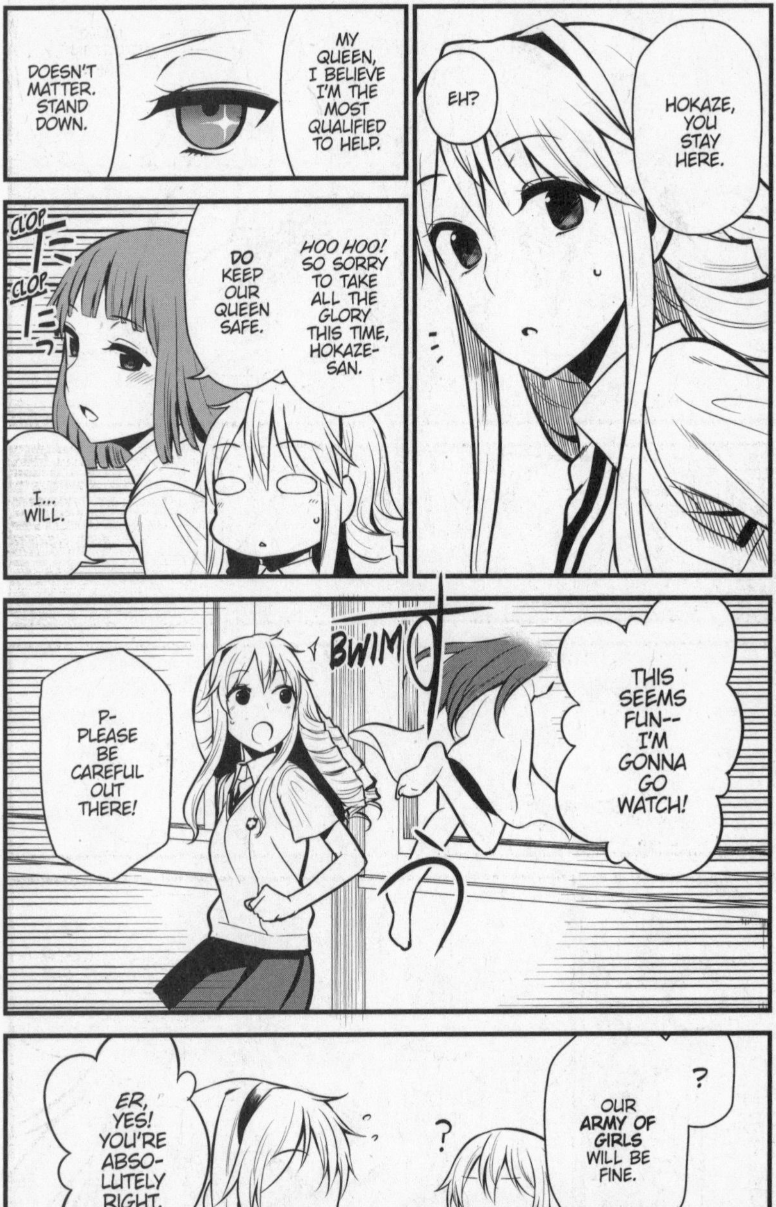
HOKAZE, YOU STAY HERE.
EH?
MY QUEEN, I BELIEVE I'M THE MOST QUALIFIED TO HELP.
DOESN'T MATTER. STAND DOWN.
HOO HOO! SO SORRY TO TAKE ALL THE GLORY THIS TIME, HOKAZE-SAN.
DO KEEP OUR QUEEN SAFE.
CLOP CLOP
I... WILL.
BWIM
THIS SEEMS FUN-- I'M GONNA GO WATCH!
P-PLEASE BE CAREFUL OUT THERE!
?
OUR ARMY OF GIRLS WILL BE FINE.
?
ER, YES! YOU'RE ABSO-LUTELY RIGHT.
HA HA!

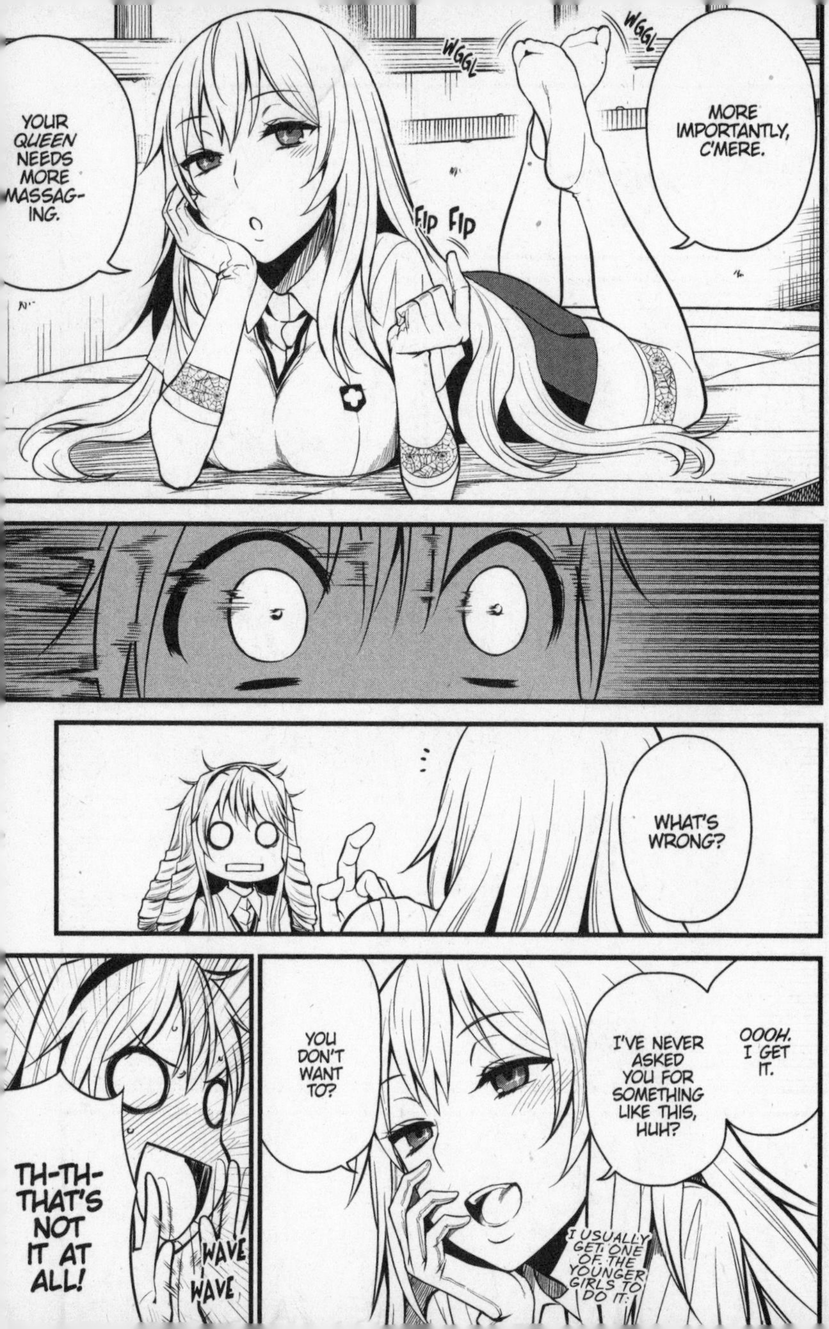
MORE IMPORTANTLY, C'MERE.
WGGL
WGGL
YOUR QUEEN NEEDS MORE MASSAG-ING.
FIP FIP
WHAT'S WRONG?
OOOH. I GET IT.
I'VE NEVER ASKED YOU FOR SOMETHING LIKE THIS, HUH?
YOU DON'T WANT TO?
I USUALLY GET ONE OF THE YOUNGER GIRLS TO DO IT.
TH-TH-THAT'S NOT IT AT ALL!
WAVE
WAVE

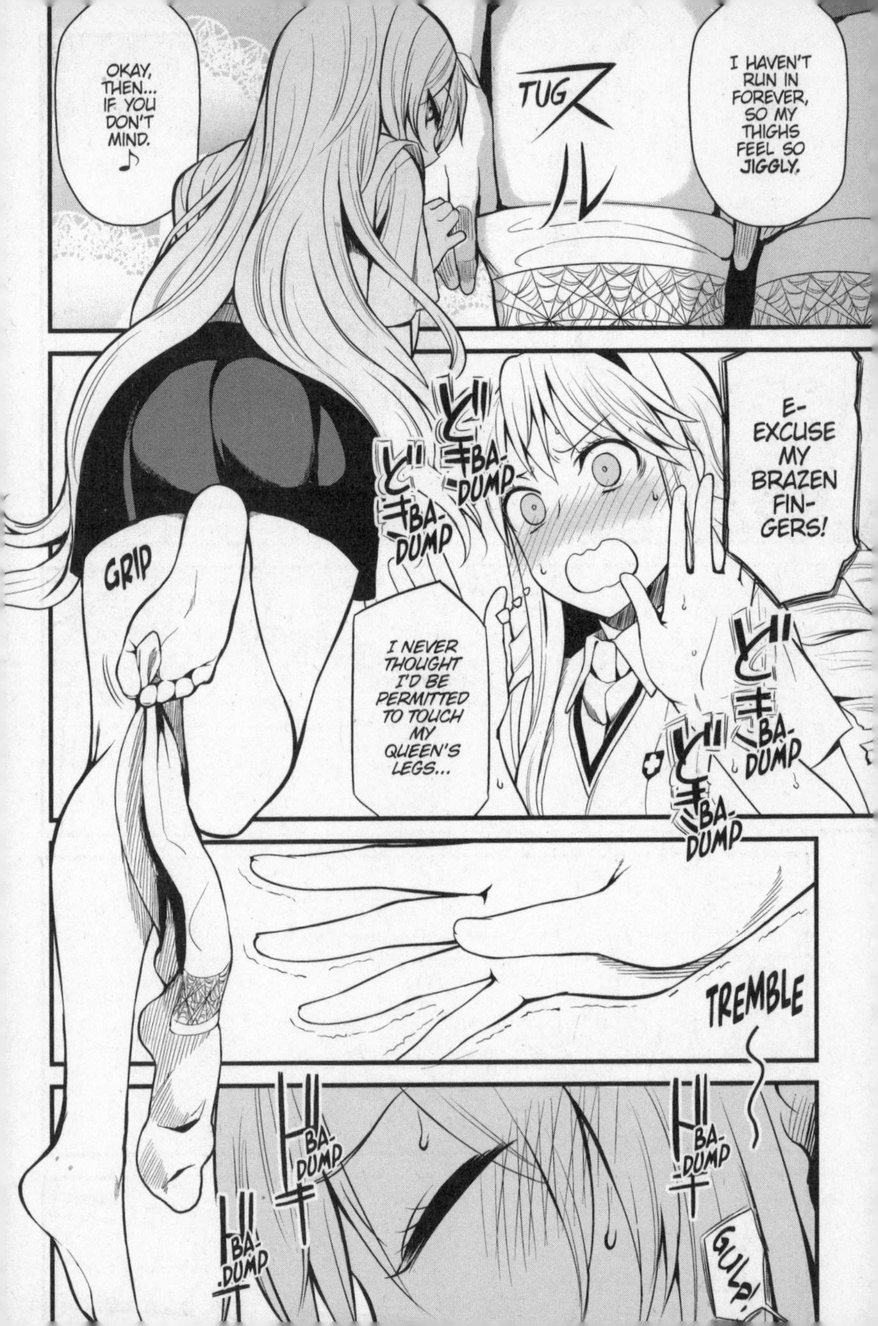
I HAVEN'T RUN IN FOREVER, SO MY THIGHS FEEL SO JIGGLY.
TUG
OKAY, THEN... IF YOU DON'T MIND. ♪
E-EXCUSE MY BRAZEN FINGERS!
BA-DUMP BA-DUMP
BA-DUMP BA-DUMP
I NEVER THOUGHT I'D BE PERMITTED TO TOUCH MY QUEEN'S LEGS...
GRIP
TREMBLE
BA-DUMP BA-DUMP BA-DUMP
GULP!

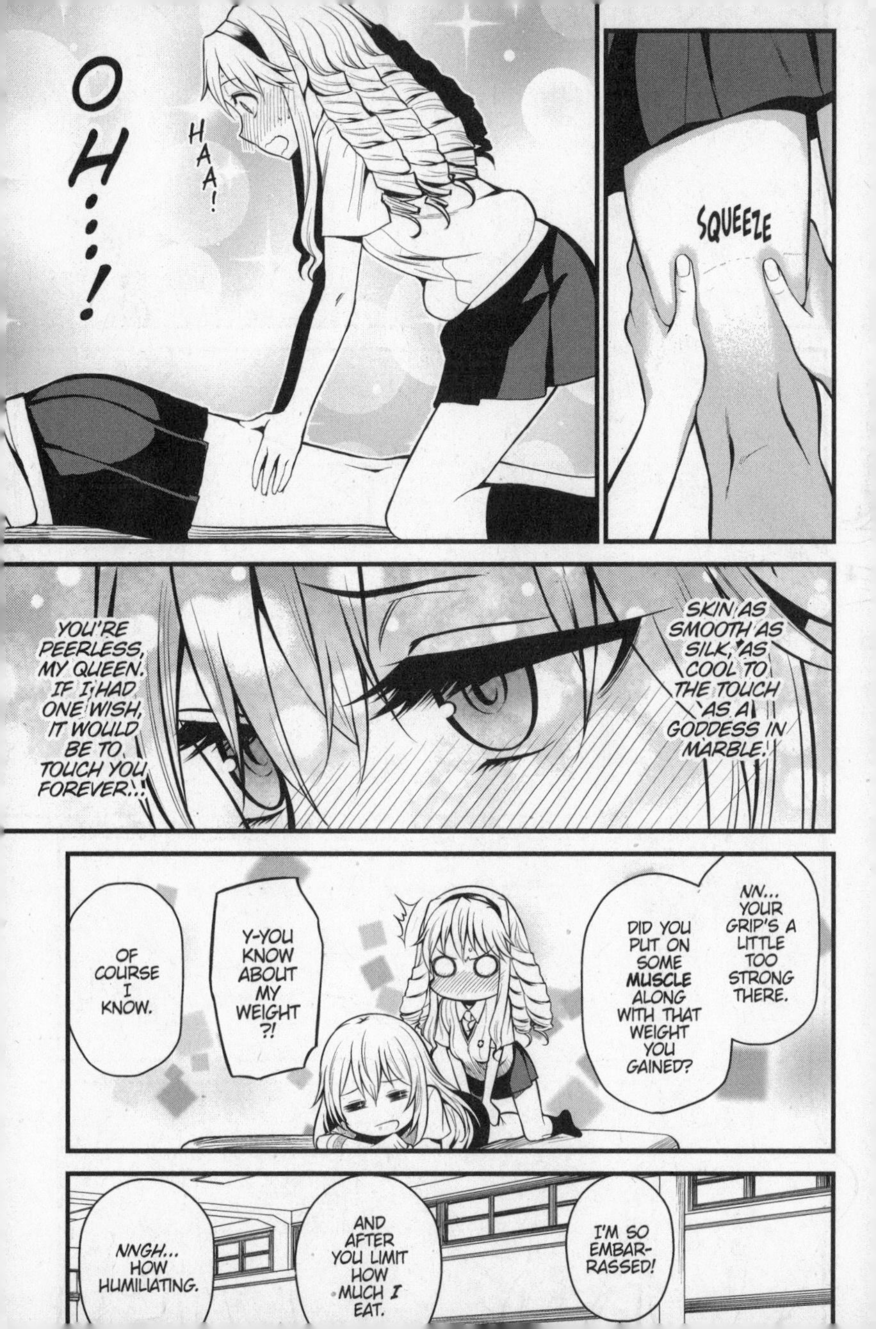
SQUEEZE
HAA!
OH...!
SKIN AS SMOOTH AS SILK, AS COOL TO THE TOUCH AS A GODDESS IN MARBLE.
YOU'RE PEERLESS, MY QUEEN. IF I HAD ONE WISH, IT WOULD BE TO TOUCH YOU FOREVER...
NN... YOUR GRIP'S A LITTLE TOO STRONG THERE.
DID YOU PUT ON SOME **MUSCLE** ALONG WITH THAT WEIGHT YOU GAINED?
Y-YOU KNOW ABOUT MY WEIGHT?!
OF COURSE I KNOW.
I'M SO EMBAR-RASSED!
AND AFTER YOU LIMIT HOW MUCH *I* EAT.
NNGH... HOW HUMILIATING.

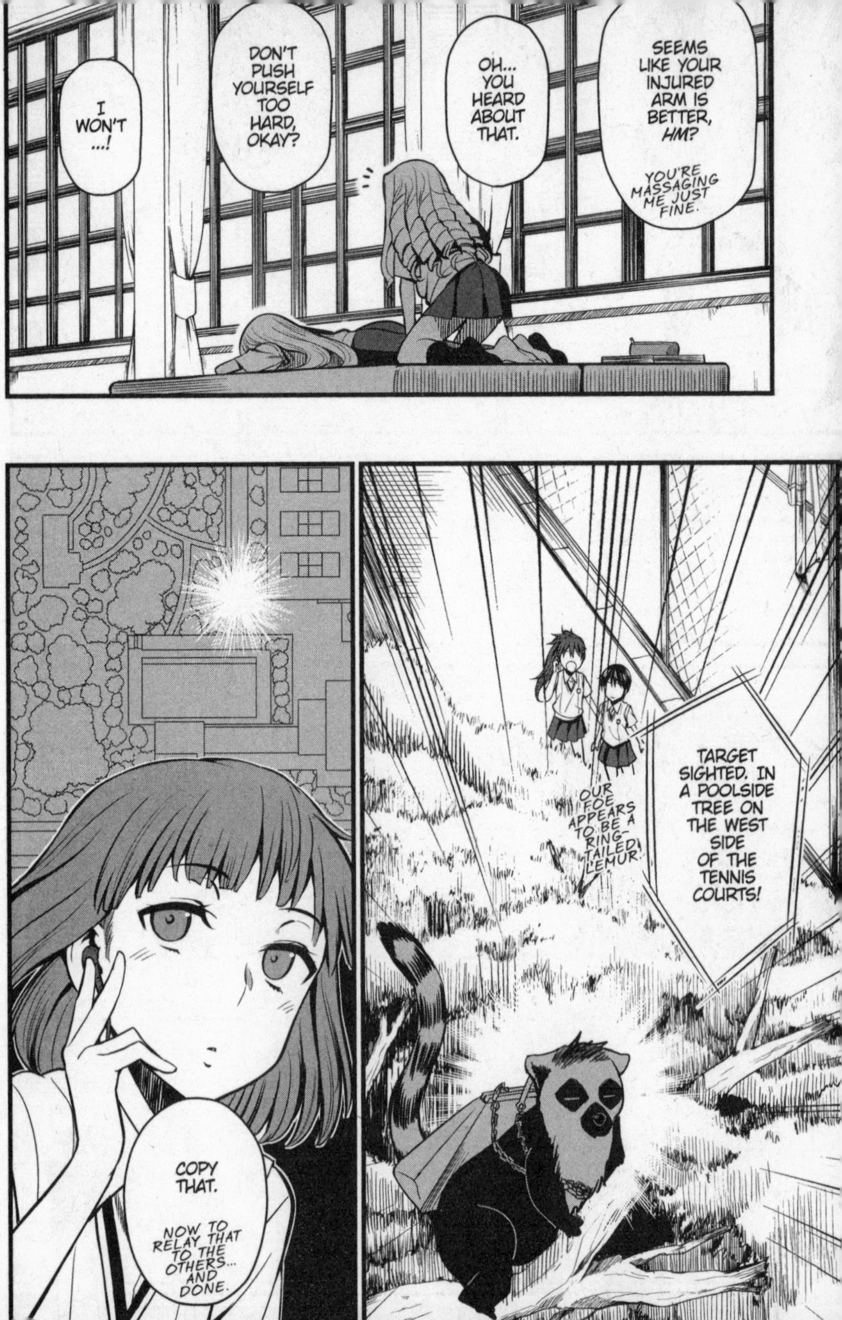
SEEMS LIKE YOUR INJURED ARM IS BETTER, HM?
YOU'RE MASSAGING ME JUST FINE.
OH... YOU HEARD ABOUT THAT.
DON'T PUSH YOURSELF TOO HARD, OKAY?
I WON'T ...!
TARGET SIGHTED. IN A POOLSIDE TREE ON THE WEST SIDE OF THE TENNIS COURTS!
OUR FOE APPEARS TO BE A RING-TAILED LEMUR.
COPY THAT.
NOW TO RELAY THAT TO THE OTHERS... AND DONE.

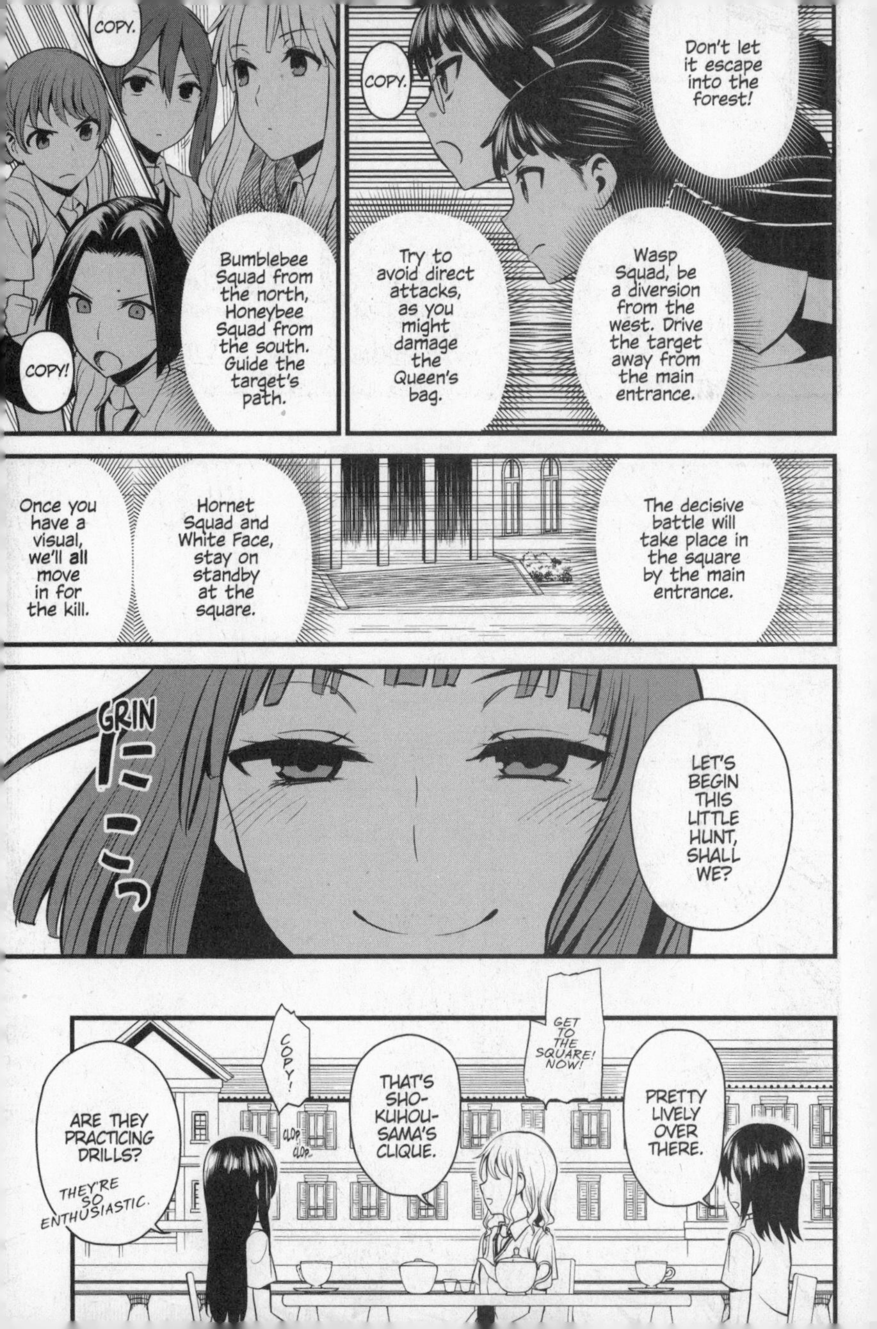
Don't let it escape into the forest!
COPY.
Wasp Squad, be a diversion from the west. Drive the target away from the main entrance.
Try to avoid direct attacks, as you might damage the Queen's bag.
COPY.
Bumblebee Squad from the north, Honeybee Squad from the south. Guide the target's path.
COPY!
The decisive battle will take place in the square by the main entrance.
Hornet Squad and White Face, stay on standby at the square.
Once you have a visual, we'll all move in for the kill.
LET'S BEGIN THIS LITTLE HUNT, SHALL WE?
GRIN
GET TO THE SQUARE! NOW!
PRETTY LIVELY OVER THERE.
COPY!
THAT'S SHOKUHOU-SAMA'S CLIQUE.
CLOP CLOP
ARE THEY PRACTICING DRILLS?
THEY'RE SO ENTHUSIASTIC.

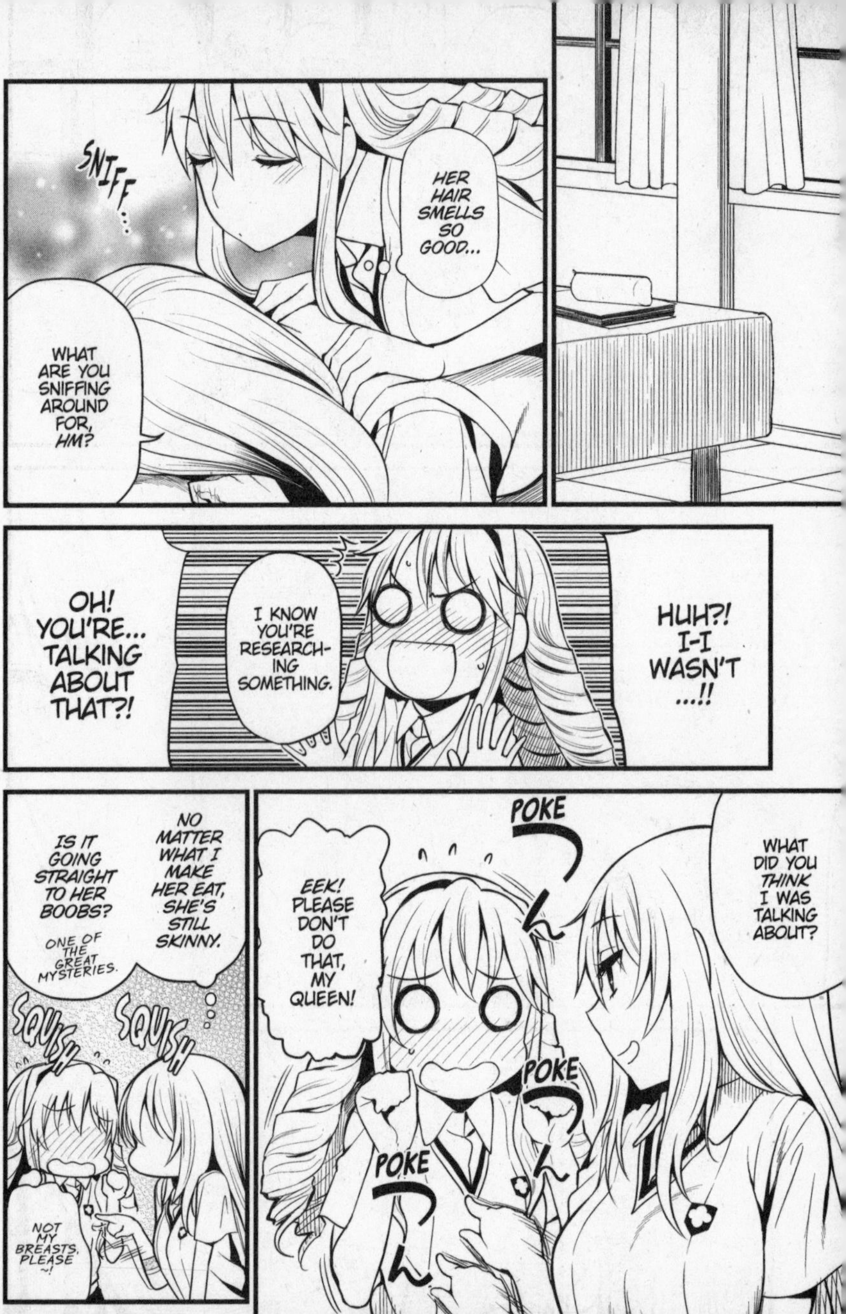
HER HAIR SMELLS SO GOOD...
SNIFF...
WHAT ARE YOU SNIFFING AROUND FOR, HM?
HUH?! I-I WASN'T ...!!
I KNOW YOU'RE RESEARCH-ING SOMETHING.
OH! YOU'RE... TALKING ABOUT THAT?!
WHAT DID YOU THINK I WAS TALKING ABOUT?
POKE
EEK! PLEASE DON'T DO THAT, MY QUEEN!
POKE
POKE
NO MATTER WHAT I MAKE HER EAT, SHE'S STILL SKINNY.
IS IT GOING STRAIGHT TO HER BOOBS?
ONE OF THE GREAT MYSTERIES.
SQUISH
SQUISH
NOT MY BREASTS, PLEASE ~!

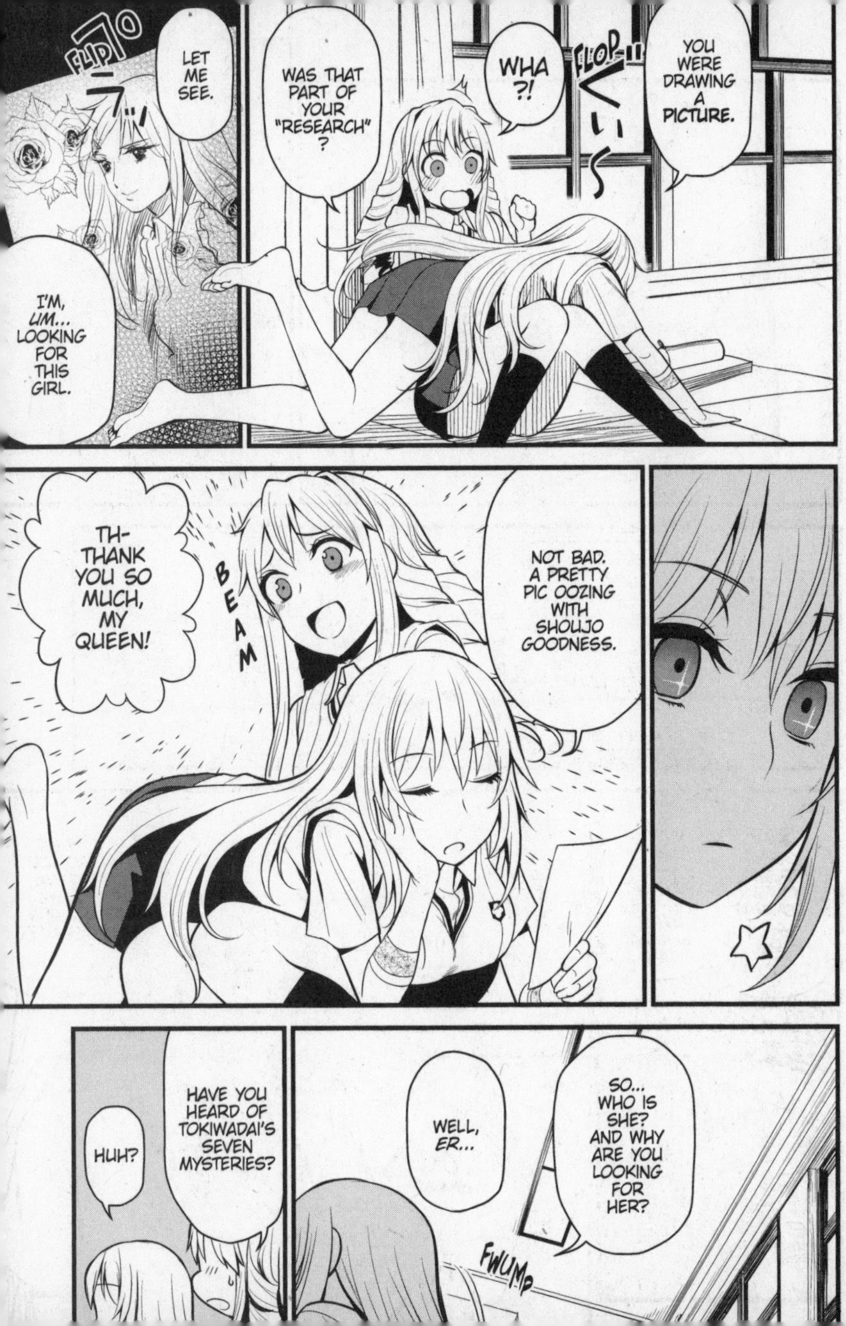
YOU WERE DRAWING A PICTURE.
FLOP
WHA ?!
WAS THAT PART OF YOUR "RESEARCH" ?
LET ME SEE.
FLIP
I'M, UM... LOOKING FOR THIS GIRL.
NOT BAD. A PRETTY PIC OOZING WITH SHOUJO GOODNESS.
BEAM
TH-THANK YOU SO MUCH, MY QUEEN!
SO... WHO IS SHE? AND WHY ARE YOU LOOKING FOR HER?
FWUMP
WELL, ER...
HAVE YOU HEARD OF TOKIWADAI'S SEVEN MYSTERIES?
HUH?

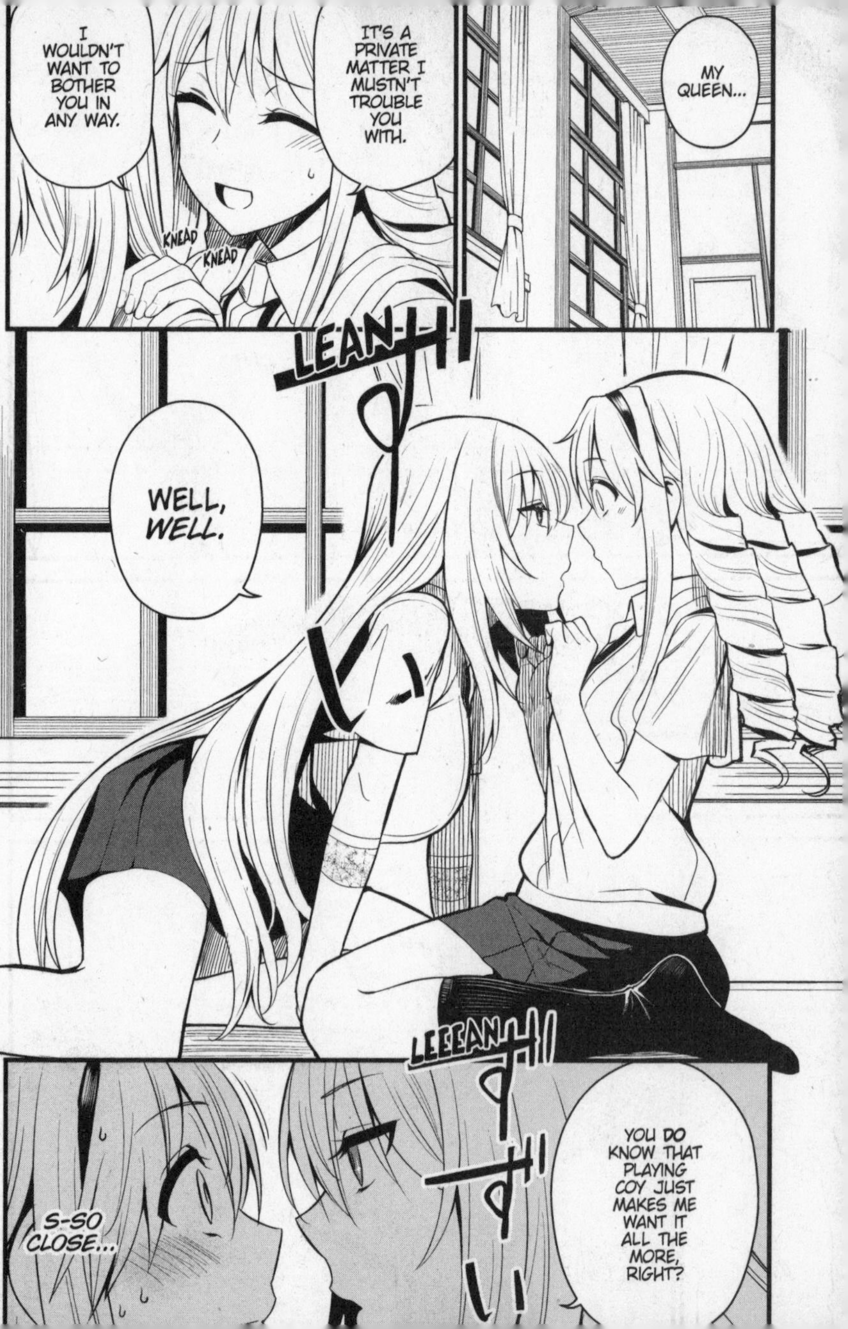
MY QUEEN...
IT'S A PRIVATE MATTER I MUSTN'T TROUBLE YOU WITH.
I WOULDN'T WANT TO BOTHER YOU IN ANY WAY.
KNEAD
KNEAD
LEAN
WELL, WELL.
LEEEAN
YOU DO KNOW THAT PLAYING COY JUST MAKES ME WANT IT ALL THE MORE, RIGHT?
S-SO CLOSE...

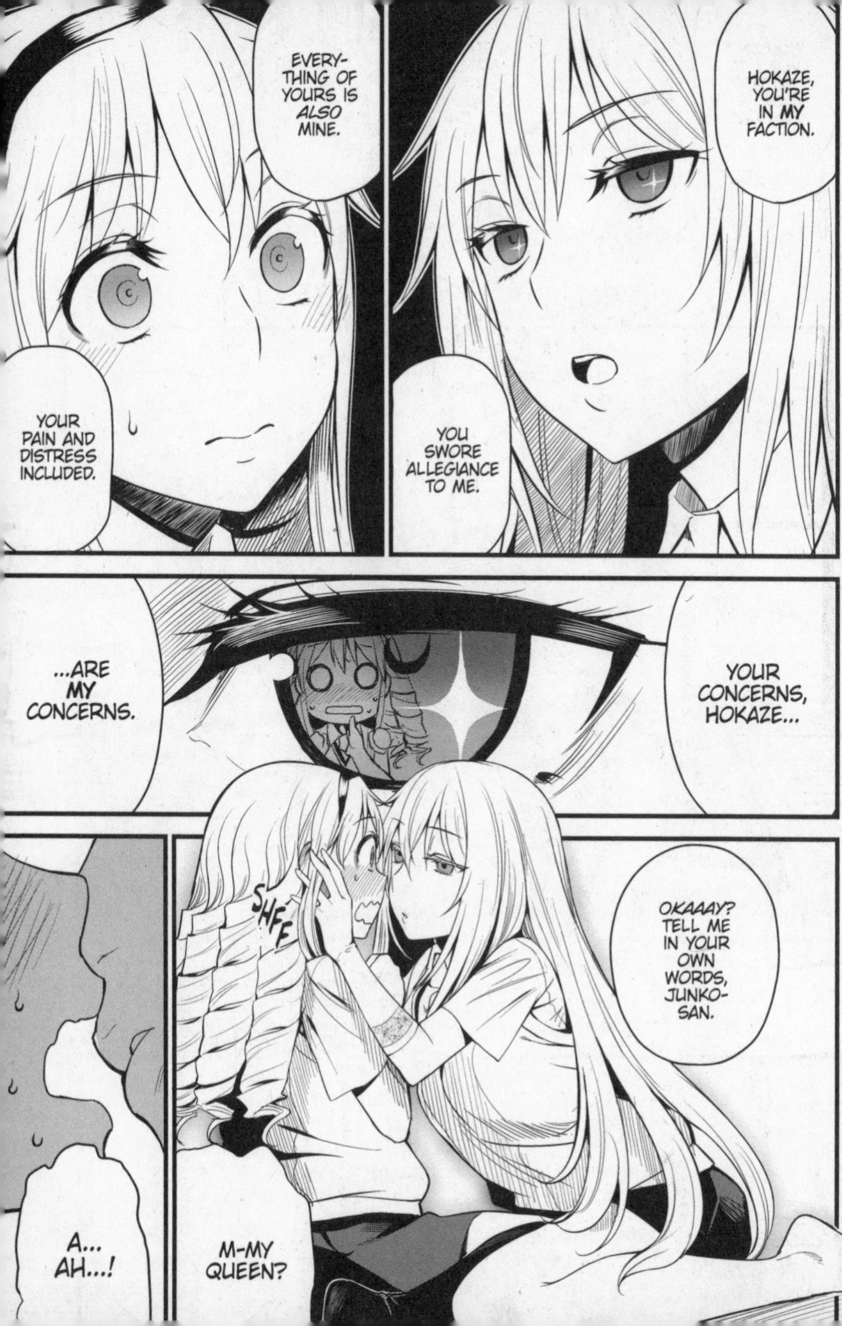
HOKAZE, YOU'RE IN MY FACTION.
YOU SWORE ALLEGIANCE TO ME.
EVERY-THING OF YOURS IS *ALSO* MINE.
YOUR PAIN AND DISTRESS INCLUDED.
YOUR CONCERNS, HOKAZE...
...ARE MY CONCERNS.
OKAAAY? TELL ME IN YOUR OWN WORDS, JUNKO-SAN.
SHFF
M-MY QUEEN?
A... AH...!

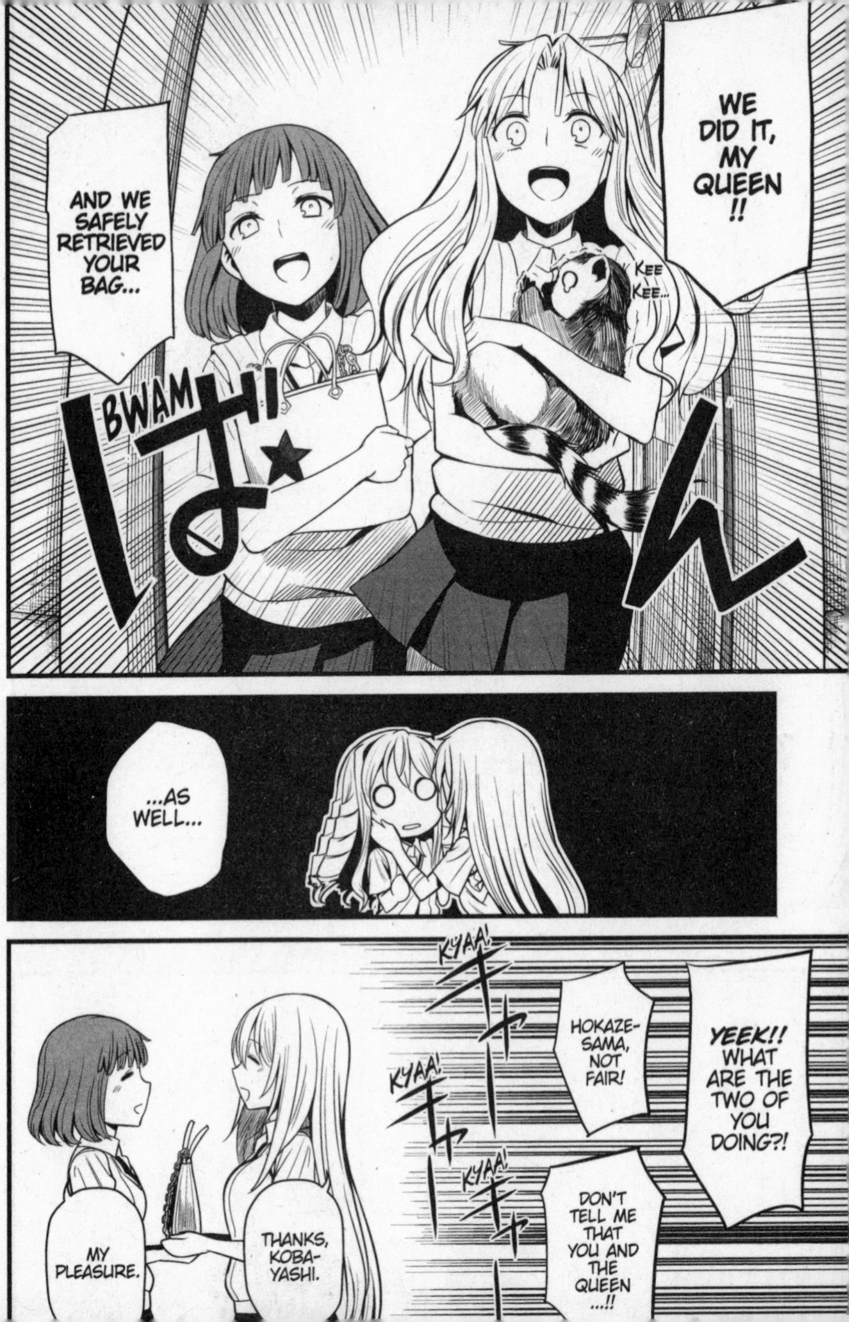

WE DID IT, MY QUEEN!!
AND WE SAFELY RETRIEVED YOUR BAG...
KEE KEE...
BWAM
ばん
...AS WELL...
YEEK!! WHAT ARE THE TWO OF YOU DOING?!
HOKAZE-SAMA, NOT FAIR!
KYAA!
KYAA!
KYAA!
DON'T TELL ME THAT YOU AND THE QUEEN ...!!
THANKS, KOBA-YASHI.
MY PLEASURE.

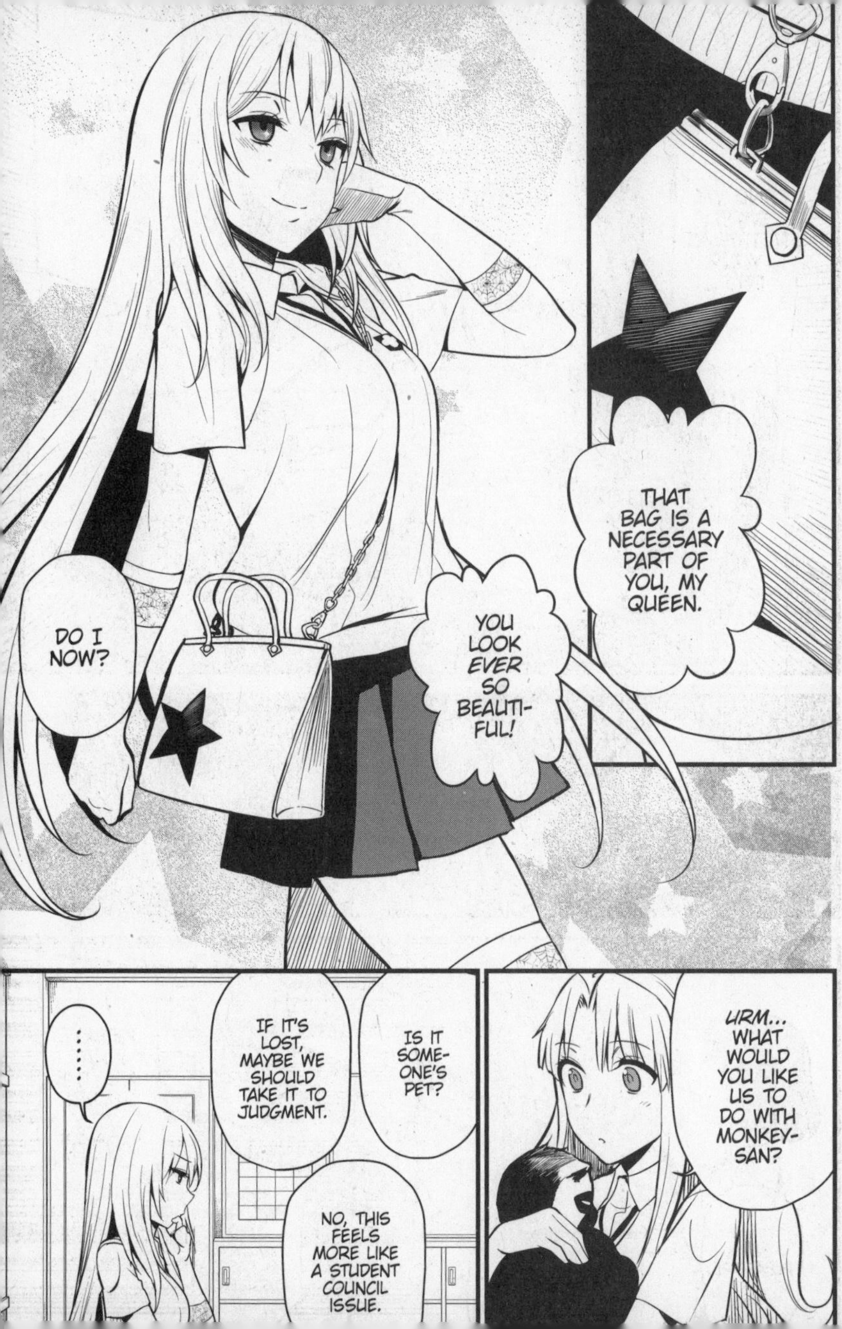
THAT BAG IS A NECESSARY PART OF YOU, MY QUEEN.
YOU LOOK *EVER* SO BEAUTIFUL!
DO I NOW?
URM... WHAT WOULD YOU LIKE US TO DO WITH MONKEY-SAN?
IS IT SOMEONE'S PET?
IF IT'S LOST, MAYBE WE SHOULD TAKE IT TO JUDGMENT.
NO, THIS FEELS MORE LIKE A STUDENT COUNCIL ISSUE.
......

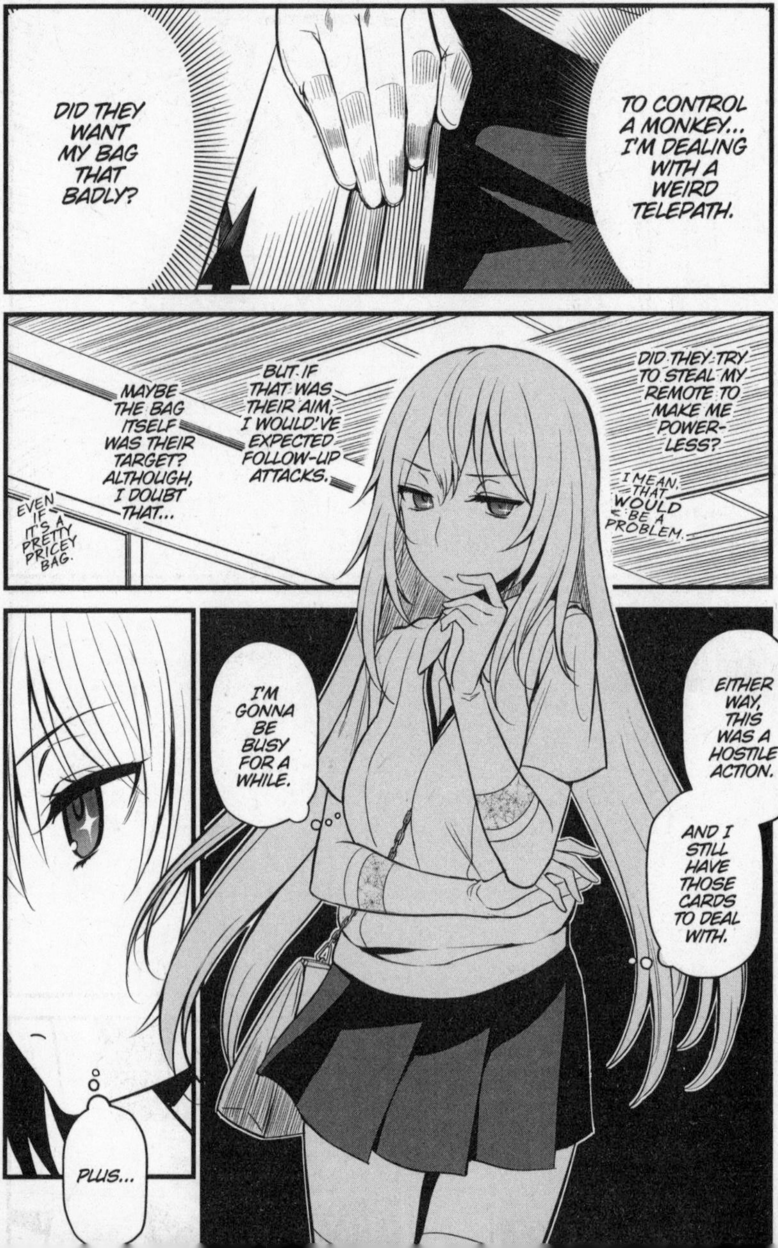
TO CONTROL A MONKEY... I'M DEALING WITH A WEIRD TELEPATH.
DID THEY WANT MY BAG THAT BADLY?
DID THEY TRY TO STEAL MY REMOTE TO MAKE ME POWER-LESS?
I MEAN, THAT WOULD BE A PROBLEM.
BUT IF THAT WAS THEIR AIM, I WOULD'VE EXPECTED FOLLOW-UP ATTACKS.
MAYBE THE BAG ITSELF WAS THEIR TARGET? ALTHOUGH, I DOUBT THAT...
EVEN IF IT'S A PRETTY PRICEY BAG.
EITHER WAY, THIS WAS A HOSTILE ACTION.
AND I STILL HAVE THOSE CARDS TO DEAL WITH.
I'M GONNA BE BUSY FOR A WHILE.
PLUS...

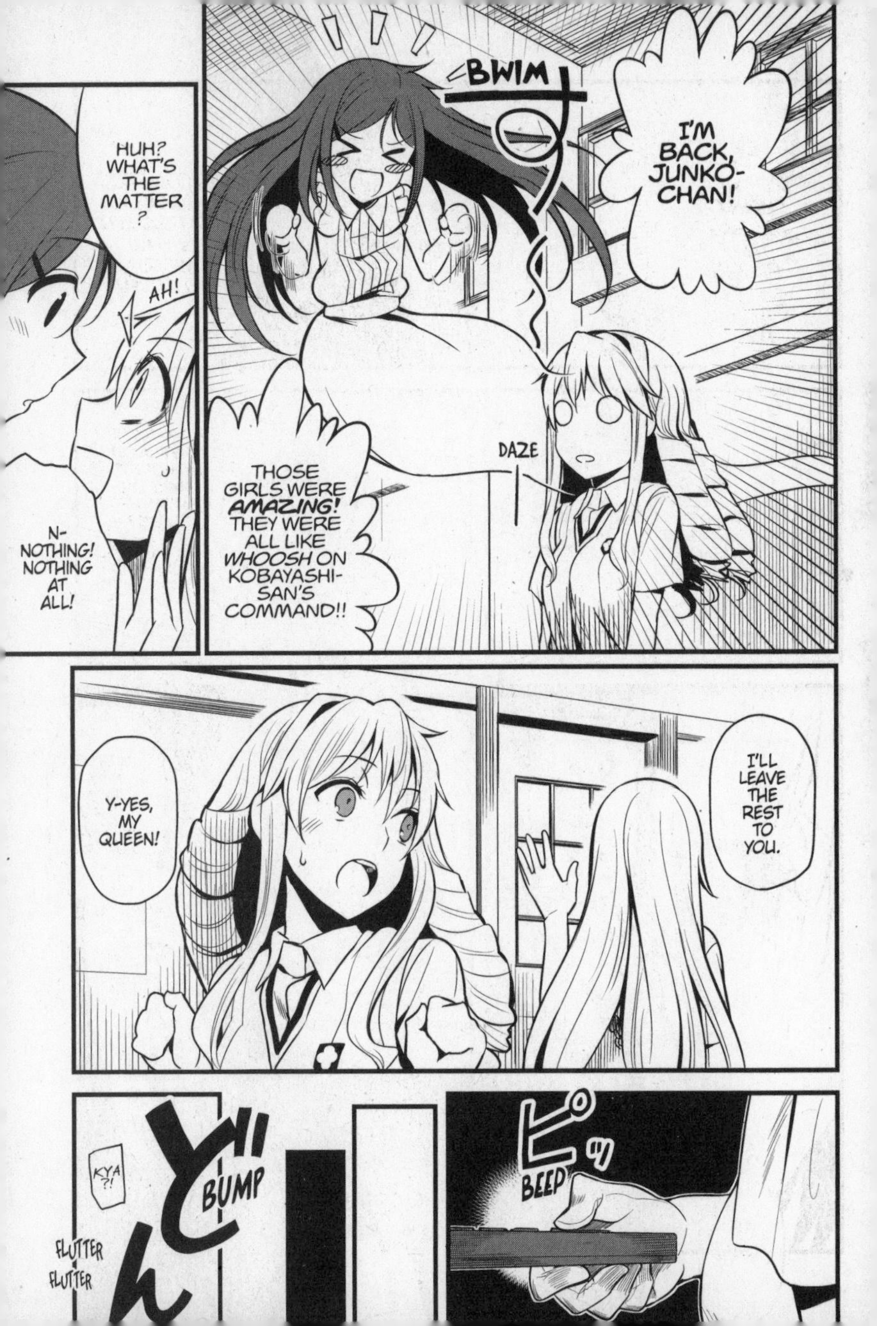
BWIM
I'M BACK, JUNKO-CHAN!
THOSE GIRLS WERE *AMAZING!* THEY WERE ALL LIKE *WHOOSH* ON KOBAYASHI-SAN'S COMMAND!!
DAZE
HUH? WHAT'S THE MATTER?
AH!
N-NOTHING! NOTHING AT ALL!
I'LL LEAVE THE REST TO YOU.
Y-YES, MY QUEEN!
BEEP
BUMP
KYA?!
FLUTTER FLUTTER

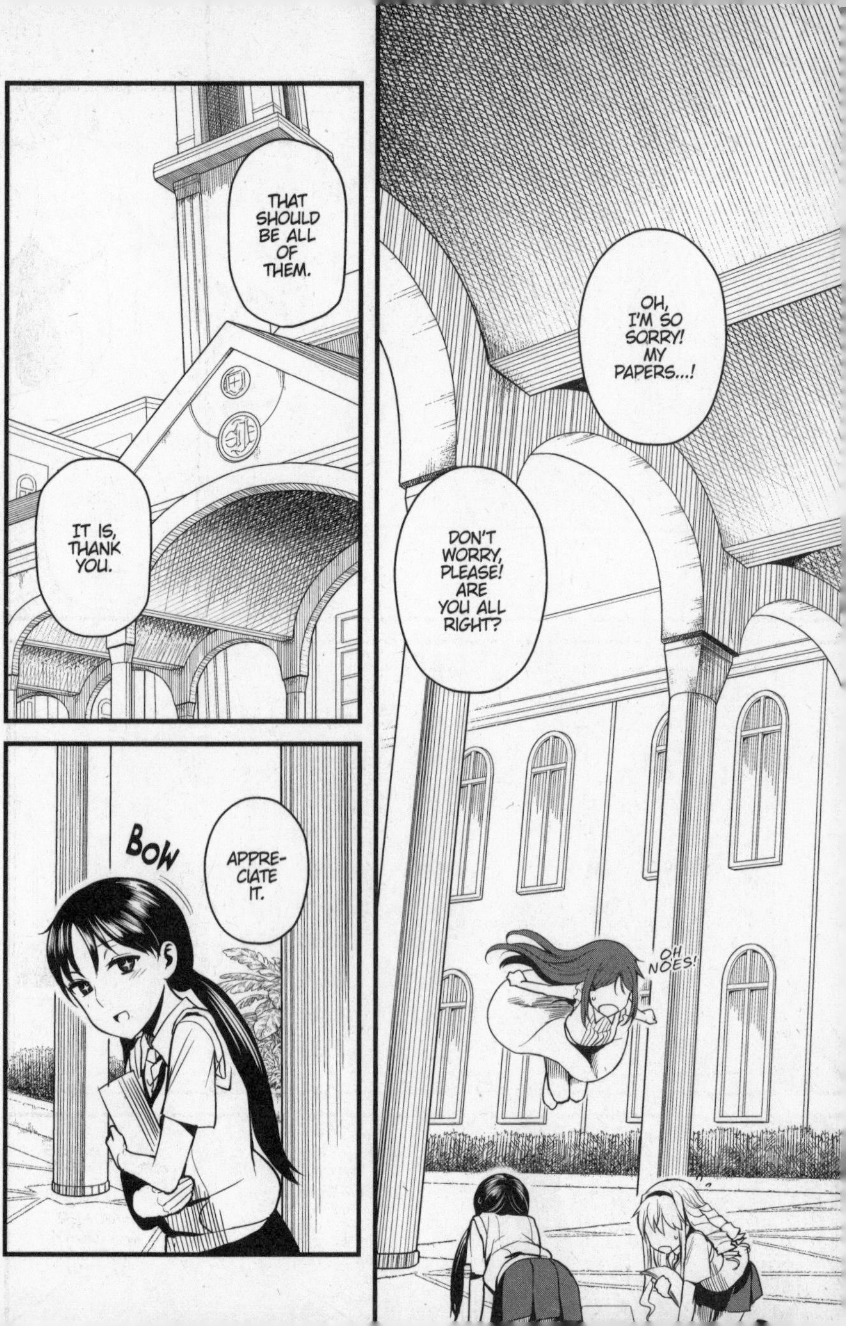
OH, I'M SO SORRY! MY PAPERS...!
DON'T WORRY, PLEASE! ARE YOU ALL RIGHT?
OH NOES!
THAT SHOULD BE ALL OF THEM.
IT IS, THANK YOU.
BOW
APPRE-CIATE IT.

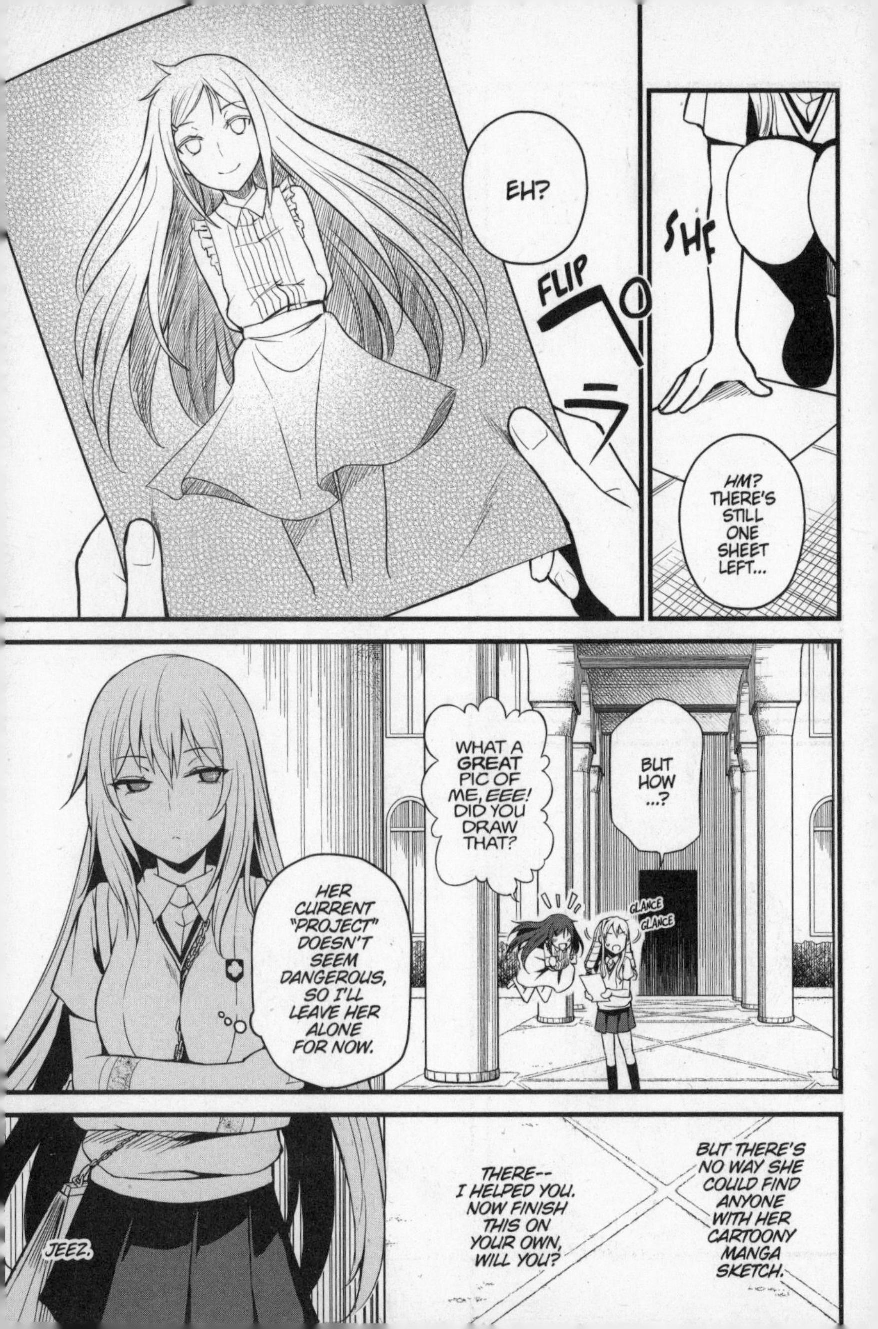
HM? THERE'S STILL ONE SHEET LEFT...
SHF
FLIP
EH?
BUT HOW ...?
WHAT A GREAT PIC OF ME, EEE! DID YOU DRAW THAT?
GLANCE
GLANCE
HER CURRENT "PROJECT" DOESN'T SEEM DANGEROUS, SO I'LL LEAVE HER ALONE FOR NOW.
BUT THERE'S NO WAY SHE COULD FIND ANYONE WITH HER CARTOONY MANGA SKETCH.
THERE-- I HELPED YOU. NOW FINISH THIS ON YOUR OWN, WILL YOU?
JEEZ.

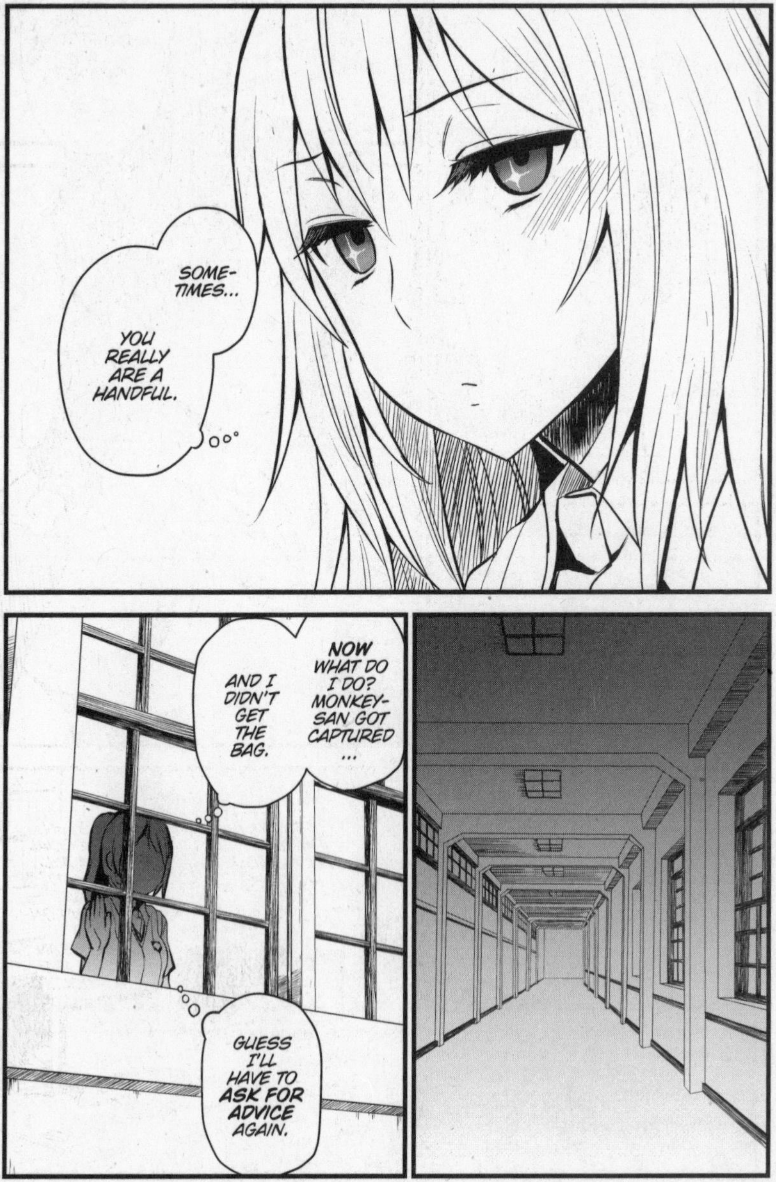
SOME-TIMES...
YOU REALLY ARE A HANDFUL.
NOW WHAT DO I DO? MONKEY-SAN GOT CAPTURED ...
AND I DIDN'T GET THE BAG.
GUESS I'LL HAVE TO ASK FOR ADVICE AGAIN.

CHAPTER 4: I'm Not Sure if I'll Be of Any Assistance, but...

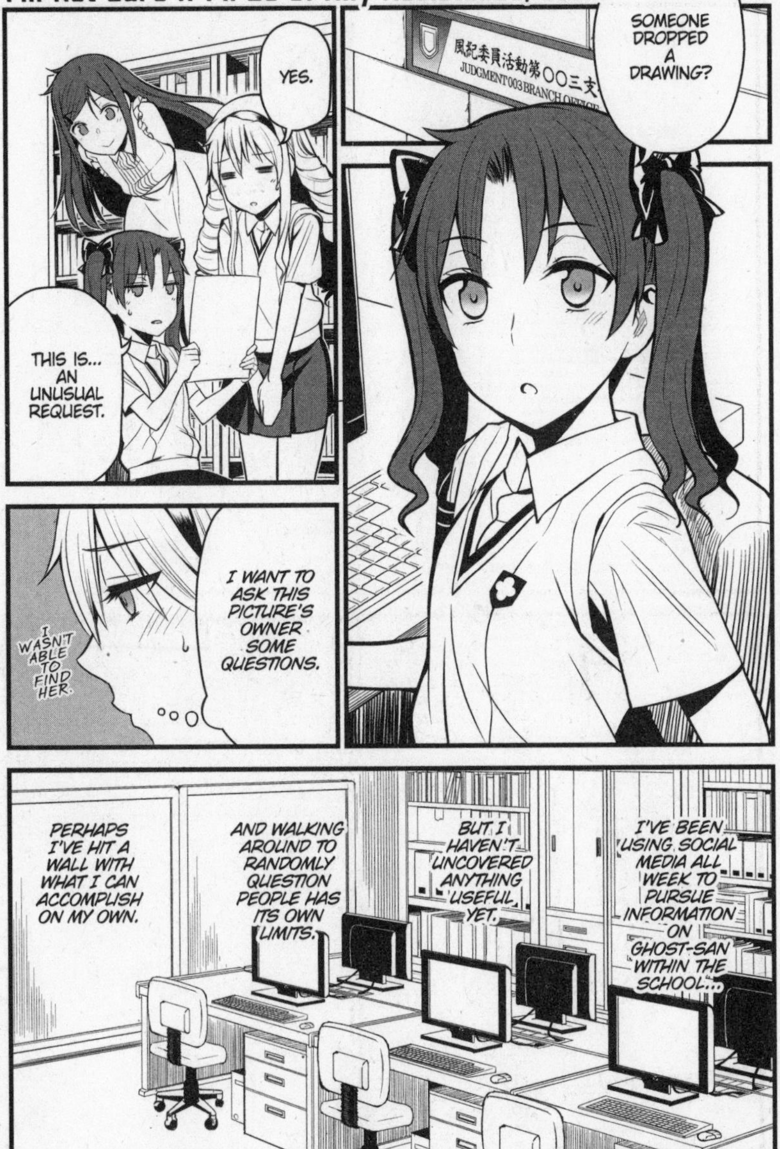
SOMEONE DROPPED A DRAWING?
風紀委員活動第〇〇三支
JUDGMENT 003 BRANCH OFFICE
YES.
THIS IS... AN UNUSUAL REQUEST.
I WANT TO ASK THIS PICTURE'S OWNER SOME QUESTIONS.
I WASN'T ABLE TO FIND HER.
I'VE BEEN USING SOCIAL MEDIA ALL WEEK TO PURSUE INFORMATION ON GHOST-SAN WITHIN THE SCHOOL...
BUT I HAVEN'T UNCOVERED ANYTHING USEFUL YET.
AND WALKING AROUND TO RANDOMLY QUESTION PEOPLE HAS ITS OWN LIMITS.
PERHAPS I'VE HIT A WALL WITH WHAT I CAN ACCOMPLISH ON MY OWN.

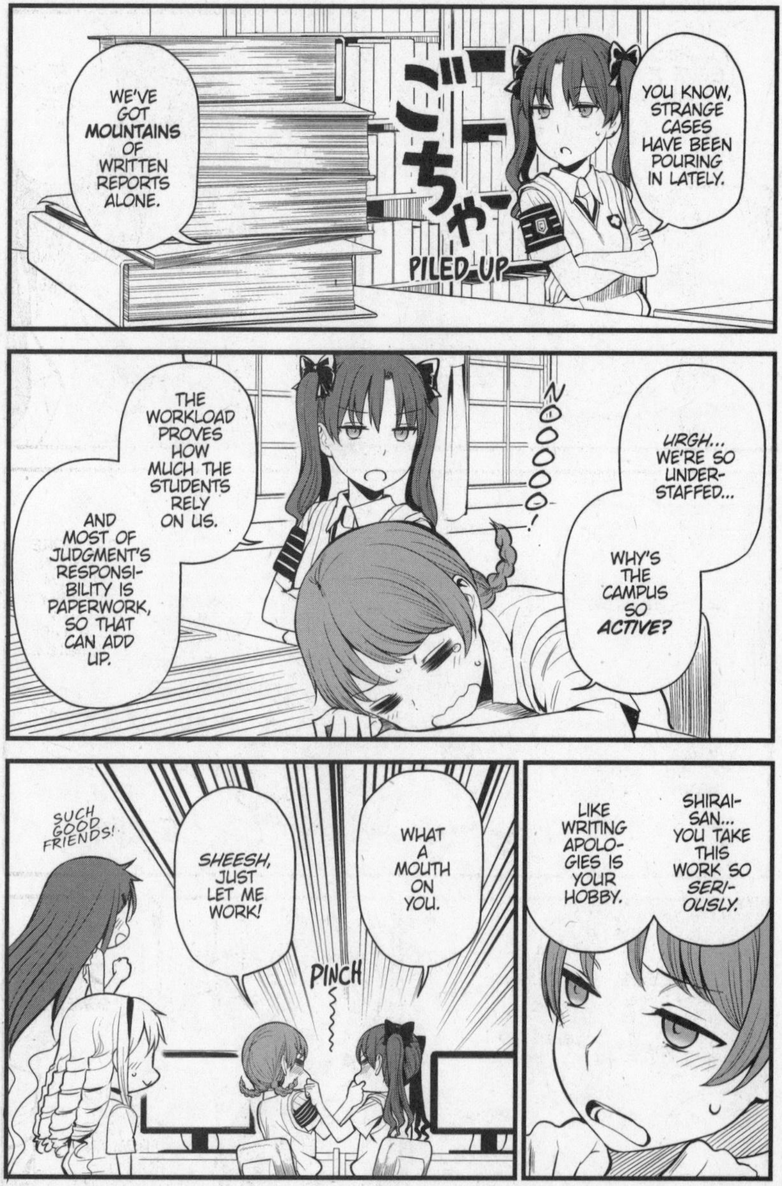
YOU KNOW, STRANGE CASES HAVE BEEN POURING IN LATELY.
ごちゃー
PILED UP
WE'VE GOT MOUNTAINS OF WRITTEN REPORTS ALONE.
URGH... WE'RE SO UNDER-STAFFED...
WHY'S THE CAMPUS SO ACTIVE?
NOOOOOO!
THE WORKLOAD PROVES HOW MUCH THE STUDENTS RELY ON US.
AND MOST OF JUDGMENT'S RESPONSI-BILITY IS PAPERWORK, SO THAT CAN ADD UP.
SHIRAI-SAN... YOU TAKE THIS WORK SO SERI-OUSLY.
LIKE WRITING APOLO-GIES IS YOUR HOBBY.
WHAT A MOUTH ON YOU.
PINCH
SHEESH, JUST LET ME WORK!
SUCH GOOD FRIENDS!

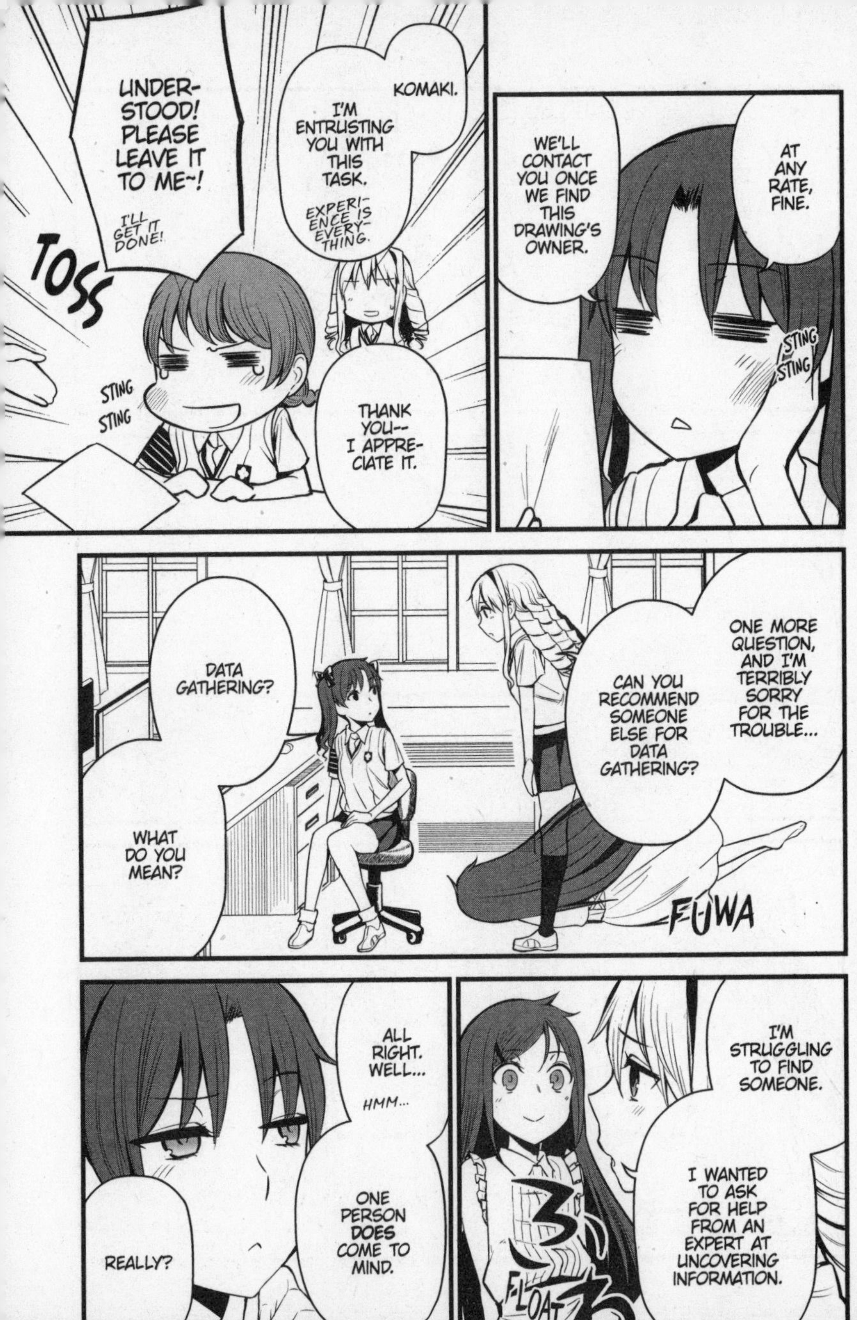
AT ANY RATE, FINE.
WE'LL CONTACT YOU ONCE WE FIND THIS DRAWING'S OWNER.
STING STING
KOMAKI.
I'M ENTRUSTING YOU WITH THIS TASK.
EXPERIENCE IS EVERYTHING.
UNDERSTOOD! PLEASE LEAVE IT TO ME~!
I'LL GET IT DONE!
TOSS
THANK YOU-- I APPRECIATE IT.
STING STING
ONE MORE QUESTION, AND I'M TERRIBLY SORRY FOR THE TROUBLE...
CAN YOU RECOMMEND SOMEONE ELSE FOR DATA GATHERING?
FUWA
DATA GATHERING?
WHAT DO YOU MEAN?
I'M STRUGGLING TO FIND SOMEONE.
I WANTED TO ASK FOR HELP FROM AN EXPERT AT UNCOVERING INFORMATION.
F-LOAT
ALL RIGHT. WELL...
HMM...
ONE PERSON DOES COME TO MIND.
REALLY?

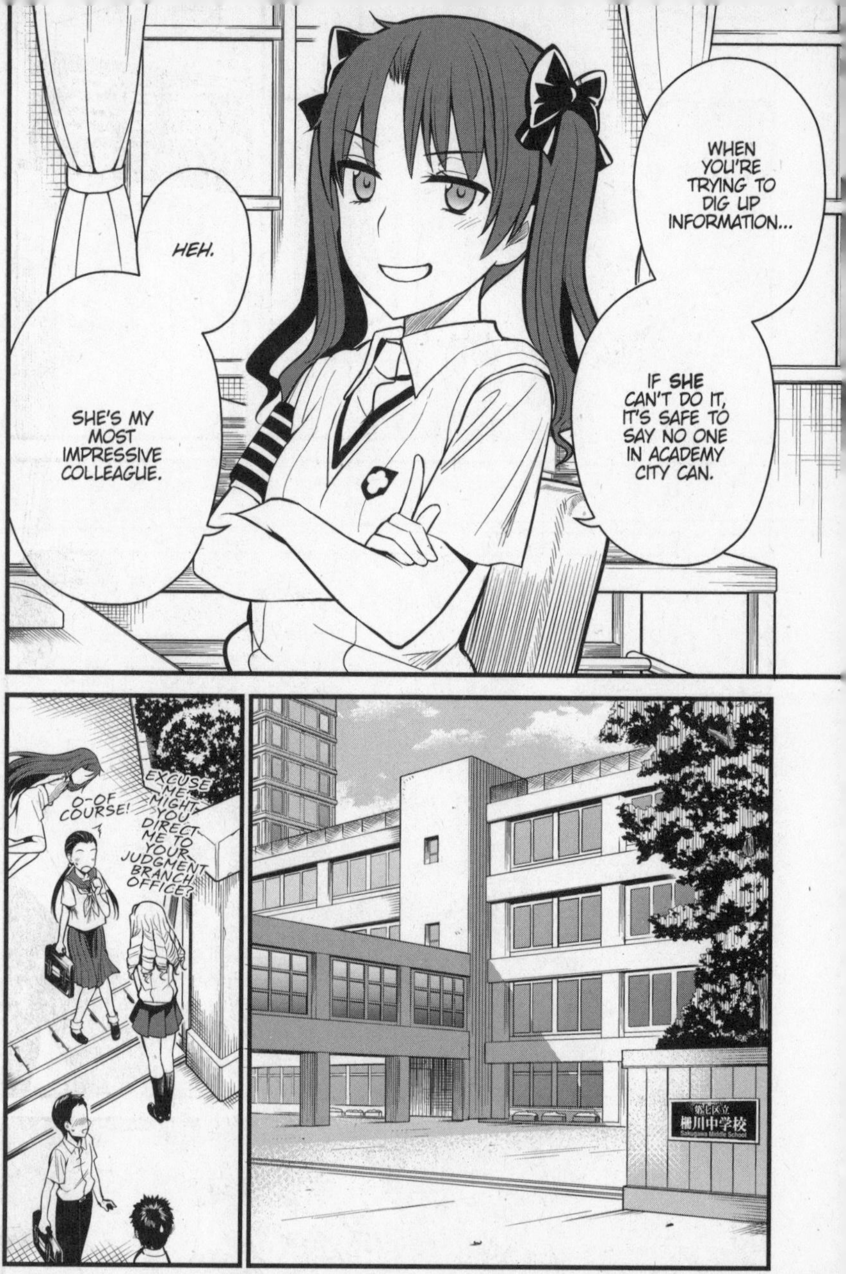
WHEN YOU'RE TRYING TO DIG UP INFORMATION...
IF SHE CAN'T DO IT, IT'S SAFE TO SAY NO ONE IN ACADEMY CITY CAN.
HEH.
SHE'S MY MOST IMPRESSIVE COLLEAGUE.
第七区立
柵川中学校
Sakugawa Middle School
EXCUSE ME. MIGHT YOU DIRECT ME TO YOUR JUDGMENT BRANCH OFFICE?
O-OF COURSE!

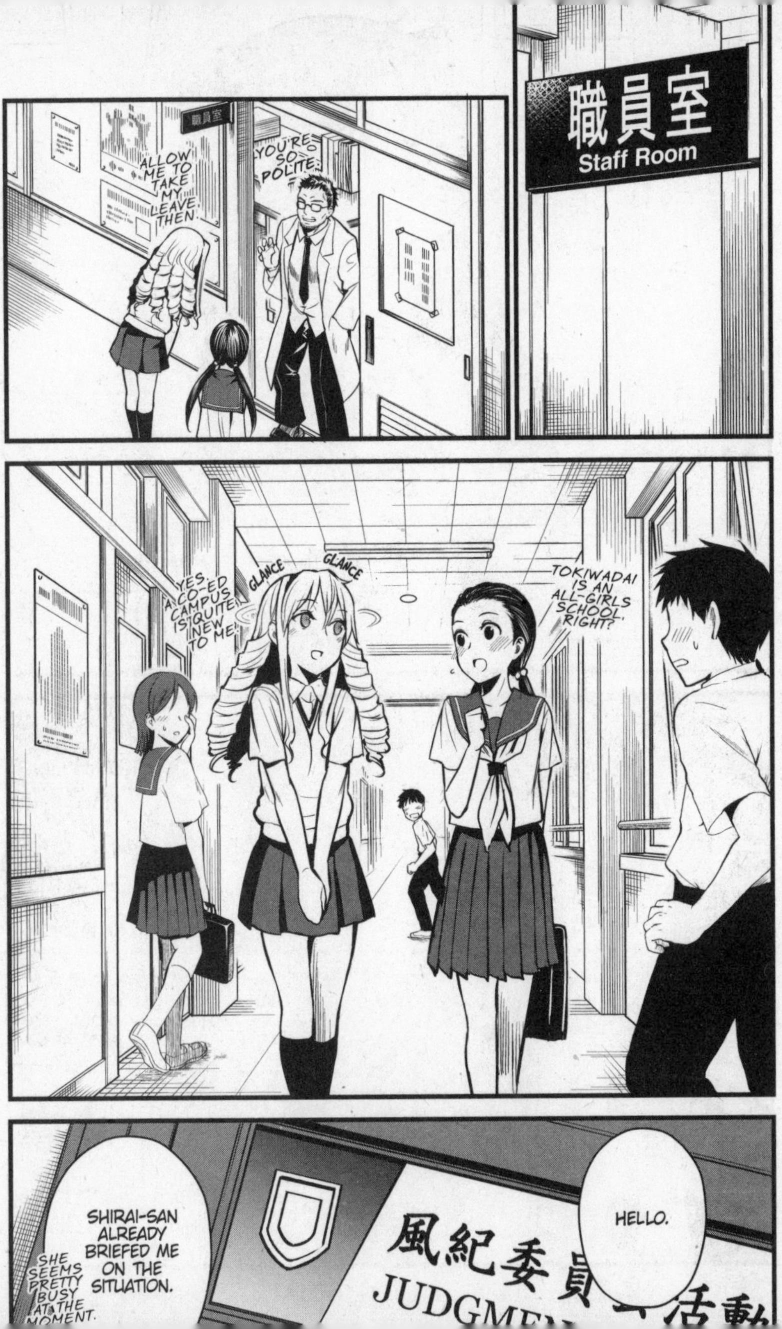
職員室
Staff Room
YOU'RE SO POLITE.
ALLOW ME TO TAKE MY LEAVE THEN.
TOKIWADAI IS AN ALL-GIRLS SCHOOL, RIGHT?
GLANCE
GLANCE
YES. A CO-ED CAMPUS IS QUITE NEW TO ME!
HELLO.
風紀委員
JUDGMEN
活動
SHIRAI-SAN ALREADY BRIEFED ME ON THE SITUATION.
SHE SEEMS PRETTY BUSY AT THE MOMENT.

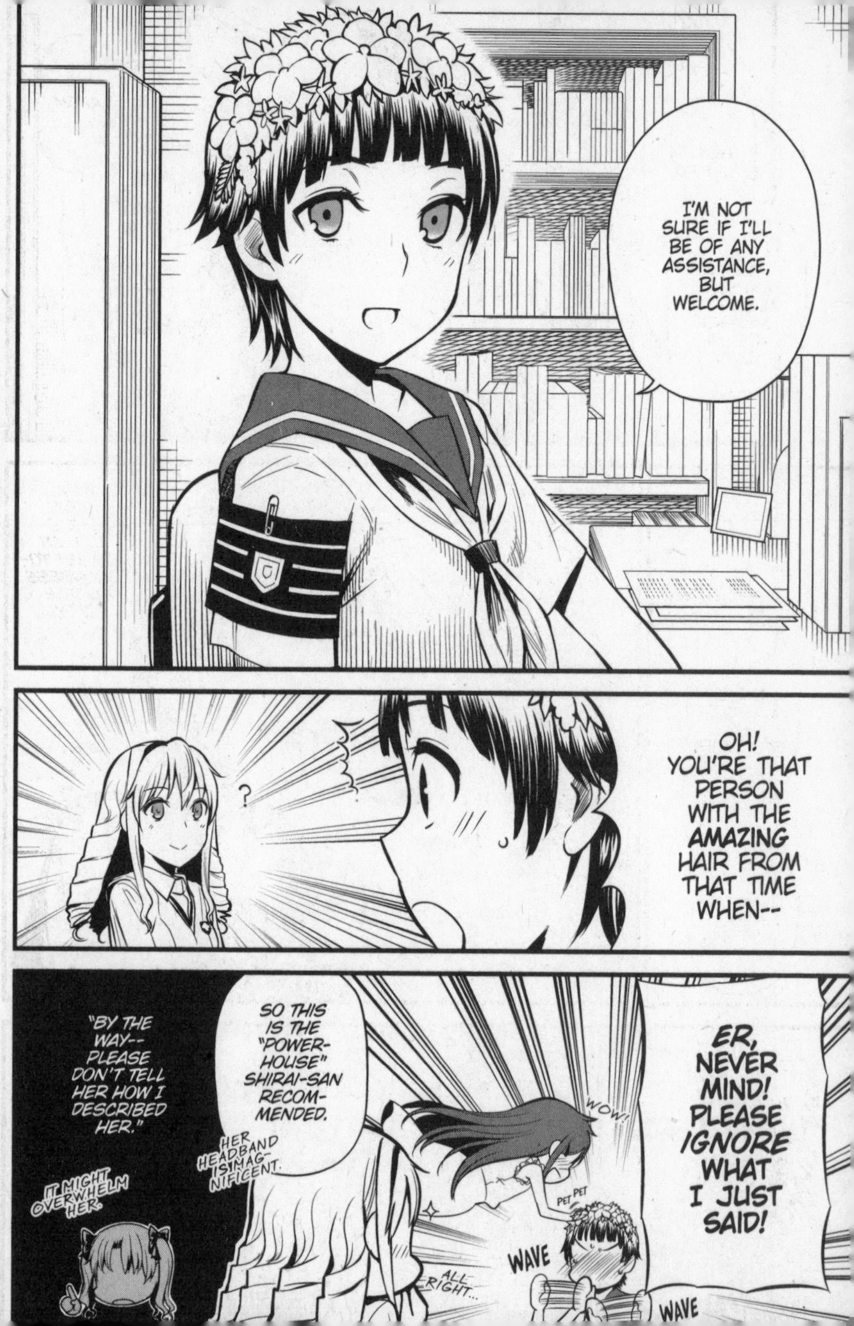
I'M NOT SURE IF I'LL BE OF ANY ASSISTANCE, BUT WELCOME.
?
OH! YOU'RE THAT PERSON WITH THE AMAZING HAIR FROM THAT TIME WHEN--
ER, NEVER MIND! PLEASE IGNORE WHAT I JUST SAID!
WAVE
WAVE
PET PET
WOW!
ALL RIGHT...
SO THIS IS THE "POWER-HOUSE" SHIRAI-SAN RECOMMENDED.
HER HEADBAND IS MAG-NIFICENT.
"BY THE WAY-- PLEASE DON'T TELL HER HOW I DESCRIBED HER."
IT MIGHT OVERWHELM HER.

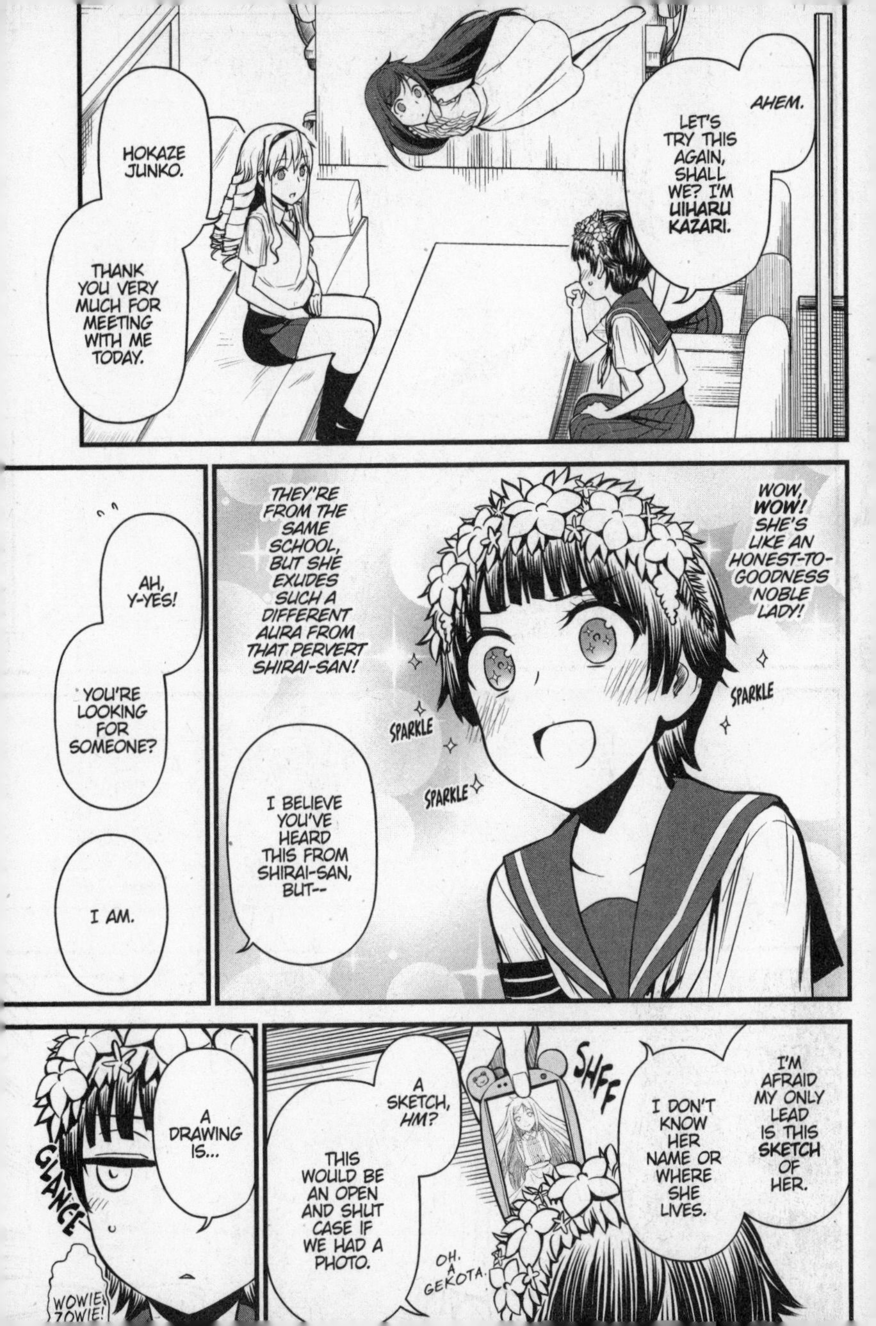
AHEM.
LET'S TRY THIS AGAIN, SHALL WE? I'M UIHARU KAZARI.
HOKAZE JUNKO.
THANK YOU VERY MUCH FOR MEETING WITH ME TODAY.
WOW, WOW! SHE'S LIKE AN HONEST-TO-GOODNESS NOBLE LADY!
THEY'RE FROM THE SAME SCHOOL, BUT SHE EXUDES SUCH A DIFFERENT AURA FROM THAT PERVERT SHIRAI-SAN!
SPARKLE
SPARKLE
SPARKLE
I BELIEVE YOU'VE HEARD THIS FROM SHIRAI-SAN, BUT--
AH, Y-YES!
YOU'RE LOOKING FOR SOMEONE?
I AM.
I'M AFRAID MY ONLY LEAD IS THIS SKETCH OF HER.
SHFF
I DON'T KNOW HER NAME OR WHERE SHE LIVES.
A SKETCH, HM?
THIS WOULD BE AN OPEN AND SHUT CASE IF WE HAD A PHOTO.
OH. A GEKOTA.
A DRAWING IS...
GLANCE
WOWIE ZOWIE!

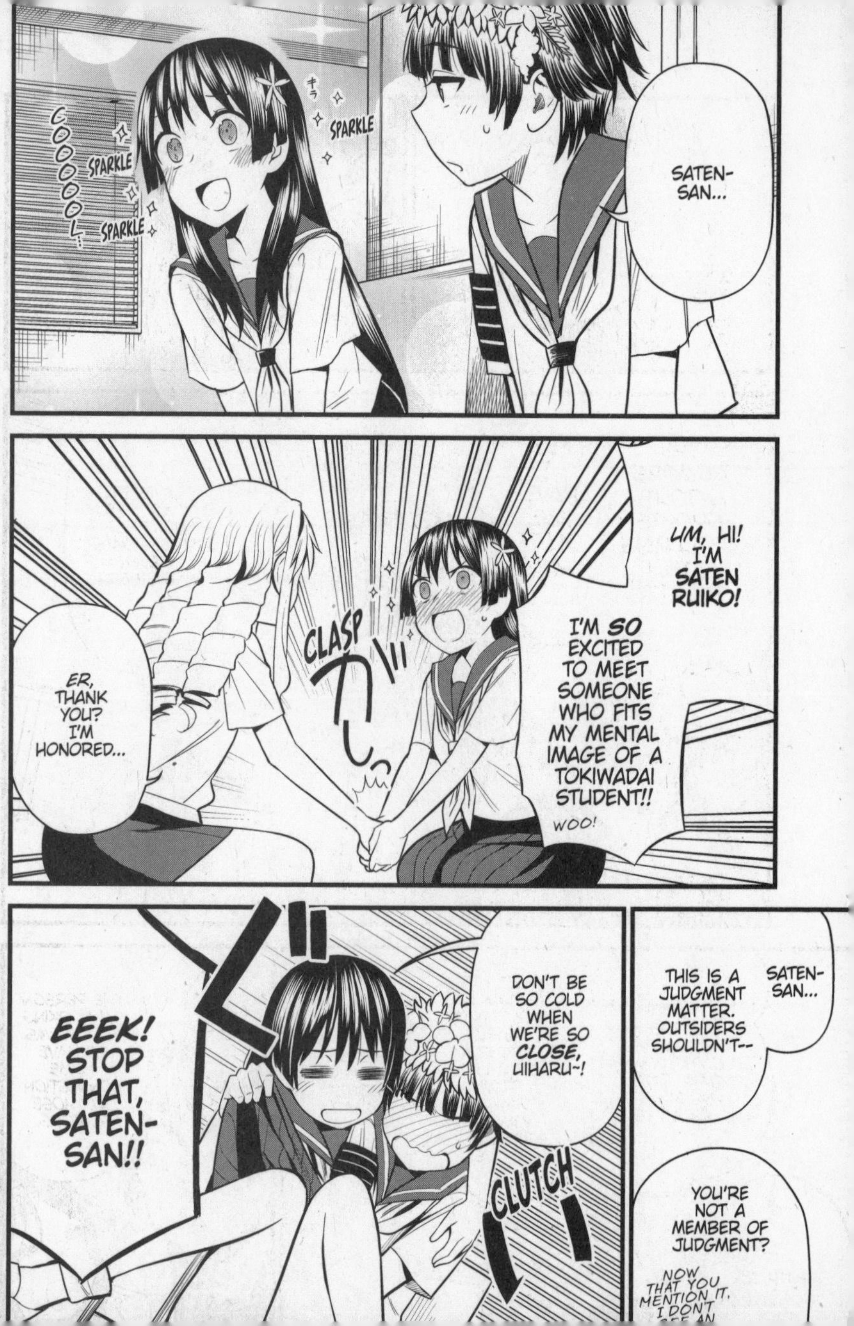
SATEN-SAN...
キラ
SPARKLE
SPARKLE
SPARKLE
COOOOOOOL...
UM, HI! I'M SATEN RUIKO!
I'M SO EXCITED TO MEET SOMEONE WHO FITS MY MENTAL IMAGE OF A TOKIWADAI STUDENT!!
WOO!
CLASP
ER, THANK YOU? I'M HONORED...
SATEN-SAN...
THIS IS A JUDGMENT MATTER. OUTSIDERS SHOULDN'T--
YOU'RE NOT A MEMBER OF JUDGMENT?
NOW THAT YOU MENTION IT, I DON'T
DON'T BE SO COLD WHEN WE'RE SO CLOSE, UIHARU~!
CLUTCH
EEEK! STOP THAT, SATEN-SAN!!

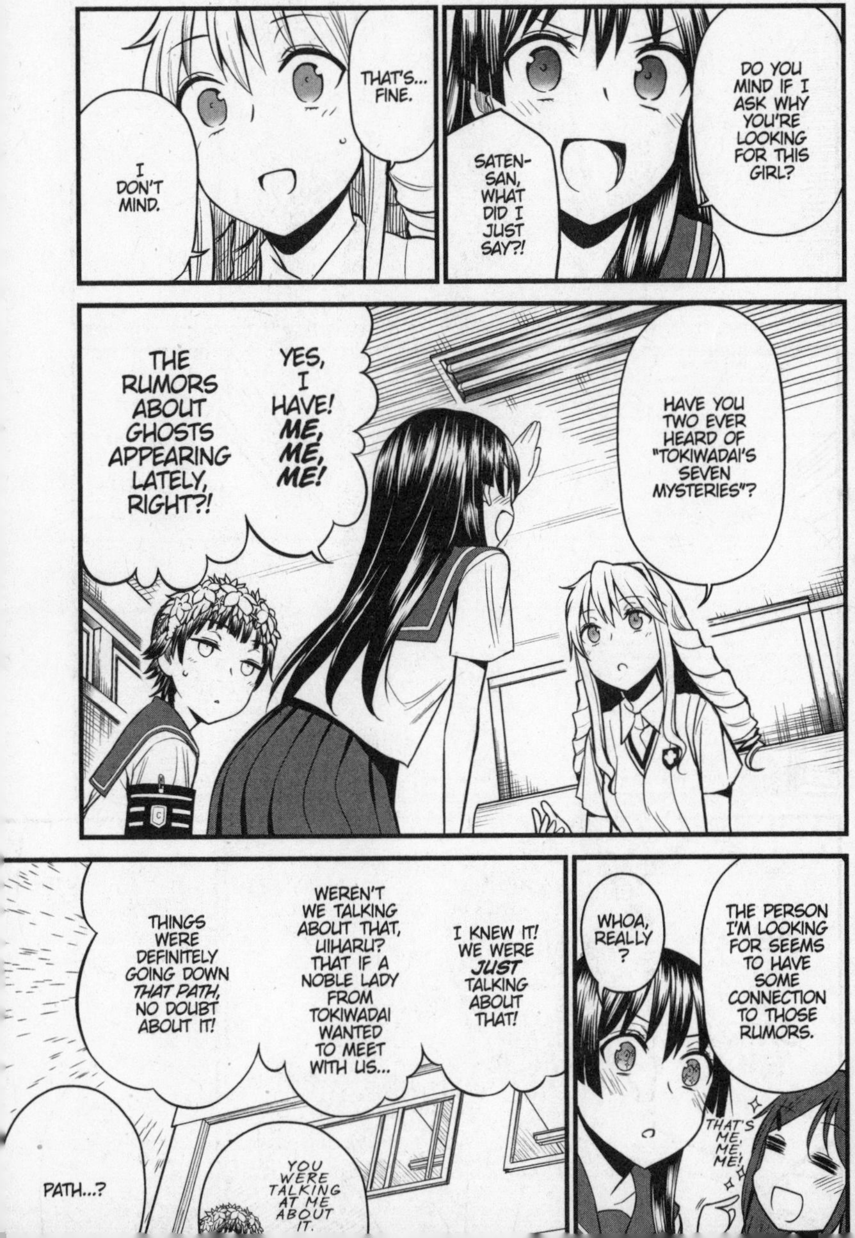
DO YOU MIND IF I ASK WHY YOU'RE LOOKING FOR THIS GIRL?
SATEN-SAN, WHAT DID I JUST SAY?!
THAT'S... FINE.
I DON'T MIND.
HAVE YOU TWO EVER HEARD OF "TOKIWADAI'S SEVEN MYSTERIES"?
YES, I HAVE! *ME, ME, ME!*
THE RUMORS ABOUT GHOSTS APPEARING LATELY, RIGHT?!
THE PERSON I'M LOOKING FOR SEEMS TO HAVE SOME CONNECTION TO THOSE RUMORS.
WHOA, REALLY?
THAT'S ME, ME, ME!
I KNEW IT! WE WERE *JUST* TALKING ABOUT THAT!
WEREN'T WE TALKING ABOUT THAT, UIHARU? THAT IF A NOBLE LADY FROM TOKIWADAI WANTED TO MEET WITH US...
THINGS WERE DEFINITELY GOING DOWN *THAT PATH*, NO DOUBT ABOUT IT!
YOU WERE TALKING AT ME ABOUT IT.
PATH...?

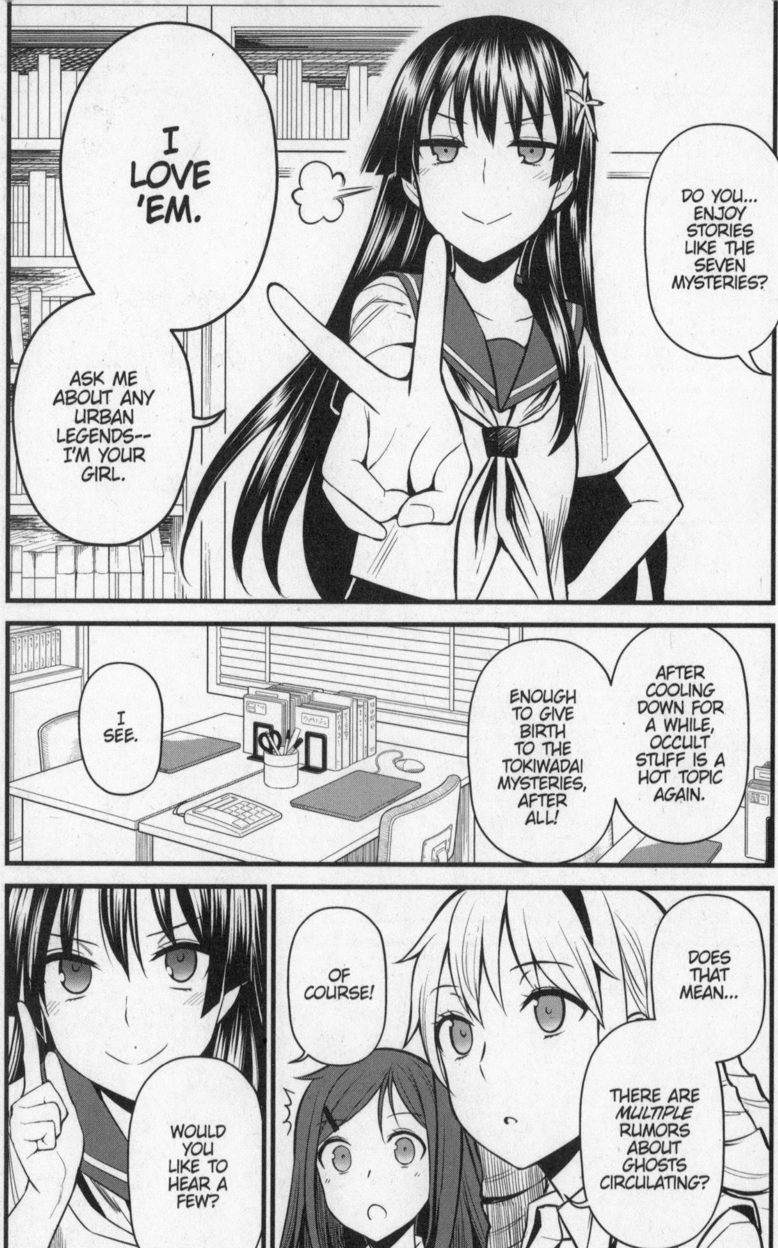
DO YOU... ENJOY STORIES LIKE THE SEVEN MYSTERIES?
I LOVE 'EM.
ASK ME ABOUT ANY URBAN LEGENDS-- I'M YOUR GIRL.
AFTER COOLING DOWN FOR A WHILE, OCCULT STUFF IS A HOT TOPIC AGAIN.
ENOUGH TO GIVE BIRTH TO THE TOKIWADAI MYSTERIES, AFTER ALL!
I SEE.
DOES THAT MEAN...
THERE ARE *MULTIPLE* RUMORS ABOUT GHOSTS CIRCULATING?
OF COURSE!
WOULD YOU LIKE TO HEAR A FEW?

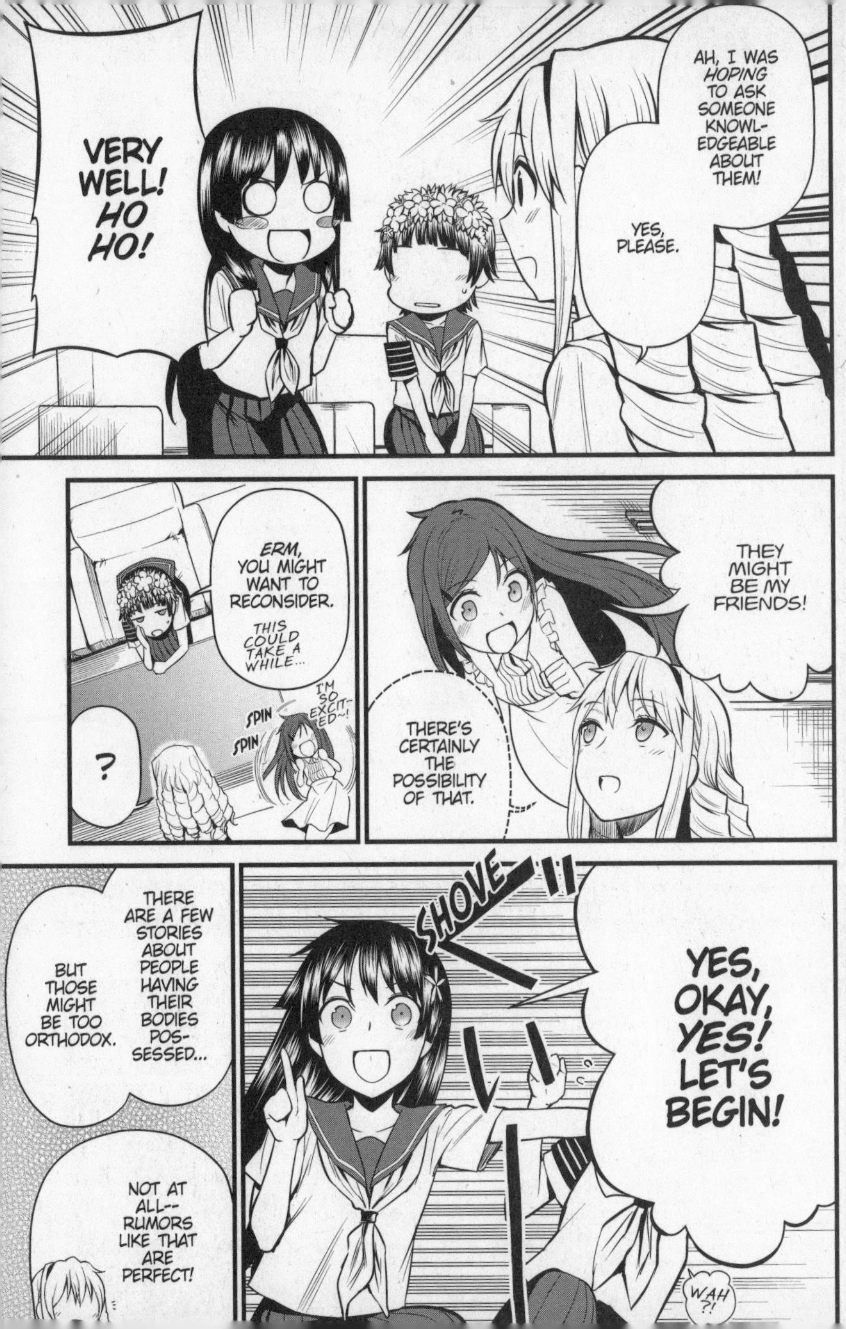
AH, I WAS HOPING TO ASK SOMEONE KNOWLEDGEABLE ABOUT THEM!
YES, PLEASE.
VERY WELL! HO HO!
THEY MIGHT BE MY FRIENDS!
THERE'S CERTAINLY THE POSSIBILITY OF THAT.
ERM, YOU MIGHT WANT TO RECONSIDER.
THIS COULD TAKE A WHILE...
I'M SO EXCITED~!
SPIN
SPIN
?
YES, OKAY, YES! LET'S BEGIN!
SHOVE
WAH?!
THERE ARE A FEW STORIES ABOUT PEOPLE HAVING THEIR BODIES POSSESSED...
BUT THOSE MIGHT BE TOO ORTHODOX.
NOT AT ALL-- RUMORS LIKE THAT ARE PERFECT!

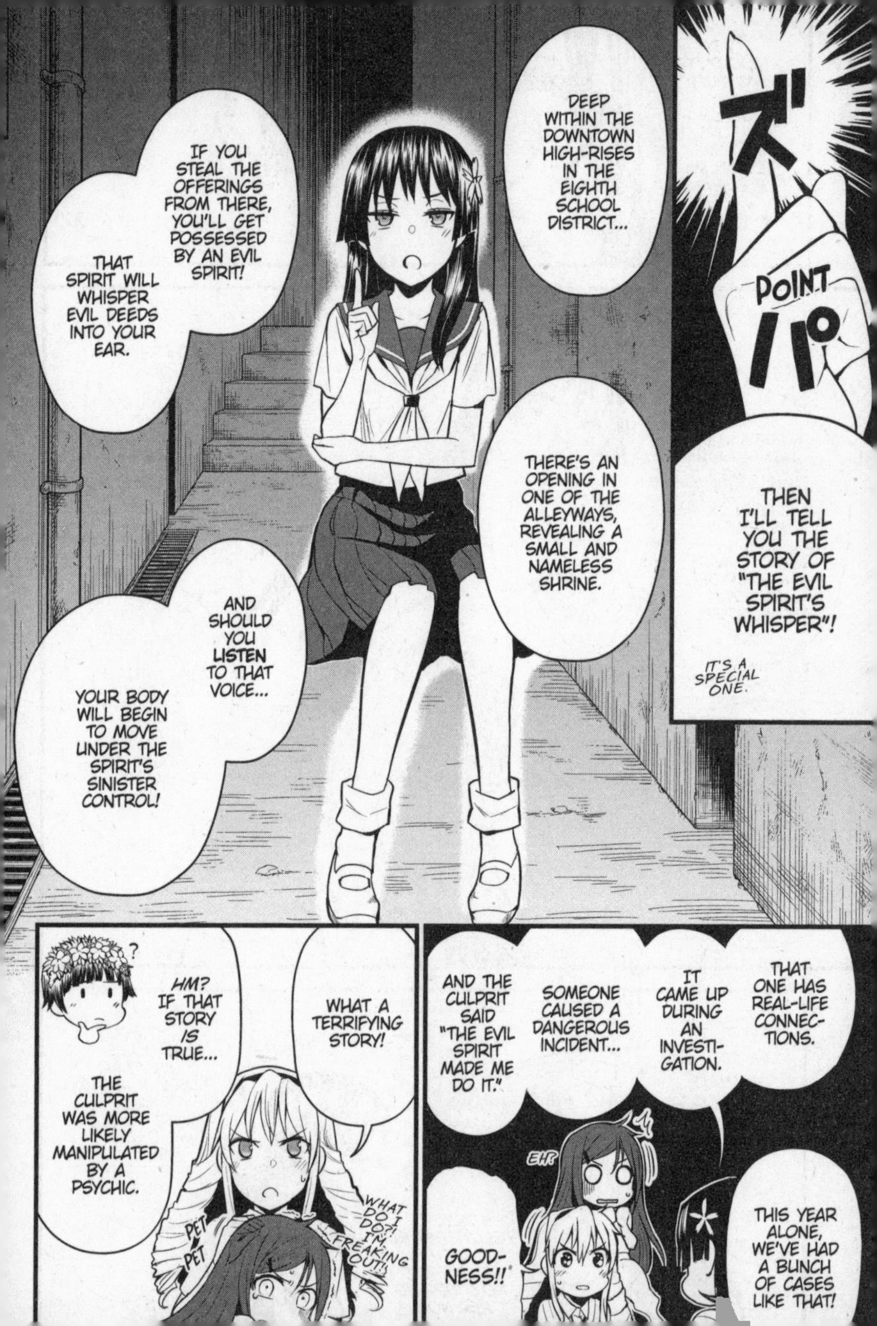
ズ
POINT
パ
THEN I'LL TELL YOU THE STORY OF "THE EVIL SPIRIT'S WHISPER"!
IT'S A SPECIAL ONE.
DEEP WITHIN THE DOWNTOWN HIGH-RISES IN THE EIGHTH SCHOOL DISTRICT...
THERE'S AN OPENING IN ONE OF THE ALLEYWAYS, REVEALING A SMALL AND NAMELESS SHRINE.
IF YOU STEAL THE OFFERINGS FROM THERE, YOU'LL GET POSSESSED BY AN EVIL SPIRIT!
THAT SPIRIT WILL WHISPER EVIL DEEDS INTO YOUR EAR.
AND SHOULD YOU LISTEN TO THAT VOICE...
YOUR BODY WILL BEGIN TO MOVE UNDER THE SPIRIT'S SINISTER CONTROL!
THAT ONE HAS REAL-LIFE CONNECTIONS.
IT CAME UP DURING AN INVESTIGATION.
SOMEONE CAUSED A DANGEROUS INCIDENT...
AND THE CULPRIT SAID "THE EVIL SPIRIT MADE ME DO IT."
EH?
THIS YEAR ALONE, WE'VE HAD A BUNCH OF CASES LIKE THAT!
GOODNESS!!
WHAT A TERRIFYING STORY!
?
HM? IF THAT STORY IS TRUE...
THE CULPRIT WAS MORE LIKELY MANIPULATED BY A PSYCHIC.
WHAT DO I DO?! I'M FREAKING OUT!!
PET PET

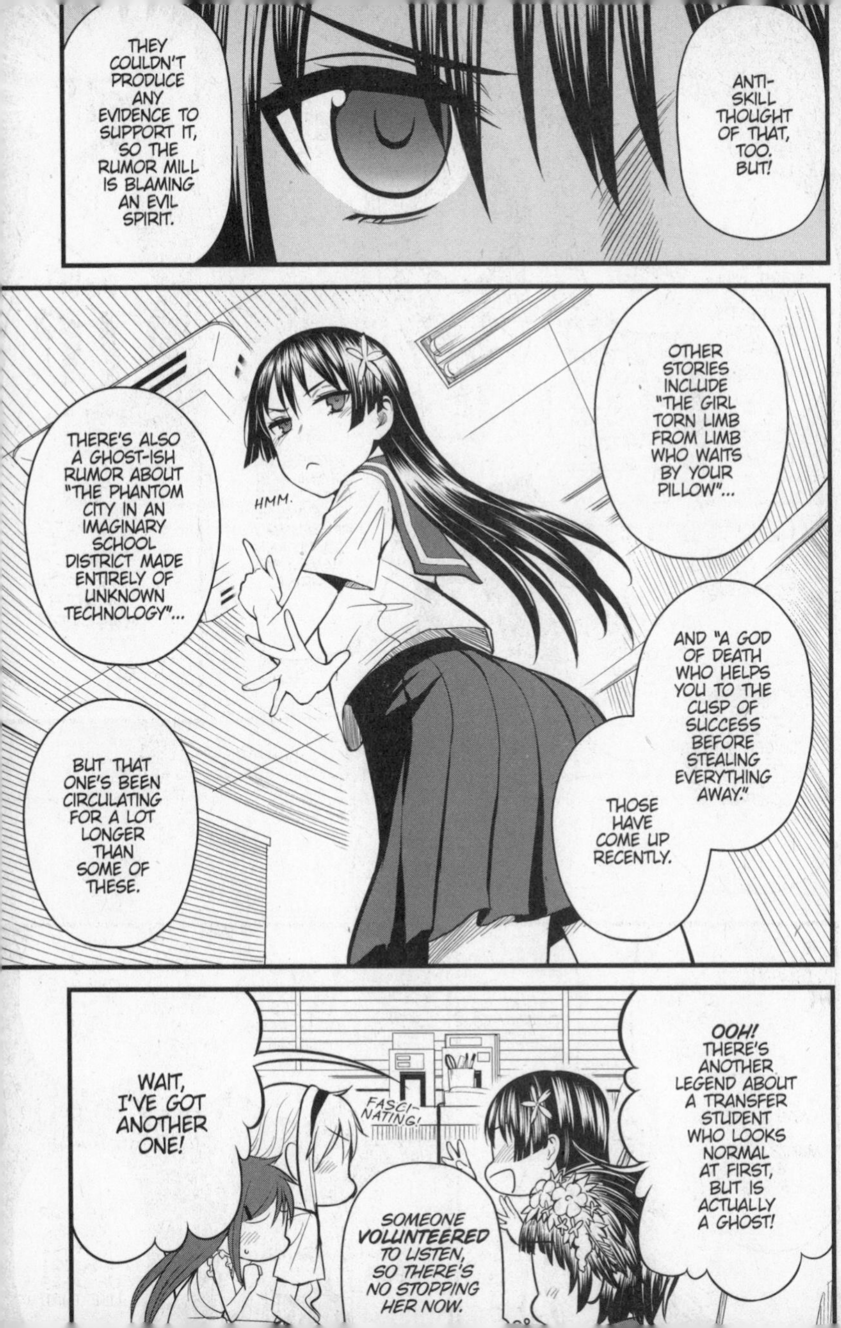
ANTI-SKILL THOUGHT OF THAT, TOO. BUT!
THEY COULDN'T PRODUCE ANY EVIDENCE TO SUPPORT IT, SO THE RUMOR MILL IS BLAMING AN EVIL SPIRIT.
OTHER STORIES INCLUDE "THE GIRL TORN LIMB FROM LIMB WHO WAITS BY YOUR PILLOW"...
AND "A GOD OF DEATH WHO HELPS YOU TO THE CUSP OF SUCCESS BEFORE STEALING EVERYTHING AWAY."
THOSE HAVE COME UP RECENTLY.
HMM.
THERE'S ALSO A GHOST-ISH RUMOR ABOUT "THE PHANTOM CITY IN AN IMAGINARY SCHOOL DISTRICT MADE ENTIRELY OF UNKNOWN TECHNOLOGY"...
BUT THAT ONE'S BEEN CIRCULATING FOR A LOT LONGER THAN SOME OF THESE.
OOH! THERE'S ANOTHER LEGEND ABOUT A TRANSFER STUDENT WHO LOOKS NORMAL AT FIRST, BUT IS ACTUALLY A GHOST!
FASCI-NATING!
WAIT, I'VE GOT ANOTHER ONE!
SOMEONE **VOLUNTEERED** TO LISTEN, SO THERE'S NO STOPPING HER NOW.

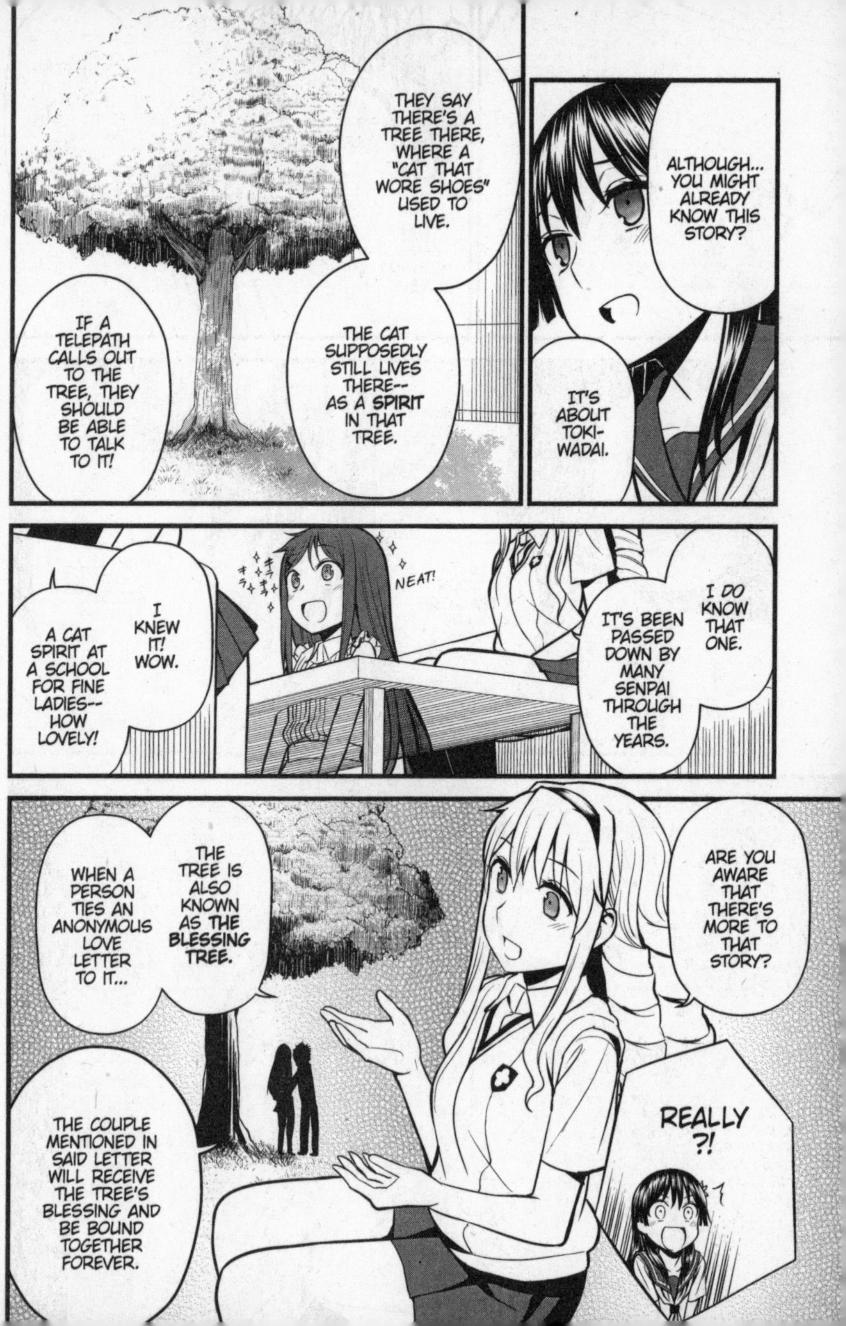
ALTHOUGH... YOU MIGHT ALREADY KNOW THIS STORY?
IT'S ABOUT TOKI-WADAI.
THEY SAY THERE'S A TREE THERE, WHERE A "CAT THAT WORE SHOES" USED TO LIVE.
THE CAT SUPPOSEDLY STILL LIVES THERE-- AS A **SPIRIT** IN THAT TREE.
IF A TELEPATH CALLS OUT TO THE TREE, THEY SHOULD BE ABLE TO TALK TO IT!
I *DO* KNOW THAT ONE.
IT'S BEEN PASSED DOWN BY MANY SENPAI THROUGH THE YEARS.
NEAT!
I KNEW IT! WOW.
A CAT SPIRIT AT A SCHOOL FOR FINE LADIES-- HOW LOVELY!
ARE YOU AWARE THAT THERE'S MORE TO THAT STORY?
THE TREE IS ALSO KNOWN AS **THE BLESSING TREE.**
WHEN A PERSON TIES AN ANONYMOUS LOVE LETTER TO IT...
THE COUPLE MENTIONED IN SAID LETTER WILL RECEIVE THE TREE'S BLESSING AND BE BOUND TOGETHER FOREVER.
REALLY?!

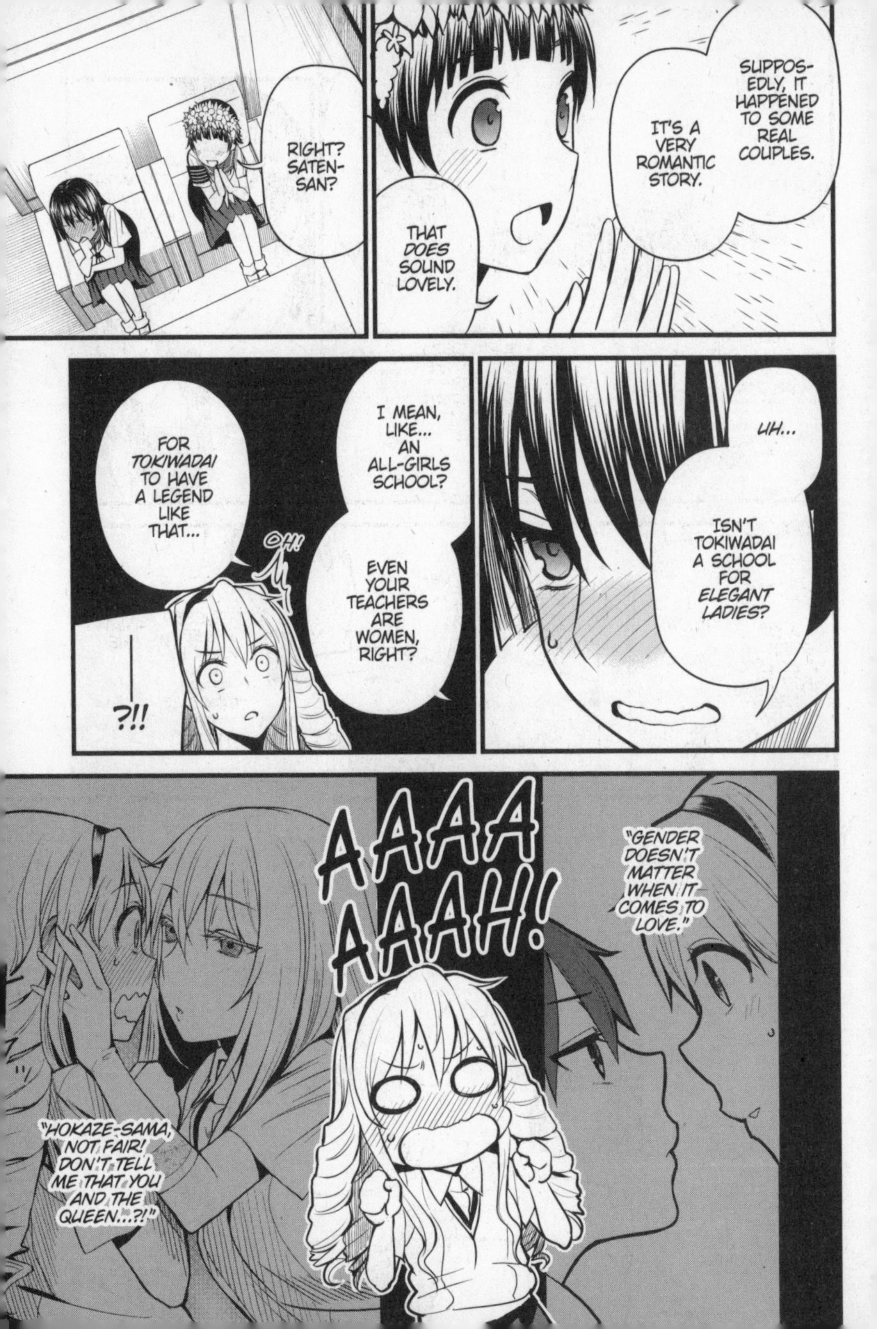
SUPPOSEDLY, IT HAPPENED TO SOME REAL COUPLES.
IT'S A VERY ROMANTIC STORY.
THAT *DOES* SOUND LOVELY.
RIGHT? SATEN-SAN?
UH...
ISN'T TOKIWADAI A SCHOOL FOR *ELEGANT LADIES?*
I MEAN, LIKE... AN ALL-GIRLS SCHOOL?
EVEN YOUR TEACHERS ARE WOMEN, RIGHT?
FOR *TOKIWADAI* TO HAVE A LEGEND LIKE THAT...
OH!
—?!!
"GENDER DOESN'T MATTER WHEN IT COMES TO LOVE."
AAAA AAAH!
"HOKAZE-SAMA, NOT FAIR! DON'T TELL ME THAT YOU AND THE QUEEN...?!"

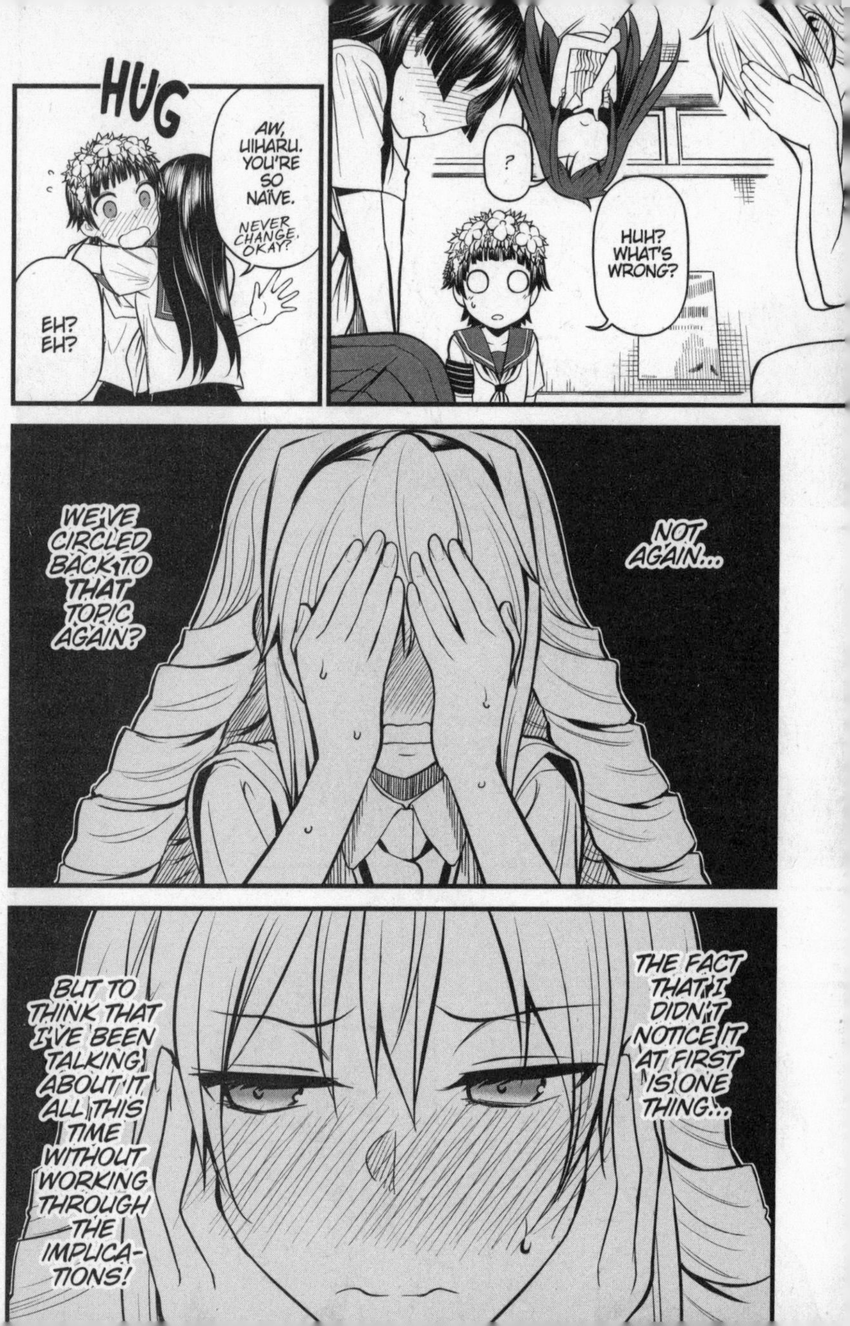
?
HUH? WHAT'S WRONG?
HUG
AW, UIHARU. YOU'RE SO NAÏVE.
NEVER CHANGE, OKAY?
EH? EH?
NOT AGAIN...
WE'VE CIRCLED BACK TO THAT TOPIC AGAIN?
THE FACT THAT I DIDN'T NOTICE IT AT FIRST IS ONE THING...
BUT TO THINK THAT I'VE BEEN TALKING ABOUT IT ALL THIS TIME WITHOUT WORKING THROUGH THE IMPLICATIONS!

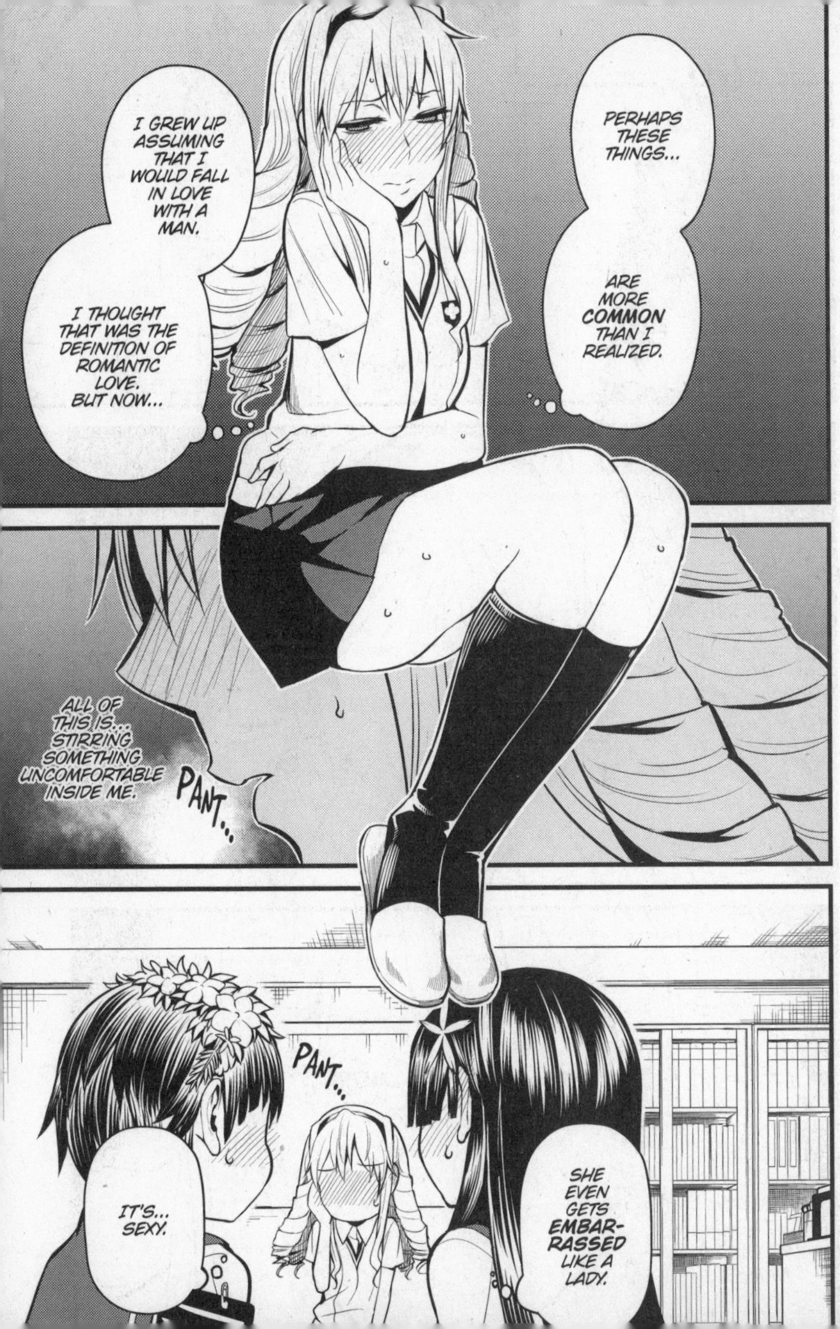
PERHAPS THESE THINGS...
ARE MORE COMMON THAN I REALIZED.
I GREW UP ASSUMING THAT I WOULD FALL IN LOVE WITH A MAN.
I THOUGHT THAT WAS THE DEFINITION OF ROMANTIC LOVE. BUT NOW...
PANT...
ALL OF THIS IS... STIRRING SOMETHING UNCOMFORTABLE INSIDE ME.
PANT...
SHE EVEN GETS EMBARRASSED LIKE A LADY.
IT'S... SEXY.

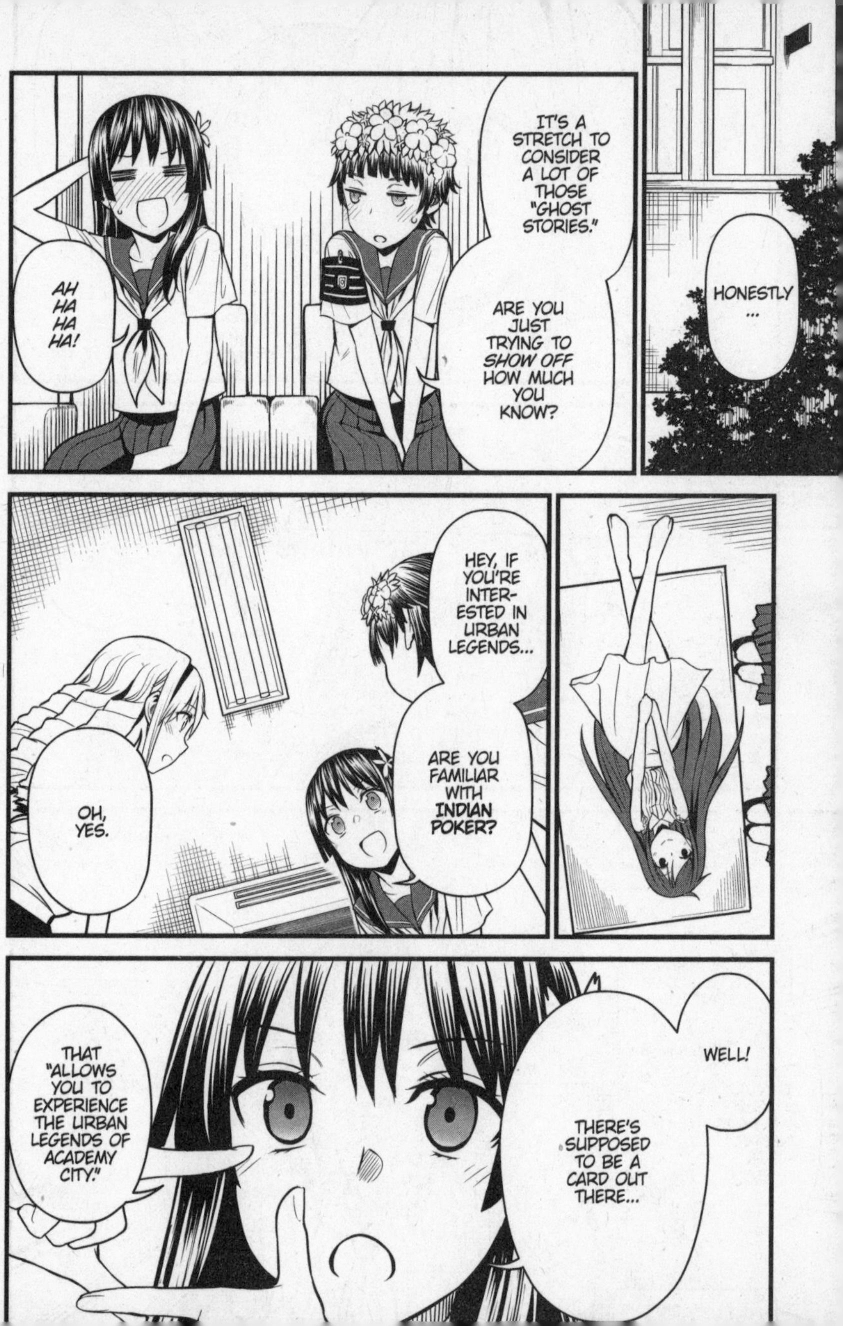
HONESTLY ...
IT'S A STRETCH TO CONSIDER A LOT OF THOSE "GHOST STORIES."
ARE YOU JUST TRYING TO SHOW OFF HOW MUCH YOU KNOW?
AH HA HA HA!
HEY, IF YOU'RE INTER-ESTED IN URBAN LEGENDS...
ARE YOU FAMILIAR WITH INDIAN POKER?
OH, YES.
WELL!
THERE'S SUPPOSED TO BE A CARD OUT THERE...
THAT "ALLOWS YOU TO EXPERIENCE THE URBAN LEGENDS OF ACADEMY CITY."

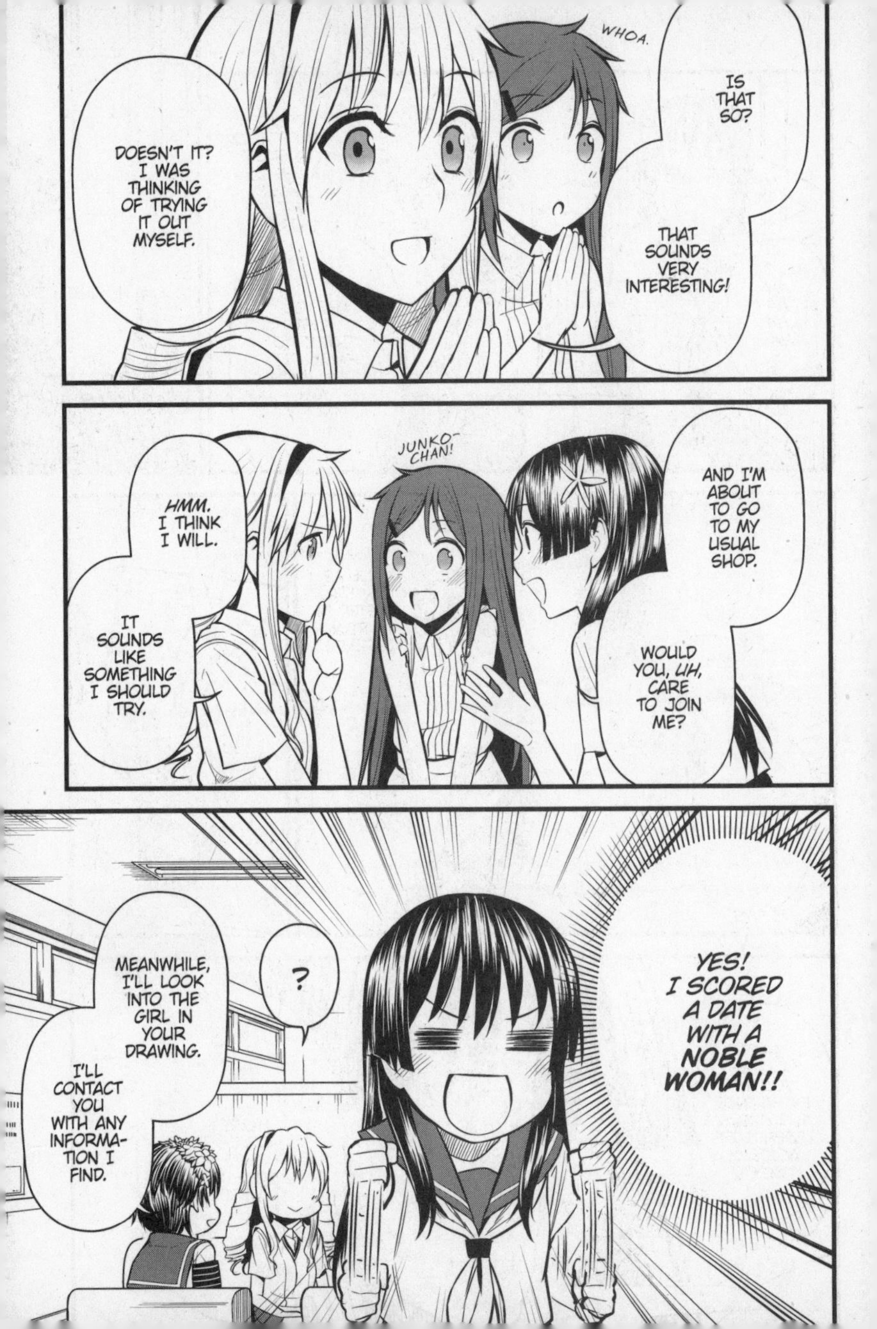
WHOA.
IS THAT SO?
THAT SOUNDS VERY INTERESTING!
DOESN'T IT? I WAS THINKING OF TRYING IT OUT MYSELF.
AND I'M ABOUT TO GO TO MY USUAL SHOP.
WOULD YOU, *UH*, CARE TO JOIN ME?
JUNKO-CHAN!
HMM. I THINK I WILL.
IT SOUNDS LIKE SOMETHING I SHOULD TRY.
YES! I SCORED A DATE WITH A **NOBLE WOMAN!!**
?
MEANWHILE, I'LL LOOK INTO THE GIRL IN YOUR DRAWING.
I'LL CONTACT YOU WITH ANY INFORMATION I FIND.

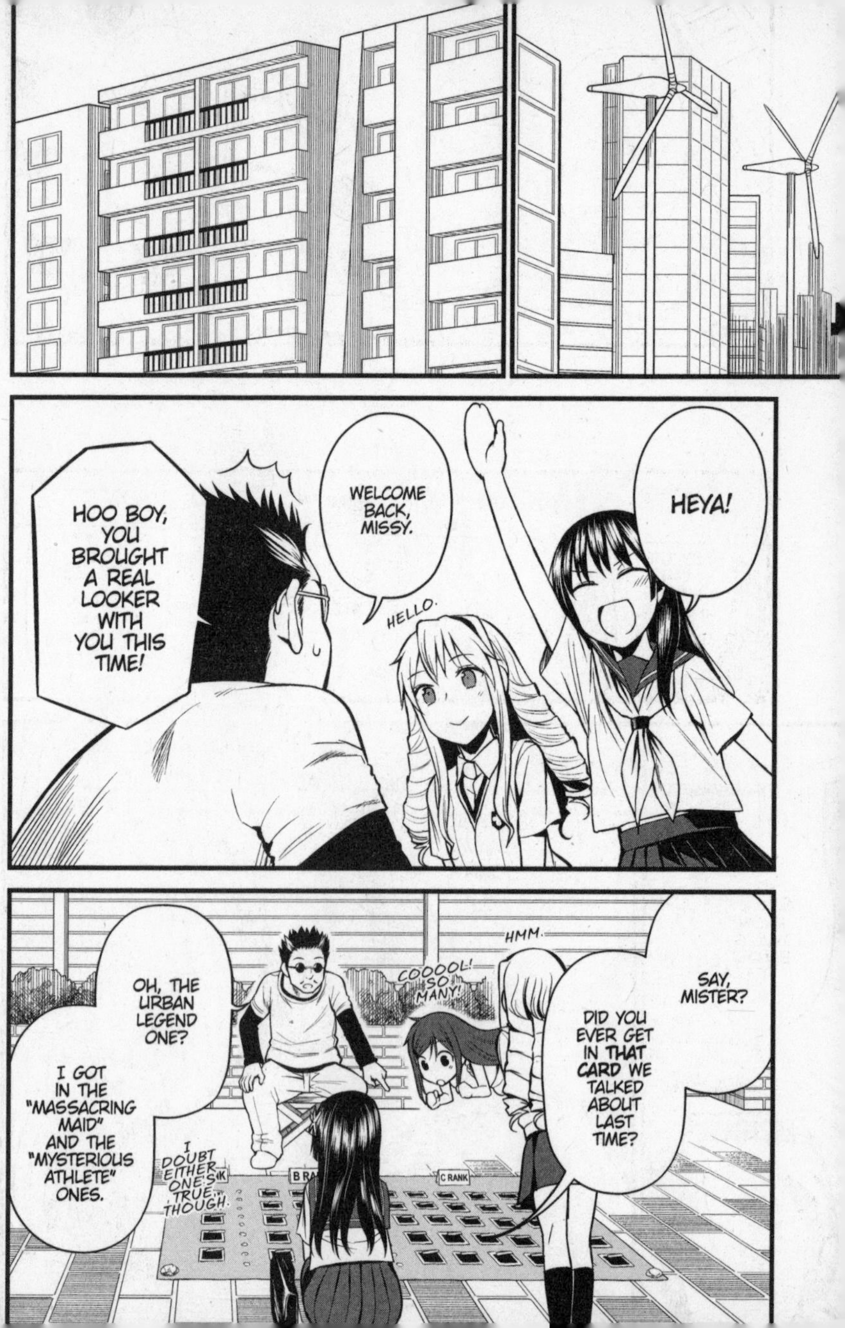
HEYA!
HELLO.
WELCOME BACK, MISSY.
HOO BOY, YOU BROUGHT A REAL LOOKER WITH YOU THIS TIME!
SAY, MISTER?
DID YOU EVER GET IN THAT CARD WE TALKED ABOUT LAST TIME?
HMM.
COOOOL! SO MANY!
C RANK
B RANK
OH, THE URBAN LEGEND ONE?
I GOT IN THE "MASSACRING MAID" AND THE "MYSTERIOUS ATHLETE" ONES.
I DOUBT EITHER ONE'S TRUE, THOUGH.

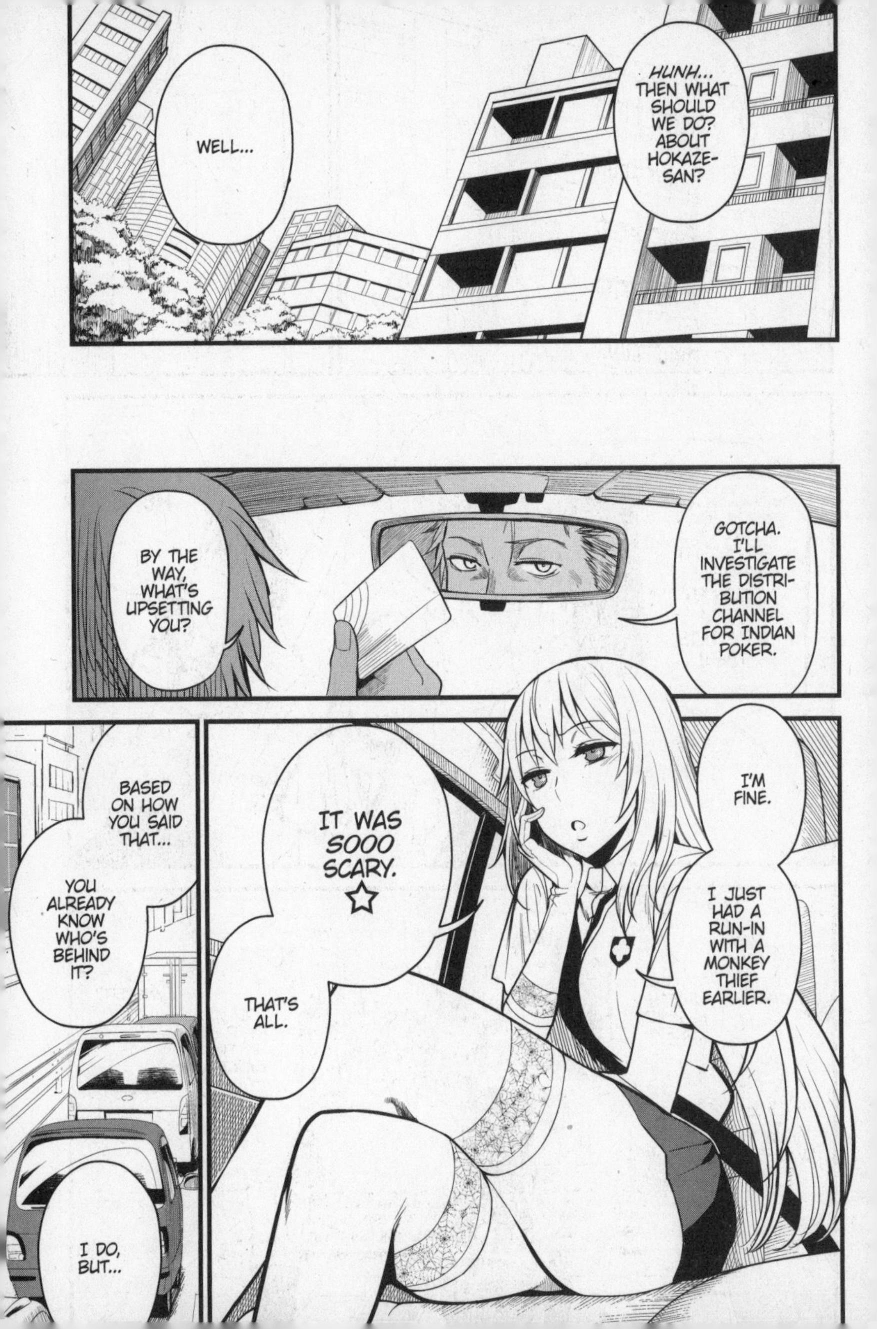
HUNH... THEN WHAT SHOULD WE DO? ABOUT HOKAZE-SAN?
WELL...
GOTCHA. I'LL INVESTIGATE THE DISTRIBUTION CHANNEL FOR INDIAN POKER.
BY THE WAY, WHAT'S UPSETTING YOU?
I'M FINE.
I JUST HAD A RUN-IN WITH A MONKEY THIEF EARLIER.
IT WAS SOOO SCARY. ☆
THAT'S ALL.
BASED ON HOW YOU SAID THAT...
YOU ALREADY KNOW WHO'S BEHIND IT?
I DO, BUT...

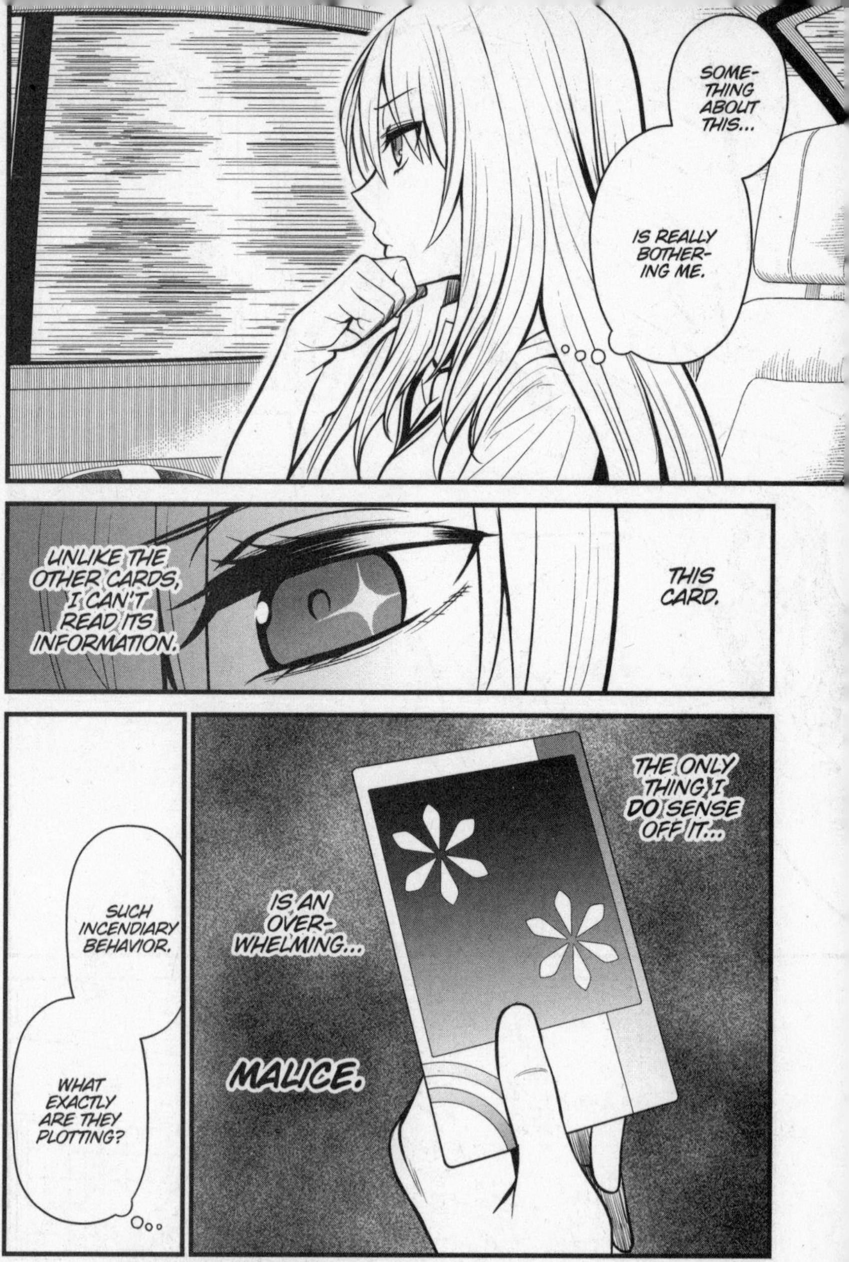
SOMETHING ABOUT THIS...
IS REALLY BOTHERING ME.
THIS CARD.
UNLIKE THE OTHER CARDS, I CAN'T READ ITS INFORMATION.
THE ONLY THING I DO SENSE OFF IT...
IS AN OVERWHELMING...
MALICE.
SUCH INCENDIARY BEHAVIOR.
WHAT EXACTLY ARE THEY PLOTTING?

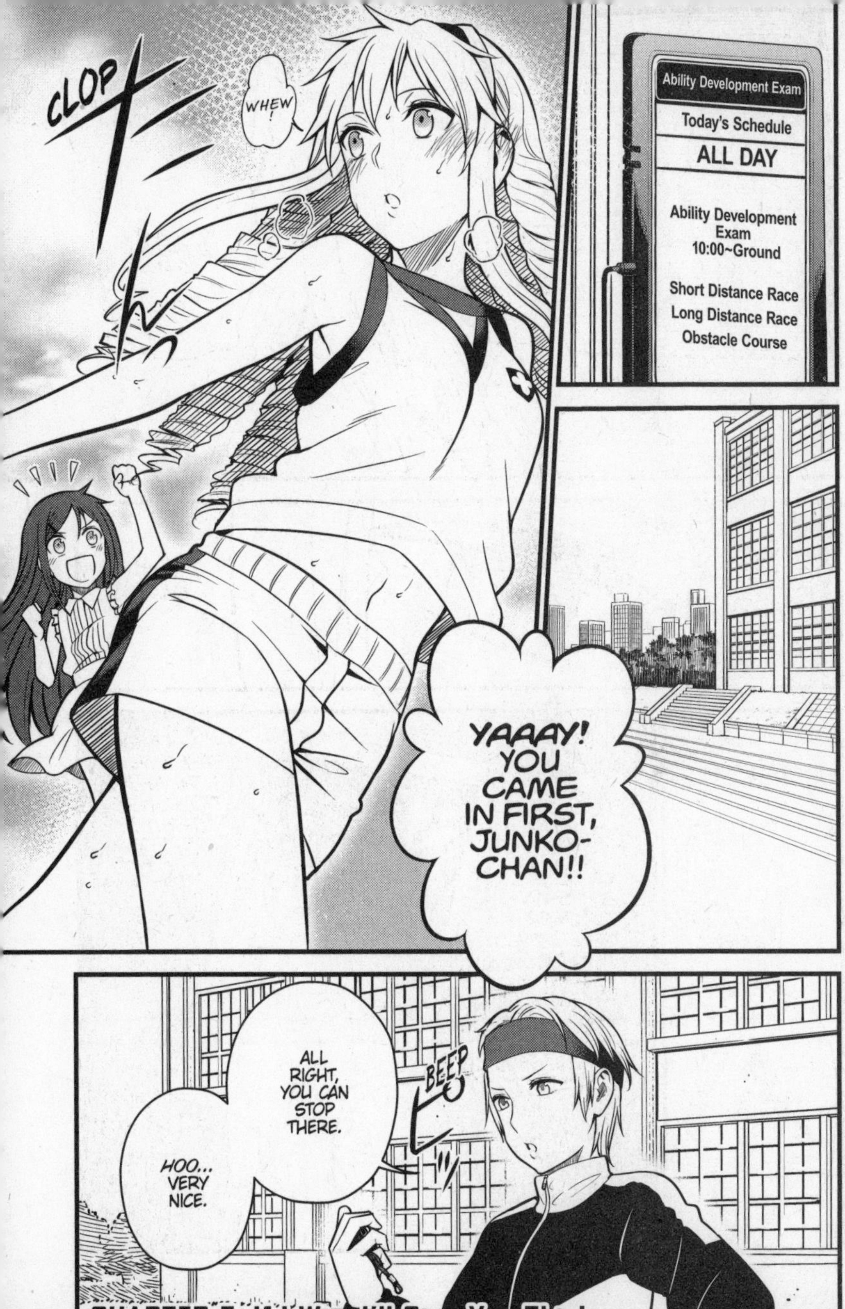
Ability Development Exam
Today's Schedule
ALL DAY
Ability Development Exam 10:00~Ground
Short Distance Race
Long Distance Race
Obstacle Course
CLOP
WHEW!
YAAAY! YOU CAME IN FIRST, JUNKO-CHAN!!
BEEP
ALL RIGHT, YOU CAN STOP THERE.
HOO... VERY NICE.

CHAPTER 5: If I Win, I'll Give You This!

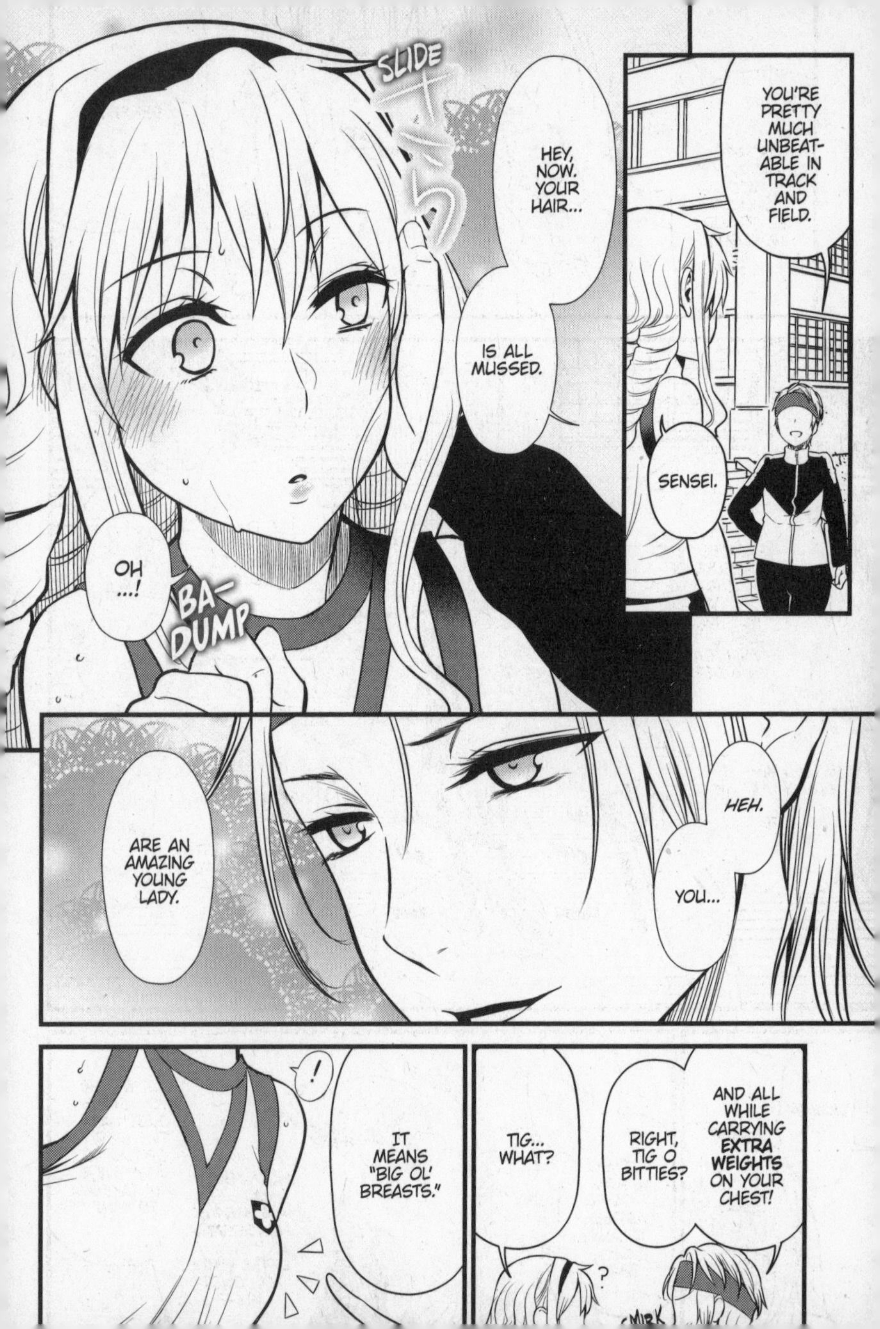

YOU'RE PRETTY MUCH UNBEAT-ABLE IN TRACK AND FIELD.
SENSEI.
HEY, NOW. YOUR HAIR...
IS ALL MUSSED.
SLIDE
OH ...!
BA-DUMP
HEH.
YOU...
ARE AN AMAZING YOUNG LADY.
AND ALL WHILE CARRYING **EXTRA WEIGHTS** ON YOUR CHEST!
RIGHT, TIG O BITTIES?
TIG... WHAT?
?
!
IT MEANS "BIG OL' BREASTS."

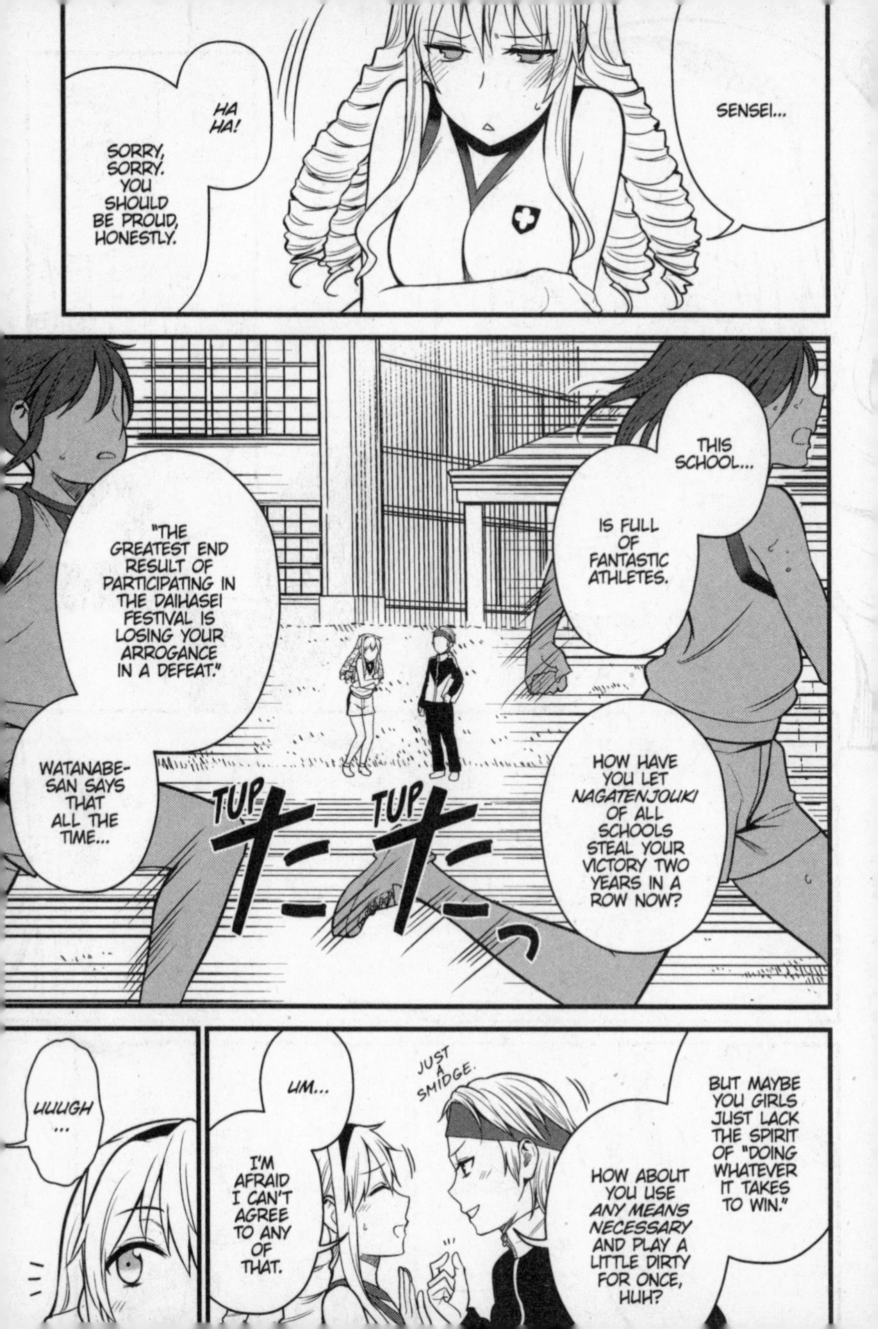
SENSEI...
HA HA!
SORRY, SORRY. YOU SHOULD BE PROUD, HONESTLY.
THIS SCHOOL...
IS FULL OF FANTASTIC ATHLETES.
HOW HAVE YOU LET *NAGATENJOUKI* OF ALL SCHOOLS STEAL YOUR VICTORY TWO YEARS IN A ROW NOW?
"THE GREATEST END RESULT OF PARTICIPATING IN THE DAIHASEI FESTIVAL IS LOSING YOUR ARROGANCE IN A DEFEAT."
WATANABE-SAN SAYS THAT ALL THE TIME...
TUP
TUP
BUT MAYBE YOU GIRLS JUST LACK THE SPIRIT OF "DOING WHATEVER IT TAKES TO WIN."
HOW ABOUT YOU USE *ANY MEANS NECESSARY* AND PLAY A LITTLE DIRTY FOR ONCE, HUH?
JUST A SMIDGE.
UM...
I'M AFRAID I CAN'T AGREE TO ANY OF THAT.
UUUGH...

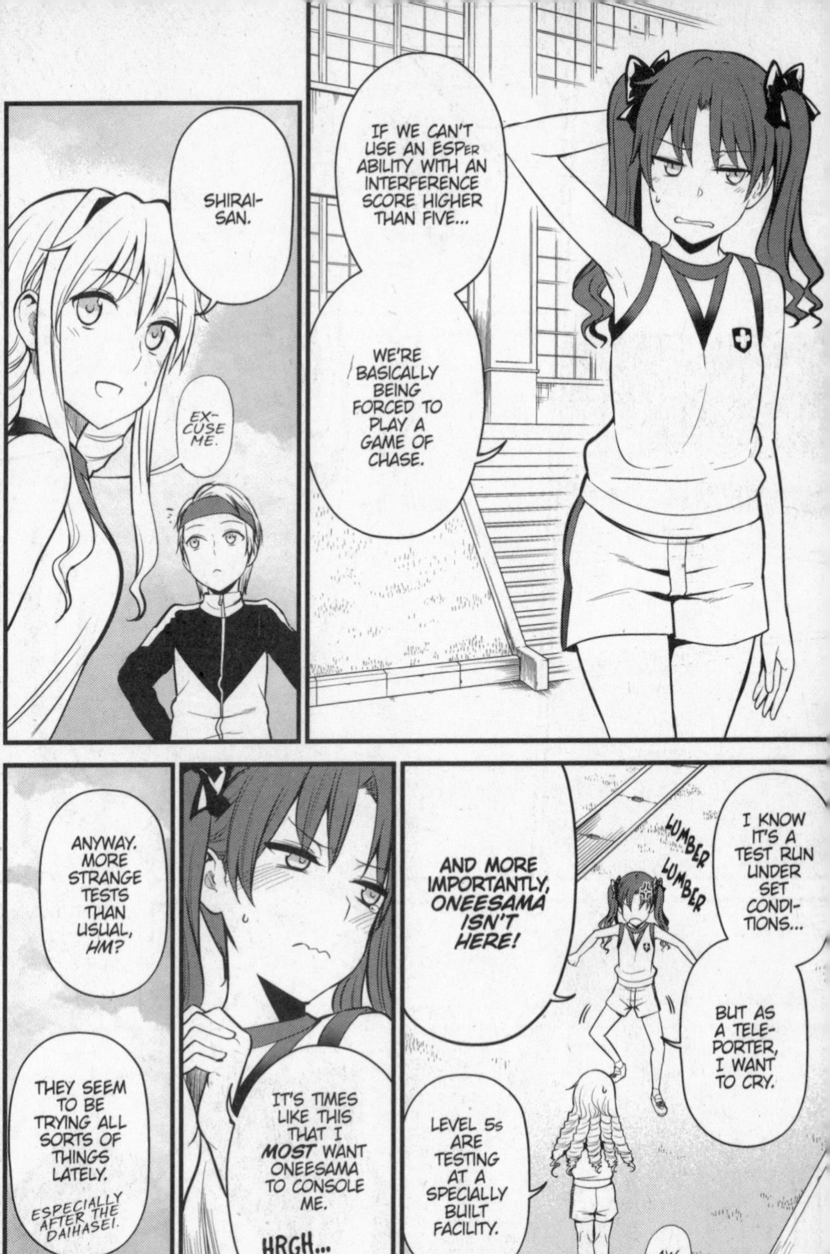

IF WE CAN'T USE AN ESPer ABILITY WITH AN INTERFERENCE SCORE HIGHER THAN FIVE...
WE'RE BASICALLY BEING FORCED TO PLAY A GAME OF CHASE.
SHIRAI-SAN.
EX-CUSE ME.
I KNOW IT'S A TEST RUN UNDER SET CONDITIONS...
BUT AS A TELE-PORTER, I WANT TO CRY.
LUMBER LUMBER
AND MORE IMPORTANTLY, *ONEESAMA ISN'T HERE!*
LEVEL 5s ARE TESTING AT A SPECIALLY BUILT FACILITY.
AW, TOO HARD?
IT'S TIMES LIKE THIS THAT I *MOST* WANT ONEESAMA TO CONSOLE ME.
HRGH...
ANYWAY. MORE STRANGE TESTS THAN USUAL, *HM?*
THEY SEEM TO BE TRYING ALL SORTS OF THINGS LATELY.
ESPECIALLY AFTER THE DAIHASEI.

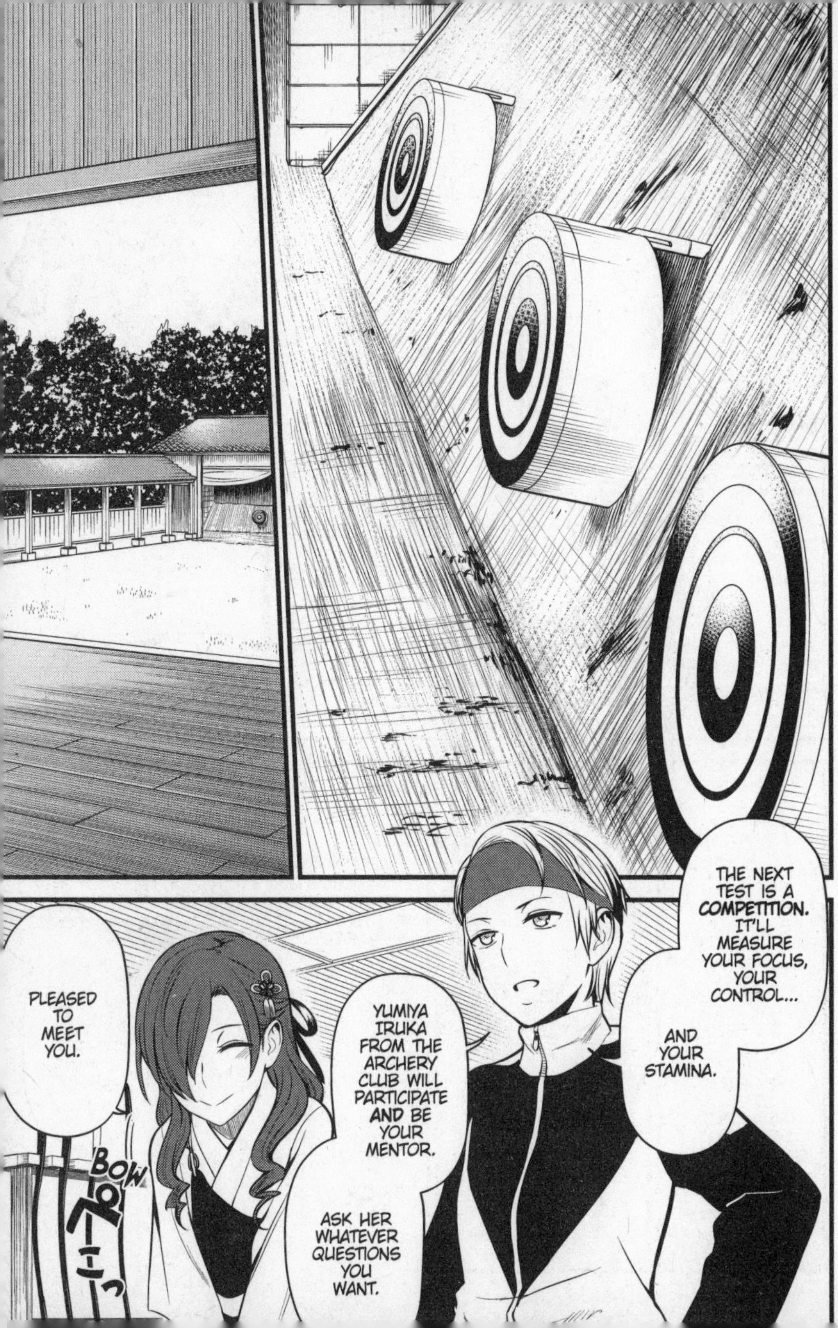
THE NEXT TEST IS A COMPETITION. IT'LL MEASURE YOUR FOCUS, YOUR CONTROL...
AND YOUR STAMINA.
YUMIYA IRUKA FROM THE ARCHERY CLUB WILL PARTICIPATE AND BE YOUR MENTOR.
ASK HER WHATEVER QUESTIONS YOU WANT.
PLEASED TO MEET YOU.
BOW

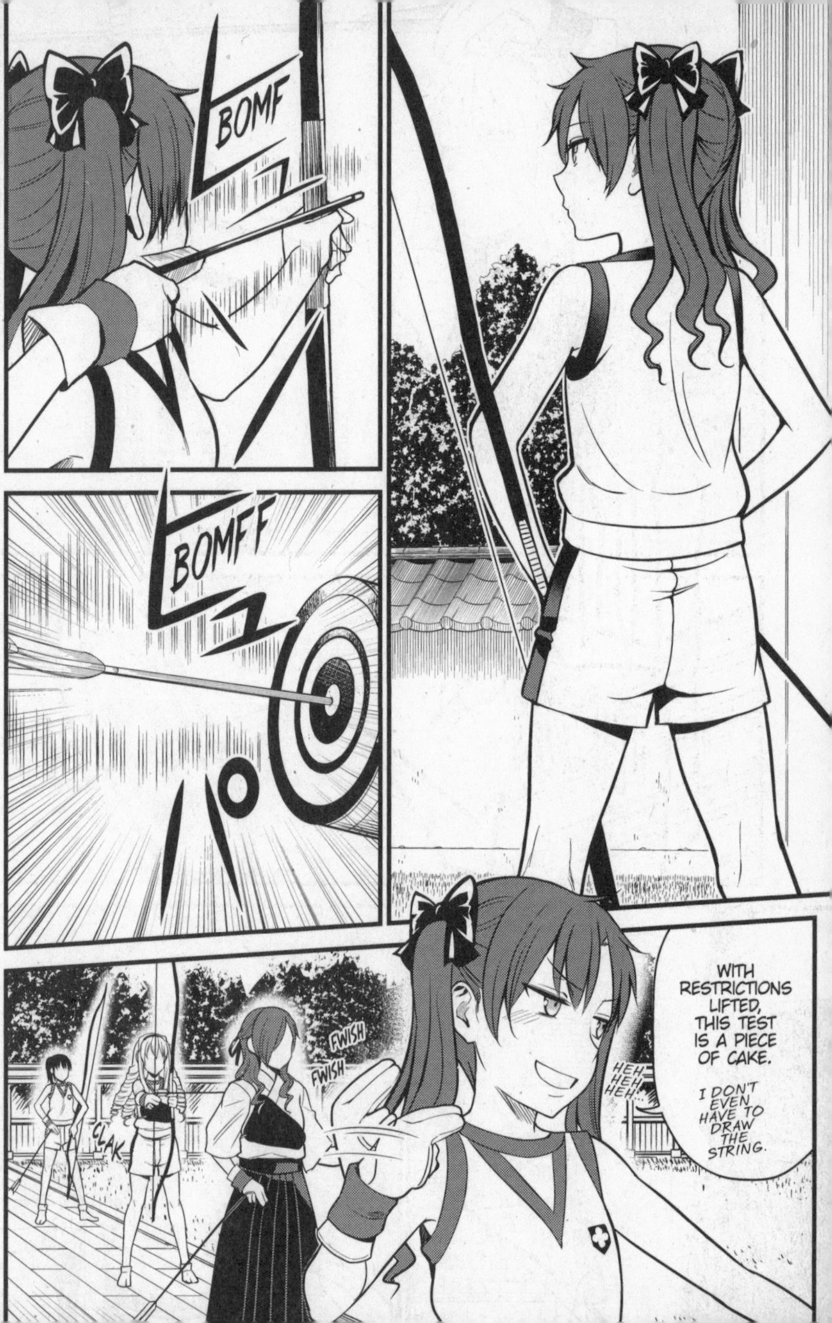
BOMF
BOMFF
WITH RESTRICTIONS LIFTED, THIS TEST IS A PIECE OF CAKE.
I DON'T EVEN HAVE TO DRAW THE STRING.
HEH HEH HEH...
FWISH
FWISH
CLAK

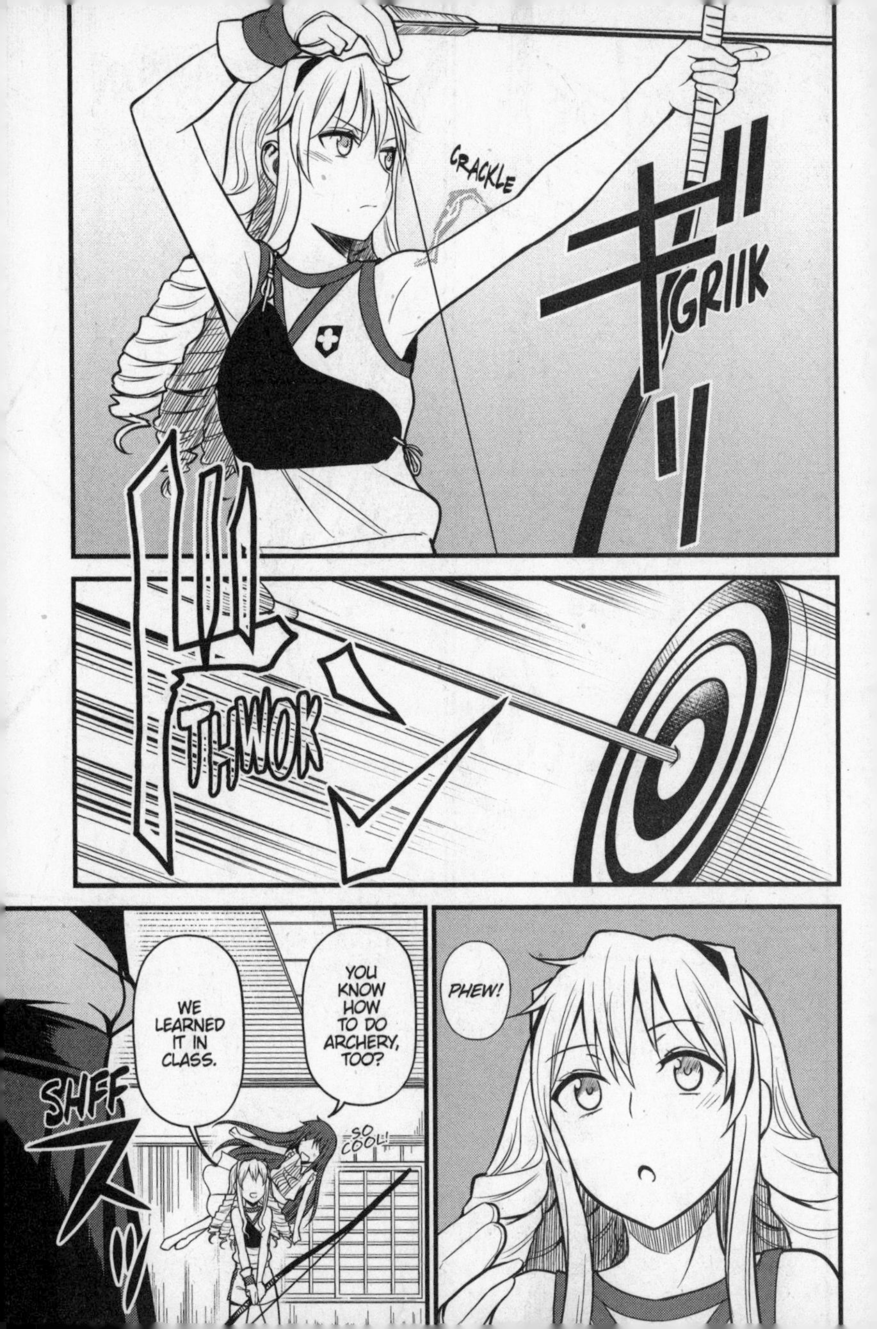
CRACKLE
GRIIK
THWOK
PHEW!
YOU KNOW HOW TO DO ARCHERY, TOO?
SO COOL!!
WE LEARNED IT IN CLASS.
SHFF

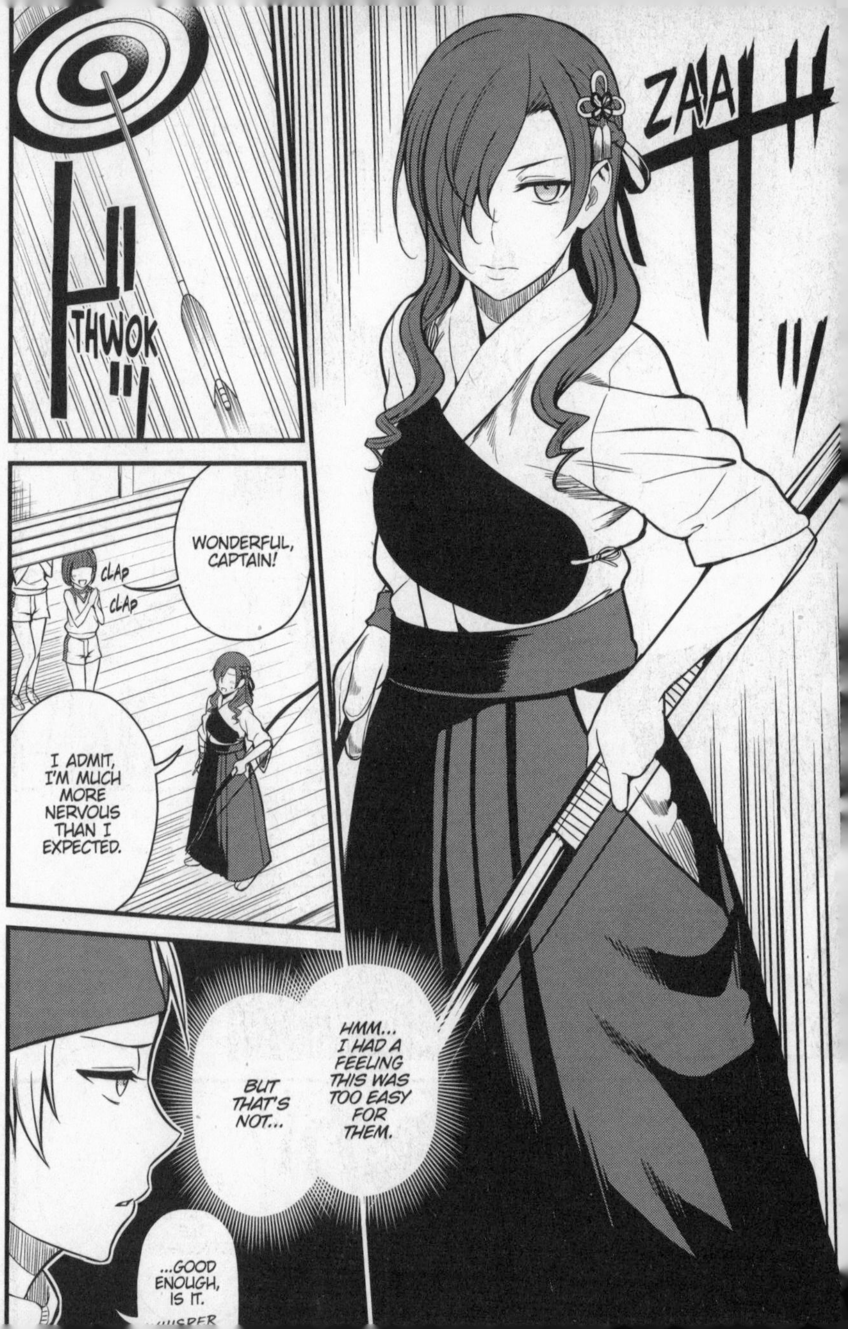
ZAAHH
THWOK
WONDERFUL, CAPTAIN!
CLAP
CLAP
I ADMIT, I'M MUCH MORE NERVOUS THAN I EXPECTED.
HMM... I HAD A FEELING THIS WAS TOO EASY FOR THEM.
BUT THAT'S NOT...
...GOOD ENOUGH, IS IT.

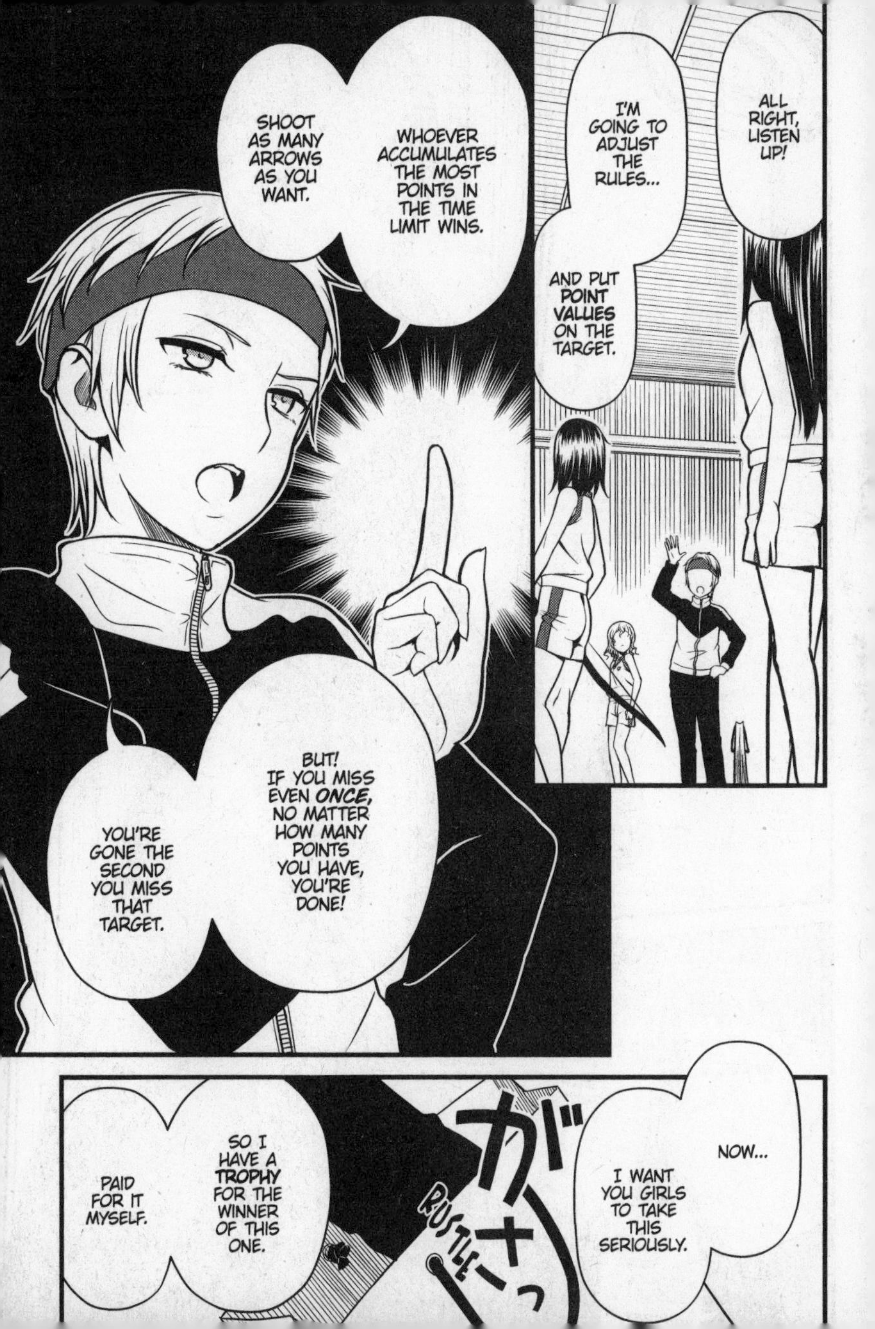
ALL RIGHT, LISTEN UP!
I'M GOING TO ADJUST THE RULES...
AND PUT POINT VALUES ON THE TARGET.
WHOEVER ACCUMULATES THE MOST POINTS IN THE TIME LIMIT WINS.
SHOOT AS MANY ARROWS AS YOU WANT.
BUT! IF YOU MISS EVEN ONCE, NO MATTER HOW MANY POINTS YOU HAVE, YOU'RE DONE!
YOU'RE GONE THE SECOND YOU MISS THAT TARGET.
NOW...
I WANT YOU GIRLS TO TAKE THIS SERIOUSLY.
がさっ
RUSTLE—
SO I HAVE A TROPHY FOR THE WINNER OF THIS ONE.
PAID FOR IT MYSELF.

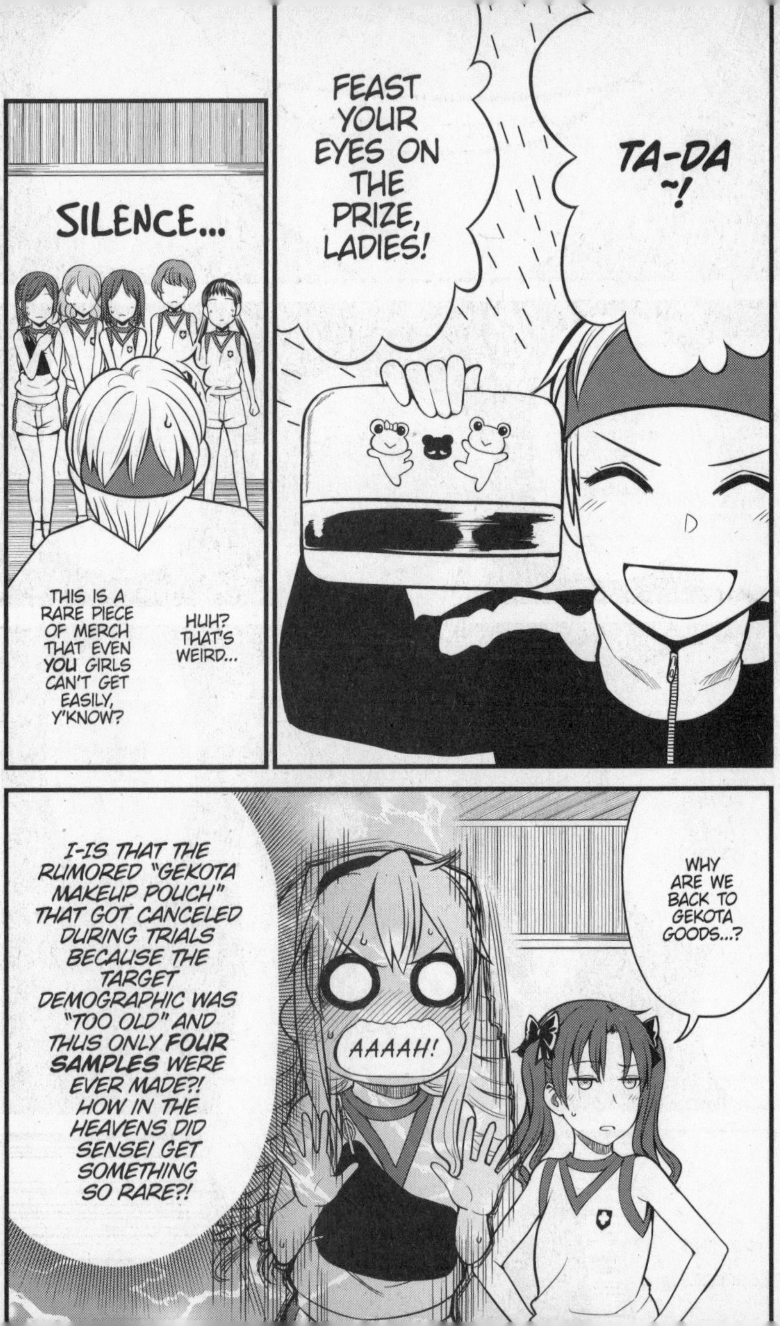
TA-DA ~!
FEAST YOUR EYES ON THE PRIZE, LADIES!
SILENCE...
HUH? THAT'S WEIRD...
THIS IS A RARE PIECE OF MERCH THAT EVEN **YOU** GIRLS CAN'T GET EASILY, Y'KNOW?
WHY ARE WE BACK TO GEKOTA GOODS...?
AAAAH!
I-IS THAT THE RUMORED "GEKOTA MAKEUP POUCH" THAT GOT CANCELED DURING TRIALS BECAUSE THE TARGET DEMOGRAPHIC WAS "TOO OLD" AND THUS ONLY **FOUR SAMPLES** WERE EVER MADE?! HOW IN THE HEAVENS DID SENSEI GET SOMETHING SO RARE?!

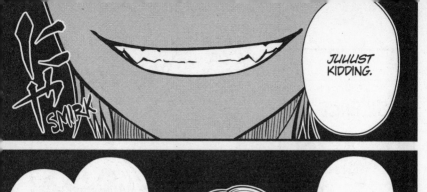

SMIRK

JUUUST KIDDING.

I KNEW I'D GET A RESPONSE LIKE THAT.

FOR THOSE IN THE KNOW, THIS IS EXTREMELY VALUABLE...

BUT FOR THOSE WHO AREN'T, IT'S LIKE, "WHO CARES"?

LISTEN UP.

YOU'RE ABOUT TO LEARN THE TRUE POWER OF THIS LITTLE POUCH...

AND YOU WILL CARE.

IF YOU USE THIS THING CORRECTLY...

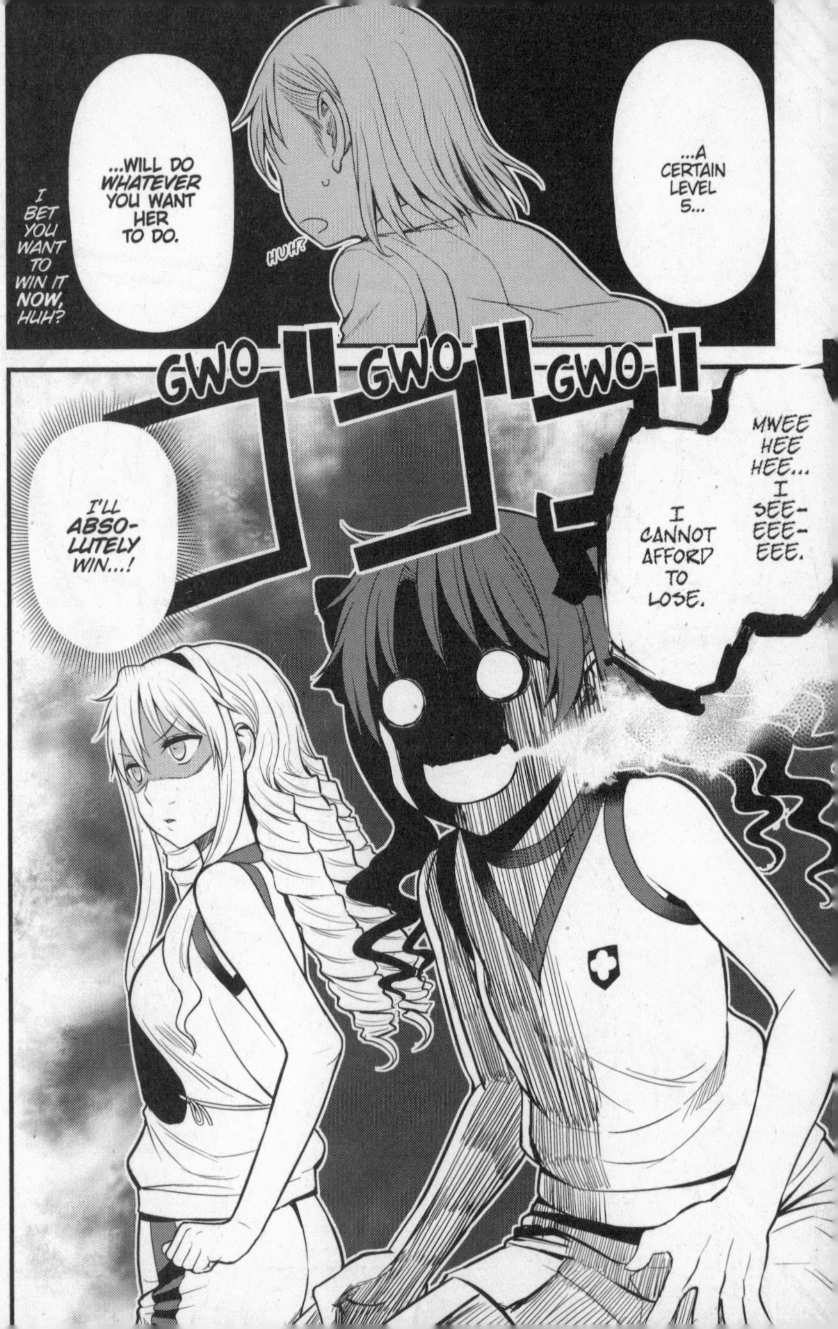
...A CERTAIN LEVEL 5...
...WILL DO WHATEVER YOU WANT HER TO DO.
HUH?
I BET YOU WANT TO WIN IT NOW, HUH?
GWO GWO GWO
MWEE HEE HEE... I SEE-EEE-EEE.
I CANNOT AFFORD TO LOSE.
I'LL ABSOLUTELY WIN...!

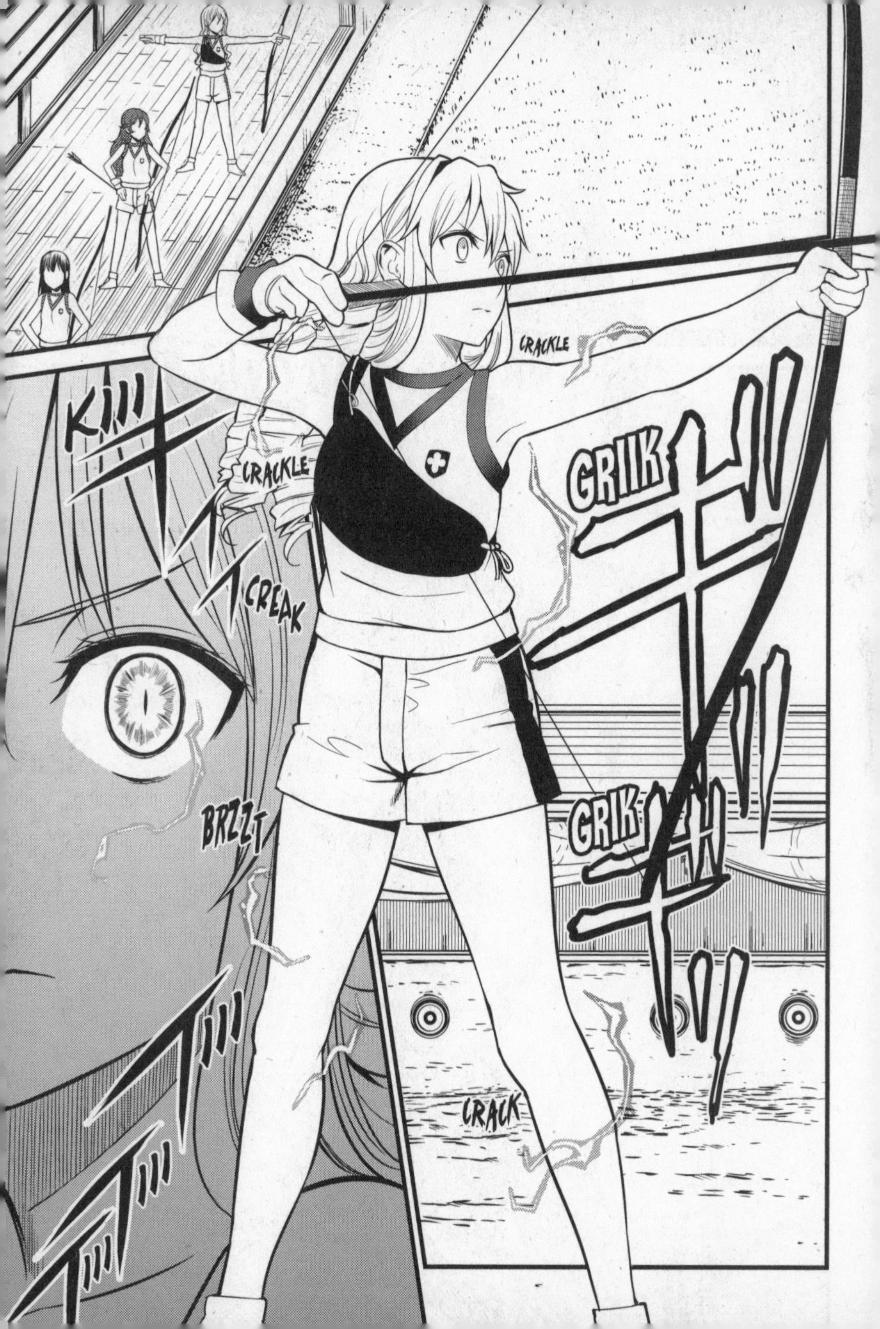
CRACKLE
KIII
CRACKLE
CREAK
GRIIK
BRZZT
GRIK
CRACK

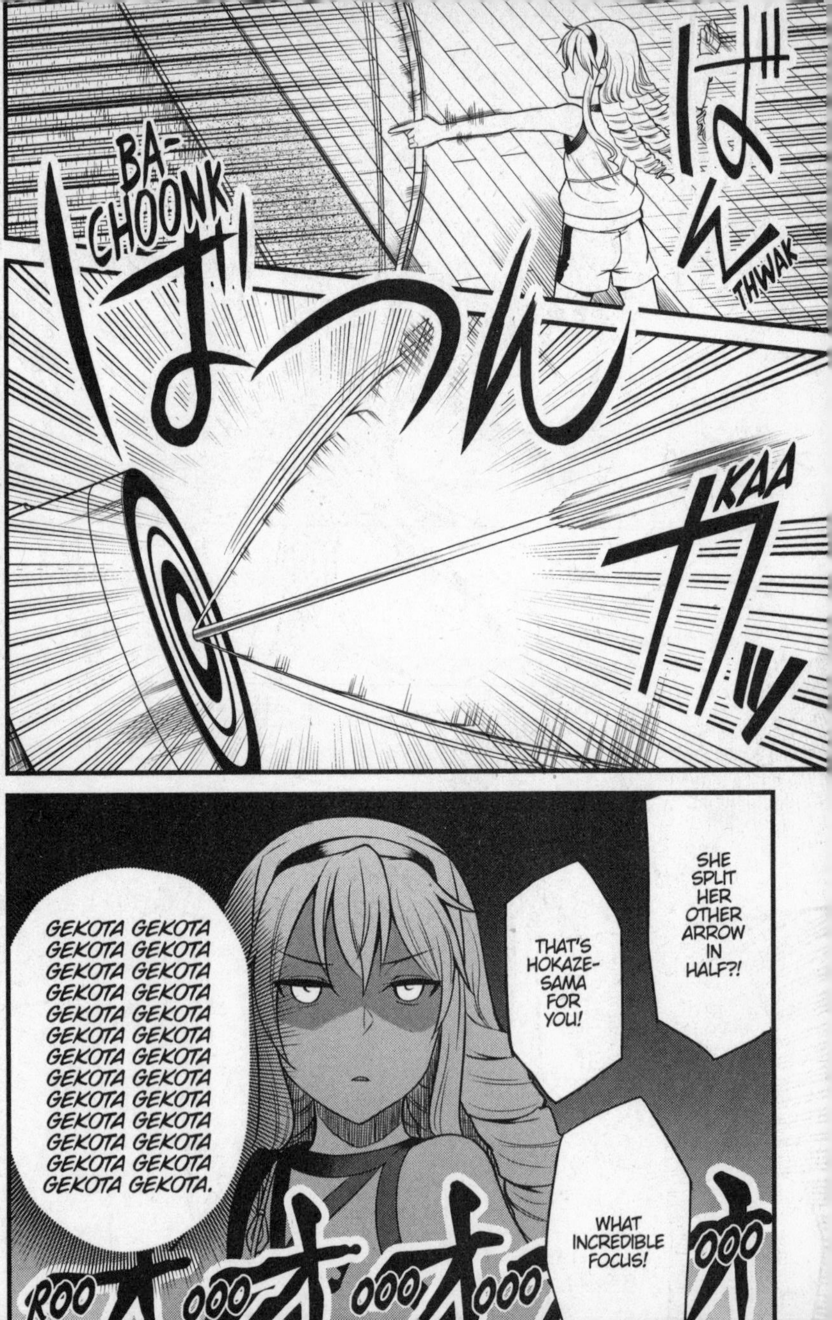
THWAK
BA-CHOONK
KAA
SHE SPLIT HER OTHER ARROW IN HALF?!
THAT'S HOKAZE-SAMA FOR YOU!
GEKOTA GEKOTA.
WHAT INCREDIBLE FOCUS!
ROO OOO OOO OOO OOO

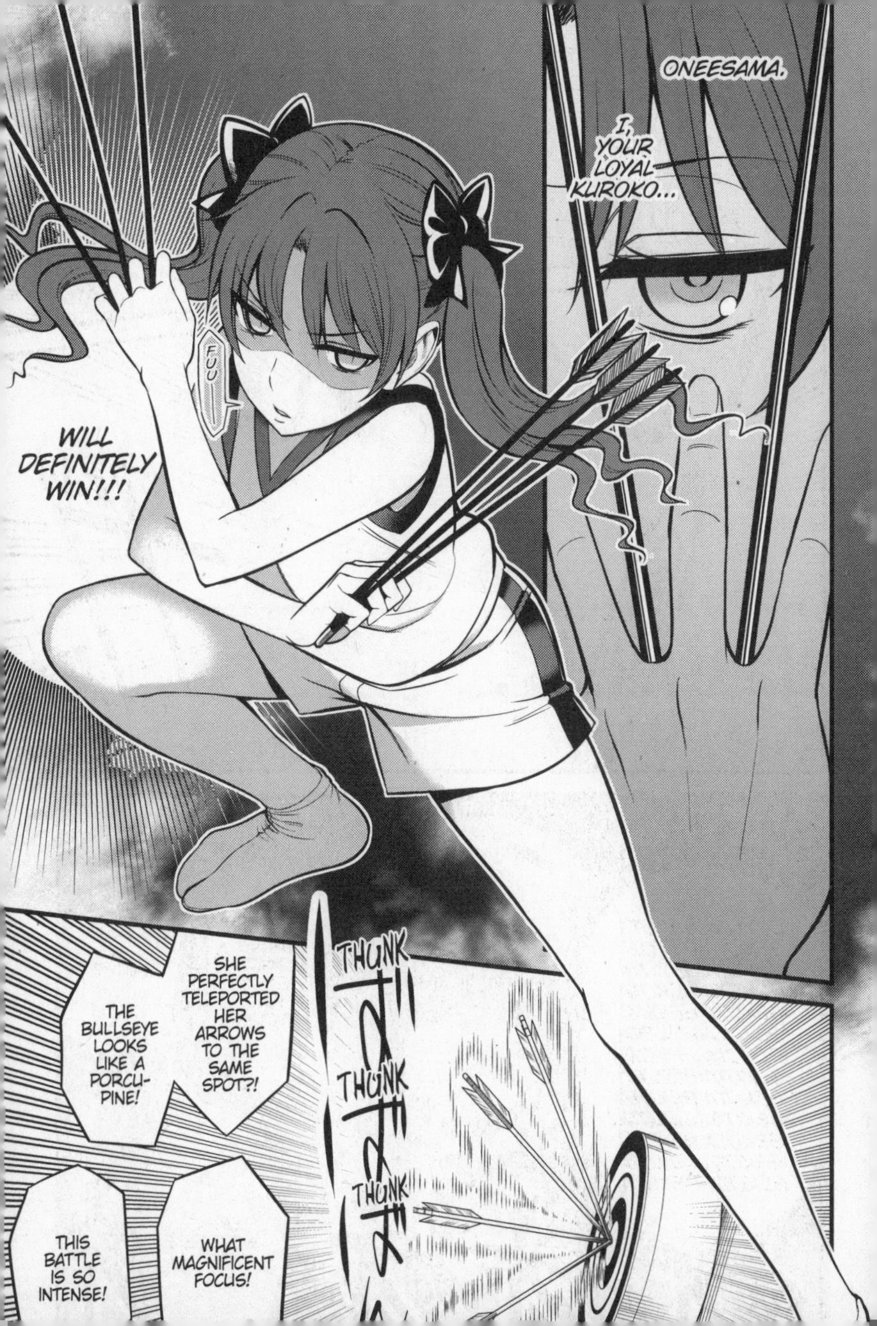
ONEESAMA.
I, YOUR LOYAL KUROKO...
FUU
WILL DEFINITELY WIN!!!
THUNK
THUNK
THUNK
SHE PERFECTLY TELEPORTED HER ARROWS TO THE SAME SPOT?!
THE BULLSEYE LOOKS LIKE A PORCU-PINE!
WHAT MAGNIFICENT FOCUS!
THIS BATTLE IS SO INTENSE!

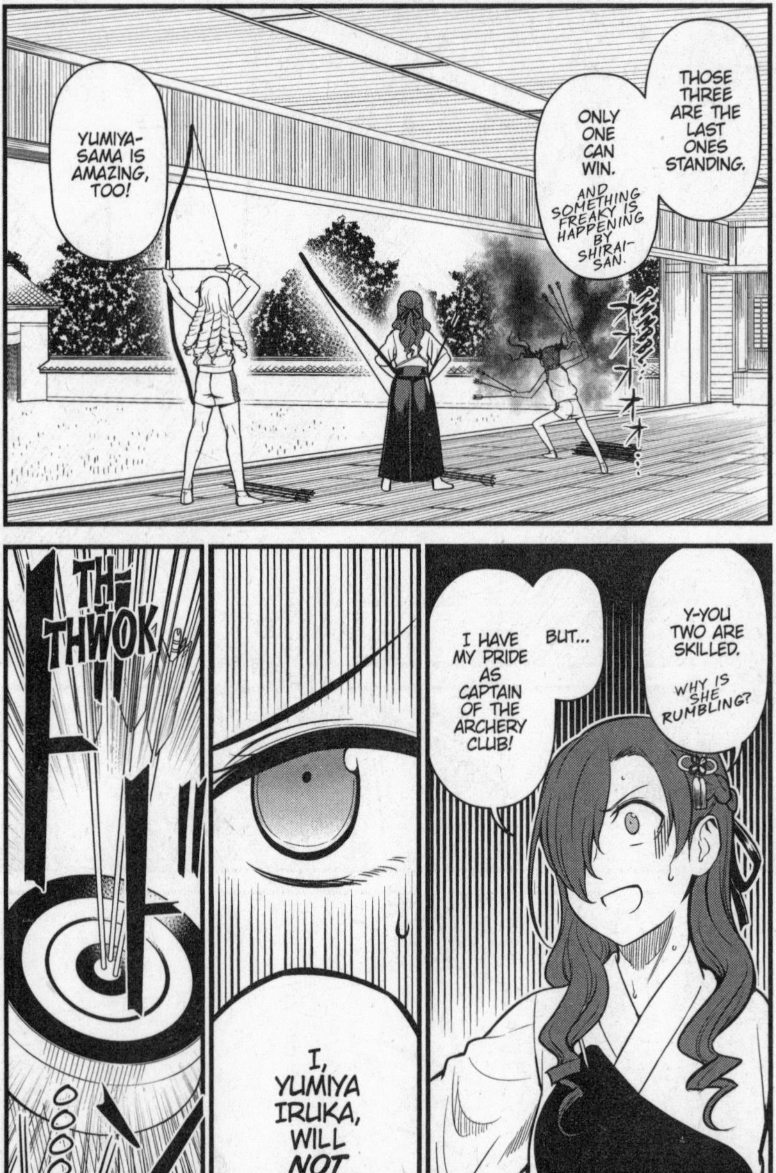
THOSE THREE ARE THE LAST ONES STANDING.
ONLY ONE CAN WIN.
AND SOMETHING FREAKY IS HAPPENING BY SHIRAI-SAN.
RMMBBL...
オオオオオ...
YUMIYA-SAMA IS AMAZING, TOO!
Y-YOU TWO ARE SKILLED.
WHY IS SHE RUMBLING?
BUT...
I HAVE MY PRIDE AS CAPTAIN OF THE ARCHERY CLUB!
I, YUMIYA IRUKA, WILL *NOT* LOSE!
TH-THWOK
OOOOOOOH

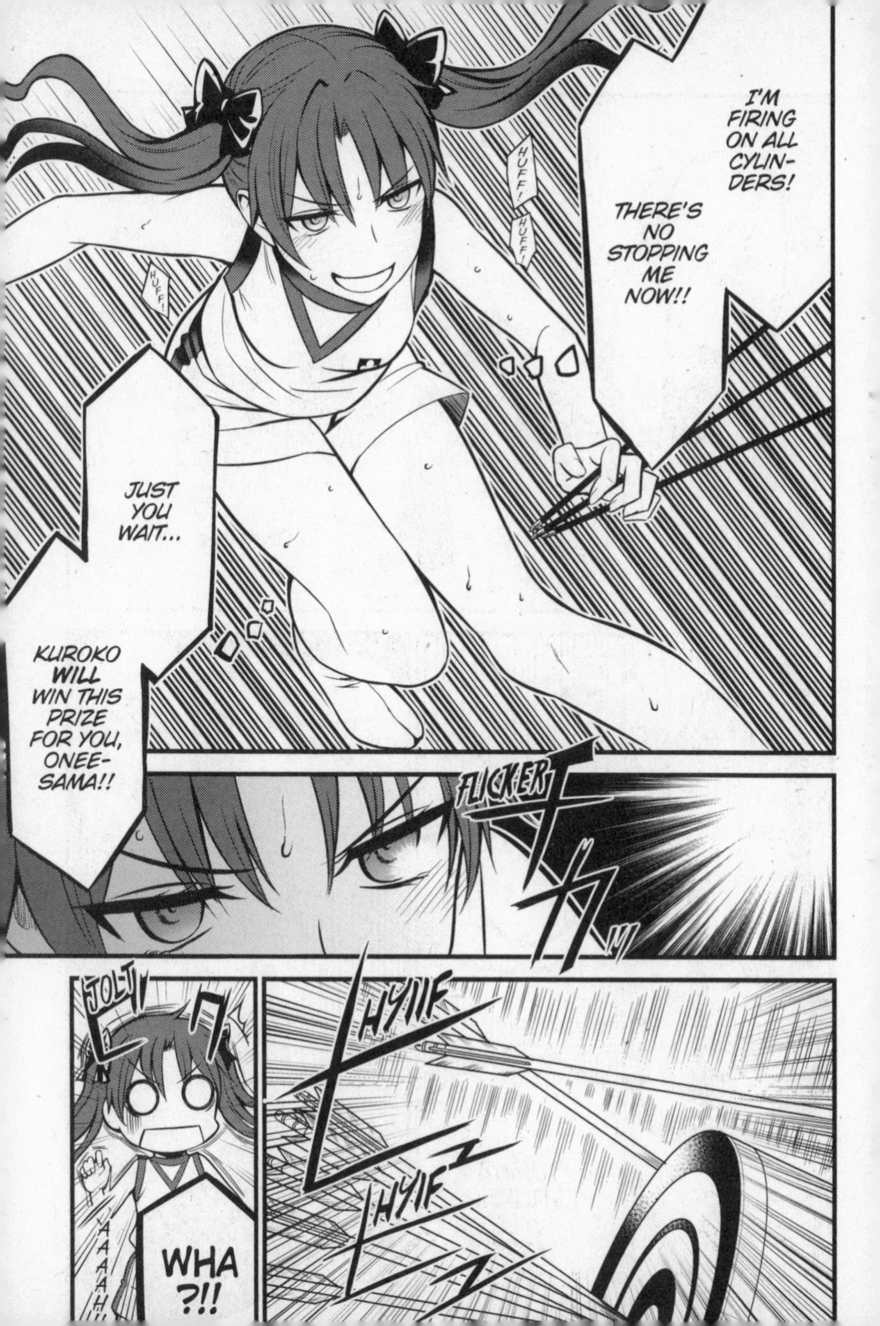
I'M FIRING ON ALL CYLIN-DERS!
HUFF! HUFF!
HUFF!
THERE'S NO STOPPING ME NOW!!
JUST YOU WAIT...
KUROKO WILL WIN THIS PRIZE FOR YOU, ONEE-SAMA!!
FLICKER
HYIIF
HYIF
JOLT
WHA ?!!
AAAAAH!

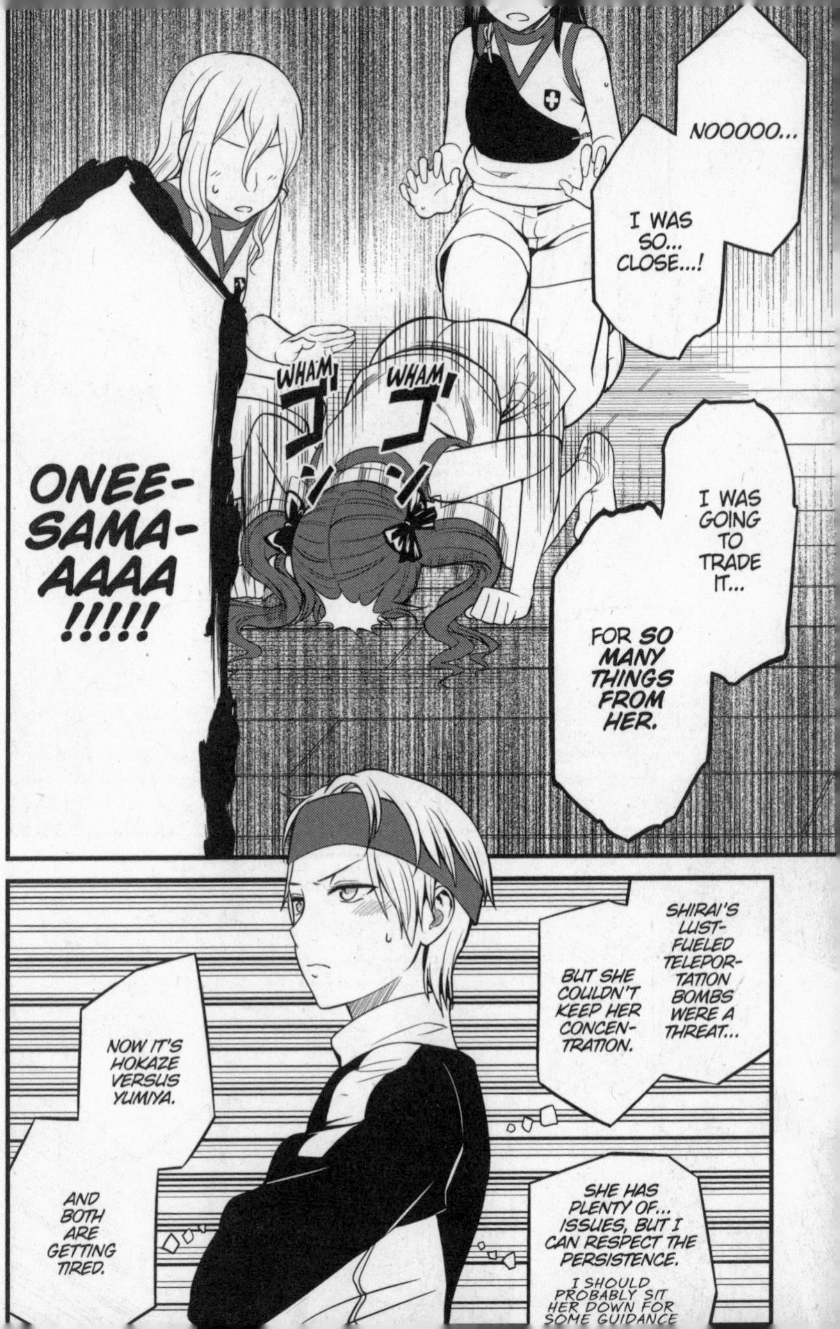
NOOOOO...
I WAS SO... CLOSE...!
WHAM
WHAM
I WAS GOING TO TRADE IT...
FOR SO MANY THINGS FROM HER.
ONEE-SAMA-AAAA!!!!!
SHIRAI'S LUST-FUELED TELEPORTATION BOMBS WERE A THREAT...
BUT SHE COULDN'T KEEP HER CONCENTRATION.
NOW IT'S HOKAZE VERSUS YUMIYA.
AND BOTH ARE GETTING TIRED.
SHE HAS PLENTY OF... ISSUES, BUT I CAN RESPECT THE PERSISTENCE.
I SHOULD PROBABLY SIT HER DOWN FOR SOME GUIDANCE

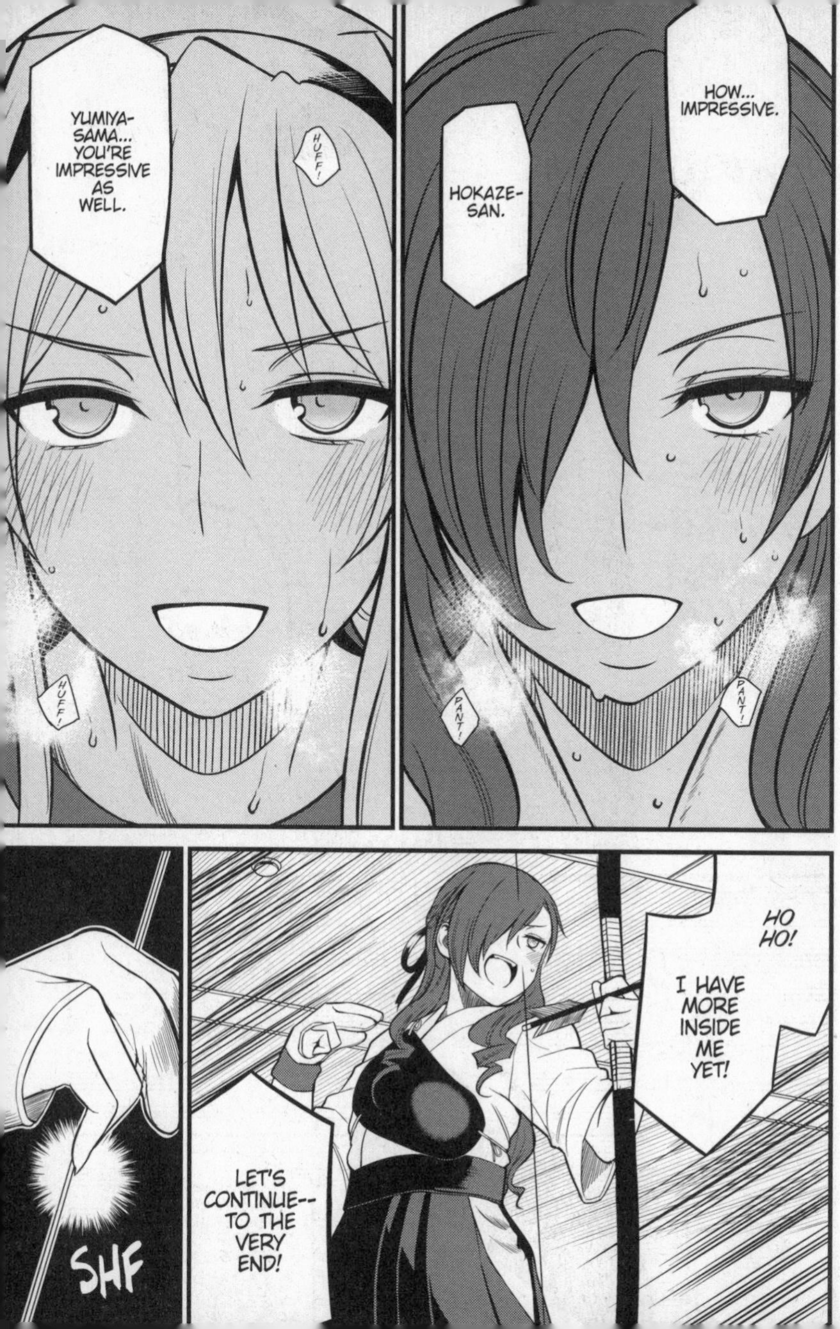
HOW... IMPRESSIVE.
HOKAZE-SAN.
PANT!
PANT!
YUMIYA-SAMA... YOU'RE IMPRESSIVE AS WELL.
HUFF!
HUFF!
HO HO!
I HAVE MORE INSIDE ME YET!
LET'S CONTINUE-- TO THE VERY END!
SHF

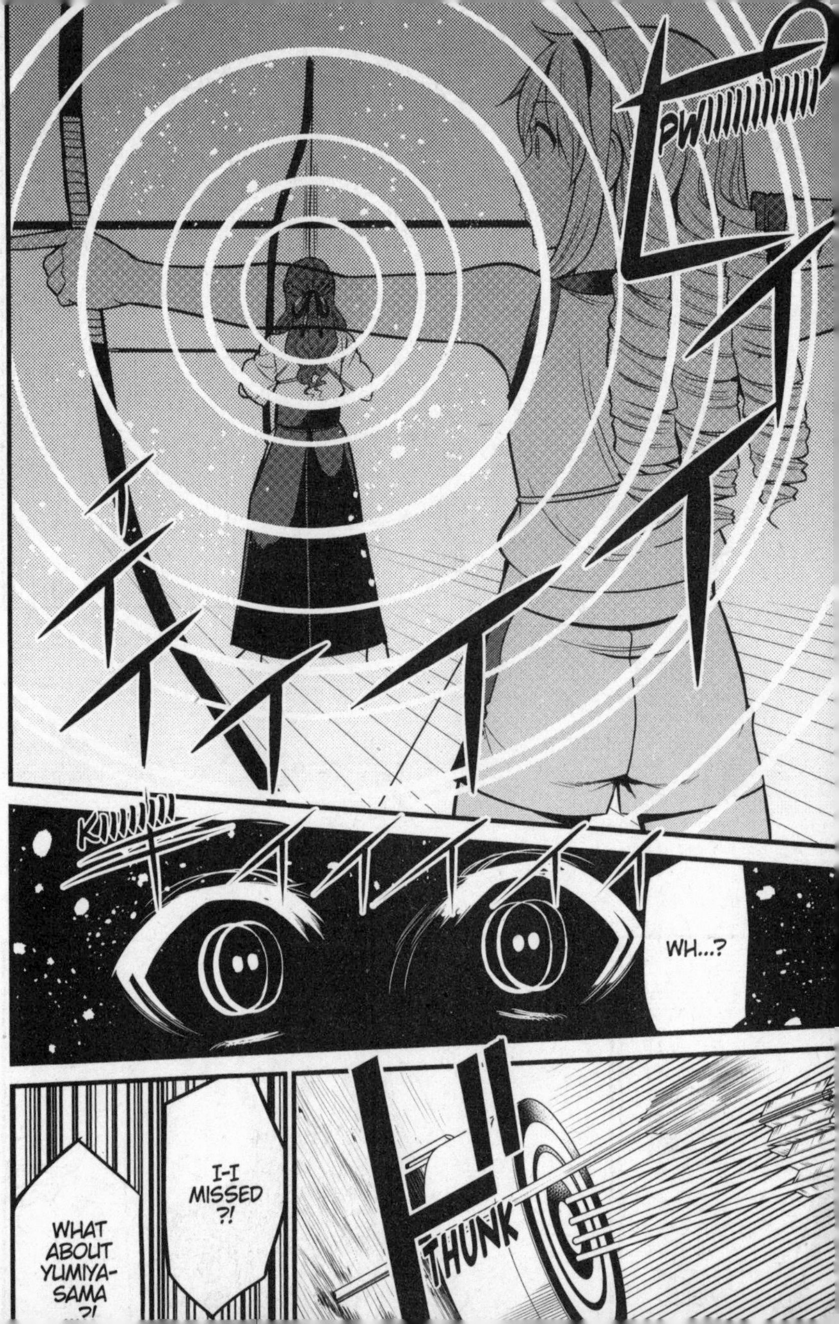
PWIIIIIIIIIIIII
KIIIIIII
WH...?
THUNK
I-I MISSED?!
WHAT ABOUT YUMIYA-SAMA?!

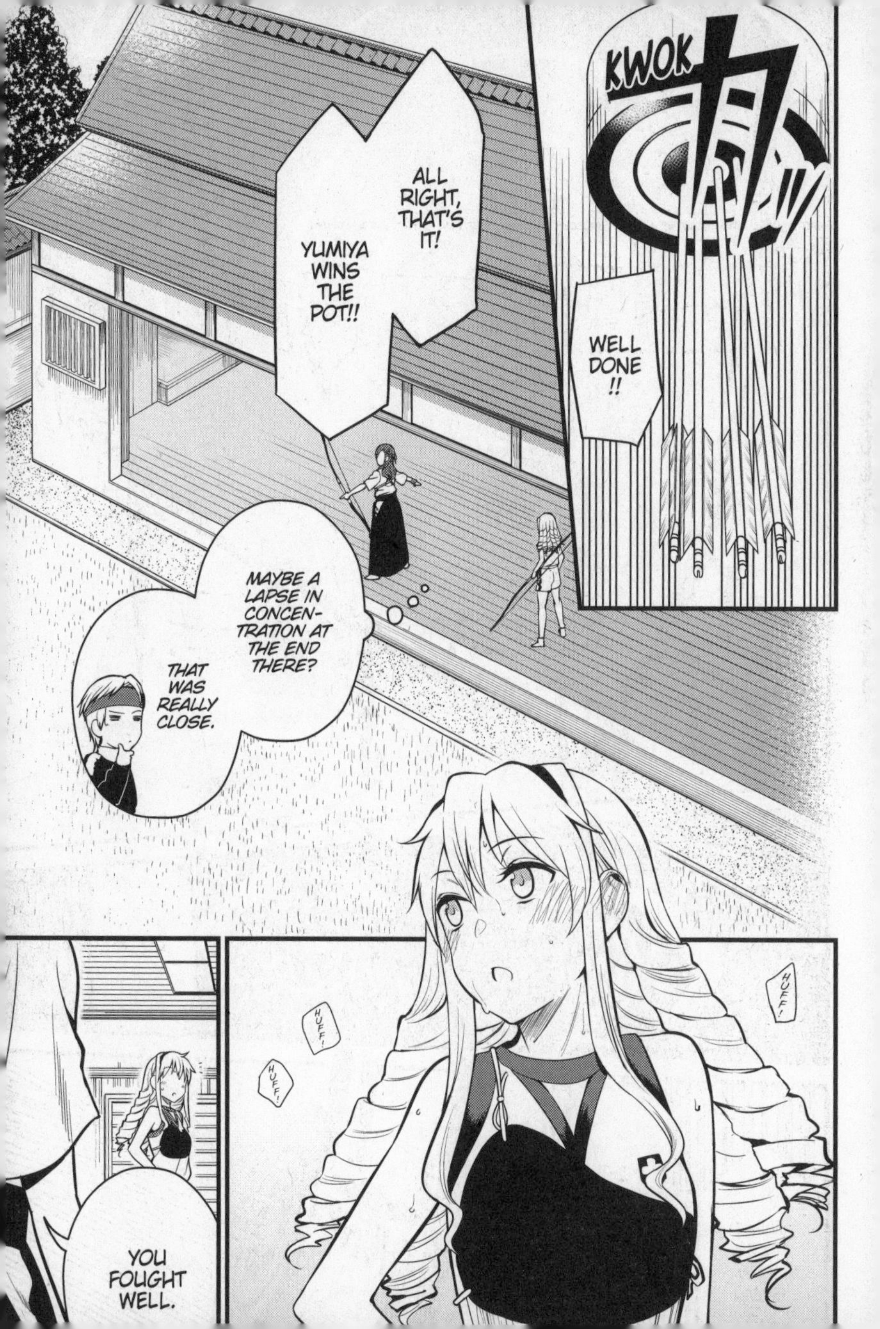
KWOK
WELL DONE!!
ALL RIGHT, THAT'S IT!
YUMIYA WINS THE POT!!
MAYBE A LAPSE IN CONCENTRATION AT THE END THERE?
THAT WAS REALLY CLOSE.
HUFF!
HUFF!
HUFF!
YOU FOUGHT WELL.

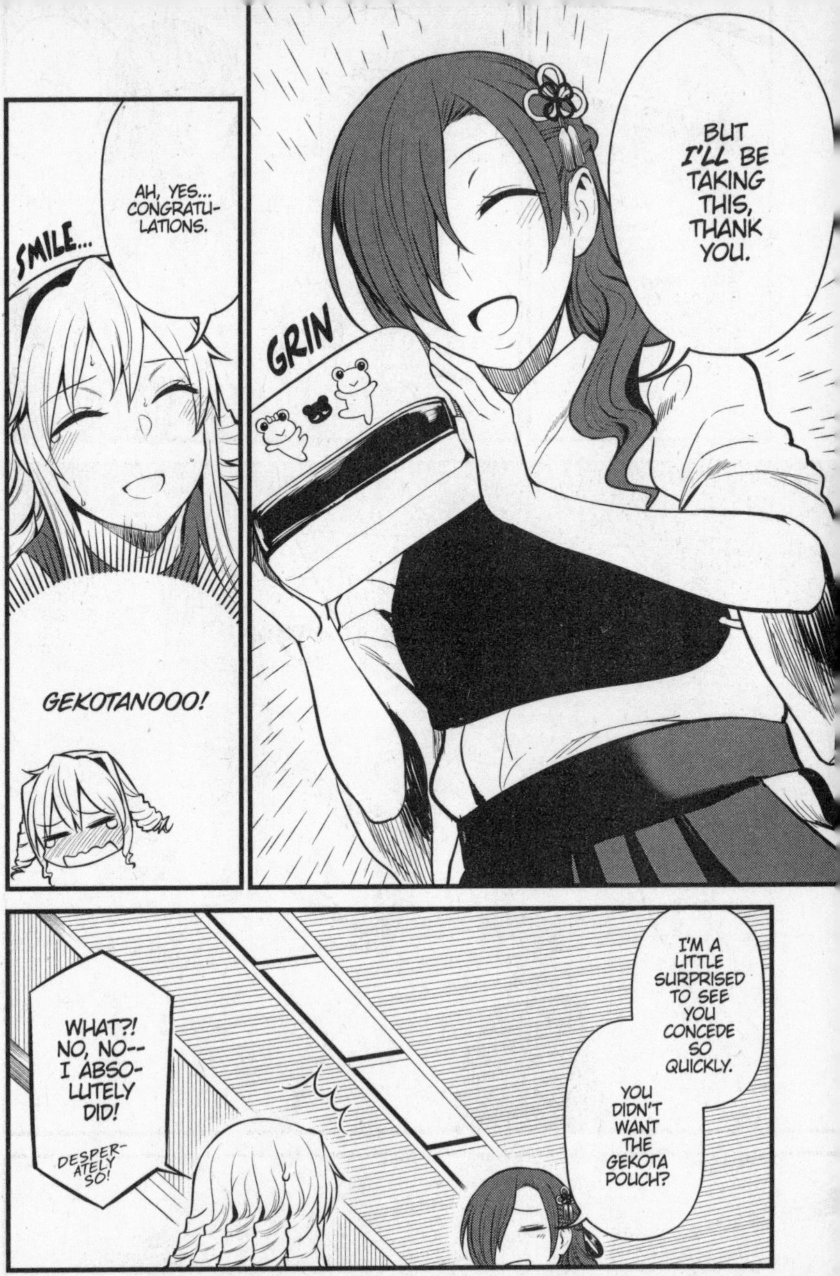
BUT I'LL BE TAKING THIS, THANK YOU.
GRIN
SMILE...
AH, YES... CONGRATU-LATIONS.
GEKOTANOOO!
I'M A LITTLE SURPRISED TO SEE YOU CONCEDE SO QUICKLY.
YOU DIDN'T WANT THE GEKOTA POUCH?
WHAT?! NO, NO-- I ABSO-LUTELY DID!
DESPER-ATELY SO!

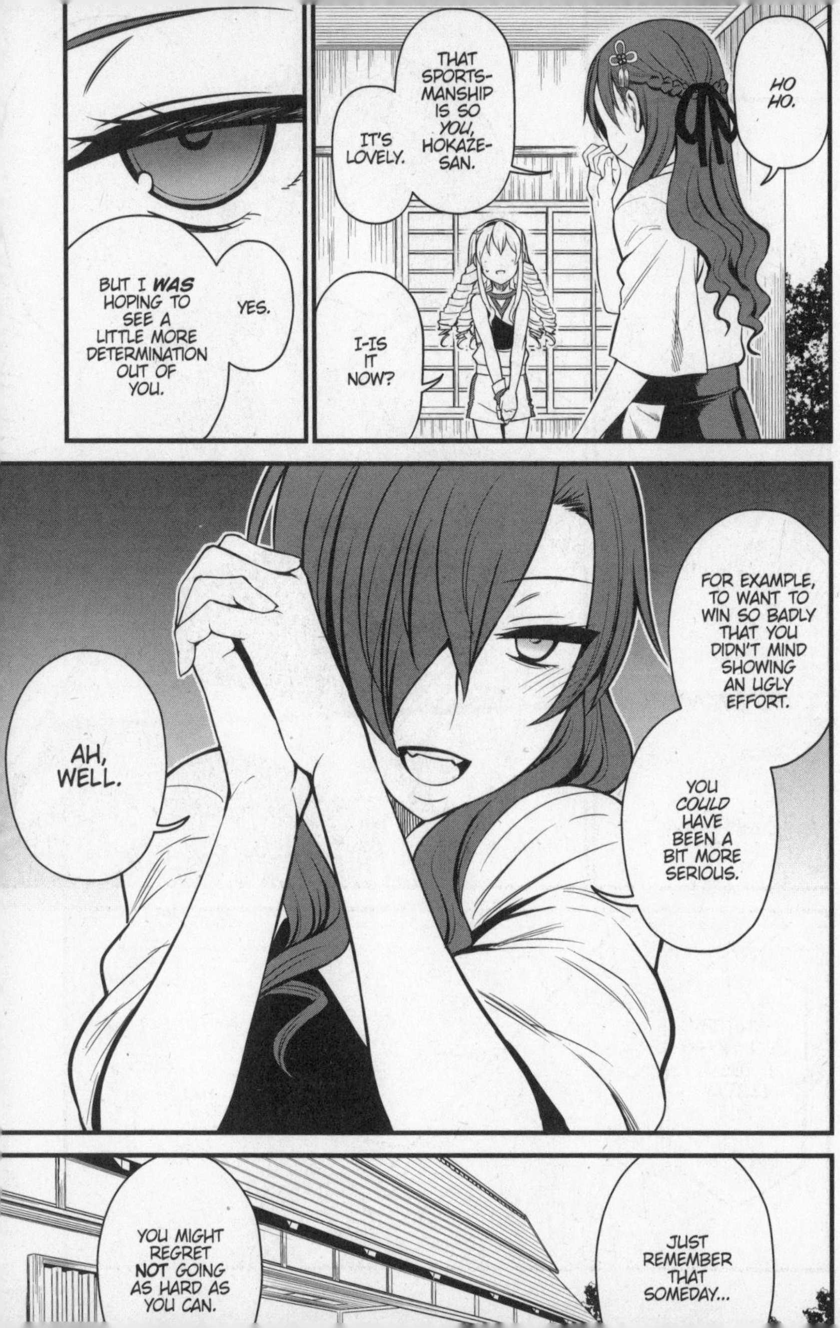
HO HO.
THAT SPORTS-MANSHIP IS SO *YOU*, HOKAZE-SAN.
IT'S LOVELY.
I-IS IT NOW?
YES.
BUT I **WAS** HOPING TO SEE A LITTLE MORE DETERMINATION OUT OF YOU.
FOR EXAMPLE, TO WANT TO WIN SO BADLY THAT YOU DIDN'T MIND SHOWING AN UGLY EFFORT.
YOU *COULD* HAVE BEEN A BIT MORE SERIOUS.
AH, WELL.
JUST REMEMBER THAT SOMEDAY...
YOU MIGHT REGRET **NOT** GOING AS HARD AS YOU CAN.

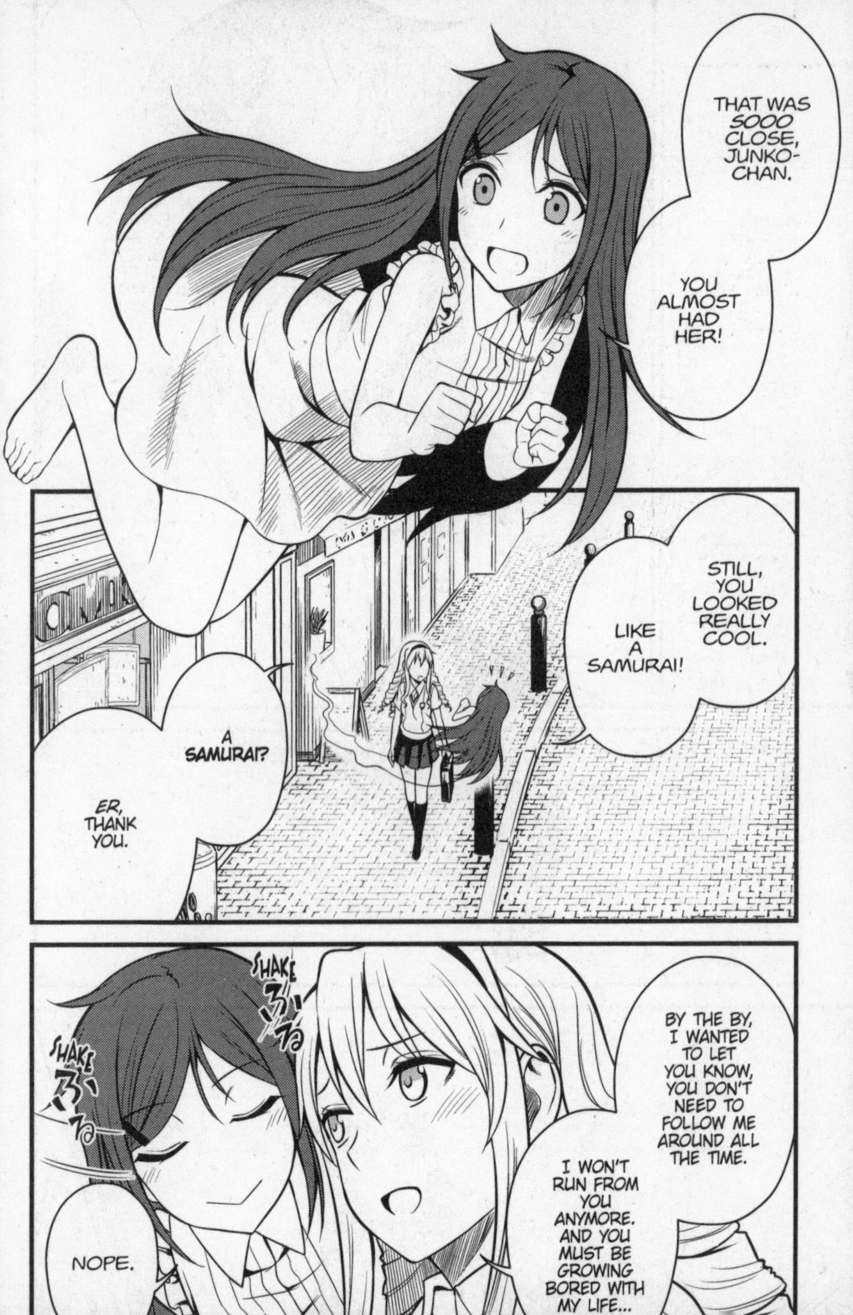
THAT WAS SOOO CLOSE, JUNKO-CHAN.
YOU ALMOST HAD HER!
STILL, YOU LOOKED REALLY COOL.
LIKE A SAMURAI!
A SAMURAI?
ER, THANK YOU.
BY THE BY, I WANTED TO LET YOU KNOW, YOU DON'T NEED TO FOLLOW ME AROUND ALL THE TIME.
I WON'T RUN FROM YOU ANYMORE. AND YOU MUST BE GROWING BORED WITH MY LIFE...
SHAKE
SHAKE
NOPE.

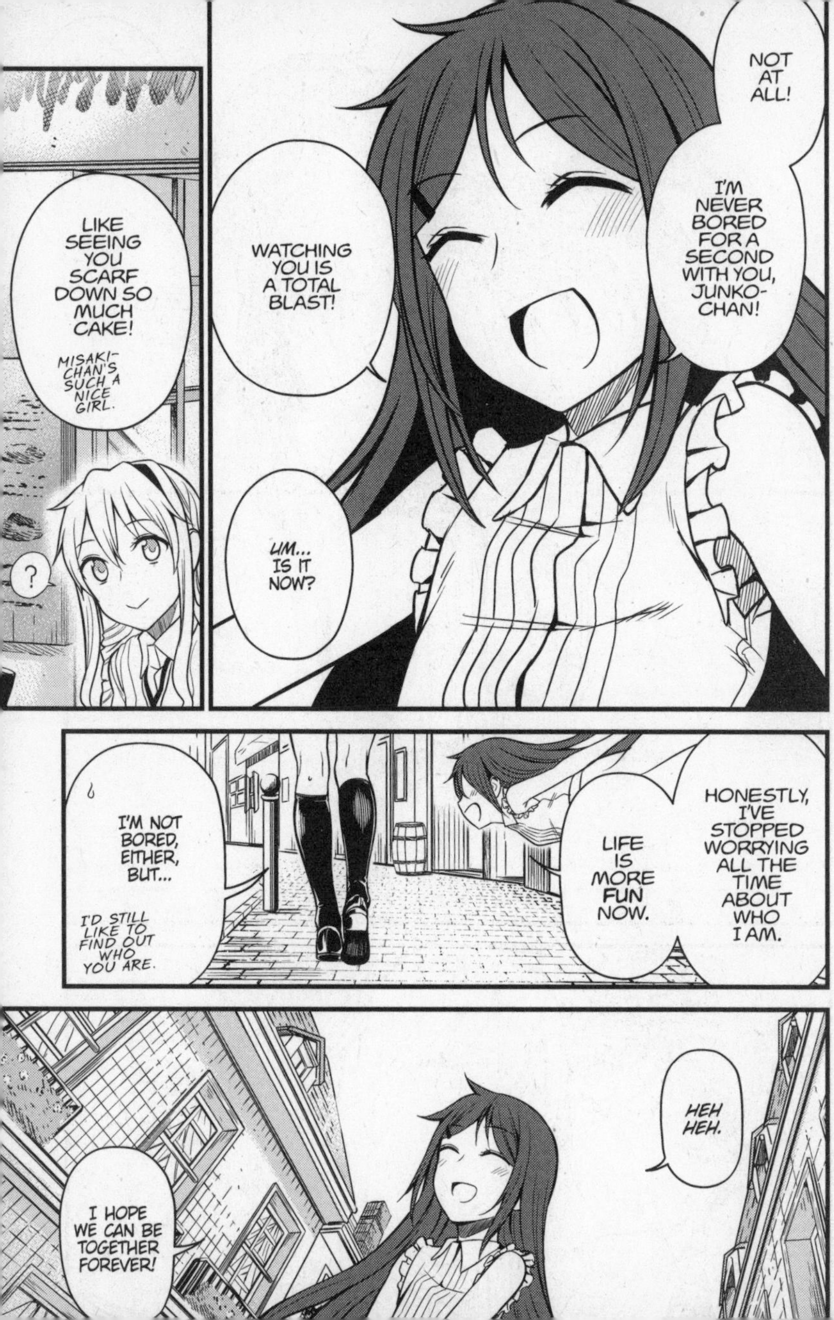
NOT AT ALL!
I'M NEVER BORED FOR A SECOND WITH YOU, JUNKO-CHAN!
WATCHING YOU IS A TOTAL BLAST!
UM... IS IT NOW?
LIKE SEEING YOU SCARF DOWN SO MUCH CAKE!
MISAKI-CHAN'S SUCH A NICE GIRL.
?
HONESTLY, I'VE STOPPED WORRYING ALL THE TIME ABOUT WHO I AM.
LIFE IS MORE FUN NOW.
I'M NOT BORED, EITHER, BUT...
I'D STILL LIKE TO FIND OUT WHO YOU ARE.
HEH HEH.
I HOPE WE CAN BE TOGETHER FOREVER!

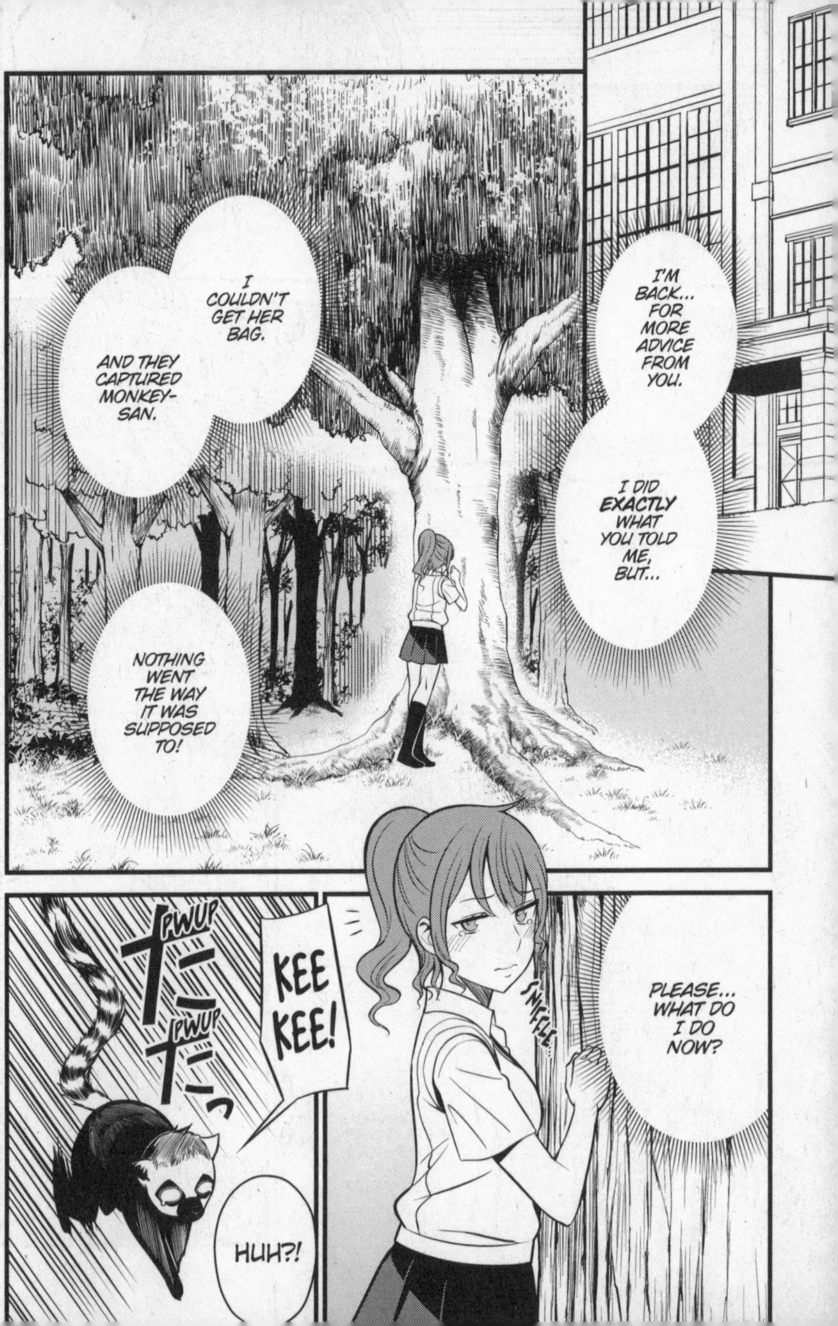
I'M BACK... FOR MORE ADVICE FROM YOU.
I DID EXACTLY WHAT YOU TOLD ME, BUT...
I COULDN'T GET HER BAG.
AND THEY CAPTURED MONKEY-SAN.
NOTHING WENT THE WAY IT WAS SUPPOSED TO!
PLEASE... WHAT DO I DO NOW?
SNIFFLE...
KEE KEE!
PWUP
PWUP
HUH?!

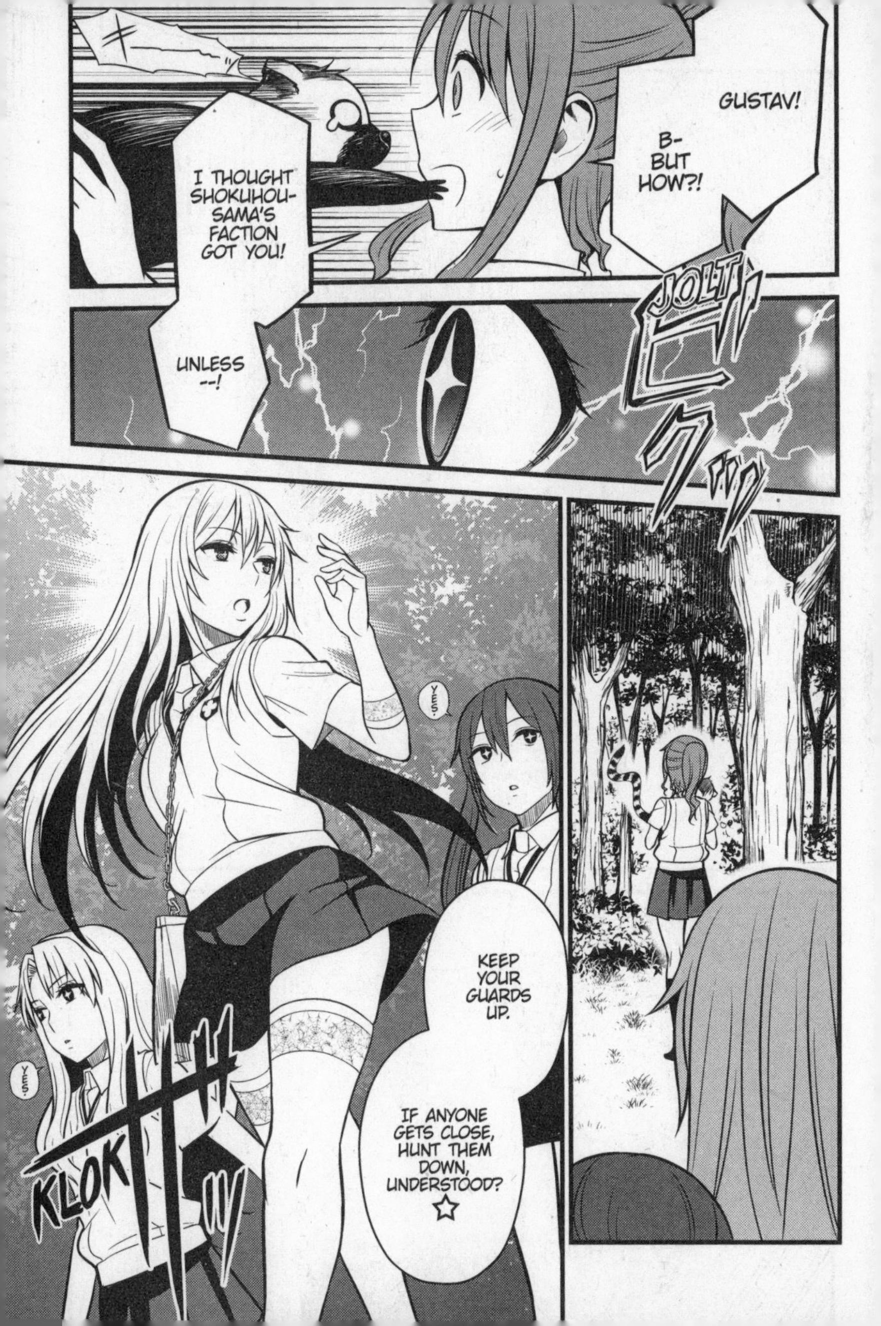
GUSTAV!
B-BUT HOW?!
I THOUGHT SHOKUHOU-SAMA'S FACTION GOT YOU!
UNLESS --!
JOLT
YES.
KEEP YOUR GUARDS UP.
IF ANYONE GETS CLOSE, HUNT THEM DOWN, UNDERSTOOD? ☆
YES.
KLOK

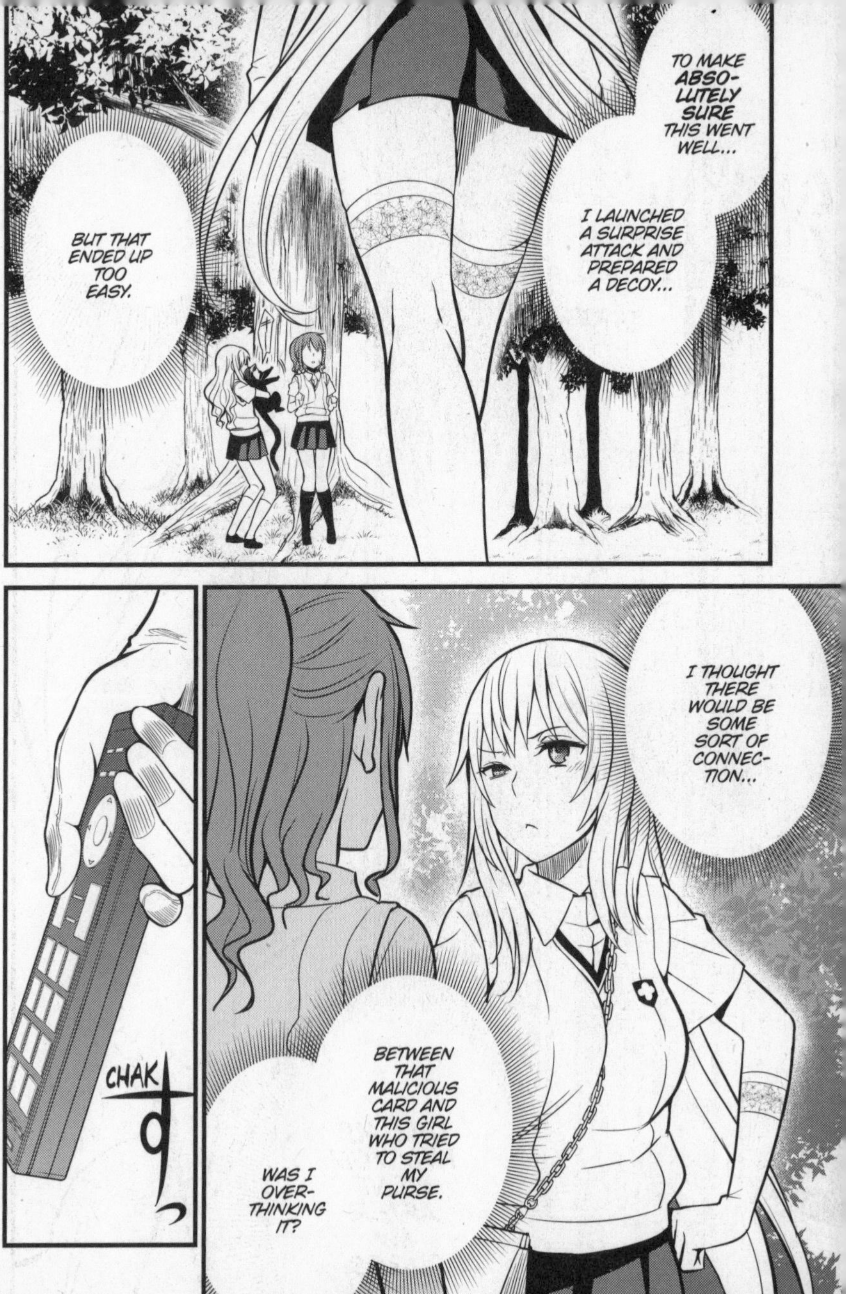
TO MAKE ABSOLUTELY SURE THIS WENT WELL...
I LAUNCHED A SURPRISE ATTACK AND PREPARED A DECOY...
BUT THAT ENDED UP TOO EASY.
I THOUGHT THERE WOULD BE SOME SORT OF CONNECTION...
BETWEEN THAT MALICIOUS CARD AND THIS GIRL WHO TRIED TO STEAL MY PURSE.
WAS I OVERTHINKING IT?
CHAK

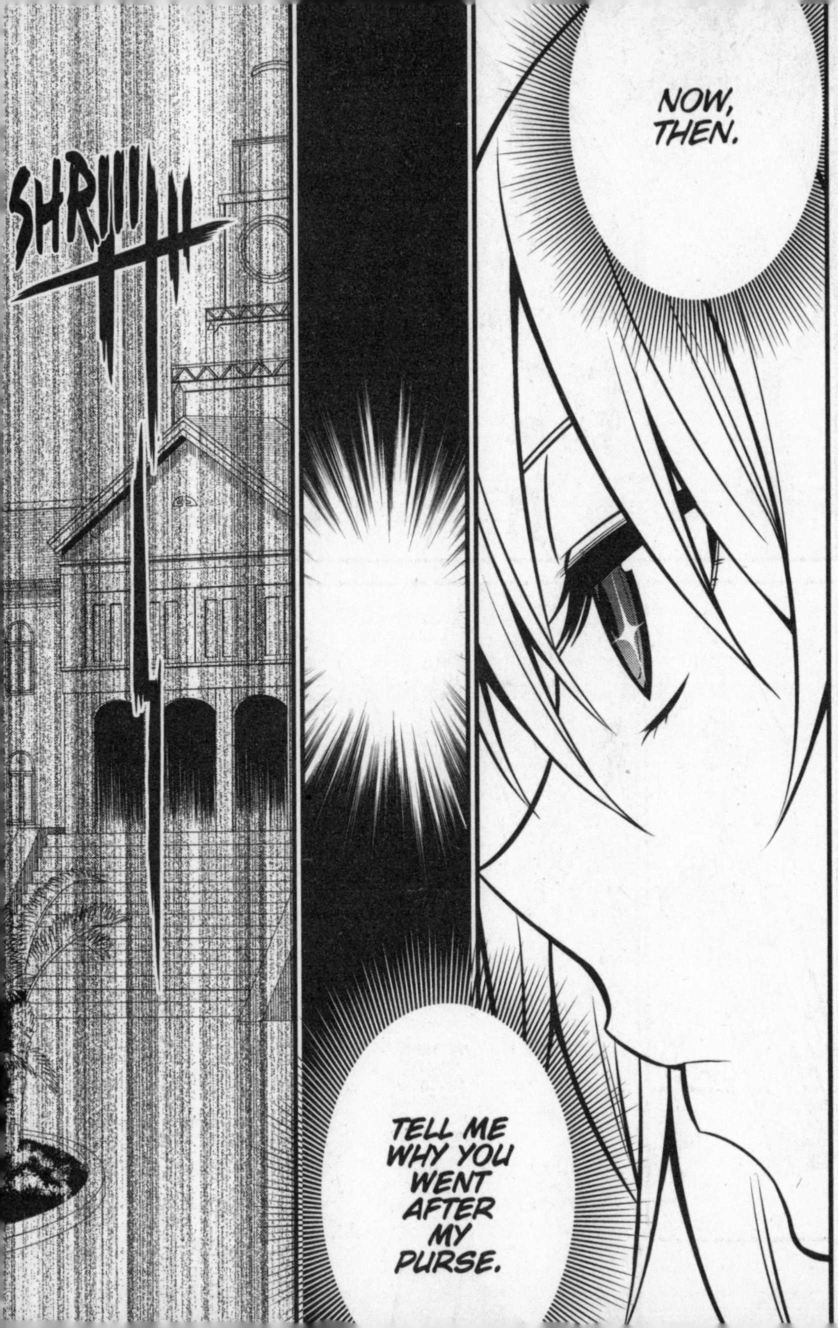
NOW, THEN.
TELL ME WHY YOU WENT AFTER MY PURSE.

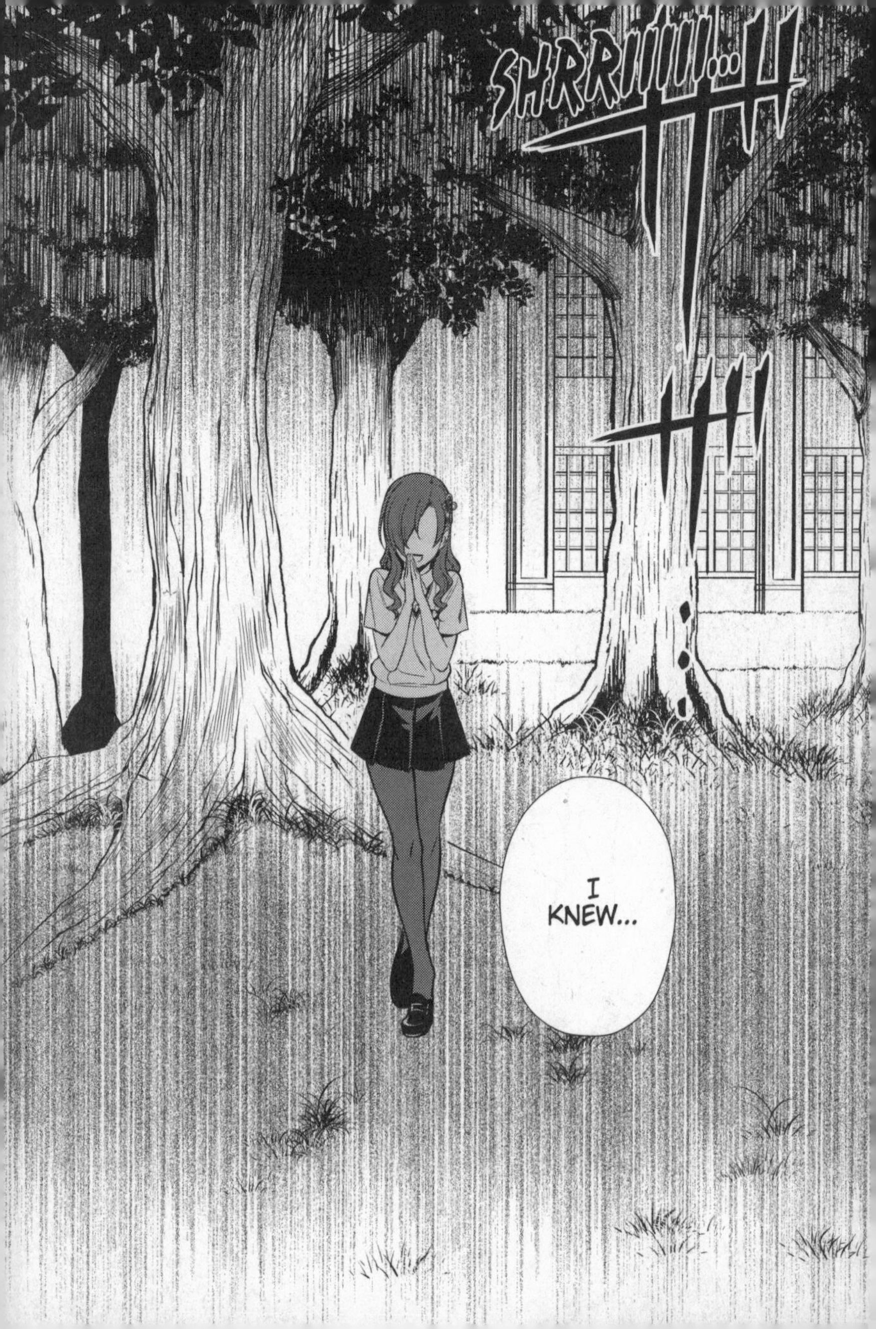
SHRIIIIII...II
I KNEW...

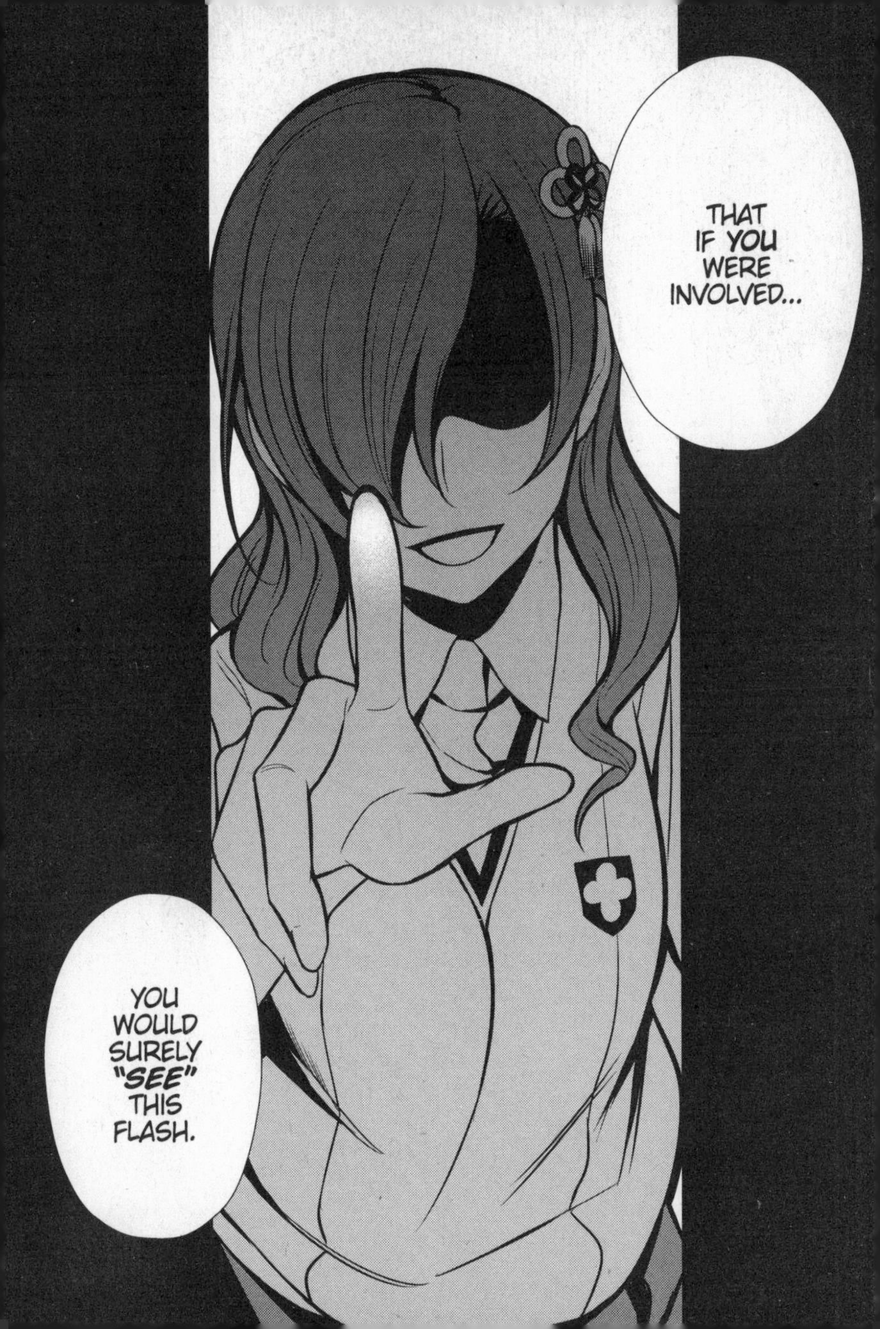
THAT IF YOU WERE INVOLVED...
YOU WOULD SURELY "SEE" THIS FLASH.

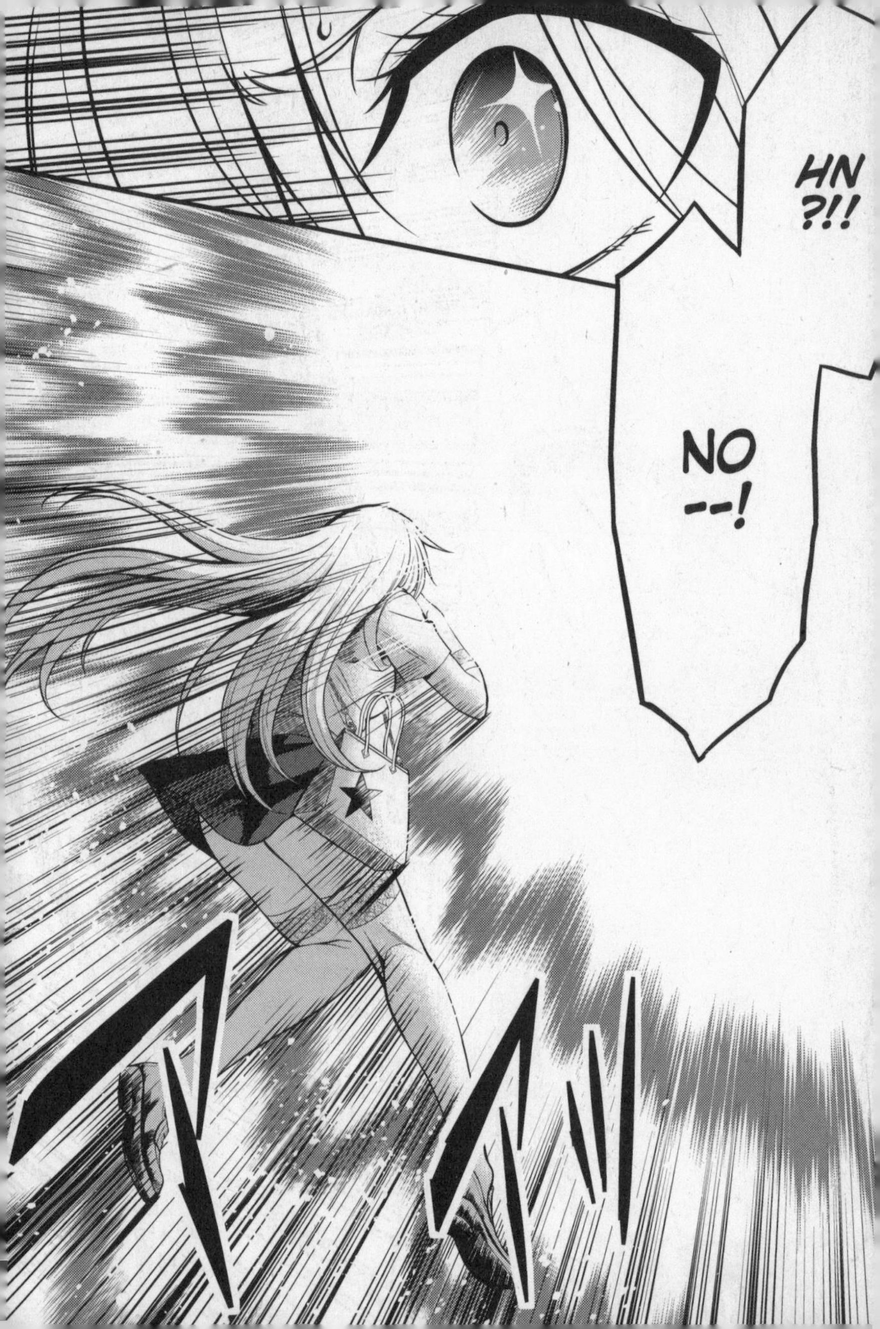
HN ?!!
NO --!

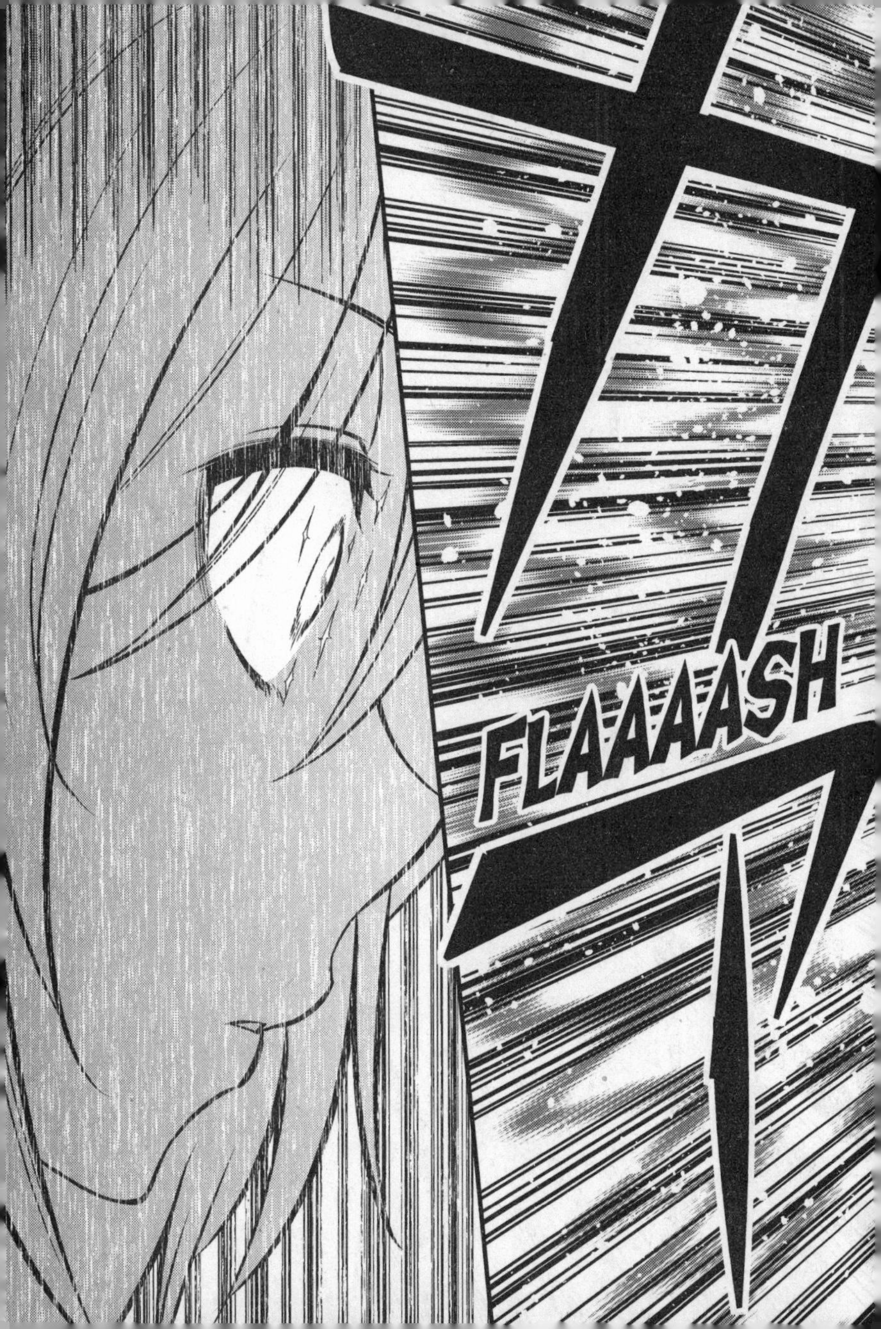
FLAAAASH

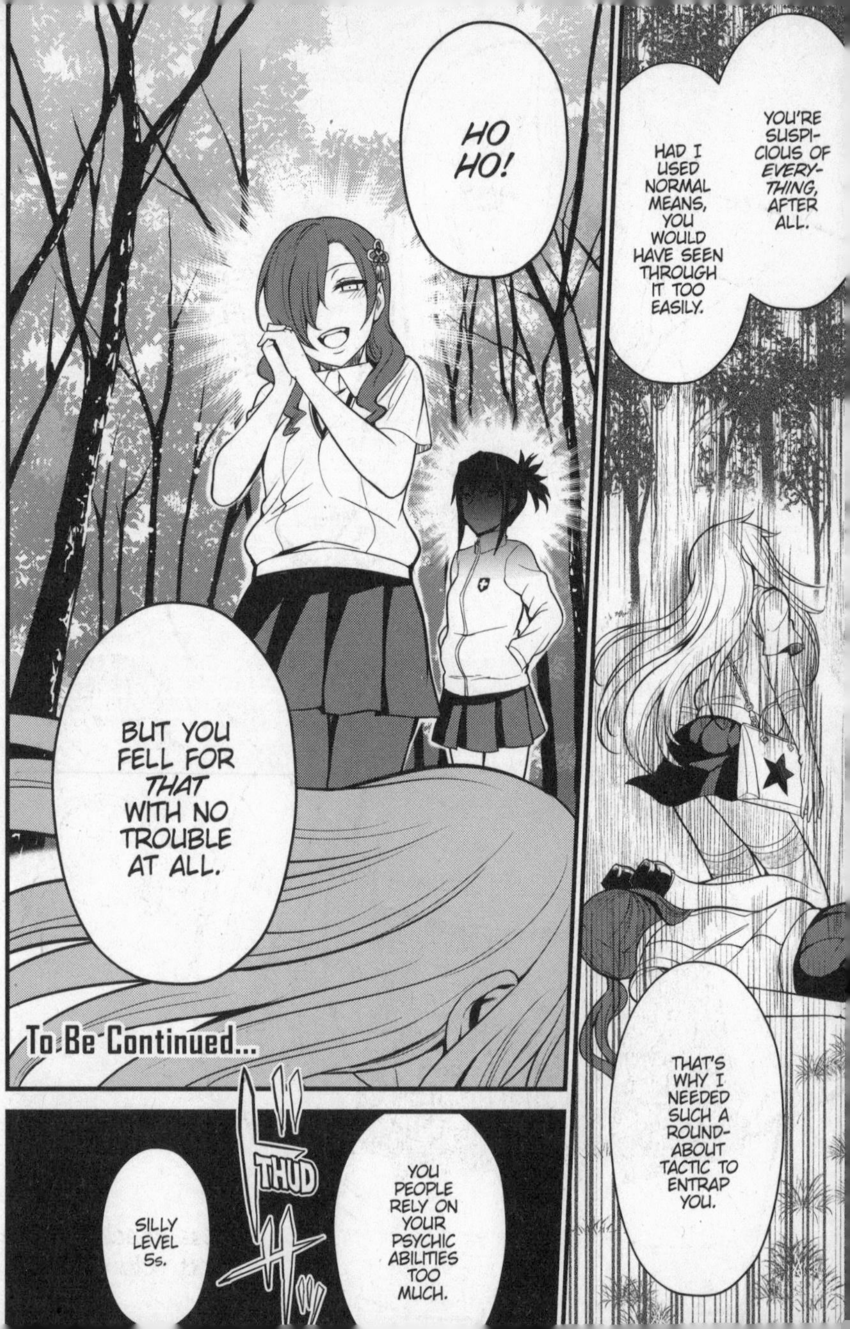

YOU'RE SUSPICIOUS OF *EVERYTHING*, AFTER ALL.
HAD I USED NORMAL MEANS, YOU WOULD HAVE SEEN THROUGH IT TOO EASILY.
THAT'S WHY I NEEDED SUCH A ROUNDABOUT TACTIC TO ENTRAP YOU.
HO HO!
BUT YOU FELL FOR *THAT* WITH NO TROUBLE AT ALL.
To Be Continued...
YOU PEOPLE RELY ON YOUR PSYCHIC ABILITIES TOO MUCH.
THUD
SILLY LEVEL 5s.

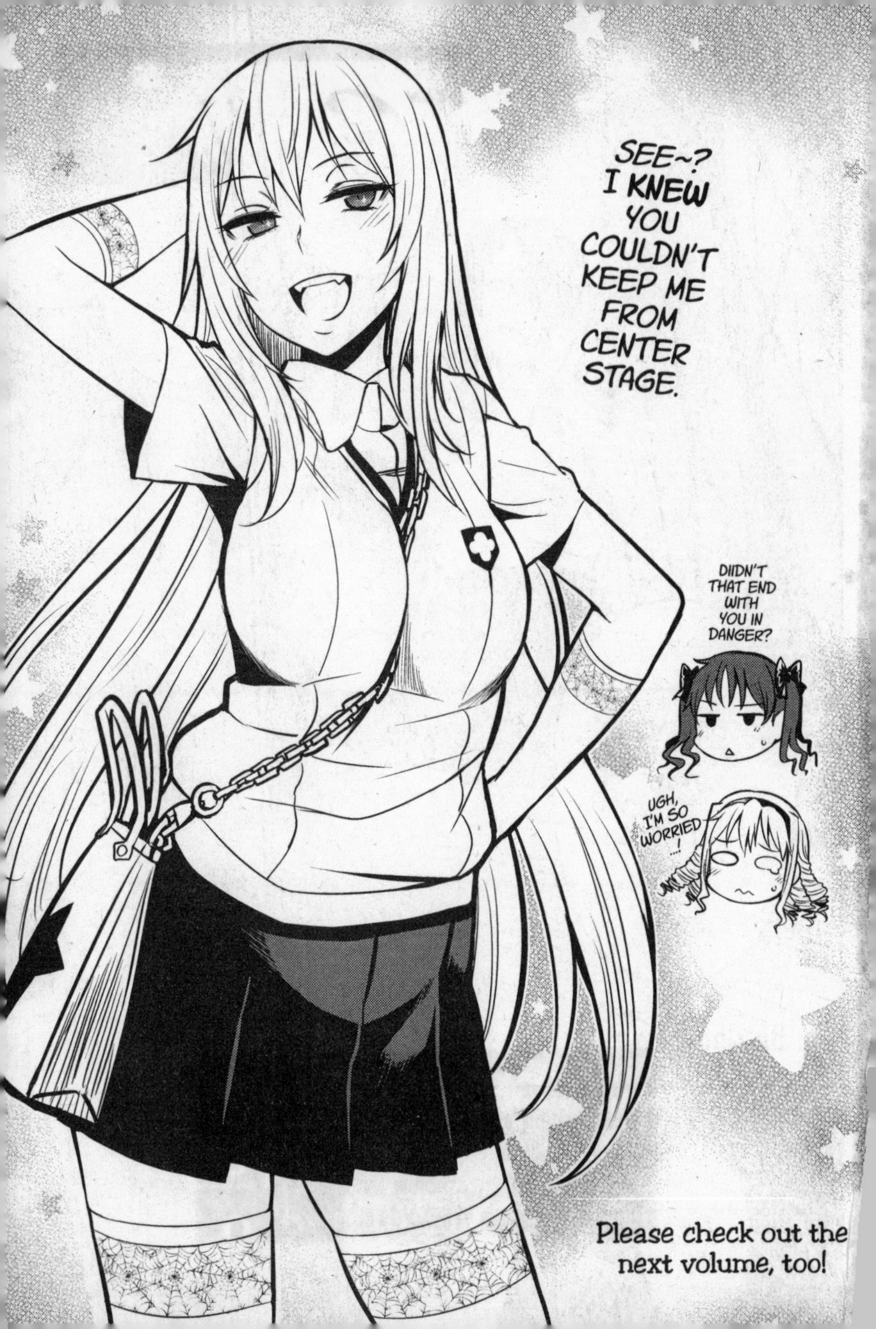
SEE~? I KNEW YOU COULDN'T KEEP ME FROM CENTER STAGE.
DIIDN'T THAT END WITH YOU IN DANGER?
UGH, I'M SO WORRIED...!
Please check out the next volume, too!

SEVEN SEAS ENTERTAINMENT PRESENTS

A CERTAIN SCIENTIFIC RAILGUN Astral Buddy

story: KAZUMA KAMACHI / art: YASUHITO NOGI / character designs: KIYOTAKA HAIMURA VOLUME 1

TRANSLATION
Nan Rymer

ADAPTATION
Maggie Danger

LETTERING AND RETOUCH
Roland Amago
Bambi Eloriaga-Amago

COVER DESIGN
Nicky Lim

PROOFREADER
Kurestin Armada
Janet Houck

EDITOR
Shannon Fay

PRODUCTION MANAGER
Lissa Pattillo

EDITOR-IN-CHIEF
Adam Arnold

PUBLISHER
Jason DeAngelis

First published in 2017 by KADOKAWA CORPORATION, Tokyo.
English translation rights arranged with KADOKAWA CORPORATION, Tokyo.

ISBN: 978-1-64275-036-2

Printed in Canada

First Printing: February 2019

10 9 8 7 6 5 4 3 2 1

READING DIRECTIONS

This book reads f
If this is your firs
reading from the
take it from there
numbered diagra
first, but you'll get the hang of it! Have fun!!

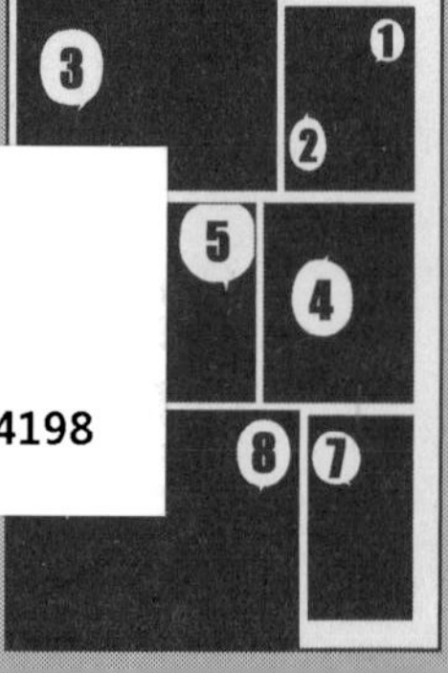
3
1
2
5
4
8
7